Race and Resistance in Boston

Race and Resistance in Boston

A Contested Sports History

EDITED BY ROBERT CVORNYEK
AND DOUGLAS STARK

Foreword by Devin McCourty

University of Nebraska Press
LINCOLN

The University of Nebraska Press is part of a land-grant institution
with campuses and programs on the past, present, and future
homelands of the Pawnee, Ponca, Otoe-Missouria, Omaha, Dakota,
Lakota, Kaw, Cheyenne, and Arapaho Peoples, as well as those
of the relocated Ho-Chunk, Sac and Fox, and Iowa Peoples.

Library of Congress Cataloging-in-Publication Data

Names: Cvornyek, Robert, editor. | Stark, Douglas, editor.
Title: Race and resistance in Boston: a contested sports history / Edited
by Robert Cvornyek and Douglas Stark; Foreword by Devin McCourty.
Description: Lincoln: University of Nebraska
Lincoln, [2024] | Includes index.
Identifiers: LCCN 2024023490
ISBN 9781496232687 (paperback)
ISBN 9781496242235 (epub)
ISBN 9781496242242 (pdf)
Subjects: LCSH: Sports—Massachusetts—Boston—History—
20th century. | African American athletes—Massachusetts—Boston—
History—20th century. | African Americans—Massachusetts—
Boston—Social conditions—20th century. | Discrimination in
sports—Massachusetts—Boston—History—20th century. |
Boston (Mass.)—Race relations—History—20th century. | Boston
(Mass.)—History—20th century. | BISAC: SOCIAL SCIENCE /
Ethnic Studies / American / African American &
Black Studies | SPORTS & RECREATION / History
Classification: LCC GV584.5.B6 R33 2024 |
DDC 796.09744/61—dc23/eng/20240718
LC record available at https://lccn.loc.gov/2024023490

Set in Arno Pro by Scribe Inc.

For Dorothy and Rob:

Each sheltered the other through the darkest storms
with steadfast love and hope. Forever Mother and Son.

For Melanie:

No truer a soul has lived than my wife.

CONTENTS

FOREWORD

DEVIN MCCOURTY

In March 2023, I decided to retire after thirteen years of playing for the New England Patriots. As a player, I was proud of what I had accomplished: three-time Super Bowl champion, twelve-time team captain, Pro Bowl selection as both a cornerback and a safety, and three-time second-team All-Pro. I loved every minute—punishing practices, preparing for games, and competing against the best players every week. It was an experience I will forever cherish.

With retirement comes reflection. I'm grateful that my career with the Patriots allowed me to create a platform to address the racial and economic injustices that restrict opportunities for Blacks in Boston and around the nation. As I reflect on my years in New England, I realize that my time off the field, when I engaged in various social justice movements, proved just as meaningful as my time on the field. Activism led me to become a more informed and well-rounded citizen. I asked myself what I could do to help but also understood the need to educate myself about the issues of the day, and that meant uncovering the history of how we arrived at this divisive moment in our country. History tells us that African Americans have always felt a sense of disaffection, but this sentiment led Black communities to develop tactics and strategies designed to achieve racial uplift and combat the inequities they faced. You cannot ignore what is happening around you today, but you must take time to study the resilient history of the African American journey. It is filled with sorrow, protest, reform, and transformation. The past will always shape and inform the present. This is especially true of Boston's Black athletic history. The city's African American players resisted segregation and racial discrimination during the Jim Crow era and later fought to secure cultural representation during the ongoing freedom movement.

My appreciation for Black history started with my maternal grandmother, Emma Lee King. Born in Virginia in the 1920s, she witnessed segregation firsthand, supported the civil rights movement, and followed its progress in the Black press. My mother, Phyllis Harrell, confirmed her message and guided my education with a strong but loving hand. Black teachers, especially in middle school, opened my eyes to the courageous acts of those who came before me. I learned that Martin Luther King Jr. and Malcolm X, both of whom lived in Boston during formative moments in their lives, offered multiple paths to freedom. Both men, along with a combination of Black writers, artists, and scholars, highlighted the diversity of thought and experience that thrived in Black communities, households, and schools. It wasn't until later that I realized the pivotal role that athletes played in the advancement of American race relations. *Race and Resistance in Boston: A Contested Sports History* deepens our awareness of Black athletic activism in the Hub, a story that remained underappreciated until now.

This book highlights stories about players, teams, and communities that provide an authentic expression of the city's racial past from an African American sports perspective. In Boston, the collision of race and sport has been examined mostly through baseball and basketball. Studies on the Boston Red Sox and Boston Celtics have established a dominant narrative and narrowed the conversation surrounding Black participation in a broad range of sporting activities at the amateur and professional levels. Traditionally, this narrative represents the opposites, with the Red Sox being the last Major League Baseball team to integrate with Pumpsie Green in 1959, and the Celtics, behind Bill Russell, sitting at the forefront of racial integration. This book constructs a counternarrative that examines the multiple ways African American athletes negotiated Boston's racial boundaries. Some of the topics include soccer, cricket, boxing, golf, tennis, baseball, basketball, hockey, front-office executives, and the busing crisis in the 1970s. For the first time, these topics are presented in one volume in a series of critical essays that provide greater historical context, shed light on heartbreak, and ultimately end with a message of hope and a call to action. This approach provides a lens to further understand subjects such as urbanization, immigration, labor, politics, demographics, and race relations. Furthermore, previous scholarship centered on the city's Black sporting community had concentrated on the mid-twentieth century. The authors in this book expand the focus from the late nineteenth to the twenty-first century, covering a 150-year period.

Before joining the Patriots, I understood that Boston had an uneasy racial reputation. My mother had visited the city and warned me that she encountered two very different versions of city life. Boston was an educated and cultured place that often embodied progressive values and ideals. But it also possessed a menacing side, one that tolerated—and, at times, encouraged—racism. When I left Rutgers University for the Patriots, teammates and friends cautioned me that Boston might be a tough town for a Black man.

Equipped with this knowledge, I drew inspiration from Celtics legend Bill Russell. He navigated Boston's racial landscape with honesty and openness. Russell defied the barriers Black athletes experienced during the 1950s and 1960s, and I am the proud beneficiary of his efforts. He was equally vocal about Boston's dismal record on race. He advocated for an underserved community that battled residential segregation, inadequate schools, and economic deprivation. His legacy extended far beyond his championship days on the court. Russell, along with other activists including Jim Brown, Muhammad Ali, Kareem Abdul-Jabbar, Tommie Smith, John Carlos, and LeBron James, established a tradition that I decided to emulate. I did not realize that local hometown male and female athletes performing at the amateur and professional levels played similar roles in Boston. After reading the stories in this book, I now consider myself part of this local legacy too. It is one of which I am immensely proud.

Many current Boston athletes have joined this tradition by assisting me in my work with organizations like Boston Uncornered and the Players Coalition. Our relationship with people of color living in Greater Boston, including Mattapan, Dorchester, and Roxbury, has been a loving and productive one. We visited churches, schools, and community centers, listening and learning. We exposed injustices like juvenile incarceration and inadequate education. We brought these issues to the attention of city and state lawmakers. My leadership role on the Patriots taught me to take responsibility for our team's success on the field, and these same leadership skills have led me to accept accountability for those suffering racial and economic discrimination.

A while back, I participated in a panel discussion on race and gender in sports held at Boston University and hosted by sports analyst and National Football League (NFL) journalist Andrea Kremer. I expressed certainty that sports represent a microcosm of American society and, at various historical moments, reflect the nation's existing attitudes and opinions. My belief is that sport also possesses the power to challenge and change the status quo. The athletes represented in this book, along with the rise and revolt of the modern Black athlete, exercised the power to transform society. We are all proud to be a part of this long and significant history.

ACKNOWLEDGMENTS

This book would not have been possible without the support of our contributors. When we approached them about an edited volume regarding race and sports in Boston, each immediately provided their support and encouraged us to pursue this much-needed topic to help correct a prevailing narrative that was limited in scope and interpretation. Some of our contributors proved so enthusiastic that they started to research and write their articles before we even had a book contract. We wish to thank each of them for their patience as we have gone back and forth with suggestions, edits, and questions. Your dedication and effort have made this a thoroughly enjoyable process. And your essays have shed light on a previously unexplored topic.

A project of this nature took many twists and turns. What started out as a one-volume project has since become a multi-volume series. We continually found new leads, unearthed topics, and found contributors willing to share their talents. As the project deepened, we confronted several challenges that involved finishing this book, conceptualizing a multivolume series, and presenting a topic that, in many instances, was being researched for the first time. The historiography of Black sports in Boston was spotty at best, and the lack of resources proved challenging. Furthermore, the *Boston Chronicle*, the city's Black newspaper, was missing the early years, lost to time, and has not been digitized, making it difficult for our contributors to access Boston's lone Black newspaper. Our hope is that the surviving issues of the *Boston Chronicle*, currently on microfilm, will one day be digitized and available to everyone.

Nonetheless, we benefited from wonderful conversations with a wide range of individuals, including Dick Johnson at the Sports Museum, Charlie Titus at UMass Boston, Alfreda Harris at the Shelburne Community Center, Jeff Gerson at UMass Lowell, Ted Fay at UMass Boston, and Richard Lapchick at the University of Central Florida. Many other individuals proved equally helpful during this process. There are too many to name, but know that your assistance, no matter how big or small, was much appreciated.

We wish to acknowledge the professional and guiding support of Rob Taylor and Courtney Ochsner at the University of Nebraska Press. Rob championed this book from the outset and helped shape its content and structure. Courtney kept the process moving along in a timely fashion and ensured that all necessary parts were in hand and ready to go. Taylor Martin joined us mid-stream and was instrumental in getting this project over the proverbial hump. To all three, many thanks for this wonderful opportunity.

We also wish to thank those who helped us secure images, including Brian Bunk, Spencer Grant, and Aaron Horne at the Boston Public Library; Andy Krause at Getty Images; James E. Spencer at the Smithsonian; and Dave Walberg, assistant director of athletics for Sports Communication and Event Management, UMass Boston.

To our proofreaders, Eileen and Michelle Moon, an extremely talented mother-daughter editing team, many thanks for your close readings of each essay and your insightful comments, which made this a much stronger book.

Our manuscript readers were equally up to the challenge, and our heartfelt thanks go to Leslie Grinner, Kathryn Leann Harris, Dave Hecht, Dick Johnson, and Greg Tranter. Each of you provided a different angle as you approached our work. Your comments proved very helpful as we strengthened the book and its overall argument.

Robert's thoughts move to his mother, Lorraine, for the tender way she introduced and supported his interest in sport, and to his loving family—Dorothy, Robert, Elizabeth, Philip, and Isabella—for their innate goodness as people and partners in life.

From Doug: I wish to thank my family, always supportive of my writing projects even if it takes some time away from our family activities. To my wife, Melanie, and children, Ben and Tessa, many thanks for your support. I hope one day you understand the joy these projects give me.

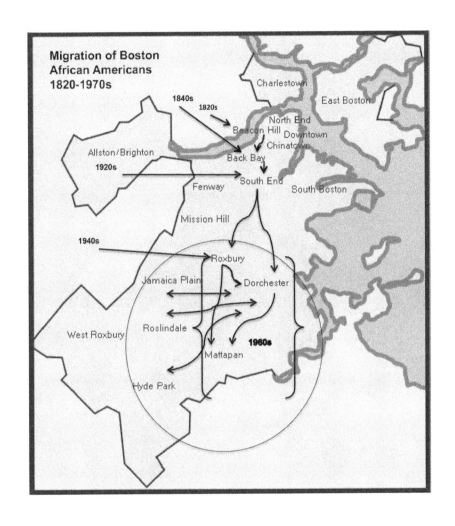

Map 1. *Historical Patterns of Black Migration in Boston.* From Robert E. Weir, "Constructing Legends: Pumpsie Green, Race, and the Boston Red Sox," *Historical Journal of Massachusetts* 42, no. 2 (Summer 2014): 60.

Introduction

ROBERT CVORNYEK AND DOUGLAS STARK

The collision of race and sport in present-day Boston resonates with stories and events connected to the past. Though known as the "Cradle of Liberty," Boston rarely escaped the combined indignities of racism and segregation fueled, in part, by economic and residential conflicts between the city's working-class ethnics and Black Americans. These tensions revealed themselves in most aspects of the city's life, including the social and cultural world of sport. Historian Zebulon Miletsky aptly concludes that "as a symbol, Black Bostonians have always been emblematic of that distinctly American of dilemmas—the curious conundrum of what it means to be Black in the cradle of Liberty."[1] The juxtaposition of Boston's liberal tradition and troubled racial past provides the historical backdrop for many of the chapters in this book.

In sport, this juxtaposition has traditionally focused on the city's premier professional teams, the Celtics in basketball and Red Sox in baseball. The relationship between Boston and these clubs mirrored the city's tense racial history and has been the focus of much scholarly attention. The distinctive approach to racial integration that each club pursued encouraged authors to contrast the binary policies of both teams and highlight the individuals who navigated the city's color line in mid-twentieth-century America. Boston sport during the modern civil rights era remains a familiar trope. The Celtics drafted the first Black player in the National Basketball Association (NBA), Chuck Cooper, in 1950, whereas the Red Sox were the last Major League Baseball team to integrate, signing Elijah "Pumpsie" Green in 1959. During this nine-year interim, the Celtics signed Bill Russell, the person who delivered the team eleven championships but was never fully accepted in the city he represented. Russell's encounters with racial hostility as a Celtic led him to label Boston a "flea market for racism."[2] The interrelationship among the Celtics, the Red Sox, and the city of Boston framed a dominant narrative that helped explain the city's racial complexities. This story occupied center stage and largely overlooked the wider contexts of race and sport in the city.

This volume's collection acknowledges this customary account but offers a counternarrative that examines the influence that generations of Black athletes, teams, sportswriters, and front-office executives exercised to shape the city's racial identity. Long before Chuck Cooper, Bill Russell, and Pumpsie Green tested Boston's racial consciousness, Black athletes participated in a variety of individual sports and created teams of their own making. These athletes retained their focus on racial integration, but they concurrently utilized sport as a form of racial pride, resistance, and cultural expression. Boston's Black athletes strengthened racial solidarity and created opportunities for race-based economic uplift for themselves and others. In return, the Black community nurtured its own teams and sportspersons within a city that repeatedly sought to narrow or exclude equal athletic participation.

In 1959, two competing narratives unfolded to illustrate the variety of approaches to interpret race and sport in Boston. During the spring of 1959, Pumpsie Green, the first African American ballplayer to wear a Red Sox uniform, captivated the attention of national sportswriters and subsequent historians. Not since Jackie Robinson's ill-fated tryout with the Red Sox in 1945 had the team entertained interest in a Black player. Green would indeed finish what Robinson started when he joined the Red Sox as the final player to integrate a Major League Baseball team.[3] Green's courageous journey, however, delineates only one route to understanding the city's intersection of race and sport. Boston's Black athletes struggled in the trenches, fighting racism for decades before and after Green's arrival.

Green's appearance in Boston coincided with another narrative, a story fixed deeply within the city's Black community. In April 1959 the Amateur Athletic Union selected John Curtis Thomas as the indoor track season's most outstanding performer.[4] As a seventeen-year-old student attending Boston University, Thomas set a new indoor record in the high jump at the Knights of Columbus track meet in Boston and then became the first person to clear seven feet at the Millrose Games in New York City.[5] *Sports Illustrated* magazine touted him as "America's bright new hope against the Russians" in the upcoming 1960 Olympics.[6] Thomas participated in the 1960 and 1964 Cold War Olympics as one of several Black American athletes who personified the paradox of representing a nation that marginalized and discriminated against people of color.[7]

Thomas was born in Cambridge, Massachusetts, across the Charles River from Boston. His father, Curtis, drove a city bus, and his mother, Ida, worked in the kitchen at Harvard University. As a high school student at Rindge Technical School, he exemplified the dreams and determination of many African Americans living in Greater Boston. At Boston University, "he was always fighting to be the best," and despite a devastating ankle injury that nearly ended his career, Thomas later competed successfully in the 1960 Olympics.[8] Thomas's talent, spirit, and determination ensured his induction as the first African American member of the Boston Athletic Association. According to former association spokesperson Thomas Grilk, "For those of us growing up in Greater Boston in the 1950s and 1960s, John Thomas in the high jump was our personal connection to national, international, and Olympic track and field."[9] Equally important, local Black neighborhoods applauded his achievements and comforted his disappointments. He acknowledged his neighbors' support by spending his life in service to the community as the athletic director at Roxbury Community College, as a trustee at the Brockton Public Library, and as a volunteer at the local YMCA. Thomas was one of Boston's own, and the recollection of his accomplishments remains a proud fixture in the Black community's collective memory.

The Green-Thomas scenario affirms the conclusion reached by historians David Wiggins and Ryan Swanson—namely, that scholars remain more interested in integration and historic firsts "rather than the individual athletes and various events and organizations integral to the development of a black national sporting culture."[10] This volume, through a collection of new and critical assessments, asserts the historical significance of race and sport in local sporting culture while positioning Boston within a broader regional and national Black sporting tradition. The chapters include a range of topics, themes, and sport personalities that strengthen our understanding of race relations in Boston and contribute to the growing scholarship on urban race and sport. The book's focus is certainly on race, but several of the chapters occupy space in the intersectional realm of race, gender, class, and sexual orientation.

The volume is divided into three separate but related sections. Part 1, "Framing Race, Community, and Resistance in Boston," contains chapters that introduce the reader to two foundational themes—resistance and community—that help define Boston's Black sporting experience. Both themes are intertwined closely in the chapters within this section. The opening essay belongs to Bijan Bayne, a leading authority on the impact of busing on the redistribution of Boston's schoolboy and collegiate athletic talent. Joseph Cooper, author of *Legacy of African American Resistance and Activism through Sport*, argues that Black sportspersons in Boston have enacted a range of activism and actions of resistance to champion racial and social justice through sport. He examines the struggle for racial freedom in Boston through his African American sport activism typology (AASAT) and African American resistance typology (AART), the latter an intergenerational analysis of social change. Notable sports figures, including Kittie Knox, Mabray "Doc" Kountze, Bill Russell, and Alfreda Harris, are featured in his chapter. They represent a portion of the variety of athletes, coaches, sportswriters, and front-office personnel who personify Boston's legacy of resistance against racial oppression. Cooper's chapter provides a timely blueprint for future activism through sport at the local, regional, national, and international levels.

In their chapter, Marcis Fennell, C. Keith Harrison, and Kelly Dwyer explicate how sport strengthened Boston's Black neighborhoods and helped establish the city's racial identity. The authors conclude that Boston serves as an illustrative example of the intersections among sport, social class, and Black culture at the community level. They identify Charles Titus, former vice chancellor for athletics, recreation, and special programs at the University of Massachusetts Boston, as someone who represents the connection between sport and Boston's Black community. Titus's leadership and commitment to equal opportunity are examined against a thematic backdrop that includes physical culture, race, and class.

In part 2, "Legitimacy in the Jim Crow Era," the authors analyze the roles that Black athletes, sportswriters, and teams played to challenge the exclusion or segregation of Black Americans from a diversity of Boston sports. During the late nineteenth and first half of the twentieth centuries, resistance expressed itself in the simultaneous desire to create all-Black teams to strengthen community solidarity and to integrate local sports to achieve wider legitimacy and recognition. Both efforts provided a strong foundation to contest racial inequality throughout Greater Boston.

In part 2's opening chapter, historians Brian Bunk and Edward Farnsworth discuss the first African Americans to integrate soccer in New England. The authors argue that the popularity of soccer in Greater Boston and Fall River, Massachusetts, quickly spread beyond white British immigrant workers who introduced it to native-born males who took up the game and transformed it into a leading sport. Among the earliest American-born soccer players were brothers Oliver and Fred Watson, the first documented African American soccer players in the United States. Both held industrial jobs in Pawtucket, Rhode Island, but maintained strong family roots in Boston and throughout New England. As professionals, they competed at the highest levels of the game.

Violet Showers Johnson's innovative chapter on cricket complements the soccer experience and delivers an insightful interpretation of how Afro-Caribbean immigrants in Boston and Cambridge aspired to achieve success both on the game field and in the broader society where they lived as people of African descent. Johnson describes how cricket developed in the West Indian Greater Boston community and later served as an identity marker that differentiated Black "foreigners" from American-born African Americans. Through cricket, West Indians and African Americans discovered revealing but unexpected answers about the limitations their sport encountered on the road to recognition and the stark realities of their contested identity in Boston and America.

In the next chapter, Andrew Smith examines the history of prizefighting in Boston through the lens of racial identity and race relations. During the late nineteenth and early twentieth centuries, Black migrants from within and without the borders of the United States embraced the "sweet science" as entertainment and as a potential source of employment. Black boxers influenced the dynamics of the sport and made the Hub a fitting case study for an analysis of changes over time in race relations and the written rules and unwritten mores of American prizefighting. Smith focuses on the careers of several prominent Black fighters who called Boston home.

The story of Black baseball in Boston reveals an added dimension to the game's history. Robert Cvornyek concludes that although Boston never hosted a professional team in the traditional Negro Leagues, the city produced several of the finest amateur teams, semiprofessional teams, and players in New England. Cvornyek contends that scholars have overlooked the players, owners, and promoters who developed the local game and ensured its intimate social and cultural presence in the Black community. African Americans in Boston resisted the indignities of segregation during the Jim Crow era by creating and supporting successful baseball teams that reflected the strength and vitality of their neighborhoods. Boston fans found a dignity and consistency in their Black players, who shaped racial identity and reinforced the notion that the struggle for racial equality can be found in several different arenas, including the baseball diamond.

Donna Halper's chapter on sportswriter Mabray "Doc" Kountze confirms how Black journalists shaped our understanding of contemporary sport and later framed the historical interpretation of Black sport in Boston. Kountze covered sports in Greater Boston for more than four decades, reporting for two local Black newspapers as well as the Associated Negro Press. He was a repository of knowledge about Black semipro baseball, and he covered professional sports too. In fact, he was the first Black sportswriter to be given a press pass by the Boston Red Sox. Besides writing about baseball, Kountze used his columns to promote the accomplishments of Black collegiate athletes in Greater Boston.

The final chapter in part 2 belongs to Marvin P. Dawkins and Jomills H. Braddock II. Their chapter foreshadows the important changes that World War II would eventually make to American race relations and examines the significance of the 1941 United Golfers Association (UGA) Negro National Open Golf Championship Tournament, held in Canton, Massachusetts. The authors conclude that the event served as a crossroads for distinguishing "early" and "late" Black golf pioneers. The 1941 tournament signaled a generational change among leading Black golfers in America. After the UGA suspended operation during the war years (between 1942 and 1945), a new cadre of Black golfers emerged to replace an older generation of Black golf champions.

The chapters in part 3, "Power and Performance in the Freedom Movement," survey topics traditionally associated with the strategies and tactics of the civil rights and Black liberation eras. Multiple themes including identity formation and intersectionality inform the work of authors who assess resistance in the Black athletic body from several social and cultural perspectives.

Historian Aram Goudsouzian's initial chapter reminds readers that even as Bill Russell led the Boston Celtics to a remarkable eleven NBA championships in thirteen seasons, he had a fraught relationship with the city of Boston. When he first arrived in the city in 1956, he possessed a liberal optimism about the community and his place in it. As the Celtics added Black players, the team earned plaudits for demonstrating the power of racial integration. Russell, however, grew disenchanted with Boston, labeling it a racist city. He immersed himself in Boston's Black community and injected himself into the city's racial politics. The city impacted Russell's racial consciousness and identity, and he, in turn, impacted race relations in the city he represented.

George Fosty combines his considerable research on Black hockey in Canada and the United States to trace Willie O'Ree's journey to become the first Black player in the National Hockey League (NHL). O'Ree made his professional debut with the Boston Bruins on January 18, 1958. O'Ree, often referred to as the "Jackie Robinson of hockey," has been the focus of renewed interest by scholars during the past decade. Fosty contends that O'Ree's legacy and achievements remain notable, but his impact on the sport fell short of expectations.

In his chapter on Black tennis in Boston, Sundiata Djata concludes that most tennis clubs, including those in the Boston area, refused admission to African Americans well into the twentieth century. Boston's Black tennis players chose to participate in a league of their own and helped establish the East Coast–driven American Tennis Association (ATA). In Boston, the Sportsmen's Tennis Center (STC) was founded in 1961 as the first indoor nonprofit tennis club built by and for the Black community. The center hosted several ATA National Championships, stimulating interest in the sport in Black neighborhoods. Boston's Longwood Cricket Club staged integrated national tournaments featuring tennis stars like anti-apartheid activist Arthur Ashe.

Jaime Loke critically examines fan and media reaction to the decision by Boston Celtic Jason Collins to openly declare his sexual orientation while working as an active basketball player. Drawing from over twenty-five thousand online news readers' comments, Loke examines the differing receptions to self-outing experienced by African American basketball players Jason Collins and Brittney Griner. Relying on a thematic textual analysis, she discovered that the public's perception of and reactions to the two athletes vastly differed. Collins's announcement was greeted with great jubilation, whereas Griner's revelation was much less celebrated in the press and was also the subject of heavy disapproval.

Donna Halper returns with a second chapter, this time to discuss race, sport, and radio. She notes that Boston had Black entertainers on the radio as early as 1922, but there were no Black announcers until 1948. Boston was also late in having a Black-formatted radio station; while there were some early experiments in 1952, it wasn't until 1961 that WILD debuted and began exclusively serving Boston's Black community. But while WILD tried its best, it was only on the air from sunrise to sunset, leaving the community to rely for its news on Black-owned newspapers like the *Bay State Banner* and the occasional public service program on Boston's predominantly white radio stations. The same was true with sports: while the exploits of Black athletes were covered, news about how they were treated in society (and in Boston) was often ignored, because nearly every sports-talk host and play-by-play announcer was white. Not only was racism downplayed; certain outspoken white talk show hosts sometimes made overtly racist remarks on the air, something that might not have occurred had there been more diversity among Boston's sports announcers.

The final chapter belongs to coauthors Eileen Narcotta-Welp and Elisabeth Erickson. They offer a theoretical interpretation of Allison Feaster, former Women's National Basketball Association (WNBA) standout and now director of player development for the Boston Celtics, through the constructs of the American Dream and Michel Foucault's theory of the docile body. In particular, the coauthors examine the postfeminist and postracial nexus of the late 1990s and early 2000s (years that spanned Feaster's college and professional basketball careers), concentrating on ideological narratives that promoted individualism and a white, middle-class, heterofeminine subject who can "act as if" she belongs in order to achieve the American Dream. Narcotta-Welp and Erickson discuss how Feaster was subject to cultural surveillance in both her personal and professional lives and examine how cultural changes in the American political, cultural, and social contexts of the late 2010s and early 2020s shifted narratives surrounding her, allowing Blackness and individualism to come into the foreground of her story.

In addition to the fifteen chapters, the book includes a foreword and an afterword. The foreword is written by former New England Patriot Devin McCourty. Since his arrival in Boston, McCourty has become a leading spokesperson for racial reform in the city, especially in education. He understands and honors the long tradition of Black athletes who used sport as a means to achieve racial uplift. In her afterword, Kathryn Leann Harris offers a sophisticated analysis of how Boston has chosen to commemorate or erase the achievements of its local Black sports personalities, many of whom are mentioned in this book. Although the stories of Black athletes continue to reverberate in the city's minority neighborhoods, most have not been told to a broader audience.

We attempted to assemble a book that acknowledges the influence that sport has exerted over the historical and cultural construction of race in Boston. We envisioned this project as an essential first step to understanding how local teams and athletes and the mass media reshaped the city's racial identity. Black athletic performance, representation, activism, and resistance have, at various historical moments, mirrored and informed Boston's racial politics. As McCourty reminds us, African American athletes have left a strong imprint on the struggle for social justice and equality, both on and off the field of play. It is our sincere hope that this volume will encourage new ways of thinking about the interplay of race and sport in a northern city with a troubled racial past and the intricate ways athletics intersect with fundamental issues that impact Black Bostonians.

Notes

1. Zebulon Vance Miletsky, *Before Busing: A History of Boston's Long Black Freedom Struggle* (Chapel Hill: University of North Carolina Press, 2022), 190.
2. Bill Russell and Taylor Branch, *Second Wind: The Memoirs of an Opinionated Man* (New York: Random House, 1979), 183.
3. "Green Ends What Robinson Started," *Boston Globe*, July 22, 1959, 35.
4. Joseph M. Sheehan, "Thomas Track Season's Top Man; High Jumper Named for Indoor Prize–Schoolman Hailed," *New York Times*, April 7, 1959, 44.
5. For information on Thomas's early life and career, see Alex Haley, "The Jumpingest Man on Earth," in *Alex Haley: The Man Who Traced America's Roots, His Life His Works* (New York: Reader's Digest, 2007), 28–34; and Bob Ryan, "Thomas Has Set High Standards," *Boston Globe*, January 31, 2003, 79, 84. For contemporary accounts of Thomas's achievements, see Harold Kaese, "Happiest Man in the World Says Record Wrecker: Very Relaxed, Very Modest, Amazing Really," *Boston Globe*, February 2, 1959, 19; "Crack Field of Track Stars Enter A.C. Meet," *New York Age*, February 4, 1959, 19; "Boston's Youth Breaks World's High Jump Mark," *Los Angeles Tribune*, February 6, 1959, 24; Jerry Nason, "Thomas on B.A.A. Spot," *Boston Globe*, February 7, 1959, 13; "Boston High Jump Sensation Became Jumper by Accident," *Los Angeles Tribune*, February 13, 1959, 23; and "John Thomas Drops Out of Boston U," *Los Angeles Tribune*, May 29, 1959, 23.
6. Kenneth Rudeen, "Seven Feet Up: The World's Best High Jumper Comes Back from Surgery to Pass the Magic Mark Once Again," accessed June 27, 2023, https://vault.si .com/vault/1960/01/25/seven-feet-up.
7. David K. Wiggins, Kevin B. Witherspoon, and Mark Dyreson, *Black Mercuries: African American Athletes, Race, and the Modern Olympic Games* (Lanham MD: Rowman and Littlefield, 2023), 102–18.
8. Susan Seligson, "Track and Field Icon John Thomas Dies at 71: Set World High-Jump Record as BU Freshman," *BU Today*, January 22, 2013, https://www.bu.edu/articles/ 2013/track-and-field-icon-john-thomas-dies-at-71/.
9. Guilk, quoted in "Obituary: John Thomas of Brockton Two-Time Olympian Dies," accessed June 29, 2023, https://www.baystatebanner.com/2013/01/23/obituary-john -thomas-of-brockton-two-time-olympian-dies/.
10. David K. Wiggins and Ryan Swanson, eds., *Separate Games: African American Sport behind the Walls of Segregation* (Fayetteville: University of Arkansas Press, 2016), 16.

PART 1

Framing Race, Community, and Resistance in Boston

1

Integration in Sport

How Busing Reshaped Athletic Talent

BIJAN C. BAYNE

One cannot tell the athletic history of Greater Boston without addressing race relations and Black athletes. From the story of world-class local track-and-field heroes like Louise Stokes, Eddie Dugger, Charlie Jenkins, Phil Reavis, and John Thomas to the pioneering careers of hockey's Willie O'Ree and pro basketball's Chuck Cooper, Black participants figure prominently. Hundreds more Black and Afro-Latin athletes achieved sports fame by representing local professional teams or playing for the city's many universities. In addition to the players themselves, Blacks have been an integral element of Hub sports history, from team owners such as semipro baseball's Clara Muree Jones; to journalists like Mabray "Doc" Kountze, Larry Whiteside, and Jimmy Myers; to coaches like Arthur "Fat" Johnson. Not to be forgotten are those Boston-area athletes who went on to fame in other locales, such as longtime *Chicago Defender* sportswriter Fay Young, who grew up in Cambridge and Malden and helped found the Negro National (baseball) League.

The culture and national image of race relations in Boston may be divided into two periods: before and after Judge Arthur Garrity's 1974 decision to enforce busing as a means of desegregating Boston's public schools. Before the mandate, Boston's nickname was "The Cradle of Liberty," and the city was remembered as a locus of abolition. After Garrity's decision, racist opposition to busing defined the city's reputation. Black Bostonians cannot count the number of times people from other cities or regions have said to them, "You're from Boston. I heard it's so racist."

As sport is a microcosm of the larger society, this anthology examines various realms of Black sports participation in Greater Boston through the stories of its participants. To better understand the nuances that shaped the city that hosted these teams, associations, and events and was home to these athletes, coaches, and administrators, it helps to know the tale of the two cities before and after the busing decision. National preconceptions about Boston, influenced by the violent images of the first months of forced school busing in and out of Roxbury, Dorchester, Hyde Park, South Boston, and Charlestown, informed fan and media reactions to statements about racist fans or hecklers made by visiting Black athletes such as Adam Jones of the Baltimore Orioles and Kyrie Irving, then of the Brooklyn Nets. Given the city's reputation, how many National Basketball Association (NBA) followers realize that Kyrie Irving's father, Dedrick, was a basketball star at Boston University or that Kyrie spent summer vacations on nearby Martha's Vineyard?

Even today, Boston's Black community regards busing as a critical turning point in the formation of the city's racial identity. Starting in the 1960s, the landscape of Greater Boston scholastic sports was dramatically reorganized by two major forces: federally mandated school busing programs aiming to achieve racial diversity in individual schools and the Metropolitan Educational Opportunity (METCO) program, a grant-funded grassroots initiative to advance opportunities for urban students by placing them in suburban districts. As different as the goals and shapes of the public busing mandate and the voluntary METCO initiative were, taken together, they served to shake up the demographics and power structures of local scholastic sports.

At the time of the busing decision, Boston's Black population had been growing for more than a century. Though the game of basketball was invented in the state in 1891, the city was not a hotbed of schoolboy basketball until the mid-twentieth century. Track and field was the more prominent arena for high school competition. Stars like sprinter Eddie Dugger, hurdler Fran Washington, dash man Lloyd Bell, and Olympians Charlie Jenkins (1952, 400 meters) and John Thomas (1964, high jump) competed in this event. In the 1950s, most local Black basketball talent was distributed among three schools: Boston Tech, with star players like Eddie Gates; Roxbury Memorial, led by Manny Texeira, Roscoe Baker, Hewie Joyner, and Albie Rue (the latter three later played collegiate basketball at Delaware State); and Boston Latin, the oldest high school in the United States. The successes of Bob Cousy and Bill Russell's dynastic Boston Celtics in the 1950s triggered a growing interest in basketball among city youth. The best Black players matriculated at historically Black universities, with some exceptions: Ed Washington and Eddie Gates, who played on Boston University's 1958 National Collegiate Athletic Association (NCAA) Tournament Elite Eight team (bowing in the tourney to Jerry West's squad from the University of West Virginia).

Even before mandatory busing, student athletes experienced plenty of reshuffling in high school sports: Roxbury Memorial closed its doors in 1960, and Boston Tech moved into its former building. Roxbury High School opened in 1969, only to close in 1973. Jeremiah Burke in Dorchester became a coeducational high school in 1972; the same year, Boston English opened to girls. Brandeis High in the South End closed after 1954, and Don Bosco Tech moved into that facility.

As the reality of busing approached, white neighborhoods like Southie, Charlestown, and Hyde Park—as well as racially diverse Roxbury, Dorchester, the South End, Mattapan, and Jamaica Plain—steeled themselves for what seemed inevitable. So did most of the city's parents, scholastic coaches, and athletes. What they had seen on their television screens from Birmingham, Selma, and the University of Mississippi a decade prior was coming closer to home: crisis, confrontation, and conflict lines drawn in the proverbial sand. Town ways were threatened. Media was in the middle of it all—first local, then national and international. Louise Day Hicks, chair of the Boston School Board at the time and an ardent segregationist, didn't budge or flinch. She encouraged the angry parents of South Boston High students not to flinch as well.[1]

I was born in 1959 and lived in Roxbury until right before the school year of 1965. Had my family not moved to Washington DC, I may have been a high school sophomore in Roxbury, the first year of forced busing. As it was, my relatives and contemporaries were impacted. On the first day of school in 1974, only thirteen students assigned to bus from Southie High, a working-class and ethnically Irish white neighborhood, showed up to attend school in Roxbury. They were met with no violence. Only 100 of the 1,300 pupils reassigned from mostly Black Roxbury turned up at Southie. Their reception was the opposite. Mobs pelted the teenagers with eggs, bottles, and bricks. Buses were turned over and set afire. Both the state police and the Massachusetts National Guard were deployed on Southie's campus, which became the site of national network news coverage in the fall of 1974. Those images stayed with viewers, reinforced by newspapers and weekly news magazines. Among the most striking and enduring was a 1976 image by *Boston Herald American* photographer Stanley Forman showing a white Joseph Rakes brandishing an American flag to attack Black lawyer Theodore Landsmark near city hall. Its caption read "The Soiling of Old Glory," and it won Forman a 1977 Pulitzer Prize.[2] It couldn't have done worse damage to Boston's image if it had been staged. These depictions helped fuel the national mindset that "Boston is racist"—despite its being the capital of a state that, though only 4 percent Black, had twice elected Ed Brooke to serve as the first Black U.S. senator since Reconstruction. Three decades later, by electing Deval Patrick, Massachusetts became the only U.S. state to have had both a Black U.S. senator and a Black governor.

A total of eighteen thousand students were bused from their neighborhoods to schools in other communities. Another thirty thousand left the public school system to attend parochial or prep schools.[3] Some of those students made their athletic marks on their new schools. In the early 1970s, Bobby Carrington became the first Black student at Archbishop Williams of Braintree, where he was a basketball star. Joe Streater was a standout player in the Dual County League for Lincoln-Sudbury. There were also Black athletes at Newton North High School and its smaller counterpart, Newton South, but most of them lived in Newton or Newton Centre before METCO or during its inception. The 1970s METCO executive director, Bob Hayden, raised his children, Karen and Bobby Junior, in Newton. So did Alvin Fortune. A former Colorado State wide receiver and defensive back, Fortune was hired as basketball coach by Newton High School in 1964, becoming the first Black head coach at a Boston-area public school. His wife, Isabel, was future senator Ed Brooke's secretary, a profession she acquired in the 1950s as one of the first two young Black women admitted to Fisher Business College. In the early 1970s, Fortune helped design the school busing program for Prince George's County, Maryland, where he had been named principal of Fairmont Heights High School.

METCO continues to exist, allowing city students to attend public schools in other communities that have opted in to the program. In 1987, two founding officials, Ruth Batson and Bob Hayden, wrote *A History of METCO*, a pamphlet chronicling the program's development and successes. In 2019, a state study reported that about 98 percent of METCO participants graduated from high school, contrasted with between 60 to 70 percent of students in other Boston schools. Some 90 percent plan to attend college, whereas only 59 percent of non-METCO students in Boston do.[4] Its many significant alums include Marilyn Mosby, the Baltimore state's attorney in the Freddie Gray case, and Audie Cornish, cohost of *All Things Considered* on National Public Radio. These points received strong support from several scholars and journalists, including Alana Semuels in her 2019 article in the *Atlantic* titled "The Utter Inadequacy of America's Efforts to Desegregate Schools."

METCO was not the only option; community-run schools also played an important role in providing high-quality education for Black students. Former University of Colorado basketball player Phil Hart founded and ran the Federation of Boston Community Schools in the 1970s. The three schools in the federation were New School for Children, Highland Park Free School, and Roxbury Community School, all founded by Black parents in the late 1960s as a response to racism in Boston's public schools. Jonathan Kozol began his teaching career in 1964 as a fourth grade teacher in an inner-city school. He was fired for lecturing about a Langston Hughes poem.[5] In 1967, his first book describing his experience in Boston's public schools, *Death at an Early Age: The Destruction of the Hearts and Minds of Negro Children in the Boston Public Schools*, won the 1968 National Book Award. Kozol then joined with Black parents when the New School for Children was founded in 1968, where he also taught. Chuck Lawrence was the principal of another community-controlled K–8 school, the Highland Park Free School. An attorney and law professor, Lawrence was one of the architects of critical race theory.[6] Roxbury's St. Joseph Community School was featured in a documentary film produced in 1975 by Tanya and Phil Hart titled *We Learn by Love*. Boston's 2021 acting mayor Michelle Janey attended a Roxbury free school.

School Sports Transformed

Three years into the mandated busing plan, Southie High had a much lower enrollment and many tiny, racially integrated classes. Local white parents had pulled their kids out. Students grew accustomed to the smaller scale. The teachers remained. Roxbury transfer students woke up early (in the dark in autumn), boarded their buses, and were still "greeted" by Massachusetts state troopers outside the building. Overall attendance at Boston's public schools, which had been one hundred thousand students, fell to sixty thousand, then forty thousand.[7] Many of the best athletes were cropping up in Catholic schools, private schools, and the suburbs. Even before the Garrity decision, upwardly mobile Black families had been departing Roxbury and Dorchester for Framingham, Newton, and Natick to the west or towns and cities such as Milton, Malden, Randolph, and Medford.

As these transitions unfolded, sports went on. Children who grew up on Bobby Orr, John Havlicek, and Carl Yastrzemski weren't going to be stopped by relocation—they were disheartened maybe, and feeling displaced, but far from inactive. When busing was in full stride, former Roxbury resident Bruno Giles was starring in basketball at Natick High School, Joe Streater at Lincoln-Sudbury was playing in the Dual County League, and Rufus Harris was a Boston Globe All-Scholastic performer for Framingham South, where he teamed with future Israeli League standout and Cleveland Cavaliers coach David Blatt. Harris went on to become the greatest player in the annals of the University of Maine (in a Yankee Conference that still included the University of Connecticut and Boston University).[8]

In some instances, after the dust settled, it seemed that the relocations might have been for the best. In the late 1960s, college basketball recruiters hadn't paid much attention to Boston basketball, viewing the talented Jimmy Walker of Boston Trade High School as an anomaly. But all that would change in the age of Mel King, Tommie Atkins, and Elma Lewis, due in part to the creation of two outlets for the town's hoop talent—the Boston Neighborhood Basketball League (BNBL), a summer program founded in 1969, and the legendary Boston Shootout.

Most of these players and their contemporaries played summer ball, beginning with 1969's Boston Neighborhood Basketball Association (BNBA), composed of community summer leagues in West Roxbury, North End, East Boston, Savin Hill, Lower Mills, Parker Hill, and Roxbury. Roxbury had a powerhouse team called the Titans, run by Al Brodsky, who was an assistant boys' basketball coach at Cathedral High. In those days, Roxbury's Washington Park was the most competitive city spot for pickup games. Bruce Clark played for Brighton High in the District League, with stars Leland "Lee-Lee" Pope, Willie Ames, and Floyd Thames. Clark recalls,

> During my senior year they put me in Dorchester High because of the busing thing. I was only there for the first marking term. . . . I couldn't learn anything due to the fact everyone was messing up and not getting the work done. . . . That school was so crazy . . . I couldn't hear the teachers. Every class was a joke. . . . We had so many students that the seniors and juniors went from 7:20 to 12 noon and the sophomores and freshmen went from 1 p.m. to 4:30. I was never so happy to get back to Brighton. I was trying to get into Mass Art, and my art teacher from BHS made it happen.[9]

From the BNBA grew the BNBL.

Scholastic players who learned their game on Boston's battlegrounds helped the city capture the storied Boston Shootout, a summer intercity All-Star tournament against the nation's premier urban high school competition. In 1971, three years before forced busing, NBA referee Ken Hudson, ball handler Rudy Cabral, and streetball stars–turned–Roxbury Clubhouse board members Roscoe Baker and "Jeep" Jones began organizing the Boston Shootout to showcase the city's best to the rest of the hoops world. The Shootout took place in 1972, the same summer that *Morgan v. Hennigan* (the case that resulted in mandatory busing) was filed. It was repeated in 1985, 1989, and 1995. All those years, the locals were decided underdogs, and America's top streetball students from New York City, LA, Chicago, Washington DC, and Atlanta expected easy pickings. Thanks to a steady stream of guard talent (in his four years, Patrick Ewing's teams never won the Shootout) and a boost from the home crowd, Boston kids put themselves on the basketball map for something other than Celtic championships. By the middle 1970s, Oregon, Holy Cross, Minnesota, Boston College, Florida State, and Rutgers gave scholarships to Greater Boston basketball stars such as Felton Sealy of Don Bosco, David Thompson of Stoughton, and James Bailey of Xaverian. A poorly devised social plan inadvertently shifted the power balance of scholastic basketball.

The Boston Six

Boston's 1972 inaugural Shootout squad featured some of basketball's best-kept secrets, including King Gaskins of Catholic Memorial, Carlton Smith of English High, Lexington High's Ronnie Lee (Russell's brother), "Smooth" Bobby Carrington of Archbishop Williams, post-man Billy Collins of Don Bosco, and Will Morrison of Tech High. Carrington was recruited by Oregon, University of Southern California, Utah, Syracuse, New Mexico, and the University of San Francisco but had been attending Boston College games since his sophomore year of high school.

After going through teams from DC (starring burly All-Everything Adrian Dantley) and New York (with Rutgers signee and future All-American Phil Sellers), the host team faced a finals matchup with Connecticut, led by Walter Luckett of Bridgeport Kolbe Cathedral (who averaged thirty-nine points per game in high school and graced the cover of the *Sports Illustrated* college basketball preview—as a freshman).[10] Boston copped the inaugural Shootout championship in a 72–71 nail-biter.

That historic Shootout championship team became known as the Boston Six, serving notice that the urban game was alive and very well at places such as Washington Park. In fact, the centerpiece of the Washington Park scene was not one of the Six but a player a year ahead of them, Dorchester High grad Stevie Strother, whose moves inspired the park's summer cry, "Run the Show, Stro', Run the Show."[11] Fans from across the city, including sportswriters and members of the Celtics, flocked to Washington Park to witness Strother's handle, Gaskins's deadly crossover dribble, Smith's silky jump shot, and Collins's monstrous dunks.

In high school, "Smooth" Bobby Carrington scored more than 1,500 points, earning a reputation as a force to be reckoned with on the court.

He was cocaptain of the 1971–72 team that won the Catholic Conference Championship. Carrington went on to star at Boston College. When he left school, he was the Eagles' all-time leading scorer with 1,849 points. Carrington led the 1974–75 team to a 21-9 record, averaging 20.9 points per game. They made the NCAA Tournament. Carrington later played in the American Basketball Association (ABA) and NBA.

Soon the city was producing 1970s superstars such as Felton Sealy of Don Bosco, Mimi James and Paul Little of Rindge, Dwan Chandler of English, and "Jammin'" James Bailey of Xaverian. Names such as Tommy Ford, Lee-Lee Pope, Perry Adams, and "Fast Eddie" Anderson were better known to blacktop aficionados than avid readers of the *Boston Globe* and *Herald American* sports pages. All were battle-tested outdoors; Adams's outdoor jump shot was so sure, he earned the nickname Ching for the sound the ball made against the chain nets. Out-of-towners who had come to play for Harvard, Boston College (BC), Boston University (BU), Northeastern, and even the Celtics were impressed by the level of homegrown talent. Guys with street cred took their game to the next level, strengthening Boston's "rep." Ron Lee made All-American at Oregon and played for the Phoenix Suns. King Gaskins began at Holy Cross, while Carrington, Collins, and Morrison signed at Boston College as a group. James Bailey made the big time with Rutgers and the Nets, followed by Butch Wade at Michigan.

The Golden Age

About six years into the busing program and fifteen years after METCO began, Eastern Massachusetts experienced a golden age of high school sports. In 1981 the most recruited hockey player in the country was Bobby Carpenter of Danvers's St. John's Prep, and the most recruited male basketball player was Pat Ewing of Cambridge Rindge and Latin. There were many other outstanding athletes, such as running back Jay McGee of Brockton (class of '82, on a football team ranked number one nationally) and Brockton's tight end Mark Bavaro (class of '81), who also starred in track and field and later became a Notre Dame All-American and played in two Pro Bowls.[12] Glen Gonsalves of Falmouth was high-jumping seven feet three inches at major Eastern track-and-field meets in 1981.[13] There was Brookline High basketball ace Fred Hill, Natick High quarterback (and basketball star) Doug Flutie, and girls basketball stars Medina Dixon of Rindge, Michelle Edwards of Cathedral, and Robin Christian of Jamaica Plain—all of whom went on to star at prominent university programs and played professionally. Included in this list are established players such as Eugene Miles from Dorchester, Craig Walker from Chelsea, Peter Wynne from Beverly, and Stu Primus from Lynn. In 1980, Lynn Classical, featuring Primus and Pancho Bingham, beat Rindge and Latin in a scrimmage at Milton High.[14] Primus went on to play basketball at BC, Bingham at BU. Butch Wade (class of '82) was staring at Boston Tech before a standout career at the University of Michigan. Wade enrolled in Michigan the same fall as Bourne High School running back Bob Perryman.

A few years later, former Roxbury youth basketball teammates Tony Bogarty and Demetriouse "Meechie" Russell emerged as star guards for Cohasset High School and Newton South High School, respectively. Bogarty's teammate Bryan Edwards set a state career scoring record for boys (2,563 points, passing mid-1970s Catholic Memorial sharpshooter Ronnie Perry) before playing for Boston College. Greater Boston scholastic sports was experiencing an unprecedented renaissance. A generation of children were reared on stories of Bob Cousy and Ted Williams and raised watching the Bobby Orr Bruins on TV 38. Youth were weaned on the sports columns of Bud Collins, Wil McDonough, Bob Ryan, Leigh Montville, Peter Gammons, and Dan Shaughnessy. And that was just in the *Boston Globe*. They saw Len Berman and Dick Stockton before they went national. The Bobby Orr rinks helped fuel the explosion. So did basketball opportunities such as the BNBL and the Boston Shootout.

This dispersal of talent, particularly in basketball, was fostered by Black upward mobility embodied in migration from Roxbury, Dorchester, Jamaica Plain, and Mattapan to Randolph, Newton, Framingham, Natick, Milton, and Stoughton. In addition, forced public school busing pushed Roxbury's athletes to South Boston, Charlestown, and Hyde Park high schools. By 1981 it was in full force. When the twelfth graders of 1981 had been sixth graders, the experiment resulted in violent attacks on Black students attending Southie High, Charlestown, and Hyde Park Irish American enclaves.[15] And under

METCO, now the largest and second-oldest continuously running voluntary school diversity program in the United States, parents of city teens took advantage of opportunities to enroll them in upscale or suburban schools.

Redistribution of Scholastic Sports Wealth

At the time METCO was founded, a future 1981 high school senior would have been three years old. In its initial year, seven schools participated, involving 220 students.[16] By the middle 1970s, this redistribution benefited the Black athletes, the white athletes, and their coaches. In basketball, Bobby Carrington had starred at Archbishop Williams of Braintree, David Thompson at Stoughton, and LeJuan "Buddy" Brantley at Bishop Feehan in Attleboro. Billy Raynor and King Gaskins of Catholic Memorial's early 1970s teams—and Felton Sealy, a Parade All-American who graduated Don Bosco in 1976—exemplified an influx into the local Catholic programs. Now suburban and private schools boast BNBL-level talent. And promising white stars such as Ronnie Perry of Catholic Memorial and Bob Bigelow of Winchester ventured into Roxbury to test their mettle against local players. Roxbury community leaders such as Alfreda Harris, Jeep Jones, and Roscoe Baker shepherded talent at centers such as Norfolk House, the Shelburne Center, and the Cooper Community Center. There were places to play. Boston entered sports teams in the National Youth Games and the Junior Olympics.[17]

It was a generation of youth raised eating Big Yaz Bread. During the dramatic 1975 World Series, the class of '81 were sixth graders, up late and on the edge of their seats when Pudge Fisk's homer won Game Six. On October 2, 1978, when Bucky Dent broke their hearts with his homer in the American League East division tiebreaker game, they were fourteen- or fifteen-year-old high school students and already competitive in sports. The 1978 Patriots were 11-5, led by quarterback Steve Grogan, fullback Sam "Bam" Cunningham, wide receivers Stanley Morgan and Harold Jackson, defensive backs Mike Haynes and Raymond Clayborn, and Pro Bowlers tight end Russ Francis, guard John Hannah, and offensive tackle Leon Gray. The students grew up on competitive football teams. Stanley Cup winners in hockey. NBA champs starring John Havlicek and Dave Cowens. "We were at the tail end of a great era in Boston sports—the Big Bad Bruins; Havlicek, Cowens & the Celtics;

the Sox and Fred Lynn and Jim Rice; heck, even the Patriots were piling up wins on the way to respectability. All of us wanted to grow up and be them, and all of us went out to our parks, heck, I went out to our street, and tried to play like them!" said Jay Ash, former Chelsea High School basketball player, Chelsea City manager, and former Housing and Economic Development secretary for Governor Baker.[18]

Standing Pat

Pat Ewing came to Cambridge from Jamaica at age thirteen, after having been raised on soccer and cricket. Cambridge in 1976 was the ideal place for him to be mentored in a new sport—basketball. The local high school star, Paul Little of Rindge, was a Parade High School All-American. The athletic tradition at Rindge long predated Little and Ewing. The school produced several of Greater Boston's Black semipro baseball stars of the 1930s. It also graduated John Thomas, the first athlete to high-jump seven feet indoors, and Charlie Jenkins, 1952 Olympic 400-meter dash gold medalist. Community basketball talent was often tutored by an older alum named Francis "Rindge" Jefferson. One of his mentees at the Cambridge Community Center was a small guard named Mike Jarvis. The heavy pickup games took place at Hoyt Field and Corporal Burns Park.

In 1962, Rindge (then "Rindge Tech"), a primarily Black squad, won the state Tech Tournament at the Boston Garden. "Rindge" Jefferson was a smooth, six-foot-two-inch wing player for the semipro Boston (Colored) Bruins, a former star at Kentucky State. It was he who tutored a husky Roxbury fourteen-year-old named Jimmy Walker in the finer elements of the game. Rindge's hours with Walker paid off in the latter leading the nation in scoring as a Providence College guard. That status earned him a number-one overall NBA Draft selection in 1967 (eighteen years before Ewing, having been mentored by Jarvis, garnered the same distinction).

When Ewing was an eighth grader, his physical education teacher, Steve Jenkins, introduced him to Jarvis, who was then an assistant college coach. Pat started learning the basics and went to Hoyt and Burns to watch pickup runs. One day he saw Xaverian High alum and Rutgers All-American Jammin' James Bailey play there. Northeastern assistant coach and former Huskies player Joe Delgardo and others worked young Ewing out at the Roxbury Youth Center. Toughened him up. He would need it, and not just on the court.

Jarvis became the head boys' basketball coach at Rindge, Steve Jenkins his assistant. Ewing enrolled in the ninth grade, and the team was making television news two or three times a week during his sophomore season. It was by no means a one-person team. Rindge benefited from excellent guard play by performers Karl Hobbs, who controversially transferred from Jeremiah Burke; Kevin Headley; and Ladon Adair. Early in Pat's career, they had a strong forward named Billy Ewing (unrelated). With success came haters. At away games, students threw rocks and bricks at their team bus or slashed its tires. The Rindge players were called racial slurs by opposing fans. Skirmishes even broke out on the court.[19]

Rindge persisted, running off a thirty-four-game winning streak. The loss (65–58) was to perennial New Haven power Wilbur Cross in 1980, at New Haven Coliseum. Wilbur Cross had a six-foot-nine-inch center named Jeff Hoffler who had faced Ewing a couple years earlier at a summer tournament in Detroit. Years later Jarvis told a New York paper Ewing had been ill with the flu and shouldn't have played.[20] In 1981, Bostonians hoped Pat Ewing would stay home and continue his basketball career at BC. On February 3, 1981, Ewing, his parents, Jarvis, and Jenkins held a press conference before 200 onlookers, 150 of them media, at Satch's Restaurant (owned by former Boston Celtic Satch Sanders). Ewing announced his decision to enroll at Georgetown University, where he would play for former Celtic John Thompson. Jarvis was asked if the decision was final, and Ewing replied, "There is no doubt in my mind that this is it." Maryland Coach Lefty Driesell said, "If I were (Georgetown Coach) John (Thompson), I wouldn't relax until the day he registers for classes."[21] A decade after busing began, Xavierian's 1985 Shootout backcourt of Dana Barros (a Mattapan native) and Rindge's Rumeal Robinson typified the city's history of premier guard play, characterized by a legacy of great ballhandling.

Today, though 54 percent of Bostonians are white, Boston's public schools are just 14 percent white. By 2018, more than half of Boston's public schools were evaluated to be highly segregated. Many have 90 percent non-white enrollments.[22] Despite this fact, the schools in Roxbury, Dorchester, and the South End are not particularly basketball powers, as they were from 1965 to 1975 when they were similarly imbalanced by ethnicity. For reasons beyond complexion, the better players flock to prep and private schools, much as they did from the period between James Bailey's mid-1970s stardom at Xaverian and that of Dana Barros in the mid-1980s at the same school. The more things change, the more they remain the same.

Local sports fans have similarly showered love and support on athletes as varied as 1970s Red Sox pitcher Luis Tiant, Brockton-raised boxer Marvelous Marvin Hagler, and Dominican baseball heroes Manny Ramirez, Pedro Martinez, and David Ortiz. Former Celtics such as Satch Sanders and Cedric "Cornbread" Maxwell still call the area home. When short-time 1960s Celtics center Wayne Embry retired as general manager of the Milwaukee Bucks, his primary mailing address was on Martha's Vineyard.[23] As for isolated incidents, in Game Six of the 1962 NBA Finals, Elgin Baylor of the Los Angeles Lakers scored a (still) Finals record 61 points against Boston before fouling out late in the game. Hub fans honored Baylor with a standing ovation; every Celtic player on the bench shook his hand. Though people still conflate the horrific violence associated with forced busing with the Red Sox being the last big league team to racially integrate its roster in 1959, the Celtics and the Bruins were the first teams in their respective sports to sign Black players. The Celtics were also the first to hire a Black coach (Bill Russell).[24] To date they have had seven Black coaches—more than any other NBA franchise. There are bigoted fans and all-white school enclaves and communities across the United States. While not perfect, Boston has been a place for Black athletes from all over the world to showcase their gifts—long before and long after the busing mandate.

Notes

1. James Aliosi, "Louise Day Hicks: 'You Know Where I Stand,'" *Commonwealth Beacon*, October 16, 2013, https://commonwealthbeacon.org/politics/012-louise-day-hicks-you-know-where-i-stand/.
2. "Desegregation Busing," Boston Research Center, accessed March 20, 2023, https://bostonresearchcenter.org/projects_files/eob/single-entry-busing.html.
3. Kio Herrera, "The Lasting Legacy of Boston's Busing Crisis," Prism, January 11, 2023, https://prismreports.org/2023/01/11/lasting-legacy-boston-busing-crisis/.

4. Alena Semuels, "The Utter Inadequacy of America's Efforts to Desegregate Schools," *Atlantic*, April 2019, https://www.theatlantic.com/education/archive/2019/04/boston -metco-program-school-desegregation/584224/.

5. Efe Igho-Osagie Shavers, "'No One Worked Harder Than Us Metro Kids, We Had to Figure Out the Rules on Our Own like Wild Animals': The Impact of the Metro Program on Black Students" (PhD diss., Boston College, 2024), https://open.bu.edu/ bitstream/handle/2144/48768/Shavers_bu_0017E_19172.pdf?sequence=6&isAllowed =y.

6. Alex Granados, "Jonathan Kozol: The Savage Inequalities of Public School," *EdNC*, October 26, 2017, https://www.ednc.org/savage-inequalities-public-school/.

7. Charles R. Lawrence, "Unconscious Racism Revisited: Reflections on the Impact and Origins of the Id, the Ego, and Equal Protection," Georgetown Law Faculty Publications and Other Works, 2008, https://scholarship.law.georgetown.edu/facpub/339/.

8. See "Boundary Adjustment Comment Form" and "Boston Public Schools—Implemented 1974, Terminated 1988," Resources Finalsite, accessed August 16, 2024, https:// resources.finalsite.net/images/v1643234176/beavertonk12orus/jcrzpe3xzgvdrnkpedzg/ 12116PublicComment.pdf.

9. Julia Spitz, "They've Got the Game, Not the Hoopla," *MetroWest Daily News*, May 5, 2007, https://www.metrowestdailynews.com/story/news/2007/05/15/spitz-they-ve -got-game/41224152007/.

10. Bijan C. Bayne, *Martha's Vineyard Basketball: How a Resort League Defied Notions of Race and Class* (Washington DC: Rowman and Littlefield, 2015).

11. George Hassett, "Summer Hoops Special: Searching for Stro," DigBoston, July 13, 2016, https://digboston.com/summer-hoops-special-searching-for-stro/. See also Jordan Horrobin, "As Luck Would Have It: Walter Luckett, the Story of Ohio's Sports Illustrated Cover Athlete Who Overcame Injury and Found Success after Basketball," *The Post*, October 5, 2017, https://projects.thepostathens.com/SpecialProjects/homecoming -2017/as-luck-would-have-it.html.

12. Brian Costello, "Mark Bavaro: Charlie Hustle," *Notre Dame News*, 2005, https://news .nd.edu/news/charlie-hustle/.

13. "Greg Gonsalves: Falmouth/High Mump," MSTCA, accessed August 16, 2024, https:// mstca.org/hall-of-fame/athletes/85.

14. "Lynn Classical vs. Rindge," *Lynn Journal*, May 27, 2021, https://lynnjournal.com/2021/ 05/27/the-stuff-of-legends-classical-basketball-superstar-stu-primus-recalls-the-rams -march-to-greatness/.

15. Chris Lovett, "Documentary Revisits the 'Trauma' of the Busing Era," *Dorchester Reporter*, September 13, 2023, https://www.dotnews.com/2023/documentary-revisits-trauma -busing-era. See also Paul Delaney, "Blacks' Anger Rising in South Boston as Violence over Schools Spreads," *New York Times*, May 2, 1976, https://www.nytimes.com/1976/ 05/02/archives/blacks-anger-rising-in-south-boston-as-violence-over-schools.html.

16. "METCO's History," Metropolitan Council for Educational Opportunity, accessed August 16, 2024, https://metcoinc.org/about/metco-history/.

17. See "Felton Sealey," Basketball Reference, 2022, https://www.basketball-reference .com/players/s/sealefe01.html.
18. Bijan C. Bayne, "Special Throwback Feature: Classic Scholastic," *DigBoston*, June 11, 2021, https://digboston.com/special-throwback-feature-classic-scholastic/.
19. Noah Perkins, "Ewing, Jarvis Rewind the Time," *Milford Daily News*, June 25, 2020, https://www.milforddailynews.com/story/sports/pro/2020/06/25/patrick-ewing -talks-racism-basketball-and-being-part-of-greatest-team-at-cambridge-rindge-and -latin-/42476307/.
20. Chip Malafronte, "New Haven 200: The Day Wilbur Cross Beat Patrick Ewing," *New Haven Register*, June 29, 2013, https://www.nhregister.com/connecticut/article/NEW -HAVEN-200-The-day-Wilbur-Cross-beat-Patrick-11422019.php.
21. Michael Wilbon, "7 Foot Center Ewing Elects to Play for Hoyas," *Washington Post*, February 2, 1981, https://www.washingtonpost.com/archive/sports/1981/02/03/7 -foot-center-ewing-elects-to-play-for-hoyas/50ea2d7d-3748-4a80-8037-e78cad561a7f/.
22. "Desegregation Busing," Boston Research Center, accessed August 16, 2024, https:// bostonresearchcenter.org/projects_files/eob/single-entry-busing.html.
23. Bijan Bayne interview of Wayne Embry, September 20, 1997, Boston, Massachusetts.
24. Richard Johnson, "Celtics Select Chuck Cooper as NBA's First Black Player Drafted," sportsmuseum.org, accessed August 16, 2024, https://www.sportsmuseum.org/curators -corner/celtics-select-chuck-cooper-as-nbas-first-black-player-drafted/; and "Willie O'Ree: The Jackie Robinson of Hockey," sportsmuseum.org, accessed August 16, 2024, https://www.sportsmuseum.org/curators-corner/willie-oree-the-jackie-robinson-of -hockey/.

2

Black Activism in Boston Sports

JOSEPH N. COOPER

The racial history of Boston is one of complexity and contradictions, a chronicle that provides important context to the study of Black activism in sports. On one hand, Boston is the bedrock of the American Revolution and the capital of a state that advocated for the abolition of slavery long before the Civil War. During the antebellum era—the period that preceded the Civil War—the city of Boston was a destination for people of African descent who were fleeing slavery.[1]

Boston is also the birthplace of American public education, a progressive city in which prominent Black leaders like historian and sociologist W. E. B. Du Bois and civil rights hero Rev. Martin Luther King Jr. acquired higher education and rose to international renown. From the late 1800s to the present, Black people have found gainful employment and achieved upward mobility in Boston and the New England region when similar opportunities were limited elsewhere—particularly in the South.[2] And since the 1960s, numerous Black immigrants from the Caribbean Islands and West Africa have settled in Boston.[3]

On the other hand, Boston is also a place where Blacks who fought on behalf of the British during the American Revolution (when the British promised them freedom from slavery in exchange for their service) were vilified and denounced. Later, the third stanza of the *Star-Spangled Banner*, written by Francis Scott Key in 1814, celebrates the deaths of the "hireling and slave."

Throughout American history, Blacks have been subjected to residential segregation, economic deprivation, physical and psychological violence, inferior access to quality health care, educational neglect, and mass incarceration.[4] The paradoxes of race relations in Boston reflect the contradictions that exist in our country: a nation that professes democracy, freedom, justice, and equality for all while deeply entrenched in capitalistic, neoliberal, and white racist beliefs and systems. Therein lies the reason why the color line has endured in Boston and the United States from the nation's founding to the twenty-first century.[5]

In the seminal text titled *Boston Riots: Three Centuries of Social Violence*, historian Jack Tagger documents 103 riots in Boston between the years 1700 and 1976. Common themes associated with the riots are political resentment, economic tensions, and communal social violence. Tager explains the phenomenon of communal social violence in these terms:

> Communal social violence . . . applies to a self-identified collection of people sharing a common cultural heritage with others, but who have a stronger allegiance to their group than to their larger society. . . . Pertinent local conditions also play an important role in producing specific factions of riotous citizens. . . . Feeling stifled, they might use violence to express themselves. . . . Thus, those who perceive themselves as powerless, either momentarily or habitually, regardless of their class, sometimes become violent to rectify their problems. They might wish to restore lost prerogatives, maintain the status quo, or vent anger and frustration at governance structures that are either impotent or unjust.[6]

The combination of deindustrialization, domestic and international conflicts, large-scale migration shifts, and economic instabilities resulted in civil unrest in Boston and numerous other urban environments throughout the United States during the twentieth century. Two important points to note about Tager's concept of communal social violence as it pertains to Boston are the prevalence of riotous behavior across race, ethnicity, and social class (i.e., inter- and intraclass group conflicts) and the contrasting reasons for these demonstrations (i.e., maintaining versus changing the status quo). Throughout the nineteenth century, Boston was considered one of the most racially segregated cities in the United States, and this reputation continued into the twentieth century.[7] The impact of racism on social class in Boston is illustrated by the fact that in 1930, 77 percent of Blacks worked in low-paying manual jobs compared to 46 percent of white European immigrants.

During and after the Great Depression, discrimination against Black workers continued despite numerous protests to democratize the workplace.[8] Racial tensions in Boston were commonplace from the eighteenth century to the early twenty-first century due to residential segregation and economic competition between Blacks and whites of the working class.[9]

One prominent example of civil unrest in Boston along racial lines occurred in the 1970s with the antibusing crisis. Scholars have agreed that the primary reason for the antibusing crisis was anti-Black racism.[10] Despite civil rights milestones like *Brown v. Board of Education of Topeka, Kansas* (1954), the U.S. Supreme Court decision outlawing segregation in public schools, and the passage of further civil rights protections under the Civil Rights Acts of 1964, 1965, and 1968, the number of racially imbalanced public schools in Boston increased from forty-six in 1966 to seventy-five in 1973.[11] In 1972, the National Association for the Advancement of Colored People (NAACP) filed a lawsuit against the city of Boston for denying Black students equal access to public education. Two years later, in 1974, the courts ruled in favor of the NAACP.[12] The anti-Black racism from whites toward Blacks in South Boston led to student walkouts, parent protests, and physical violence. White protesters believed that court-ordered busing to achieve school desegregation was unjust and socially detrimental. This discontent was grounded in the fact that white parents felt that the presence of Black students in the same schools as white students would decrease the quality of education and pose a threat to "innocent" white children.[13] The concern for student safety was so high that mayor Kevin White requested 125 federal marshals to maintain order, but federal judge W. Arthur Garrity declined the request. Subsequently, three hundred state police and one hundred riot-trained officers were deployed during the antibusing crisis. From the 1970s to the 1990s, numerous incidents of violence occurred between Blacks and whites in South Boston (particularly in Charlestown, Dorchester, and Hyde Park), and more than a dozen people were killed, underscoring the intensity of racial conflict in the city.

In subsequent years, white flight increased, and the student population in Boston's public schools became predominantly Black and Latino. The educational inequalities among public, private, and suburban schools in the Boston area widened the economic divides between race, income, and wealth. The institutionalized racism embedded in Boston's residential, educational, and economic policies resulted in a staggering stratification of the population along racial lines. A recent Federal Reserve Bank of Boston report reveals that Black households own two cents of liquid assets for every one dollar owned by white households.[14] Additional findings from the report indicate that Blacks are more likely to experience poorer long-term housing and retirement outcomes due to lack of homeownership, lack of home equity, and lower retirement savings compared to whites. This brief historical overview provides a necessary context for exploring the conditions in Boston that elevated the importance of sports in achieving change through resistance and activism at the local, state, national, and international levels.

Sports is one area of Boston history where racism has been perpetually challenged. Boston is widely recognized as a pioneering city for racial integration in sports.[15] For Blacks in Boston, achievement in sports generates racial pride, community, entertainment, revenue, and racial uplift. During the early to mid-twentieth century, the concept of racial uplift was embodied in the "muscular assimilationism" ethos shared by many African Americans.[16] This ethos rested on the belief that success in areas such as sports would improve race relations across all facets of society.[17] For whites in Boston, racial integration in sports presented a veneer of interracial harmony while maintaining inequitable structural arrangements that included the underrepresentation of Blacks in ownership and top-level management positions, a lack of Black-owned businesses, and inferior residential housing in predominantly Black neighborhoods.[18] Since the late nineteenth century, sport has served as a platform for disrupting the racial status quo, making it a space where Black sportspersons—athletes, coaches, administrators, journalists, and marketers, among others—could strategically align their efforts with broader social movements to champion racial uplift in overt and subtle ways.[19] The success of African Americans in sports previously dominated by whites ruptures the ideology of white superiority and serves as an example of the racial possibilities in the United States when barriers are removed and merit is equitably assessed. Within this chapter, I utilize the African American resistance typology (AART) and African American sport activism typology

(AASAT) to highlight the various ways in which Black Boston sportspersons championed racial justice in sports and beyond.[20]

Typologies of Resistance and Sports Activism

African Americans have engaged in intergenerational resistance against racial oppression since the seventeenth century. Various social movements such as the Black liberation struggle through Reconstruction (1600s–1890s), New Negro movement (1900s–1940s), civil rights movement (1950s–1960s), Black Power and Black feminist movements (1970s–1980s), hip-hop movement (1980s–2000s), and Black Lives Matter movement (2010s–2020s) influenced and were influenced by African American sportspersons.[21] Sociologist Harry Edwards categorizes Black athlete activism during the twentieth and twenty-first centuries into four distinct waves: gaining legitimacy (1900–1945), acquiring political access and positional diversity (1946–early 1960s), demanding dignity and respect (mid-1960s–1970s), and securing and transferring power via economic and technological means. Across these different eras, African American sportspersons relied on different strategies and resources to pursue racial progress.[22]

To understand the diversity of approaches utilized by African American sportspersons, I developed the AART.[23] The AART is composed of eight forms of resistance: agency, pioneering, advocacy, hybrid, activism, social movement, revolutions / social transformations, and sustained cultural empowerment. The following definition of *resistance* informs the eight-category typology: "intentional and/or unintentional actions by individuals, groups, organizations, and/or institutions that challenge oppressive systems and ideological hegemony."[24] The AART provides a broader framework for understanding how, when, why, and where African Americans resist racial oppression in intentionally disruptive ways for a collective aim (*activism*) as well as in less intentionally disruptive ways for both personal and, at times, collective aims (*borderline activist actions*). In other words, all forms of resistance are not activism, but activism is one primary form of resistance.

The difference between borderline activist actions and activism is based on intention and context. For example, Joseph Cooper and colleagues define *activism* as "engagement in intentional actions that challenge a clearly defined opposition and disrupt hegemonic systems perpetuating oppression, injustice, and inequity while simultaneously promoting empowerment among those historically oppressed, fairness/equity, human dignity, and demands for a shift in power relations in concert with broader social justice movements."[25] The five criteria of activism include intentionality for igniting change for a collective group, the presence of clear opposition, disruption to a status quo, the expression of concrete demands, and a connection to a broader social movement.[26] Therefore, resistance actions such as *agency, pioneering*, and *advocacy* are not inherently activism unless these five criteria are met. Stated differently, when determining whether an action is activist or not, context always matters; it should not be misinterpreted as a measure of effectiveness in achieving a progressive aim. As I have stated elsewhere, both activism and borderline activist actions can advance social justice aims under certain conditions.[27]

In terms of borderline activist actions, agency refers to the use of personal choice and/or group actions to express a sense of individuality and/or socio-cultural disposition within a specific context. In many instances, agency is an expression of personal interests rather than collective aims and thus only deemed activism if all five criteria are fulfilled. Throughout U.S. history, African Americans like famous Black heavyweight boxing champions Jack Johnson in the early 1900s and Muhammad Ali in the 1960s have utilized their agency to express their humanity and challenge rigid pathologies mapped onto them. Pioneering involves being the first of a social identity group to accomplish a particular feat. While barrier breaking often contributes to collective progress, the intention of all pioneers (in sports or otherwise) is not always focused on this goal. Therefore, like the category of agency, pioneering is deemed as a borderline activist action unless all five activism criteria are met.

Advocacy involves intentional actions taken by an individual or group to generate awareness of and galvanize support for addressing specific social issues and conditions. Advocacy efforts are often conflated with activism, but in many instances, these actions do not involve direct opposition to or result in a concrete disruption of a status quo. In oppressive societies, advocacy is more widely promoted and accepted precisely because it is less disruptive of and threatening to the foundations of hegemonic systems and structures. *Hybrid resistance* refers to an engagement in multiple forms of resistance across time, space, and context. *Social movement* is defined as sustained collective efforts against oppressive forces and systems by an oppressed group for a concentrated period, typically but not exclusively lasting for one year or more. Both the AART and AASAT posit that activism is inextricably linked to broader social movements. *Revolutions / social transformations* are counteroppressive efforts that result in a restructuring of societal hierarchies and a shift in political, economic, military, and social power from oppressor groups to oppressed groups. *Sustained cultural empowerment* refers to the elimination of all forms of anti-Black racism and the presence of Black-centered ways of thinking, doing, and being.

My purpose in creating the AART and the AASAT is to develop a framework in which to understand the nuanced differences that exist across activist actions. The AASAT describes ten types of activism: symbolic, scholarly, grassroots, mass mobilization, economic, legal, political/civic, media, music and art, and military.[28] *Symbolic activism* refers to coordinated public acts of disruption to redress social injustices. Protests are a popular form of symbolic activism and are widely recognized in previous literature on African American athlete activism.[29] *Scholarly activism* refers to the challenging of hegemonic norms that support the existing power structure via teaching, research, and sociopolitical analyses like autobiographies, memoirs, and ethnographies. All activist efforts are undergirded by philosophical and paradigmatic foundations, which are presented in the form of scholarly contributions. *Grassroots activism* refers to locally organized disruptive actions for social justice. These actions typically occur within a specific organization, institution, community, or city. *Mass mobilization activism* involves the formation of people across multiple geographical regions for the purpose of generating widespread social, political, legal, and/or economic change. Activism on the interstate, national, and international levels has been an integral source of strength for groups who have been subjected to oppressive conditions across time, space, and context.[30]

Economic activism refers to financial divestment from oppressive entities and/or fiscal investment in politically and culturally empowering entities.[31]

The presence of Black economies in segregated neighborhoods has served as a lifeline for African Americans dating back to Reconstruction.[32] *Legal activism* involves the strategic use of the judicial system at the local, state, federal, and international levels to change laws for social justice aims. In the United States, a common demand across all eras of Black resistance has been the institution of legal protections for human and civil rights. *Political/civic activism* refers to directly challenging government power structures for social change, such as the release of political prisoners. The creation of voting blocs and counterhegemonic political organizations to demand justice in governmental policies and practices are examples of *political activism*. *Media activism* refers to the use of newspapers, radio, television, and digital communications platforms to achieve social justice goals. During the early and mid-twentieth century, the role of the Black press was significant in galvanizing support for racial justice causes in sports and beyond.[33] *Music* and *art activism* emerged as Black social justice–oriented cultural expressions. A common feature of the Black aesthetic is the interplay among sports, music, and art; each of these expressions has been used as a tool of resistance.[34] *Military activism* refers to the use of combat, violence, and technology to challenge oppressive regimes and systems. This form of violence has been a central component of the battle for Black liberation in the United States and beyond. Collectively, the AART and AASAT provide a framework for examining how, when, why, and where Black sportspersons in Boston have challenged racial and social injustices in sports and beyond.

Intergenerational Black Resistance and Activism

Consistent with my sociological orientation, in this section I examine select intergenerational instances of Black resistance and activism in Boston sports and connect them with broader Black social movements in the United States that occurred at the same time. Based on the selected examples, the following Black social movements are highlighted: the Black liberation struggle through Reconstruction (mid- to late 1800s) and New Negro movements (1900s–1940s), the civil rights (1950s–1960s) and Black Power movements (1970s–1980s), and the post–civil rights and Black Power movements (1980s–2020s).[35]

Resistance in Liberation and New Negro Movements

One of the earliest forms of Black resistance and activism in Boston sports occurred with the establishment of Black independent, amateur, and semiprofessional baseball teams and leagues during the latter part of the Black liberation struggle through Reconstruction in the 1870s through the start of the New Negro movement in the early 1900s. The gentlemen's agreement in Major League Baseball (MLB) that banned the participation of Blacks (then referred to as "Colored") was also in effect at the amateur and semiprofessional levels. The Boston Resolutes were the first Black amateur baseball team formed in the city in 1870.[36] The pioneering activism of this team led to grassroots activism seven years later with the formation of the League of Colored Baseball Players.[37] Although the league was short-lived due to financial instability and lack of organizational infrastructure, this pioneering attempt served as a precedent for future efforts to create a Black baseball league.[38] Both the team and league were established as a means of commanding respect, recognition, and inclusion of Black athletes and teams into mainstream sports.

Moreover, the creation of this league embodied the ethos of the New Negro era. The term *New Negro* refers to African Americans in the postemancipation period who were focused on building institutions to challenge their racial oppression. Among these institutions were the African Society, African Masonic Lodge, Odd Fellows, and Boston Urban League.[39] While African American baseball was not a social or political organization in the traditional sense, it merits consideration as part of the ethos of the New Negro era. Historian Robert Cvornyek explains the significance of African American baseball in Boston during the early 1900s: "African Americans in Boston resisted the indignities of segregation during the Jim Crow Era by creating and supporting successful baseball teams that reflected the strength and vitality of their neighborhoods. Boston fans found a dignity and consistency in their black players that shaped racial identity and reinforced the notion that the struggle for racial equality can be found in several different arenas, including the baseball stadium."[40] The fact that Black teams were often composed of various ethnic groups also underscores how sports participation serves as an extension of African diasporic connections. For example, Black baseball teams in Boston during this period were often composed of African Americans, Cape Verdeans, Cubans, and Native Americans. Their collective identity through sport facilitated cultural empowerment in a city and a society in which anti-Blackness was ubiquitous.

Like Black independent, amateur, and semiprofessional teams in urban enclaves across the United States, the Boston Resolutes played most of their games in Black neighborhoods, where they were supported by local Black churches, fraternal organizations, and businesses. These games were an integral part of cultural life in the New Negro era: spectators wore fancy outfits, and music and social celebrations were often included. The games also served as a venue for grassroots and economic activism for racial causes beyond sports. For example, in 1941, attorney John S. R. Bourne, president of the Eastern New England Congress for Equal Opportunities, used a local baseball game to recruit patrons to support a boycott of a white store in Roxbury that refused to hire Negro girls as clerks.[41] The baseball games not only fostered a sense of collective racial identity but also served as a space for political mobilization to resist injustices in the broader community. The presence of Black community leaders that included politicians, businesspeople, clergy, and entertainers at these events underscores the cultural and political significance of Black baseball in urban areas in the North.[42]

The Resolutes' success contributed to the establishment of the National Colored League (NCL) in 1887, which included teams from New York, Boston, Philadelphia, Pittsburgh, Baltimore, and Louisville. Although the league was short-lived—it folded the same year—its establishment signified Black sportspersons' pursuit of *organizational activism* as a form of *mass mobilization activism* amid racial exclusion from white mainstream sport leagues. In 1903, the Greater Boston Colored League (GBCL) was established, which reflected organizational activism at the *grassroots* level. Teams in the GBCL included the West Medford Independents, the Boston Royal Giants, the Cambridge Washingtons, the Malden Riversides, the West Newton Athletics, and the Allstons. In the 1920s and 1930s, the GBCL included teams from Boston, Cambridge, Malden, Winchester, Everett, Lynn, and Medford. The Boston Resolutes' *hybrid resistance* (pioneering, grassroots, mass mobilization,

and economic activism) aligned with sociologist Harry Edwards's conception of the first wave of Black athlete activism focused on gaining legitimacy
through sport.

Both the intraracial games in their own neighborhoods and interracial
games in white neighborhoods generated economic gains for these Black
baseball teams. Although Blacks were excluded from participating on white
teams, it was common for Black and white semiprofessional teams to engage
in symbiotic relationships for economic and marketing purposes.[43] By
the late 1880s, the Resolutes were considered one of the best teams in the
region, which generated interracial spectator interest. As such, sporting contests served as a litmus test for broader racial integration efforts. In historian
Robert Cvornyek's apt formulation of the significance of Black baseball teams
in Boston and their interracial appeal, "the baseball diamond served as a
vital arena in the struggle for freedom and the game reflected the city's racial
flexibility and spirit."[44] Black teams viewed these contests as opportunities to
advance racial progress. In the 1880s, the Black Resolutes defeated their white
crosstown rivals 25–12, claiming the rights to the team name, since both teams
sought to be called the Resolutes.[45] This victory is symbolic of the history of
Black athletes who used sport as a platform for challenging the myth of white
superiority, as heavyweight boxing champion Jack Johnson did in defeating
Tommy Burns and Jim "The Great White Hope" Jeffries in 1908 and 1910,
respectively. Equally significant, track-and-field champion Jesse Owens won
four gold medals at the 1936 Olympics in Berlin, Germany; the Harlem Rens
basketball team defeated the Original Celtics on December 20, 1925; and the
all-Black starting five of the Texas Western men's basketball team achieved a
National Championship victory over the all-white University of Kentucky
team in 1966.[46] For Black Americans, these victories personified racial pride.

Beyond Black baseball, another important African American sports pioneer
was cyclist Katherine Towle "Kittie" Knox.[47] In the late nineteenth century,
the sport of cycling was not only racially exclusive, but it was also sexist.[48]
As a biracial African American who excelled against competitors across
gender lines, Knox was able to navigate social settings with varying degrees
of freedom due to her lighter skin compared to many African Americans.
For example, in 1893, Knox joined Boston's all-Black Riverside Cycling Club

(pioneering activism on the individual and team level). She was also selected as the first African American member of the League of American Wheelmen (LAW). As a result of her pioneering, the Wheelmen's racist organizing officials instituted a color ban in 1894 to void her membership. As noted earlier, a primary difference between borderline activist actions and activism is the presence of clear opposition. Thus, when activism is undertaken inevitably, backlash will emerge from the opposition. However, Knox's persistent hybrid resistance resulted in her membership being restored later that year.

Despite her victory, Knox continued to experience racial and gender discrimination throughout the remainder of her career.[49] As an activist, Knox utilized various media outlets to challenge the racist ban (media activism), galvanizing a group of her fellow female cyclists who were white to threaten a boycott of the LAW if her membership was not restored (grassroots activism). In addition to her activism, Knox also exercised pioneering and agentic resistance through fashion at cycling events. She routinely challenged the norms of longer skirts and plain attire for women during that period by wearing elaborate, colorful suits. Knox's courageous resistance received favorable coverage from the *Boston Journal* and *Boston Globe* in the late 1890s, and her legacy is still celebrated by USA Cycling in the twenty-first century. Kittie Knox embodied *intersectional resistance* against racism and sexism in the Black liberation struggle era and serves as an exemplar for Black athlete activists of the present and future.

Resistance in the late New Negro era shifted to an increasing reliance on the power and influence of the media. The Black press played an integral role in pressuring local and national organizations (sport and nonsport) to desegregate.[50] The strategic use of media to champion racial justice was also prevalent in Boston. In the 1940s, William "Sheep" Jackson engaged in media activism through his writings in the *Boston Chronicle* on Black baseball teams in Boston, particularly his creation of the "All-Colored Team."[51] In concert with the formation of the Negro Leagues and the surging popularity of Black news publications like the *Chicago Defender, Pittsburgh Courier, The Crisis, Indianapolis Freeman, New York Amsterdam News, Baltimore Afro-American, Kansas City Call, Associated Negro Press,* and the *Opportunity,* to name a few, Black sports journalists and historians reflected the first and second waves of Black athlete activism focused on gaining legitimacy and acquiring political access and positional diversity in various aspects of the sports industry.[52] The National Baseball Hall of Fame and Museum was established in 1936, but it was not until 1971, with the induction of famed Black baseball player Satchel Paige, that Negro League players were invited into this exclusive membership. Without the contributions of Black sports journalists and historians like William "Sheep" Jackson and Boston's Mabray "Doc" Kountze, among others, it would not have been possible to celebrate the achievements of the Black athletes and leagues who made history on their fields.

Resistance in Civil Rights and Black Power Movements

In the 1950s, following the New Negro era, African Americans transitioned into the civil rights movement. Prominent forms of resistance in the broader Black community included grassroots, mass mobilization, pioneering, symbolic, media, legal, and political activism. As it relates to Boston sports, pioneering continued to be among the most salient forms of resistance for Black sportspersons. For example, in 1950, with the fourteenth pick of Chuck Cooper, the Boston Celtics became the first team in the National Basketball Association (NBA) to draft an African American player. In 1958, the Boston Bruins selected Willie O'Ree, who became the first Black player to participate in the National Hockey League (NHL).[53] On December 26, 1965, the Celtics became the first NBA team to start five Black players (Bill Russell, Thomas "Satch" Sanders, K. C. Jones, Sam Jones, and Willie Naulls) when they defeated the St. Louis Hawks (97–84).[54] These Black players started a total of twelve games during that season. By the 1965–66 NBA season, nearly half of the league, two-thirds of the starters, and three-fourths of the All-Stars were Black.[55] Between the 1950s and 1970s, the Celtics won thirteen NBA championships, which unequivocally proved that racial integration was possible in a society founded on racial segregation and oppression.

The success of these teams also validated the activism tenet of the civil rights era that demanded equal opportunity for Blacks and asserted that when racial barriers were removed, Blacks could achieve and excel at levels comparable to whites. The combination of grassroots and mass mobilization activism outside of sports, which included the 1963 March on

Washington for Jobs and Freedom and the 1965 voting rights protest march from Selma to Montgomery, with the pioneering success of Black sportspersons in major cities like Boston paved the way for racial progress in the United States. These historical milestones in sport coincided with the successful legal and political activism of African Americans and their allies that led to the passage of the landmark Civil Rights Acts of 1964, 1965, and 1968. Stated differently, Black success in sports humanized the race in a profound manner and affirmed that the intergenerational Black liberation struggle was not in vain.

In 1966, the Celtics broke another barrier when head coach Red Auerbach named William "Bill" Felton Russell as his successor, which made Russell the first African American to occupy that role in any major sports league in the United States.[56] As a head coach, Russell led the Celtics to back-to-back NBA championships in 1968 and 1969. Russell's pioneering opened the doors for subsequent Black professional head coaches. By 2021, six Black head coaches had led their respective teams to NBA championships: Russell in 1968 and 1969 (Celtics), K. C. Jones in 1984 and 1986 (Celtics), Al Attles in 1975 (Golden State Warriors), Lenny Wilkens in 1979 (Seattle Supersonics), Doc Rivers in 2008 (Celtics), and Tyronn Lue in 2016 (Cleveland Cavaliers).[57] The fact that half of the NBA's championship-winning Black coaches were affiliated with the Celtics underscores the progressive racial leadership within this Boston franchise. In addition, at the start of the 2021–22 NBA season, Blacks occupied nearly half of all head coaching positions (thirteen out of thirty). In total, there have been seventy Black head coaches in the NBA since 1966, including nine Coach of the Year recipients.[58] These numbers far exceed all other major professional sports leagues in the United States (National Football League [NFL], MLB, NHL, Major League Soccer [MLS], and Women's National Basketball Association [WNBA]).

Russell also played an instrumental role in the appointment of Ken Hudson as the first African American NBA full-time official in 1968 (Hudson's contribution to Boston sports is highlighted later in this chapter).[59] The pioneering resistance exhibited by these Black Boston sportspersons exemplified and added credence to Edwin Bancroft Henderson's philosophy of muscular assimilationism.[60] The pioneering exhibited by the Black Boston

Celtic players and head coaches, in partnership with white franchise own-ership, general managers, and head coaches, served as a precedent for the power of strategic responsiveness to interest convergence (SRIC) to achieve racial progress in sports.[61] SRIC refers to the phenomenon that occurs when groups facing inequitable structural conditions utilize relationships and convergent interests with power wielders to optimize holistic outcomes for themselves and their collective group. Russell demanded increased African American representation in sports leadership positions and leveraged his relationship with Red Auerbach to become the first Black head coach in the NBA, subsequently using his power and influence to create opportunities for future Black head coaches and officials to secure positions and achieve credibility in the sport.

These pioneering efforts also reflected the integrationist ethos of the New Negro and civil rights movements as well as the second wave of Black ath-lete activism whereby *political access and positional diversity* were central activist aims.[62] The separation of the races in all facets of U.S. society served to protect a racist hierarchy in which whites were considered superior and Blacks were considered inferior. Thus, integration was a direct threat to the psychosocial and pseudoscientific myth of white superiority because when Blacks and whites occupied the same spaces under equitable conditions, it became evident that no innate differences in ability existed based on race. Integration would also illuminate the fact that the perceived higher status of whites in society was less about their hard work (the liberalist meritocracy myth) and more about racist policies and practices that granted them unjust enrichment.[63] The elimination of access barriers in sports, education, and other areas of society signified racial progress because African Americans were being granted opportunities to demonstrate their prowess in previously all-white spaces. The integrationist and muscular assimilationist philosophies sought to demonstrate how Black people are human beings deserving of equal rights and fair treatment (contrary to the U.S. Constitution, which once defined them as three-fifths of a person and essentially the property of white Americans in perpetuity).[64]

In addition to his pioneering accomplishments, Russell also exemplified *hybrid resistance* throughout the course of his professional sports career.

43

Historian Aram Goudsouzian vividly explains the significance of Russell's impact on U.S. society through sports: "Russell did not desegregate the NBA, but he integrated it. He became the first black superstar—the first to generate copious publicity, the first to alter the sport's texture, the first to shape a team's championship destiny. Moreover, during the civil rights movement, Russell presided over basketball's model of successful racial integration."[65] After earning four NBA championships with the Celtics, Russell utilized his platform as a high-profile athlete to advocate for Black civil rights on and off the court. For example, in 1958, he demonstrated *symbolic activism* by refusing to participate in an exhibition tour in Dallas, Texas, when event promoters sought to institute segregated housing for players.[66] In 1962, Russell again engaged in *symbolic activism* by declining to play in an exhibition game in Louisville, Kentucky, when a local restaurant declined to serve him and his Black teammates.[67] Russell acquired a reputation for *symbolic activism* in cities where racial segregation was practiced. In 1967, Russell attended the famous Ali Summit in Cleveland, Ohio, to show his support for Muhammad Ali's refusal to join the U.S. military. Russell's support of Ali and concurrent criticism of U.S. militarism highlighted how his political views were at least partially influenced by the Black Power movement of the late 1960s and early 1970s.[68] Along with Ali, Russell criticized U.S. foreign and domestic policies as being racially oppressive.[69] Russell and his fellow Black activist athletes embodied what sociologist Harry Edwards describes as leveraging their political, economic, and media power through sport.[70]

Throughout his time in Boston, Russell faced intense racial discrimination. In 1960, his house in Reading, Massachusetts, was painted with racial epithets, and feces was left on his furniture.[71] Despite these harsh realities, Russell was unwavering in his outspokenness against racism in Boston. For example, in the late 1960s, he opened a restaurant in Boston's South End and organized a boycott of another restaurant that racially discriminated against Blacks, reflecting his grassroots and economic activism.[72] As a high-profile figure in Boston, Russell's actions influenced the racial dynamics in the city as well. His celebrity status enabled him to draw undesirable media attention to racist practices in businesses and cities, including Boston, which compelled them to change. One of Russell's strengths was his keen ability to balance his stern criticism of racism in the United States with his pride in the best of American culture, demonstrating an evolving belief that racial integration could prevail. As the historian Aram Goudsouzian concluded, "Arriving in the wake of *Brown v. Board of Education* and the Montgomery Bus boycott . . . [Russell] accepted a responsibility to represent the entire race, project humble dignity and patriotic enthusiasm, and engender a spirit of racial goodwill."[73]

Russell founded and participated in numerous grassroots, mass mobilization, and political/civic activist efforts. In 1963, he organized a human rights march from Roxbury to Boston Common that attracted over ten thousand people (*grassroots activism*).[74] The same year, he participated in the famous March on Washington with civil rights leaders from across the country (*mass mobilization activism*). Leveraging his support for the voter registration campaign in the Freedom Summer of 1964 (*political/civic activism*), Russell led basketball clinics for Black and white youth in Mississippi.[75] On a personal level, Russell also exhibited *agentic resistance* through his appearance, dress, and intentional decision to not exhibit stereotypical behaviors. Goudsouzian highlights how Russell was intentional about driving a Chrysler (instead of a Cadillac), wearing oversized suits (instead of tight suits), and grooming his face with a mustache and goatee (as opposed to being fully shaved) to exercise his individuality in a society that forced Black men to assimilate to white men's standards of acceptability. In an interview, Russell described these decisions as his "own little revolution."[76] This intentional embodiment of the Black aesthetic via physical appearance was typified by those involved in the Black Power movement, which sought to celebrate natural African features and demonstrate how Black is beautiful and powerful, in part by celebrating Afros and, among men, sporting goatees and beards. Another example of Russell's agentic resistance is when he declined an opportunity to play for Abe Saperstein's Harlem Globetrotters.[77] Russell resented the way the Globetrotters reinforced negative stereotypes of Black people for white entertainment. In contrast to Russell's activist orientation, his archrival, Wilt Chamberlain, opted out of his senior year of college at the University of Kansas to earn $65,000 playing for the Harlem Globetrotters. Russell's hybrid resistance throughout his playing career and into retirement is exemplary and continues to impact Black athlete activists like LeBron James, among others, into the twenty-first century.

Two other areas of resistance exhibited during the third wave of Black athlete *activism* were *scholarly* and *media activism* through sports. In concert with prominent African American sports historians E. B. Henderson and Sol White, Mabray "Doc" Kountze published the first book on Boston sports in 1979 titled *Fifty Sports Years along Memory Lane: A Newspaperman's Research, Views, Comment & Career Story of United States, Hometown, National & International Afro-American Sports History.*[78] This seminal text broadly documented the rich history of African American sportspersons in Boston and the United States. Kountze also served as the sports editor for the *Boston Chronicle* and *Boston Guardian* and was a feature contributor for the *Associated Negro Press*. He was also a member of the Boston Museum of Afro-American History and the Association for the Study of Afro-American Life and History founded by Dr. Carter G. Woodson. The importance of the archival record of Black sportspersons and sporting events cannot be understated. The erasure and neglect of Black contributions to the United States and global societies has been one of the strongest tools of colonization and white racist oppression. Thus, the recording and celebration of this historical information reflects a powerful form of scholarly and media activism that expresses Black humanity and excellence in the face of oppression. Russell also wrote two memoirs of his life experiences, which represent another form of mainstream scholarly activism.[79] The power of writing one's own story is emblematic of the third wave of Black athlete activism, which focused on demanding dignity and respect and thus aligned with the focus of the Black Power movement of the 1970s and 1980s.[80]

Resistance in Post–Civil Rights and Black Power Movements

After the civil rights and Black Power movements, pioneering and advocacy resistance in Boston sports occurred at the intercollegiate level. One notable figure who embodied pioneering resistance through sports is Charlie Titus. A Roxbury native, Titus became the first men's basketball head coach at the University of Massachusetts in 1974. Over a forty-year career, Titus served as the athletic director and vice chancellor of athletics, recreation, and special projects and pioneered the creation of the Little East Conference in 2012 (a Division III National Collegiate Athletic Association [NCAA] conference). Titus's longevity as a Black athletic director paved the way for future Black college athletic directors in Boston such as Vaughn Williams (athletic director at Bentley College and former associate athletic director at Boston College), Peter Roby (athletic director at Dartmouth University and former athletic director at Northeastern University), and G. Anthony Grant (athletic director at Massachusetts Institute of Technology). Titus was also instrumental in establishing the Youth, Education, and Sports (YES) with Africa program that provided coaching and athletic clinics in Benin and Senegal, West Africa. More recently, Titus, along with UMass Boston chancellor emeritus Dr. J. Keith Motley, established the sport leadership and administration undergraduate program with a $5 million endowment from New Balance. Titus has been a long-standing, outspoken advocate for Black representation in athletic leadership in Boston. In 2020, he appointed Darlene Gordon as the first Black woman interim director of athletics at UMass Boston. His legacy as a champion for racial equality through sports exemplifies pioneering and advocacy resistance.

Another notable sports figure in Boston is Hall of Famer Alfreda Harris. As the founder and former administrative coordinator of the Shelburne Recreation Center and the longest-serving member of the Boston Public School Committee, Harris is a beloved community leader and advocate in Roxbury.[81] In 1980, Harris became the first women's head coach at UMass Boston (pioneering). Harris was also the first woman to coach in the legendary Boston Shootout event founded by Ken Hudson. Later, Harris's community advocacy was reflected in her service as deputy commissioner for the Boston Parks and Recreation Department, project director for the Harvard School of Public Health program Play Across Boston, and project director for the Sport in Society program at Northeastern University. Her outstanding service to the Boston community has been recognized by numerous organizations, reflecting the power of intersectional resistance through sport.[82]

From the 1970s through the early 2020s, advocacy and grassroots activism in Boston have been reflected in the growth of community-based sports organizations that were designed to foster positive youth development in predominantly Black communities. As noted earlier, during this period there was intense racial tension, and Black communities were under siege due to the backlash from the antibusing crisis and economic instability in the city. In addition, due to the emergence of neoliberalism in the United States during the late twentieth century, funding for Boston's public schools and public sports programs was reduced, which led to the creation of Black-led grassroots sports organizations. Thus, the establishment of positive sports development programs for Black youth during this period was not only an act of communalism but also an act of resistance and survival.

In the 1970s, Mike Jarvis, former head coach at Cambridge Rindge and Latin School, Boston University, George Washington University, St. John's University, and Florida Atlantic University, established the legendary Shoot Straight Program in Cambridge, Massachusetts, to provide a space where youth basketball players could develop their skills with coaches and mentors who shared their racial and cultural backgrounds.[83] Ken Hudson, the first NBA full-time official (1968), established the Boston Shootout league in 1972. In 1991, Tony Richardson created the No Books No Ball nonprofit organization to provide positive youth development through sports and mentorship for Boston youth.[84] The No Books No Ball program includes academic, psychological, and social support for Black youth in Boston. All three of these initiatives have contributed to the positive development of thousands of Black youths in Boston and have been lauded as transformative for these communities.[85] The success of these Black-owned and Black-led grassroots organizations reflects the intergenerational legacy of resistance in Boston sports dating back to the creation of the Resolutes and Black baseball amateur teams of the late 1800s.[86]

From the 1990s to the early 2020s, several Black sports leaders have continued the legacy of advocacy and grassroots activism through youth sports programming in Boston. These leaders include Al Kinett of the Shelburne Recreation Center, Jack Crump of the Haynes Crump Bruins, R. C. Pruitt of the Roxbury Boys and Girls Club, Bill Wimberly of the Roxbury YMCA, Harry and Dennis Wilson of the Roxbury Basketball Association and Roxbury Raiders, Robert Lewis Jr. (founder and CEO of the BASE), Michael Rubin of East Boston High School, Trudy Fisher of John D. O'Bryant High School,

Dennis Wilson of Madison Park High School, and Lino Sanchez of Urban Achievers Safe School. The proliferation of youth sports programs grounded in a commitment to racial justice in Boston is an important, if often over-looked, example of resistance in discussions of activism through sports. The spotlighting of these community sports leaders signifies the recognition of their efforts and contributions to improve Black life in Boston in culturally empowering and substantive ways.

Building on the foundation of predecessors such as Frank "Fay" Young, Chester L. Washington, Sam Lacy, and Wendell Smith, Black sports jour-nalists in Boston in the twenty-first century have utilized their platforms to engage in media activism.[87] In what historian Harry Edwards calls the fourth wave of Black athlete activism, these Black sports journalists have leveraged the tools of technology to disseminate their racial justice com-mentary to mass audiences. One of the most renowned sports journalists in Boston is Howard Bryant. From 2002 to 2005, Bryant served as a columnist for the *Boston Herald*. Later, he published several books that documented the personal and sports lives of prominent Black athletes. Bryant's books include *Shut Out: A Story of Race and Baseball in Boston* (2002), *The Last Hero: A Life of Henry Aaron* (2010), *Sisters and Champions: The True Story of Venus and Serena Williams* (2018), *The Heritage: Black Athletes, a Divided America and the Politics of Patriotism* (2018), and *Full Dissidence: Notes from an Uneven Playing Field* (2020). Like Jackson's journalistic contributions in the 1940s and Kountze's archival work in the 1970s, Bryant's contributions high-light the legitimacy, perseverance, and excellence of Black sportspersons.[88]

In conclusion, the history of resistance and activism through sports in Boston is undeniable. Across gender lines, Boston sportspersons from Kittie Knox to Bill Russell to Mabray "Doc" Kountze to Alfreda Harris have ignited progressive racial change in the city and beyond. The hybrid resistance exhibited by Black Boston sportspersons has broken barriers, shifted atti-tudes, and transformed communities. The evolution of resistance strategies in Boston across time and space illustrates Edwards's notion of a sustained ideology of Black athlete activism occurring in distinct waves that mirror the social movements of their time.[89] The AART and AASAT illuminate the range and effectiveness of different strategies for racial uplift through sports.

The achievements of these Black Boston sportspersons provide a blueprint for future sports activists who seek to improve the plight of Black communities locally, regionally, nationally, and internationally.

Notes

1. Historian Gerald Horne refers to this event as the "counter-revolution of 1776," in that Euro-American settler colonialists sought to preserve the institution of slavery rather than abolish it, as the British had pursued prior to the arrival of the Euro-Americans. Gerald Horne, *The Counter-revolution of 1776: Slave Resistance and the Origins of the United States* (New York: New York University Press, 2014), vii.
2. Robert C. Hayden, "A Historical Overview of Poverty among Blacks in Boston, 1950–1990," *Trotter Review* 17, no. 1 (2007): 135; Jane M. Hornburger, "Deep Are the Roots: Busing in Boston," *Journal of Negro Education* 45, no. 3 (1976): 236; Arthur O. White, "The Black Leadership Class and Education in Antebellum Boston," *Journal of Negro Education* 42, no. 4 (1973): 504.
3. Hayden, "Historical Overview," 135–36.
4. Hayden, "Historical Overview," 139–40; Horne, *Counter-revolution*, xii.
5. W. E. B. Du Bois, *The Souls of Black Folk* (Chicago: A. C. McClurg, 1903–2003), 3.
6. Jack Tager, *Boston Riots: Three Centuries of Social Violence* (Boston: Northeastern University Press, 2001), xi, 4–5.
7. Tager, *Boston Riots*, 15.
8. Hayden, "Historical Overview," 136.
9. Matthew Delmont, "Television News and the Making of the Boston Busing Crisis," *Journal of Urban History* 43, no. 2 (2017): 219; Ronald P. Formisano, *Boston against Busing: Race, Class, and Ethnicity in the 1960s and 1970s* (Chapel Hill: University of North Carolina Press, 1991), 66; Hornburger, "Deep Are the Roots," 235; Kimberly Probolus-Cedroni, "Bright Flight: Desegregating Boston's Elite Public Schools, 1960–2000," *Journal of Urban History* 48, no. 3 (2020): 7; Lynnell L. Thomas, "Civil Rights Gone Wrong: Racial Nostalgia, Historical Memory, and the Boston Busing Crisis in Contemporary Children's Literature," *Journal of Urban History* 43, no. 2 (2017): 257.
10. Formisano, *Boston against Busing*, 66; Hornburger, "Deep Are the Roots," 237.
11. Thomas, "Civil Rights," 257.
12. Ana Patricia Muñoz et. al., *The Color of Wealth in Boston* (Boston: Federal Reserve Bank of Boston Joint Publication with Duke University and the New School, 2015), 1.
13. Mabray Kountze, *Fifty Sports Years along Memory Lane: Afro-American Sports History Hometown, Local, National* (Medford MA: Mystic Valley Press, 1979), xii.
14. The term *African American* refers to the ethnic group of people of African descent in the United States who have biological lineage to ancestors who were subjected to transatlantic atrocity (often referred to as a slave trade), chattel slavery, Jim Crow, and racial oppression in the United States from the fifteenth century through the early

twentieth century. For a discussion of the term, see Darlene Clark Hine, William C. Hine, and Stanley C. Harrold, *The African-American Odyssey: Since 1965* (Upper Saddle River NJ: Pearson Prentice Hall, 2006).

15. African Americans are also the ethnic group and lineage that was the focus of the Civil War of 1861–65 and subsequent Emancipation Proclamation of 1865 and Thirteenth Amendment. The term *Black* is used in this chapter to refer to the broader racial group of people of African descent including African Americans, African Caribbeans, and African immigrants (also referred to as a diaspora term popularized by Black Power and nationalists organizations). See Stokely Carmichael and Charles Hamilton, *Black Power: The Politics of Liberation in America* (New York: Vintage, 1967).

16. Edwin Bancroft Henderson, *The Negro in Sports* (Washington DC: Associated Publishers, 1939), 41.

17. Kountze, *Fifty Sports Years*, 5.

18. Joseph N. Cooper, *A Legacy of African American Resistance and Activism through Sport* (New York: Peter Lang, 2021), 25–26.

19. Cooper, *Legacy*, 77; Joseph N. Cooper, Charles Macaulay, and Saturino H. Rodriguez, "Race and Resistance: A Typology of African American Sport Activism," *International Review for the Sociology of Sport* 54, no. 3 (2019): 151; Joseph N. Cooper, Michael Mallery Jr., and Charles D.T. Macaulay, "African American Sport Activism and Broader Social Movements," in *Passing the Ball: Sports in African American Life and Culture*, ed. Drew Brown (Jefferson NC: McFarland, 2020), 99–102.

20. Cooper, *Legacy*, 25–26.

21. Harry Edwards, "The Fourth Wave: Black Athlete Protests in the Second Decade of the 21st Century," keynote address, the North American Society for the Sociology of Sport (NASSS), Tampa Bay, Florida, 2016.

22. Cooper, *Legacy*, 77.

23. Cooper, *Legacy*, 7.

24. Cooper, Macaulay, and Rodriguez, "Race and Resistance," 154–55.

25. Cooper, Macaulay, and Rodriguez, "Race and Resistance," 155.

26. Cooper, *Legacy*, 8.

27. Cooper, Macaulay, and Rodriguez, "Race and Resistance," 151; Cooper, Mallery, and Macaulay, "African American Sport Activism," 99–102.

28. Edwards, "Fourth Wave."

29. Gerald Horne, *Negro Comrades of the Crown: African Americans and the British Empire Fight the US before Emancipation* (New York: New York University Press, 2012), 78.

30. Cooper, Macaulay, and Rodriguez, "Race and Resistance," 175.

31. Hine, Hine, and Harrold, *African-American Odyssey*, 288.

32. Doris R. Corbett and Angela B. Stills, "African Americans and the Media: Roles and Opportunities to Be Broadcasters, Journalists, Reporters, and Announcers," in *Diversity and Social Justice in College Sports: Sport Management and the Student-Athlete*, ed.

Dana D. Brooks and Ronald C. Althouse (Morgantown WV: Fitness Information Technology, 2007), 183; Cooper, *Legacy*, 256.

33. Cooper, *Legacy*, 325.

34. As noted earlier, this era started as early as the 1600s, but for the purpose of the examples highlighted in this chapter, the mid-1800s is the designated starting point of analysis.

35. For the purposes of this chapter, the hip-hop (1980s–2000s) and Black Lives Matter (2010s–20s) movement eras will be referred to as the post–civil rights and Black Power movement eras, since the examples highlighted in the chapter do not correspond with examples cited in the original text where these eras were presented.

36. See Laura Baring-Gould, "The Boston Resolutes in the News, 1887 Boston Resolutes, September 1870," *Black Ball* 3, no. 1 (2010): 90.

37. Michael E. Lomax, *Black Baseball Entrepreneurs, 1860–1901: Operating by Any Means Necessary* (Syracuse NY: Syracuse University Press, 2003), 138–40.

38. Gerald Early, "The New Negro Era and the Great African American Transformation," *American Studies* 49, nos. 1–2 (2008): 14.

39. Robert Cvornyek, "The Color of Baseball: Race and Boston's Sporting Community," *Black Ball* 6, no. 1 (2013): 70.

40. Cvornyek, "Color of Baseball," 101.

41. Lomax, *Black Baseball Entrepreneurs*, 14–16.

42. Lomax, *Black Baseball Entrepreneurs*, 42.

43. Cvornyek, "Color of Baseball," 102.

44. Cvornyek, "Color of Baseball," 72.

45. Cooper, *Legacy*, 6–14.

46. For a discussion of this athlete, see Cooper, *Legacy*, 284–86.

47. Lorenz J. Finison, *Boston's Cycling Craze, 1880–1900: A Story of Race, Sport, and Society* (Boston: University of Massachusetts Press, 2014), 12.

48. Victoria Shead, "Women's History Month: Kittie Knox," USA Cycling, last modified March 1, 2021, https://gravelnats.usacycling.org/article/womens-history-month-kittie -knox.

49. Cooper, *Legacy*, 256; Corbett and Stills, "African Americans and the Media," 183.

50. Cvornyek, "Color of Baseball," 82.

51. Cooper, *Legacy*, 257; Corbett and Stills, "African Americans and the Media," 183; Edwards, "Fourth Wave"; Lomax, *Black Baseball Entrepreneurs*, 78–82.

52. Cooper, *Legacy*, 355–56.

53. Willie O'Ree is a Black Canadian who was the descendant of African people who were enslaved in the United States. His grandparents escaped from slavery in the United States, and therefore, O'Ree has African American roots.

54. Marc Spears, "From Russell to KG to Today's Celtics: Being a Black Player in Boston," *The Undefeated*, last modified February 29, 2020, https://theundefeated.com/features/ celtics-being-a-black-player-in-boston.

55. Aram Goudsouzian, "Bill Russell and the Basketball Revolution," *American Studies* 47, nos. 3–4 (2006): 73–74.

56. Bill Russell and Taylor Branch, *Second Wind: The Memoirs of an Opinionated Man* (New York: Ballantine, 1980), 8.

57. Gilbert McGregor, "How Bill Russell's Coaching Career Opened Doors: NBA's Black Head Coaches," MSN Sports, last modified October 21, 2021, https://www.msn.com/en-us/sports/nba/how-bill-russells-coaching-career-opened-doors-for-nbas-black-head-coaches/ar-AAPKkK.

58. McGregor, "How Bill Russell's Coaching."

59. "Ken Hudson, NBA Pioneer," IAABO Black Caucus, February 21, 2019, https://iaaboblackcaucus.wordpress.com/2019/02/21/ken-hudson-nba-pioneer/.

60. Henderson, *Negro in Sports*, 41.

61. Joseph N. Cooper and Jewell E. Cooper, "I'm Running So You Can Be Happy and I Can Keep My Scholarship: A Comparative Examination of Black College Athletes' Experiences with Role Conflict," *Journal of Intercollegiate Sport* 8 (2015): 147.

62. Cooper, *Legacy*, 50–51; Early, "New Negro," 14; Edwards, "Fourth Wave."

63. Joe Feagin, *Systemic Racism: A Theory of Oppression* (New York: Routledge, 2006), xii.

64. Horne, *Counter-revolution*, 43.

65. Goudsouzian, "Bill Russell," 61.

66. Goudsouzian, "Bill Russell," 66.

67. Goudsouzian, "Bill Russell," 70; Russell and Branch, *Second Wind*, 33.

68. Carmichael and Hamilton, *Black Power*, xi.

69. Russell and Branch, *Second Wind*, 51; Bill Russell and William McSweeney, *Go Up for Glory* (New York: Dutton, 1966), 33.

70. Harry Edwards, "The Promise and Limits of Leveraging Black Athlete Power Potential to Compel Campus Change," *Journal of Higher Education Athletics & Innovation* 1, no. 1 (2016): 4–6.

71. Goudsouzian, "Bill Russell," 72; Russell and McSweeney, *Go Up for Glory*, 62.

72. Goudsouzian, "Bill Russell," 72.

73. Goudsouzian, "Bill Russell," 65.

74. Goudsouzian, "Bill Russell," 70; Russell and McSweeney, *Go Up for Glory*, 87.

75. Goudsouzian, "Bill Russell," 66.

76. Russell and McSweeney, *Go Up for Glory*, 53; Goudsouzian, "Bill Russell," 67.

77. Thomas Whalen, *Dynasty's End: Bill Russell and the 1968–69 World Champion Boston Celtics* (Boston: Northeastern University Press, 2004), 46.

78. Kountze, *Fifty Sports Years*, xii.

79. Russell and Branch, *Second Wind*, i; Russell and McSweeney, *Go Up for Glory*, i.

80. Cooper, *Legacy*, 35–37; Edwards, "Fourth Wave."

81. "Charlie Titus Bio. Hall of Fame," UMass Boston Athletics, last modified March 10, 2019, https://beaconsathletics.com/honors/umass-boston-athletics-hall-of-fame/charlie-titus/121.

82. "Alfreda Harris Bio, Hall of Fame," UMass Boston Athletics, last modified March 10, 2019, https://beaconsathletics.com/news/2022/2/28/general-beacons-athletics-honors -its-history-as-part-of-black-history-month.aspx. See also "Alfreda Harris," Lower Roxbury Black History Project 2022, last modified March 15, 2021, https://roxbury.library .northeastern.edu/harris/.

83. Noah Perkins, "Ewing, Jarvis Rewind the Time: Basketball Hall of Famer, Former Coach Mike Jarvis Talk Racism, Basketball," *Milford Daily News*, last modified June 25, 2020, https://www.milforddailynews.com/story/sports/pro/2020/06/25/patrick-ewing -talks-racism-basketball-and-being-part-of-greatest-team-at-cambridge-rindge-and -latin-/42476307/.

84. "Changemaker: Tony Richards, Founder of No Books No Ball," Boston Scope, last modified February 20, 2021, https://thescopeboston.org/3192/q-a-changemakers/ tony-richards-no-books-no-ball/.

85. "Ken Hudson"; Perkins, "Ewing"; "Changemaker."

86. Kountze, *Fifty Sports Years*, xi–xiii.

87. Cooper, *Legacy*, 256; Corbett and Stills, "African Americans and the Media," 183.

88. Howard Bryant Books, last modified January 1, 2022, https://howardbryantbooks.com.

89. Edwards, "Fourth Wave."

3

The Middle Lane

Race, Sports, Boston, Hoops, and Community

MARCIS FENNELL, C. KEITH HARRISON, AND KELLY DWYER

The intersection of sports and American culture has historically reflected the sociology of the country. The communities of Greater Boston are a prominent example of how contemporary American society has been impacted by competitive figures in Boston sports. The success these figures achieve is often expressed quantitatively on digital scoreboards or through sales reports.

Many of these achievers serve not only as representatives for their respective sports organizations but also as catalysts of achievement within the social class of their communities. Charlie Titus, former vice chancellor for athletics, recreation, and special programs at the University of Massachusetts (UMass) Boston, is one example of that influence. Our analysis, based on a personal interview with Titus featured later in this chapter, provides significant insight into the prestige of sport in Boston communities and how sociological demographics such as physical culture, race, and class impact sports in Boston. Through a critical exploration of these intersections, our intention is to highlight the stature of Titus as a Black leader in sport while illustrating the challenges Black athletes encounter within and beyond the constraints of their communities.

Boston beyond Russell and Brady

The city of Boston is considered one of the great sports cities of American history. Its reputation is supported by the success of its professional sport teams, which include eighteen National Basketball Association championships by the Boston Celtics, nine World Series titles by the Boston Red Sox, six National Hockey League Stanley Cup championships by the Boston Bruins, and six National Football League Super Bowl victories by the New

England Patriots. Represented by athletes like Bill Russell, David Ortiz, Ray Bourque, and Tom Brady, Boston possesses a sporting identity grounded in the concept of community. This identity empowers its citizens and supporters to align their perspectives with the physical culture of the city in support of the city's athletes and their sports organizations.

From a third-party perspective, Boston is as united as any other community in America. Through the lens of sports, Boston is the city of champions. Successful, high-performing athletes are accepted as members of the community despite differences in social demographics. Sociologically, the physical structure of the city delineates geographical barriers established among the communities by social class and race. Social welfare research has shown disparities in the distribution of government-allocated resources within American communities. Though these disparities are still prominent, sport has served as a figurative bridge between communities, exposing the intersection of race and class in Boston. Through sports, many individuals found success in navigating the physical culture of the microcommunities of Boston to become representatives of the macrocommunity of the city. To truly value this journey and the wisdom and resilience it requires, theoretical concepts of race and class must be explored and applied to models of success within the community.

Race, Sport, and Boston Communities

From a political standpoint, the Greater Boston area represents a beacon of progressive liberalism in modern American society. Nationally known as the hometown of the Kennedy family, Boston historically attracts bright future leaders from around the globe to attend America's most elite institutions like Harvard University and the Massachusetts Institute of Technology. One of America's most historic colonial settlements, Boston is perceived as a pioneering community grounded by American history and touted for its urban reform efforts.[1]

In the nineteenth century, settlement houses like the South End House (1891) and the Denison House (1892) were established by social reformers to combat the effects of urbanization.[2] Renowned activist Jane Addams and her fellow American settlement workers sought to make the "entire social organism democratic," the first objective of the settlement house movement.[3] Despite their efforts, industrialization and immigration fostered social and racial segregation throughout the nation.[4] Advocating for the poor, American settlement workers inverted a classic premise of charitable intervention, proposing that the moral defects of the poor were not the cause of their poverty but a consequence of their struggle for existence.[5] Contradicting the international perspective that individual freedom was enjoyed by all in America, settlement workers like Jane Addams highlighted inequities in Boston society as it moved into the twentieth century.

Though the social dynamics of contemporary Boston lean more Democratic politically, race has always been a construct that limits true equality within the liberal movement of America. Like most major cities in the United States, Boston resisted efforts to provide equal opportunities for people of color. In 1961, the Black communities of Boston, led by Ruth Batson, made a public demand to the Boston School Committee to desegregate the schools. Their civil activism led to the passing of the 1965 Racial Imbalance Act, which made segregation in Massachusetts public schools illegal.[6] Despite the legislation, the Boston School Committee willfully maintained segregation within the city's public schools, causing a group of Black parents to file suit against the Boston School Committee president James Hennigan. In the case titled *Morgan v. Hennigan*, the presiding U.S. District Court judge ruled in favor of the parents, requiring the school system to implement a busing plan to eliminate socially defined lines of segregation.[7] The historic ruling impacted the social and physical culture of Boston's communities, desegregating neighborhoods and decentralizing the civic and sport experience for all who lived there.

Modern-Day Boston

The persistence of segregation in Boston is significantly demonstrated by sociological research. Communities remain segregated along socioeconomic demographics, which are significantly correlated with racial demographics. In a 2015 study, economists found extreme disparities between the socioeconomic status of white and Black Americans in the Greater Boston region. The average total assets held by white and Black American households in

Boston are $256,500 and $700, respectively. Black Americans represent a third of the population in the Greater Boston region, most of whom reside in the city itself.[8] Considering residential data, disparities in net worth between white and Black Americans are alarming. Further exacerbating the significance of this finding, we see that racially based disparity in net worth increases as income increases.[9] The enduring racial divisions impacting Boston communities are the result of social structures rooted in racism, such as housing discrimination, gentrification, and redlining. On June 12, 2020, the Boston Public Health Commission declared racism a public health crisis, formally recognizing the historical context of racism in Boston and its impacts on the region in the present day.[10] An unexplored intersection within this crisis is sport and race in Boston.

Sport in Boston

Boston has a rich history in the early formation of interscholastic and intercollegiate sport. As early as 1833, the Primary School Committee of Boston included daily class exercise within its regulations for schoolteachers.[11] Considering the effects of urbanization in 1860, a city council committee published a report noting the physical deterioration of urban schoolchildren, mandating the implementation of physical education for "the preservation of health and the cultivation of the physical faculties as the foundation of the whole edifice of education."[12] This report led to collaborative efforts between educational institutions and sports organizations practitioners to train Boston teachers to integrate physical activity into the educational experience.

Markedly, Harvard hired the first Black American physical educator, Professor Aaron Molineaux Hewlett, a renowned Boston boxing instructor.[13] While physical training in education focused on gymnastics and martial arts, students also enjoyed sports like football, baseball, and track.[14] Recreationally, athletic sports were also prominent in Boston neighborhoods like Roxbury. The Norfolk House, now known as the Marcus Garvey House, hosted its own basketball league at its community center in 1915.[15] The embrace of athletic sports led to intracity competitions between university sports clubs and secondary school teams.[16] It was during that era that Boston gained a reputation as a city of elite sport competitions. The importance of community-based athletic sports in Boston is evidenced most prominently by the Boston Neigh-borhood Basketball League (BNBL). Established in 1969, the BNBL provides competitive basketball for participants ages six to eighteen at no cost. By providing positive sport programming within an urban environment, the BNBL served as a "curb to juvenile delinquency" amid racial rioting in the 1970s.[17] The school and neighborhood spirit fostered by the sport helped instill a sense of belonging, especially within the basketball community.

The Boston Shootout, a three-day national tournament established in 1972, brought elite athletic teams from across the United States to compete against athletes from the city's high school talent pool, highlighting Boston as a community.[18] As the premier single-elimination tournament, the Bos-ton Shootout was one of the most prominent gatherings in America from 1972 to 1999.[19] These activities enabled the community to appoint athletic heroes who achieved success as coaches, athletes, and managers. Through its transformation from intracity competitions to interscholastic sports, university sport club competitions to intercollegiate and professional sports, Boston remains a pioneering sport community. Considering the racial and social effects of racism within the transformation, athletic heroes play an important role in the battle against racism in Boston. Charlie Titus is not only a prominent athletic hero in Boston sport, but he is also a leading activist in the sport community who embodies the effort to end the public crisis of racism in Boston.

Charlie Titus, Primary Human Source

When exploring the intersection of race and sport in Boston, Charlie Titus is the primary source. Not only has he spent much of his life in the Roxbury section of Boston; he has played an intricate role in the development and establishment of intercollegiate athletics in New England. He is also well known for community service efforts across the socioeconomic boundaries of Boston communities.[20] A native of Dorchester and a representative of the Columbia Point housing project in southeast Boston, Titus became the part-time men's basketball coach at the University of Massachusetts Boston in 1974, holding the title of first and only head coach of men's basketball until 2015. Prior to his career in college athletics, Titus served as the director of youth affairs for Action for Boston Community Development (ABCD) and director of youth programs for the Lena Park Community Center.[21] Additionally, Titus was a participant in the Boston Shootout as a boys (and girls) club director.[22] Serving as the athletic director of UMass Boston athletics since 1980, Titus also served on committees at the university level as well as in collegiate athletics. He was twice named Coach of the Year in the Little East Conference (LEC), a National Collegiate Athletic Association (NCAA) Division III conference, which was established due to his leadership. He also served as the vice chancellor for student affairs at UMass Boston for two years.[23]

Titus has directly influenced institutions of sport through his community service, which includes his seats on the NCAA Division III Membership Committee, Eastern College Athletic Conference (ECAC) Board of Directors, Basketball Commemorative Officials Committee, and NCAA Regional Basketball Committee. His service has influenced the policy and culture of sport both locally and nationally. His contributions have inspired many accolades, earning him induction into the Hall of Fame of Saint Michael's College, the UMass Boston Hall of Fame, the Little East Hall of Fame, the Bay State Games Hall of Fame, and the National Association of Collegiate Directors of Athletics Hall of Fame. Now retired, Titus serves on the UMass Sport Leadership and Administration Program Advisory Board and as president of the Titus Foundation.

Reconnecting the communities of Boston to a national brand, Titus played an influential role in the recent multifaceted presence of the New Balance sports brand. New Balance serves as the official apparel sponsor for UMass Boston athletics programs and sponsor of the Track at New Balance.[24] Beyond the competitive fields, New Balance presented a $5 million pledge for the development and growth of the UMass Boston sport leadership and administration undergraduate program, including scholarship funding for students who excel in the program.[25] The brand's partnership with the university creates new and diverse career pathways for students pursuing sports management and leadership career opportunities locally and nationally.

Titus's personal and professional experience has come full circle. From a basketball player in his youth in the city of Boston to a sport leader influencing change in that same city, Titus's testimony and legacy are central to the narrative of basketball in Boston. During his youth, Titus's education was greatly affected by the busing plans enacted because of desegregation. In Boston's public schools, he experienced racism from teachers charged with educating him. On the playground, he needed to remain aware of emotional and physical threats. As a youth playing baseball, Titus shared membership on Little League teams with white players who cooperated and competed together in sport yet participated in racially based, direct confrontation away from the playing fields.

In his community efforts as a sport leader, Titus supervised citywide programs, managing an extensive budget. Pursuing a three-pronged approach to building success, Titus introduced opportunities for free education, athletics, and recreation as well as vocational training. His presence throughout the city became so obvious, community members nicknamed him "Job Man." Driven by activism, he sought institutional avenues to provide equitable opportunities through sport in his home city, which led him to UMass Boston. Despite often encountering interactions steeped in racism, his diligent service in Boston paved the way for his successful service as athletic director at UMass Boston.

Titus's testimony reflects how sport in Boston is grounded by community. His personal experience illustrates the integrity, vision, and resilience one must possess to achieve success as a Black person in Boston. He remains a central figure in regard to basketball in Boston communities. He made a profound sociocultural impact as a sports activist pioneer, affecting the city's micro- and macrocommunities alike.

Notes

1. Meg Streiff, "Boston's Settlement Housing: Social Reform in an Industrial City" (PhD diss., Louisiana State University, 2005), 12–24; John Daniels, *America via the Neighborhood* (New York: Harper and Brothers, 1920).
2. See "South End House: A Model of Possibilism and Permeation" and "Dennison House: The People's University," in Streiff, "Boston's Settlement Housing," 99–166. See also "Notes from the Archives," City of Boston, accessed July 11, 2024, https://www.boston .gov/news/notes-archives-amelia-earhart-boston.
3. Jane Addams, "The Subjective Necessity for Social Settlements," Norton, accessed July 13, 2024, https://wwnorton.com/college/history/archive/reader/trial/directory/

1890_1914/22_ch24_05.htm#:~:text=I%20have%20divided%20the%20motives,and
%20to%20bring%20as%20much.

4. Catherine Elton, "How Has Boston Gotten Away with Being Segregated for So Long,"
Boston Magazine, December 8, 2020, https://www.bostonmagazine.com/news/2020/
12/08/boston-segregation/.

5. Roy Lubove, *The Struggle for Social Security, 1900–1935* (Cambridge MA: Harvard University Press, 1968), 8, 91–112.

6. Steven J. Taylor, *Desegregation in Boston and Buffalo: The Influence of Local Leaders* (Albany: State University of New York Press, 1998), 24–25, 72–74.

7. Taylor, *Desegregation in Boston*, 48.

8. Ana Patricia Muñoz et al., "The Color of Wealth in Boston," Federal Reserve Bank of Boston, March 25, 2015, https://www.bostonfed.org/publications/one-time-pubs/
color-of-wealth.aspx.

9. Muñoz et al., "Color of Wealth."

10. Rebecca Tippett et al., "Beyond Broke: Why Closing the Racial Wealth Gap Is a Priority for National Economic Security," Issue Lab, May 2014, https://www.researchgate.net/
publication/293486028_Beyond_Broke.

11. *Third Semi-annual Report of the Superintendent of Public Schools*, City of Boston Archives, 1861, 22–23.

12. Stephen Hardy, *How Boston Played: Sport, Recreation, and Community, 1865–1915* (Knoxville: University of Tennessee Press, 2003), 109.

13. Edwin B. Henderson, "Progress and Problems in Health and Physical Education among Colored Americans," *Journal of Health and Physical Education* 6, no. 6 (June 1935): 9, 55.

14. See, for example, *Latin School Register* 9 (June 1890): 153.

15. Marie-Claire Dumornay, "The Nine Lives of the Norfolk House," Roxbury Crossing Historical Trust, May 28, 2022, http://rcht.org/the-nine-lives-of-the-norfolk-house/.

16. Hardy, *How Boston Played*, 123.

17. Daniel Sheehan, "BNBL, Now 50, Is Looking at Growth in DOT and Mattapan," *Dorchester Reporter*, May 29, 2019, https://www.dotnews.com/2019/bnbl-now-50-looking-growth
-dot-and-mattapan.

18. Abacus Reveals, "The Boston Shootout Was a Cavalcade of High School Basketball Stars," Bleacher Report, 2011, https://bleacherreport.com/articles/891337-the-boston
-shootout-a-cavalcade-of-stars-one-mans-vision.

19. Bijan C. Bayne, "The Shootout Heard around the World," *Bay State Banner*, January 31, 2012, https://www.baystatebanner.com/2012/01/31/the-shootout-heard-around-the
-world/.

20. Ed Foray, "Charlie Titus, UMass Boston Legend, Reflects on a Life Devoted to Community and Athletics," *Dorchester Reporter*, August 14, 2020, https://www.dotnews
.com/2020/charlie-titus-umass-boston-legend-reflects-life-and-career-devoted.

21. "Meet Our Team: Charlie Titus," Titus Foundation, 2024, https://titusfoundation
.org/about-us/.

22. Bayne, "Shootout Heard."
23. "Charlie Titus Bio."
24. This is a multisport athletic facility in the heart of Boston, Massachusetts, designed to accommodate sports and athletes of all ages and levels. The facility accommodates up to five thousand spectators; holds a two-hundred-meter hydraulically banked indoor track; houses a dedicated track-and-field throwing area; includes a full turf field for soccer, lacrosse, and other sports; and holds a dedicated 24,000-square-foot athlete warm-up area.
25. "UMass Boston Establishes Motley Chair to Head New Sports Leadership and Administration BA Program," New Balance Press Box, September 20, 2018, https://newbalance .newsmarket.com/archive/2018/umass-boston-establishes-motley-chair-to-head -new-sports-leadership-and-administration-ba-program/s/05f1b9e1-cc45-4dcc-bbca -0c505db9dbb4.

PART 2

Legitimacy in the Jim Crow Era

4

Gentlemen of Color

Oliver and Fred Watson and New England Black Soccer

ED FARNSWORTH AND BRIAN D. BUNK

On April 14, 1894, a match report about the Pawtucket, Rhode Island, YMCA's junior soccer team noted that Fred Watson had accidentally kicked an opponent, breaking his leg. A few months later, another newspaper reported that the YMCA's senior squad had signed Oliver Watson.[1] Notices of match incidents and club signings were commonplace, and even the fact that the two Watsons were brothers did not make the articles exceptional. What is significant is that Fred and Oliver were African Americans. The Watson brothers are the earliest documented African American soccer players in the United States. Both were born in Pawtucket, Rhode Island: Oliver in May 1872 and Fred in May 1875. During their careers, the Watsons played for several different teams and achieved several important milestones in the history of soccer in the United States. Oliver is the earliest-known African American player to compete and score in a senior club match. He was also the first to play and score in the American Cup competition. In the spring of 1901, the brothers were the first African American soccer players to win a league championship. That fall, Fred became the first to play in a professional soccer game.

The story of the Watson brothers also casts light on the complicated relationships between race, sport, and class. The Watsons grew up in an overwhelmingly white community yet were accepted as soccer players and as fellow workers. This may be one reason why newspaper reports in Pawtucket made no mention of their race during their playing careers. To the community, they were local lads in a comparatively small city playing a popular sport, one that was booming during their formative years. As young people, they played soccer with white kids, something seen as unexceptional. This may be connected to the unique history of race relations in Rhode Island. Although heavily involved in the slave trade prior to the Civil War, the state had generally been more hospitable to native-born African Americans. Native-born men of color gained the right to vote in Rhode Island in 1842, and the state mandated equality in education in 1866. As in other New England states, no legal differences existed between free Blacks and whites.[2] Despite such factors, African Americans were routinely excluded from elite social clubs in Providence. In Newport, the white population generally accepted their Black neighbors while also treating them as inferior.[3] African Americans responded to these affronts by founding their own associations, including sporting clubs. The Providence Colored Grays baseball team began play as early as 1886, while the Colored Giants formed in the city in 1905.[4] The Marathon Club organized in Providence in 1905 and sponsored a variety of Black athletic clubs in various sports, including baseball and intercollegiate football.[5] The Watson brothers gained their first significant opportunity because another organization, the local YMCA, supported a multiracial sports program.

Oliver and Fred were employed as metalworkers in Pawtucket's industrial economy. Oliver became an "expert pressman and bolt maker," and Fred also worked in a bolt factory.[6] In communities like Pawtucket, soccer teams became an area where the largely working-class members could demonstrate physical prowess and experience the camaraderie that comes with being part of a club. For the Watsons, the sporting world, like the shop floor, seemed to be a place where the men's race mattered little to their comrades, and they were accepted and evaluated based on their skill and ability. Upon his death in 1925, Oliver's coworkers at the Standard Nut and Bolt Company sent condolences along with a "huge floral column" to the family.[7] The brothers' race only drew public attention when they played in Fall River, Massachusetts, where there is no evidence of African Americans playing soccer during this period.

Oliver and Fred Watson were native New Englanders. Their father, Charles, was born in Connecticut in 1833; their mother, Lucy, in Rhode Island in 1834. A "devoted churchman," Charles was a founder of the Gaspee African Methodist Episcopal (AME) Zion Church in Providence and was employed for much of his working life by a manufacturer of pipe organs.[8]

Oliver and Fred had three brothers: Charles (b. 1864) worked on the railroad; James (b. 1867) was a laborer and crewmember on the steamer *Orient*; and Eugene (b. 1870) was a musician, newspaper reporter, and editor who was active in the local Republican Party.[9] Described as "a leader among the negroes of this city," Eugene participated in the civil rights movement, speaking at one meeting along with Frederick Douglass and Ida B. Wells.[10]

The Watsons' place as the United States' earliest documented African American soccer players puts them among the first Black players of organized soccer in the world: Robert Walker played in Scotland between 1875 and 1878; Andrew Watson (no relation) competed between 1875 and 1892 and was the first Black player to be selected for and captain a national team in Scotland before playing in England; Arthur Wharton, a goalkeeper who played between 1885 and 1892 in England, is generally considered the first Black professional player.[11] While Oliver and Fred were native-born citizens of the United States, their Black soccer forebears originally came from Britain's imperial possessions. Walker was born in Sierra Leone, Andrew Watson in British Guiana, and Wharton in Ghana before moving to the United Kingdom. Further differences in Oliver and Fred's humble working-class background are apparent compared to their predecessors. Robert Walker's white Scottish father was a merchant. Andrew Watson's white father came from a prosperous Scottish family. He owned sugar plantations and was a cousin of British prime minister William Ewart Gladstone. Wharton's mixed heritage began with his white Scottish grandfather, who was a merchant and sea captain. Wharton's father was a Glasgow-educated Methodist minister and missionary, his mother the daughter of a Scottish trader and a member of the Fante Ghanaian royal family; her family was influential in Gold Coast political, economic, and religious affairs. Andrew Watson enjoyed a "public schoolboy" education in England before his move to Scotland, where he was briefly enrolled at the University of Glasgow and received an inheritance upon turning twenty-one that allowed him, at least for a few years, "to live the life of an independently wealthy gentleman."[12] Later, he followed Robert Walker in passing the technical examinations required to begin a post-soccer career as an engineer on steamships. Wharton was sent to England as a teenager to train as a Methodist missionary before finding success as a sportsman.

The background of two contemporaries of Oliver and Fred more closely resembles the brothers' working-class origins. Scottish-born outside right Willie Clarke started his career in 1896 before signing a professional contract in 1897, while fellow countryman John Walker (no relation to Robert Walker) began playing in 1897 before turning professional in 1898, both thus following the Watson brothers in being the first native-born Black players of organized soccer in Scotland.[13] While Clarke's father was sent to Scotland to complete his education, in later life he worked as an engine fitter. Less is known about the origins of John Walker's parents. His father, who was employed as a dockworker, was a Black man who may have been born in the Spanish Caribbean, while his white mother was born in Glasgow; both were illiterate. Census records indicate that their American counterparts, Oliver and Fred, were literate, but details of their education are unknown.[14]

As Oliver and Fred came of age, soccer, or association football, was already an established pastime in Pawtucket. As in nearby Fall River, the sport had been quickly embraced by native-born players and was not viewed simply as the "English" or "Scotch" game. Soccer was first codified in England in 1863 and later tactically refined in Scotland. Precisely when soccer was first played in Rhode Island is unknown, but the state's leading team, the Pawtucket Free Wanderers, organized in 1885.[15] Formal matches began in the fall of 1886 with the founding of the Rhode Island Football Association (RIFA), which included the Free Wanderers and teams from Ashton, Lorraine, Providence, River Point, and Thornton. Some of these teams were backed by area manufacturers, underscoring links in soccer's development on the East Coast during this period to the workplace, particularly the textile industry, and immigrant workers.[16] The Free Wanderers, for example, had connections to the Conant Thread Company, the U.S. subsidiary of Scottish-based J&P Coats, the Thornton team to the British Hosiery Company, whose "workforce came from Nottingham, England."[17]

RIFA's formation followed developments across the state border in Fall River, Massachusetts, where the East Ends soccer team formed in 1883, and the Rovers and the Olympics organized in 1884. In the fall of 1885, the Bristol

County Football Association (BCFA), sponsors of the Bristol County Cup tournament, was founded.[18] The proximity of Pawtucket and Fall River made for easy communication and travel between the burgeoning soccer centers, and in May 1886 the Free Wanderers traveled to Fall River to face an all-city team, losing 2–3. Interstate contests featuring the Free Wanderers against Fall River sides continued in the spring of 1887.[19] One meeting between the Fall River Rovers and the Free Wanderers in May 1887 was preceded by a baseball game between the Providence Grays—"the colored nine"—and the Fall River Flints.[20] In January 1891 the Free Wanderers joined Fall River East Ends, Olympics, and Rovers in founding the New England League.[21]

In contrast to the emergence of Pawtucket and Fall River as leading centers for soccer in the United States, football in Boston generally meant gridiron football, the collegiate game inspired by rugby as played at Harvard University. Soccer aficionados in Fall River found "considerable amusement" in how Boston newspapers wrote as if soccer was "something new and unheard of" after the founding of the Boston Rovers in January 1888. A few months later, the *Boston Herald* reported that spectators at a Rovers practice game "were uninitiated in the mysteries of football as played under association rules."[22] Reports soon detailed other teams in the Boston area, many in textile enclaves, including the Woburn Rangers, Lowell Rovers, Lawrence Athletics, Newton Mills, and Waltham's American Watch Tool Company team. Boston teams soon traveled the fifty or so miles south to play in Pawtucket and Fall River while also hosting teams from those cities and others, including Providence.[23]

As the Free Wanderers' reputation grew, they began to face other teams from around the region, often on holidays like Decoration Day, Thanksgiving, and Christmas. Area clubs also began competing in the American Cup competition. The American Cup was first organized in 1885 by the American Football Association (AFA). The AFA modeled itself after England's Football Association and aspired to be soccer's top governing body in the United States. In fact, the AFA's reach was limited to areas on the East Coast around New York City and northern New Jersey. Despite such restrictions, the American Cup was seen as the de facto national championship, and the

1887–88 competition was the first to feature squads from New England, including the Free Wanderers.

Interest in tournament games grew in Pawtucket over the next several years. On January 12, 1889, the Free Wanderers hosted the Fall River Rovers in an American Cup semifinal match. The *Pawtucket Evening Times* called the crowd, estimated at over five thousand, "the largest ever seen at an out-door game in this city." Once again, the Rovers proved too strong for the locals, winning the match by a score of 1–2.[24] A year later, Pawtucket's Dexter Street Grounds became the first location outside of New Jersey to host the American Cup championship game.[25] On May 28, 1893, the Wanderers reached the pinnacle of U.S. soccer when they won the American Cup, defeating New York Thistle 3–1. Afterward, the club's trophies were displayed in a Broad Street shop window.[26]

In the fall of 1893, the Pawtucket YMCA team joined the RIFA and the New England League and also entered the American Cup tournament.[27] While one report described the team as "putting up an elegant article of football" and praised it for playing "a fast, scientific game," another noted that the young club was "a most peculiar one in its play, sometimes putting up a grand game, and at other times playing like schoolboys." Still, the YMCA team played well enough to best the Wanderers in the newly organized Pawtucket city championship and claim the Mayor's Cup, an impressive accomplishment against the team that had won the American Cup the previous season.[28]

We don't know when the Watson brothers began to play, but they were schoolboys when the Free Wanderers held their first matches, and they were young men when the team enjoyed its greatest success. It was their affiliation with the YMCA team, however, that brought them to public notice. At a national level, the YMCA remained segregated, but it did allow local branches to accept African American members if they chose. By the 1890s, only a handful of branches welcomed African Americans. Two of the integrated associations, Springfield and Boston, were in New England, but the position of the Pawtucket YMCA is unknown.[29] Whether or not the branch accepted Black members, the organization had no problem fielding an integrated soccer team. In September 1894, before the start of the New England League season, the *Fall River Daily Herald* reported that Pawtucket YMCA had signed thirteen players, including Oliver Watson. Five months earlier, notice appeared that Fred Watson was playing for the organization's junior team.[30] On December 22, 1894, Oliver replaced a regular starter to make his first start for the senior squad when the YMCAs traveled to Fall River to face the Olympics. The home team quickly tallied five first-half goals. "The Olympics then let up," the *Daily Globe* reported, "and the visitors, taking advantage of the chance, braced up and scored." The *Daily Herald* said of the goal, "The Pawtuckets, on a rush, succeeded in getting one, Watson putting the ball through."[31] Despite the YMCA's comeback, the Olympics finished the game 8–2 winners.

As was typical at the time, match reports did not clearly identify the goal-scoring winger, but the *Daily Globe* informed readers that "Watson, a colored man, played on the wing for the visitors. He was the first colored player ever seen in this city, and during the game he caused no end of fun by his funny talk and antics."[32] A match described as "too one-sided to be interesting" was in fact historic. Not only was Oliver Watson the first African American soccer player to appear in Fall River, but he was also the first African American to both play and score in a senior league soccer match in the United States. The language used by the *Daily Globe* echoed racist stereotypes often leveled at African Americans, especially those who played or performed in public. Yet apart from this first report, there are no newspaper accounts of Oliver or Fred receiving racist abuse from spectators or fellow players. Some spectators likely did spew racist taunts, and as was the case with Andrew Watson, Oliver and Fred probably were "on more than one occasion subjected to vulgar insults by splenetic, ill-tempered players." Despite such abuse, Andrew was admired for how he "uniformly preserved that gentlemanly demeanor which has endeared him to opponents as well as his club companions."[33] Nevertheless, critical accounts during the brothers' playing career are not marked by racist interpretation or description, and no reports questioned their right to appear alongside white players. Instead, criticism focused on their development as players or their performance in a match.

After the contest against the Olympics, Oliver next appeared in an American Cup matchup against Fall River East Ends, making him the first African American player to appear in a U.S. tournament with claims to representing a national championship. On March 9, 1895, the YMCAS won a home victory, coming from behind to dispatch the East Ends in "a remarkably fast game." Leaving behind racist caricature, the *Daily Globe* now referred to Oliver as "the gentleman of color" and praised his passing ability. With his team trailing 3–2 at the start of the second half, Oliver scored the equalizing goal. The *Daily Globe* described the play: "The home team from a fine passing streak got behind the half-backs, and Watson, getting the ball, made a break for goal. From a long shot on the right, he put one behind Cornell. A great shout went up, and both teams went into the fray in the hottest style of play."[34] The YMCA team soon took the lead as they "passed, dribbled and punted by their opponents like fiends." Oliver led the way. The next goal scorer "received the ball from Watson" before scoring. The final tally came "after a fine run down the field by Watson," who "passed splendidly" to assist the goal.[35] With the 6–3 win, the YMCA team headed to the American Cup semifinals to face hometown rivals the Free Wanderers, ultimately losing after the first game, which included another goal from Oliver, ended in a draw.[36]

When Pawtucket YMCA met the Free Wanderers in a preseason scrimmage in September 1895, a Watson was listed at fullback.[37] In the season opener at home against the Fall River Olympics on September 28, two Watsons were listed, "F. Watson" at fullback and "A. Watson" at center forward. While subsequent reports make it clear that "A. Watson" was Oliver "Allie" Watson, his obituary and burial record show his full name as Oliver Henry Arnold Watson.[38] The origin of the "Allie" nickname is unknown, but it appears he preferred that name to Oliver, the name previous reports said he was registered under with the YMCAS. "F. Watson" was Allie's younger brother, Fred. Fall River newspapers highlighted the brothers' inclusion on the YMCA roster. Ahead of their first match of the season in the Spindle City against the Rovers, the *Daily Globe* called the YMCAS "greatly strengthened" by the addition of the two "colored backs," incorrectly reporting Allie's position. The *Fall River Daily Evening News* commented, "The work of the two fast colored men recently added to the Y.M.C.A. will be watched with interest, they being the first colored men to play the game in this county."[39] Only an unknown typesetter can answer whether *county* was meant to be *country*. In the event, neither Allie nor Fred appeared in the match, a 4–2 loss.[40] Both brothers were in the lineup for an exhibition match the following week, a 2–1 win over Ashton Victors, with Fred among the players praised for their winning performance.[41]

A review of the YMCA team a few days later observed it had the kind of "good material" that could make it "one of the best teams in the country," if only "management uses good judgement in selecting the players." The article noted, "Fred Watson is improving every game he plays," while Allie would be more effective with "a little more life" in his play.[42] Allie must have taken the critique to heart because when YMCA hosted the Fall River East Ends on October 26, he found his goal-scoring form. With his team trailing 2–0 in the second half, Allie, "in the prettiest manner imaginable," bypassed the East Ends goalkeeper and "made the first goal for the local men." By the time the final whistle blew, Allie had tallied another goal in what finished as a 6–2 victory for YMCA.[43]

On November 9, 1895, YMCA met the Free Wanderers in the first round of the 1895–96 American Cup. Their places on the roster now firmly established, both Allie and Fred started for their team. After the kickoff, play moved back and forth between each goal with "astounding rapidity," but neither side could score. Then a costly error from Fred showed his inexperience: "After being dangerously near each custodian the ball was finally forced in to the Y.M.C.A. territory, and despite the efforts of their backs it was soon so near the line that Fullback Watson, thinking it was over, picked it up for a goal kick, thus allowing their opponents a free kick from which they scored after a hot scrimmage."[44] Undaunted, the YMCAs fought back, their supporters cheering "their men to an echo." Soon, Allie "tied the score on a well-placed shot." Now the "excitement was at a fever beat" as each team fought for supremacy. In the second half, "the excitement became so intense that the usually boisterous supporters forgot to shout, so eagerly did they watch each play." But with darkness falling, the score remained level at 1–1 when full time was called.[45] Fred played well in the replay, where he "blocked many brilliant attempts at scoring," but his team lost 5–3.[46]

Soccer struggled in Fall River and Pawtucket over the next few seasons due to the cumulative effects of converging debilitating factors: the economic depression following the Panic of 1893, harsh winter weather, and lingering resentment over the exodus of many top New England League players to the short-lived American League of Professional Football. Interest in the game was so low that the New England League did not meet to organize matches for the 1896–97 season. Another setback followed when the AFA formed the 1896–97 edition of the American Cup tournament without including Fall River and Pawtucket teams.[47] Fred got back on the pitch in the fall of 1898, when he lined up for "a revised Pawtucket Free Wanderers" in a cold and rainy 4–1 win over Fall River Floats on October 29.[48] The match report concluded, "Watson played a rare, good game at full back. He saved pluckily, is very fast, and kicks with good judgement."[49]

The brothers appeared together for the first time in four years on November 18, 1899, lining up for Attleboro (Massachusetts) in a 0–1 home loss to Pawtucket North End. Despite the loss, the match was the impetus for the formation of the "A. & D.," or Attleboro and Dodgeville, team, which was sponsored by the Watson & Newell Company, a manufacturer of jewelry and silverware.[50] A new league, the Rhode Island Amateur League, was organized with seven teams for the 1900–1901 season, including the A&Ds. Allie and Fred each made ten appearances for the team, playing together in nine of them. During the campaign, Allie tallied nine goals, including two hat tricks. On April 20, 1901, the brothers were on the field for a 3–2 win over the Pawtucket Rovers, a victory that gave their team the league championship, making Allie and Fred the first African American soccer players to be awarded championship medals.[51]

The Attleboro and Dodgeville team disbanded before the start of the 1901–2 season for unknown reasons.[52] By that time, the Watson brothers had moved to the Thornton squad, a picked team described in one report as "the pride of Pawtuxet valley."[53] The presence of African American players on the team was prominently reported by Fall River newspapers in previews ahead of an exhibition game in October 1901 against the New Rovers. One *Daily Globe* article noted, "They have playing with them two colored fellows who are said to be the only two regular association players of their kind in the country and they are crackerjacks at that." Another *Daily Globe* report described the Thorntons as made up of the "best players to be procured in the state of Rhode Island," adding, "The two colored players they have are the Watson brothers. One is a forward player and the other a full back." The *Daily Herald* observed the "two colored players" were "spoken of as very good men."[54]

Match reports in Fall River continued to highlight the Watsons' race: "When the game was on, the spectators saw that the two Watson brothers (colored) were with the visitors."[55] Reports also praised the brothers' work with teammates and individual play, despite their team losing 5–3. The *Daily Globe* described Fred as "a good, strong mate" for his fellow fullback. Allie, "though not holding any long suit on scrimmages, showed the ability to pass very cleverly."[56] The *Daily Herald* also praised Allie's technical skills and team play: "Watson is a colored man, as is the other Watson on the visiting team, and with his white companion played a beautiful passing game on their way down the field."[57] The *Daily Evening News* had praise for Fred: "Watson, a colored player, did well at full, and his clever work won the favor of the spectators."[58]

Unspecified disputes with the New England League eventually led the Thorntons to disband, and as a result, Fred joined the Free Wanderers. The club opened the league season at home against the Fall River Pocassets on November 9, 1901. With several starters unable to play, Fred lined up at halfback in the 4–2 loss. Soon after, the *Evening Times* reported, "16 regular professional players" had signed with the team.[59] While the report does not name the professional players, it is reasonable to conclude Fred was one of them, making him the first African American professional soccer player in the United States.

Fred's play was praised in his next appearance, a 3–0 loss on November 23 to the Fall River Pan Americans, so named because the team had won the soccer tournament at the Pan American Exposition in Buffalo in September. The rough start to the season finally took a turn for the better on Thanksgiving Day, when the Free Wanderers defeated the Fall River Oaks 5–1 at home.[60] Fred made several key defensive plays, including saving a goal. One report said his play "showed a decided improvement" and "was greatly admired."[61] A *Daily Globe* report on the 3–0 loss to the Pocassets on December 7 again highlighted the performance of "the colored fullback," observing Fred and his fellow defender "certainly put up a great game and they had to."[62]

The Pan Americans hosted the Free Wanderers at Fall River Athletic Field on Christmas Day 1901. Unaccountably for such a high-profile league match, the Free Wanderers arrived with thirteen players, three of whom were unregistered. Rather than play an unregistered player, which would result in a forfeit regardless of the outcome, the Pawtucket team played the game with only ten men. Remarkably, the shorthanded side held the Pan Americans to just one goal in the first half. Even more remarkably, the Free Wanderers scored a goal of their own minutes after the start of the second half. Soon after, Fred was badly injured. The *Daily Globe* described,

> Meikle sent the ball up the field in the air. Lynch went after it and so did Watson, the colored full-back. Lynch says the collision was almost inevitable and as he reached the ball he tried to jump to one side. While he was in the air Watson came up with a powerful kick. He kicked the ball but his foot caught Lynch squarely on the instep. Watson fell but Lynch seemed to go 10 feet in the air, turning a complete somersault and landed on the back of his neck. He got up somewhat dazed, but Watson was helpless.[63]

His leg broken, the *Daily Herald* reported Watson "was taken in the arms of several players to the gate and across the street to a small store" to await transport to the hospital. There it was found he had "sustained a simple fracture of the right leg just below the knee," although a later report said his injuries were "more serious than first thought" and included a broken bone in his ankle. The *Daily Evening News* match report noted Watson "was very popular with fans," adding, "He was a strong kicker, and played a clean sportsmanlike game."[64] The Pan American eleven, now facing only nine Free Wanderers, went on to win the game 6–1.

Several of Fred's teammates remained in Fall River after the match to visit him in the hospital. Meanwhile, the *Daily Globe* reported that members of local teams were arranging a benefit game for the injured fullback, "assisted by a number of local people who have volunteered contributions to help the cause along, as the colored fellow was one of the most popular players that ever came to this city."[65] Such matches served as an informal form of mutual aid, something common among workingman's associations of the period.[66] Pawtucket and Fall River newspapers provided updates on Fred's recovery over the next month. The same day the *Evening Times* reported Fred's discharge from the hospital, the paper announced the benefit match date for "that well known player, Fred Watson." Expectations in Fall River were that "the sale for the colored fellow will be quite a large one."[67]

The Free Wanderers lost 2–1 to the Pan Americans in the benefit match on January 25, 1902. But turnout for the match "for the popular colored full back" was strong, with "fully 3000 people spectators" on hand.[68] Indeed, the large turnout became the impetus to fund the building of a new enclosed playing field at the Free Wanderers' Dexter Street Grounds. The *Evening Times* explained, "Through the efforts of Watson's friends, a large number of tickets were sold and the injured player was netted a handsome sum. It would have been larger had the field been enclosed by a fence, for quite a number came to the game without paying a cent. These same persons, all lovers of the game, would have cheerfully paid had they been obliged to, but as they were not Watson lost a tidy sum."[69] A little more than a month later, Pan Americans manager C. C. Murphy visited Fred at his home to give him the proceeds of the benefit game. The *Fall River Daily Globe* reported, "Fred had just taken the plaster cast from his leg for good. He was much pleased to see Mr. Murphy, but when the latter turned him over a neat sum of money as the share of the benefit to which Fall River players and public contributed quite generously, the colored fellow could hardly find words to express his gratitude for the kind remembrance by the local followers of the game."[70]

After Fred's injury, the brothers' playing careers seemed to be coming to an end. Match reports featuring the Watsons appear sporadically, making it difficult to confirm if it was the brothers or someone with the same surname. Allie's last documented match took place on March 18, 1905, and Fred's two years later on March 23, 1907. Perhaps it is not surprising, as both brothers were now over thirty years old. It is unknown how many games they played over the course of their careers, and the available figures are undoubtedly incomplete. According to the best evidence, between 1894 and 1905 Allie made thirty-three appearances and scored sixteen goals across all competitions. In the years he was active from 1894 to 1907, Fred played in thirty-six games without recording a goal.

In some ways, the story of the Watson brothers is unremarkable. Industrial workers in cities across the country took up soccer and competed in local and regional competitions. It was also common for brothers and other family members to play together. What makes their story unique is that they were African American soccer players. At a time when professional baseball enforced a color line, the sport of soccer displayed a willingness to accept Black players as equals. Discrimination and prejudice, however, were not completely unknown in the sport. The Watson brothers remain the only documented African American players in the United States during the nineteenth century. The reasons for the absence of Black players are not fully known; it could be that other people of color took part in matches, but their actions were not recorded in the press. If we only read the reports from Pawtucket newspapers, we would have no indication that Allie and Fred were any different from teammates and opponents. It could also be that in many places, soccer thrived among immigrant and native-born communities that often proved unwelcoming to outsiders. The only other reference to people of color in soccer during this period has problematic overtones. A newspaper story from July 1896 notes that a club from Ilwaco, Washington, traveled with two "colored mascots."[71] Nothing more is known about these individuals or how they were treated and perceived by players and supporters.

Even as the Watsons hung up their cleats, reports from elsewhere show that more people of color were taking up the sport. When organized soccer began in Hawai'i in 1900, the participants included Chinese, Filipino, and native Hawaiians.[72] In 1908, the Spartan Athletic Club formed in New York City, offering its Black members an opportunity to play soccer. That same year a photograph of the Nomads team from Buffalo, New York, appears to include a player of color.[73] A year later, the champion Barrow School boys' soccer team of Springfield, Massachusetts, included three African Americans in the squad.[74] Although progress was slow, the 1910s to 1930s saw a boom in the number of Black clubs forming in New York. Many of these sides competed against white teams in various local competitions, including the Empire State League and the Metropolitan League.[75] Eventually, pro players of color starred in the American Soccer League and on the international stage. Gil

Heron, who has often been called the first Black professional soccer player in the United States, made his debut in 1946.

The story of the Watson brothers is an opportunity to expand the timeline of Black participation in soccer and reconsider the role of people of color in soccer history. As Allie and Fred largely faded from public view, they continued to live their lives, perhaps unaware of their role as pioneers. Allie died at the age of fifty-three in May 1925, unmarried, and survived only by his brothers Fred and Eugene. Fred married Elsie L. Watts in May 1901, and they remained together until she died in March 1931. A few years later he remarried. Like his older brothers, he had no children. Fred was sixty-six years old when he died in December 1941. Sadly, no images of either brother have been found.

Notes

1. "Injured at Football," *Fall River Daily Herald*, April 16, 1894; "Variety of Sporting," *Fall River Daily Herald*, September 26, 1894.
2. Rhode Island Black Heritage Society and 1696 Heritage Group, *A Matter of Truth: The Struggle for African Heritage and Indigenous People, Equal Rights in Providence, Rhode Island (1620–2020)* (Providence RI: Black Heritage Society, 2021), 55, 57; Robert Cottrol, *The Afro-Yankees: Providence's Black Community in the Antebellum Era* (Westport CT: Praeger, 1982), 150.
3. John Gilkeson, *Middle Class Providence, 1820–1940* (Princeton NJ: Princeton University Press, 1986), 141; Myra B. Young Armstead, *"Lord, Please Don't Take Me in August":African Americans in Newport and Saratoga Springs, 1870–1930* (Urbana: University of Illinois Press, 1999), 113, 114.
4. Leslie Heaphy, *The Negro Leagues, 1869–1960* (Jefferson NC: McFarland, 2013), 157; Robert Cvornyek and Fran Leazes, "The Price of Admission: Daddy Black, Big Dan Whitehead, and the Money Game," *Rhode Island History* 7, no. 2 (Winter–Spring 2020): 53.
5. Rhode Island Black Heritage Society and 1696 Heritage Group, *Matter of Truth*, 67.
6. "Mortuary," *Pawtucket Times*, May 26, 1925; Frederick M. Watson, "1900 U.S. Census," Ancestry.com, accessed November 19, 2020; Frederick M. Watson, "1910 U.S. Census," Ancestry.com, accessed November 19, 2020.
7. "Mortuary," *Pawtucket Evening Times*, May 26, 1925.
8. "Mortuary," *Pawtucket Evening Times*, December 17, 1915; "Charles Watson Dead," *Pawtucket Evening Times*, December 15, 1915.
9. "Mortuary," *Pawtucket Evening Times*, April 26, 1909.
10. "Which Is the 'Truly' Orator," *Pawtucket Evening Times*, January 3, 1899; "Told in Paragraphs," *Pawtucket Evening Times*, October 30, 1894.

11. Andy Mitchell, "Scotland's First Black Footballer: Robert Walker, the Curly-Haired Son of Africa," *Scottish Sports History*, October 12, 2020, https://www.scottishsporthistory .com/sports-history-news-and-blog/scotlands-first-black-footballer-robert-walker -the-curly-haired-son-of-africa; Llew Walker, *A Straggling Life: Andrew Watson, the Story of the World's First Black International Footballer* (Worthing: Pitch, 2021); Phil Vasili, *The First Black Footballer: Arthur Wharton, 1865–1930* (New York: Routledge, 1997).

12. Walker, *Straggling Life*, 55–70, 90, 76.

13. Andy Mitchell, "Willie Clarke: Scotland's Second Black Internationalist," *Scottish Sport History*, October 5, 2020, https://www.scottishsporthistory.com/sports-history-news -and-blog/willie-clarke-scotlands-second-black-internationalist. See also Mitchell, "Scotland's First Black Footballer."

14. "1900 United States Census, Pawtucket Ward 2, Providence, Rhode Island: Roll: 1511; Page: 15; Enumeration District: 0149," Ancestry.com, accessed November 19, 2020, https://www.ancestrylibrary.com/discoveryui-content/view/69417799:7602.

15. "East End Foot Ball Games," *Fall River Daily Herald*, October 22, 1884; "Foot Ball," *Evening Bulletin* (Providence), March 8, 1886; "City Chat," *Pawtucket Evening Times*, September 17, 1886; "City Chat," *Pawtucket Evening Times*, October 4, 1886.

16. See Roger Allaway, *Rangers, Rovers & Spindles: Soccer, Immigration, and Textiles in New England and New Jersey* (Howarth: St. Johann Press, 2005).

17. "Conant vs. Clarke at Football," *Evening Bulletin* (Providence), November 8, 1889; Mira Wilkins, *History of Foreign Investment in the United States to 1914* (Cambridge MA: Harvard University Press, 1989), 362; "The Victorious Thornton Club," *Evening Bulletin* (Providence), June 14, 1888; Louis McGowan, "English Immigrants to Turn-of-the-Twentieth Century Rhode Island," *Johnson Historical Society Historical Notes* 12, no. 1 (March 2006): 1.

18. "The Game of Football," *Fall River Daily Herald*, January 31, 1888; "The Champions of America," *Fall River Daily Herald*, April 16, 1888; "Hail Olympics," *Fall River Daily Globe*, April 7, 1890; "Sporting Matters," *Fall River Daily Globe*, October 26, 1885.

19. "City Chat," *Pawtucket Evening Times*, June 2, 1886; "Sporting Notes," *Fall River Daily Herald*, May 10, 1886; "City Chat," *Pawtucket Evening Times*, April 18, 1887; "City Chat," *Pawtucket Evening Times*, April 25, 1887.

20. "City Chat," *Pawtucket Evening Times*, April 18, 1887; "Foot Ball," *Evening Bulletin* (Providence), May 31, 1887; "At the North End Grounds," *Fall River Daily Evening News*, May 31, 1887.

21. "New League Formed," *Pawtucket Evening Times*, January 12, 1891.

22. "Association Football Practice," *Boston Herald*, March 4, 1888.

23. "Football Games," *Fall River Daily Herald*, March 26, 1888; "Sports of All Sorts," *Boston Daily Globe*, April 5, 1888; "City Chat," *Pawtucket Evening Times*, April 30, 1888; "Woburn Rangers Club," *Boston Herald*, June 12, 1888; "Other Football Games," *Boston Herald*, November 18, 1888; "Providence Football Team Abroad," *Evening Bulletin*

(Providence), November 30, 1888; "Irish Athletes," *Boston Daily Globe*, August 14, 1889; "Irish Athletic Club Games at Oak Island," *Fall River Daily Globe*, August 14, 1889.

24. "Home Affairs," *Pawtucket Evening Times*, January 14, 1889.

25. The match was between Fall River Olympics and Kearny Rovers. "Local Sporting," *Fall River Daily Herald*, March 10, 1890.

26. "They Win the Cup," *Pawtucket Evening News*, May 29, 1893; "Saylesville," *Evening Bulletin*, May 29, 1893; "Pawtucket," *Evening Bulletin* (Providence), June 5, 1893.

27. "American Cup-Ties," *Fall River Daily Globe*, September 5, 1893; "R.I. Football Association" and "New England League," *Fall River Daily Globe*, September 11, 1893.

28. "Football Notes," *Fall River Daily Globe*, October 14, 1893; "New England League," *Fall River Daily Herald*, January 23, 1894; "Champion Y.M.C.A's.," *Pawtucket Evening Times*, May 7, 1894.

29. Nina Mjagkij, *Light in the Darkness: African Americans and the YMCA, 1852–1946* (Lexington: University Press of Kentucky, 2003), 49.

30. "Variety of Sporting," *Fall River Daily Herald*, September 26, 1894; "Injured at Football," *Fall River Daily Herald*, April 16, 1894.

31. "On the Wane," *Fall River Daily Globe*, December 24, 1894; "Walkover for the Olympics," *Fall River Daily Herald*, December 24, 1894.

32. "On the Wane."

33. "Modern Athletic Celebrities," *Scottish Athletic Journal*, December 15, 1885.

34. "East Ends Exit," *Fall River Daily Globe*, March 11, 1895.

35. "East Ends Exit"; "Y.M.C.A. Defeats East Ends," *Pawtucket Evening Times*, March 11, 1895.

36. "Exciting Contest," *Pawtucket Evening Times*, April 22, 1895; "The Wanderers Won," *Pawtucket Evening Times*, May 6, 1895.

37. "The Game in Pawtucket," *Fall River Daily Herald*, September 23. 1895.

38. "Mortuary," *Pawtucket Evening Times*, May 26, 1925; "Return of a Death, Oliver Henry Arnold Watson," Rhode Island Division of Vital Records, accessed August 4, 2024, https://sosri.access.preservica.com/uncategorized/IO_8a1fb691-598b-487a-bed8-da26844151e6/.

39. "Football Notes," *Fall River Daily Globe*, October 11, 1895; "Football Passes," *Fall River Daily Evening News*, October 11, 1895.

40. "Rovers Win," *Fall River Daily Globe*, October 14, 1895.

41. "Y.M.C.A. Team Practice," *Pawtucket Evening Times*, October 21, 1895.

42. "Foot Ball Notes," *Pawtucket Evening Times*, October 27, 1895.

43. "East Ends Beaten," *Pawtucket Evening Times*, October 28, 1895.

44. "Association Football," *Pawtucket Evening Times*, November 11, 1895.

45. "Association Football."

46. "Free Wanderers Won," *Pawtucket Evening Times*, November 29, 1895.

47. "No Football Games," *Fall River Daily Herald*, October 10, 1896; "Frozen Out," *Fall River Daily Globe*, October 27, 1896.

48. "The C.C.'s Defeated," *Fall River Daily Globe*, November 7, 1898.

49. "Pawtucket Team Made an Excellent Showing against Fall River Floats," *Pawtucket Evening Times*, October 31, 1898; "Saturday's Game," *Pawtucket Evening Times*, October 20, 1898.

50. "North Ends Won at Attleboro," *Pawtucket Evening Times*, November 20, 1899.

51. "Game Schedule," *Pawtucket Evening Times*, December 10, 1900; "Darkness Interfered," *Pawtucket Evening Times*, November 26, 1900; "Association Football," *Pawtucket Evening Bulletin*, November 30, 1900; "Amateur Football," *Pawtucket Evening Times*, November 30, 1900; "Attleboro 7, Atherton 0," *Pawtucket Evening Times*, December 3, 1900; "League Football," *Pawtucket Evening Times*, December 17, 1900; "Attleboro Still Leading," *Pawtucket Evening Times*, December 24, 1900; "Called a Draw," *Pawtucket Evening Times*, December 31, 1900; "Amateur League Football Games," *Pawtucket Evening Times*, January 7, 1901; "No Goals Gained," *Pawtucket Evening Times*, January 28, 1901; "Schedule Off," *Pawtucket Evening Times*, April 1, 1901; "Manville Beats Attleboro Team," *Pawtucket Evening Times*, April 15, 1901; "Attleboro Wins," *Pawtucket Evening Times*, April 22, 1901.

52. "Association Football League," *Pawtucket Evening Times*, October 17, 1901.

53. "East End Echoes," *Fall River Daily Globe*, October 16, 1901.

54. "East End Echoes," October 16, 1901; "East End Echoes," *Fall River Daily Globe*, October 18, 1901; "Tomorrow's Football," *Fall River Daily Herald*, October 18, 1901.

55. "Five to Three," *Fall River Daily Globe*, October 21, 1901.

56. "Five to Three."

57. "Rovers-Thornton," *Fall River Daily Herald*, October 21, 1901.

58. "Rovers Win," *Fall River Daily Evening News*, October 21, 1901.

59. "On Association Football Fields," *Pawtucket Evening Times*, November 11, 1901; "League to Meet," *Pawtucket Evening Times*, November 15, 1901.

60. "With the Association Teams," *Pawtucket Evening Times*, November 25, 1901; "Association Football," *Pawtucket Evening Bulletin*, November 29, 1901.

61. "Football Results Association Game," *Pawtucket Evening Times*, November 29, 1901; "Goal Kicks," *Pawtucket Evening Times*, November 29, 1901.

62. "Pocassets Won," *Fall River Daily Globe*, December 9, 1901.

63. "Over Four Thousand Persons," *Fall River Daily Globe*, December 26, 1901.

64. "Christmas Football," *Fall River Daily Herald*, December 26, 1901; "Flint Village," *Fall River Daily Herald*, December 30, 1901; "Fall River 6, Pawtucket 1," *Fall River Daily Evening News*, December 26, 1901.

65. "East End Echoes," *Fall River Daily Globe*, January 30, 1902.

66. Gilkeson, *Middle Class Providence*, 108.

67. "Fred Watson Improving," *Pawtucket Evening Times*, January 2, 1902; "Fred Watson Home," *Pawtucket Evening Times*, January 16, 1902; "Ned Birt Chosen Captain," *Pawtucket Evening Times*, January 16, 1902; "Globe Gossip," *Fall River Daily Globe*, January 18, 1902; "East End Echoes," *Fall River Daily Globe*, January 21, 1902.

68. "Pan Americans 2, Free Wanderers 1," *Fall River Daily Evening News*, January 27, 1902, 5; "Pans Won the Game," *Fall River Daily Herald*, January 27, 1902.

69. "Athletics Field Contemplated," *Pawtucket Evening Times*, January 28, 1902.

70. "East End Echoes," *Fall River Daily Globe*, March 13, 1902.

71. "Football," *Daily Astorian*, July 18, 1896. The squad may have taken the practice from baseball, since by the 1880s, most teams, including those on the Pacific Coast, had mascots. Many of the earliest baseball mascots were African American boys. J. W. Stewart, "The Bat Boy or Whatever You Wish to Call Him," in *Baseball 11: New Research on the Early Game*, ed. Don Jensen (Jefferson NC: McFarland, 2020), 69, 71.

72. Brian D. Bunk, "Soccer in Paradise: The Early History of the Beautiful Game in Hawai'i," Playing Pasts: The Online Magazine for Sport and Leisure History, July 2021, https://www.playingpasts.co.uk/author/bd-bunk/.

73. Susan Rayl, "New York Renaissance Professional Black Basketball Team, 1923–1950" (PhD diss., Pennsylvania State University, 1996), 33. Nomads photograph in possession of the authors.

74. Brian D. Bunk, "The Barrow School Socker Foot Ball Team," Society for American Soccer History, last modified February 13, 2020, https://www.ussoccerhistory.org/the-barrow-school-socker-foot-ball-team/.

75. See Jermaine Scott, "Harlem's Chief Representatives: The Radical Politics of Black Soccer in New York, 1928–1949," *Journal of African American History* 6, no. 2 (Spring 2021): 196–219.

5

In Pursuit of the Boundary

Cricket in Boston's West Indian Community, 1900–1950

VIOLET SHOWERS JOHNSON

At the dawn of the twentieth century, Boston was a vibrant city in work and play. The docks and shipyards, factories, retail businesses, and service industry demonstrated the robust economy in the heart of the city and the surrounding suburbs. Leisure, in the forms of sports, recreation, and entertainment, was equally dynamic. The Boston area was bustling with dance halls, saloons and nightclubs, theaters, and amusement parks and playgrounds, and in sports, the city was a national leader. As Stephen Hardy states in his book *How Boston Played*, "Boston was at the center of America's sporting scene with such old rivals as New York or Philadelphia and emerging cities like Chicago. The self-styled 'Athens of America,' Boston nurtured a rich tradition in more than arts and literature. She was also a leader in sports and recreation."[1] This stature was reflected prominently in the variety of sports played in Boston. Almost every sport in America at the time was present in the city—baseball, football, basketball, boxing, wrestling, rowing, golf, cycling, bowling, tennis, track and field, and cricket. The last sport on the list is the focus of this essay, which discusses the centrality of cricket in the small West Indian community of Boston and Cambridge, Massachusetts, in the first half of the twentieth century. As a cultural transplant from premigration Caribbean culture, cricket served vital functions beyond the pitch, contributing to the development of an emerging community. Cricket was used consciously as a tool for projecting group identity and for responding to anti-Blackness. Starting with an overview of the Boston West Indian community, this essay will describe the development of cricket in the West Indian immigrant community and assess how West Indians used the sport to break boundaries and shield the immigrant community from the workings of race and racism in an American city.

Immigrants from the Caribbean began arriving in Boston in small numbers in the second half of the nineteenth century. In the 1880s and 1890s, only two or three hundred immigrants had come to Boston from the West Indies.[2] Those numbers increased in the early twentieth century. In 1910, the U.S. Census counted 566 West Indians living in Boston, which represented 5 percent of the total Black population. The 1920 census reflected a huge increase, with the West Indian population at 2,877. By 1952, the West Indian population was estimated at 5,000, which accounted for 12 percent of the total Black population in Boston. That number included immigrants from the Virgin Islands, Trinidad, and Guyana, but most of the Caribbean population during the first half of the twentieth century came from three English-speaking islands—Jamaica, Barbados, and Montserrat. Their migration to Boston paralleled similar waves of Caribbean immigration to New York and other destinations along the northeastern seaboard. Many of these new immigrants came directly to Boston from the Caribbean, while many were "step" migrants who arrived from intermediate destinations that included Costa Rica, Panama, Cuba, and Nova Scotia. West Indian immigration from ports in the Caribbean and Central America followed the routes of the passenger steamers, especially those of the Boston-headquartered United Fruit Company.

In Boston, West Indians settled primarily in the South End, Roxbury, and Dorchester. A smaller West Indian community also grew in Cambridge, in the vicinity of Central Square and the side streets along Massachusetts Avenue. Given their small numbers and the fact that they lived in Black neighborhoods, immigrants from the English-speaking West Indies seemed to dissolve into the larger African American population. At that time, the African American population was composed of Boston-born Blacks, including the famous "Brahmins," and migrants from Southern states, notably Georgia, North Carolina, South Carolina, and Alabama. These demographics reflected two major movements of people of African descent that occurred in the early decades of the twentieth century: migration from the American South known as the Great Migration and immigration from the Caribbean and Central America.[3]

The comparatively small number of Black immigrants from the Caribbean and Central America and their adaptation to the existing African American presence often obscured their identity as a distinct Black immigrant community. Even His Majesty's Consul General in Boston declared in 1934 that there was "no cohesive West Indian community in Boston."[4] This British diplomat was wrong. Not only was there a cohesive community, but it was also one that self-identified as British. By the 1930s, when the British consul made his pronouncement, West Indians had developed the conventional markers of community—a church, ethnic organizations and sports clubs, and a newspaper. St. Cyprian's Episcopal (Anglican) Church, which was also known as the "West Indian church," started in 1910 as a small congregation meeting in the South End home of a Jamaican woman. By 1915, the mostly Jamaican and Barbadian members of the small Anglican group had outgrown that space and began to meet in the facilities of a predominantly white Episcopalian church in Boston. In 1924, they moved to their own church building located in Lower Roxbury, in the heart of Black Boston.[5] The immigrants also organized in secular groups. A pan–West Indian association, the West India Aid Society, was created in 1915. Island-specific organizations followed, albeit much later: the Jamaica Associates in 1934; the Barbados Union Inc. in 1937; and the Montserratian Progressive League in 1939. By the time the island associations were founded, there was already an "ethnic press."

The *Boston Chronicle* was launched as a weekly newspaper in 1915 by a group of Jamaican journalists in Boston and a couple based in Jamaica under the sponsorship of the Square Deal Company.[6] Every Saturday, the pages of the *Chronicle* reflected the vibrancy of the West Indian community, which for many, including the British consul, was still a hidden ethnic enclave. The paper reported on the numerous events in the community, from special church services at St. Cyprian's to concerts, lectures, and tea parties organized by the associations. And importantly, the *Chronicle* highlighted cricket in its sports pages. In this endeavor, the newspaper played "catch-up," because cricket in the West Indian community predated the *Chronicle*, St. Cyprian's, and the island associations. Black West Indians first played organized cricket in Massachusetts in the 1890s.

West Indians did not introduce cricket to Boston. One of the oldest recreational and competitive sports in America, cricket had made its way to the city by the early 1800s, well before significant immigration from the Caribbean began.[7] By the mid-nineteenth century, Boston was developing a reputation for cricket that rivaled Philadelphia's, which was the foremost cricket-playing city at the time. Longwood Cricket Club, founded in 1877 in Chestnut Hill, Massachusetts, was one of the leading forces for this advancement. Although tennis later overtook cricket as the sport most associated with the Longwood Cricket Club, in its first two decades, the club cultivated cricket well beyond the suburb in which it was located.[8] John Isaacs (Ike) Chambers and brothers Harry and George Wright worked tirelessly to promote the club and elevate cricket in Boston to a level comparable to cricket in Philadelphia.[9]

Although Longwood gained a national reputation as an elite Massachusetts cricket club, there were more than twenty such clubs in the state. The members were exclusively white. In the late eighteenth century and the first three-quarters of the nineteenth century, New England cricket clubs, like Longwood, as well as the collegiate teams of elite institutions were regarded as recreational avenues for "men of leisure." By the end of the nineteenth century, conscious efforts were being made to secure more working-class visibility by supporting the growth of teams in factory towns like Brockton, New Bedford, Malden, Beverly, Fall River, Lynn, Lowell, Medford, Chelsea, and Everett. The members of these teams were mostly English and other European immigrant men who worked as artisans and laborers in the factories and other establishments. In Boston in 1889, the cricket establishment formed the Boston Cricket Club, which was intended to be "the working-class arm" of the Longwood Cricket Club. It was with a similar resolve that the cricket establishment reached out to West Indians living in Boston and Cambridge. Jamaica native A. Newton Service, founder of the Windsor Cricket Club, recalled that organized West Indian cricket in Boston began in 1892 with an invitation from two of the greatest bowlers in the state, Longwood Club cricketers and members of the Boston Athletic Association, George Wright and Ralph Cracknell. These men encouraged the Black immigrants to come together to form "gentlemen elevens" (cricket teams). The West Indians accepted the invitation and began to organize. After two short-lived clubs—West Indian Cricket Club and Suffolk Cricket Club—in 1898, the West India A Cricket Club was formed.[10]

The invitation from Wright and Cracknell was not far-fetched. These men had firsthand knowledge of the prominence of cricket in the popular culture and the larger society of the British West Indies. In 1886, the West Indies Cricket Team took its first international tour of North America, which included a stop, after Philadelphia, at the Longwood Cricket Club. It was a highly successful tour in which the West Indies team won twelve out of the fourteen matches it played in Canada and the United States. In January 1888, putting a team together with players from Philadelphia, Boston, New York, and the South, the United States reciprocated with a tour of the West Indies. Wright and Cracknell, who was also a *Boston Globe* sportswriter, knew first-hand the cricket roots of this group of Boston immigrants. The Gentlemen of Longwood recognized the potential of the Gentlemen of the South End, Roxbury, and Cambridge and sought to include them in the development of their homeland pastime in their new American home. Therefore, the fact that Boston's West Indian community embraced a sport transplanted to America prior to their own immigration was not surprising. What was surprising to many, however, and even an anomaly, was that a group of Blacks in a Black neighborhood in an American city in the pre–civil rights movement era was immersed in a sport that was then considered white and upper class.

The formation of other West Indian cricket teams followed quickly on the heels of the founding of West India A. The Wanderers was formed in 1901, and by 1908, there were seven additional West Indian cricket clubs: in Boston (West India B, Windsor, Windsor Minor, and Caribbean) and in Cambridge (University, Standard, and Athletics). All these teams played in the Massachusetts Cricket League, which was established in July 1904.[11] The players were recruited from the West Indian communities of the South End, Roxbury, Dorchester, and Cambridge. It was easy to build the teams because many West Indies immigrants were men who had played cricket before they emigrated. While most of them had played the game recreationally, in their yards and local fields, there were a few who had played competitively as amateurs in local home teams.[12] In their close-knit neighborhoods in Boston and Cambridge, the teams learned who to recruit by word of mouth. They recruited aggressively among established residents, new arrivals from the West Indies, and out-of-state transfers. It was common that newcomers straight from the boat, train, or bus were immediately registered on a team and offered the opportunity to play as quickly as one day after their arrival. Franklin Field was the home ground of the Boston teams, while the Cambridge teams—University, Standard, and Athletics—used the North Brighton Smith Field as their base. Franklin Field had already gained a reputation as the nerve center of Boston cricket by the time the West Indian teams were formed.[13] By the 1920s and 1930s, it had become the "home crease" of the West Indian teams, but they did not have a monopoly on the field. It was still the base for many of the matches of the Massachusetts Cricket League and the site of friendly and exhibition matches. On August 25, 1935, the *Boston Globe* described Franklin Field as a "cricket Mecca."[14]

As might be expected of sports teams in their infancy, the West Indian cricket teams started in the lower rankings in the first few years of the twentieth century. Well-established teams from the factory towns were in the lead. For example, in the 1904 season, the top teams were Everett, Lynn Wanderers, Lawrence, Brockton, and East Boston. West India A tied with Chelsea for first place in the second division. The *Boston Globe* of November 12, 1904, predicted that West Indians would become leaders of cricket in Massachusetts. In only a short time, that prediction was becoming reality. In an article titled "Some Cricket Surprises," the *Boston Globe* of May 19, 1905, reported, "The league cricket clubs are beginning to find their pace, and the surprise of the season so far is the defeat of Bunting by Merrimac and of Everett by West India."[15] In June 1907, a *Boston Herald* headline announced, "East Boston Has a Narrow Escape. West India A Gave Them a Hard Time on Their Own Ground." The *Boston Traveler* of July 30, 1915, reported on the "surprise" defeat of the Beverly Blues by the West India A Team at Beverly. On February 9, 1920, this publication affirmed the superior standing of West India, which won the 1919 championship without losing a game: "West India is the strongest cricket team that ever represented the Hub."[16]

Besides the pioneer West India A, other West Indian teams also rapidly ascended to the top of the league. In a July 15, 1915, article headlined "Wanderers Win," the *Herald* spotlighted the remarkable success of the West Indian teams: Wanderers, Windsor, Athletics, and the more familiar West India A. By the 1930s, the West Indian teams were consistently represented in the top tier of the Massachusetts Cricket League. In the 1931 season, the final match was played between two West Indian teams—Windsor and Standard. By 1939, Windsor had won the championship three times. By the 1940s, there was no denying the West Indian ascendancy. The West Indian newspaper, the *Chronicle*, as well as mainstream newspapers reported on their impressive standing. The October 5, 1941, *Globe* reported that West India CC (Cricket Club) and other "colored" teams "did a real job knocking off the all-star teams."[17] That year, the West Indian teams dominated the Massachusetts Cricket League: West India A was the champion, Windsor was second, Athletics was fourth, and Wanderers was sixth. And by that time, West India A, Windsor, and Wanderers had won all the major cricket cups in the state: the John Hayes Cup of the Massachusetts Cricket League, the Robert Burns Cup, and the Alexander Ford Cup.

Cricketers were well known in the small West Indian enclaves and state-wide in the cricket arena. Some of the household names that emerged from the sport were Lester Benn, John Bynoe, Darnley Phillips, J. Callender, Alan Parkes, Claudius "Cossy" Grant, Allan Mayers, and John Ifill. Describing them as "players of unusual skill," the press commented frequently on individual players. Lauding Claudius Grant, the *Chronicle* wrote, "He is a fearless type of cricketer, something like Barnes the Australian wicket-keeper. When Cossy is behind the sticks, the rest of the Windsors need not fear of losing the game."[18] Of the fourteen teams in the league in 1939, six were West Indian teams. Thus, by the 1930s, in both numbers and performance, West Indians were distinct in cricket in Massachusetts. The *Chronicle* proclaimed in 1939, "We must blow our own horn. For decades now our boys have been key in the Massachusetts Cricket League. While they are not the whole ship, they are a formidable anchor."[19]

Beyond the league, cricket was a formidable anchor for the West Indian community of Boston and Cambridge in the first half of the twentieth century.

It played a significant role in the development of a West Indian subculture. It provided the first opportunity for the immigrants to organize. From the onset, cricket was established as a cultural institution that transcended competitive sport. As the men formed teams to play the game, they engaged other members of the community in organizing with them. Specifically, each team created women's groups, known as a women's circle or women's auxiliary, which served as an effective tool for including families and other community institutions. As early as 1903, the teams were acknowledging publicly that the women's groups were great assets to the teams and the evolving immigrant community.[20] The women were crucial in raising much-needed funds for uniforms and sporting equipment. They catered the refreshments for the tea breaks, a requisite feature of any cricket match, and worked prominently on program planning committees for annual banquets, thanksgiving church services, musical recitals and concerts, picnics, and other social events sponsored by the cricket clubs. The women were not confined to gendered "domestic-type" contributions. Many of them were avid fans who attended matches as fully engaged spectators. Sports columnists frequently commented on the actions of women as vocal fans who understood the sport. The *Globe* of August 31, 1920, described the excitement of an avid fan of Standard who "knew more about the sport than the men."[21]

While as a sport cricket was a summer-only endeavor, given that the annual cricket season lasted from May to September, cricket in the West Indian community exerted a yearlong influence. Cricket and cricketers were at the center of the community. Starting in the 1920s, the players organized pre- and postseason thanksgiving services at St. Cyprian's, the cultural center of the West Indian community. The long-serving rector of that church, Reverend Leroy Fergusson, was a fixture at matches and social events organized by cricket clubs.[22] He used his special sermons and keynote speeches at anniversary banquets to remind cricketers of their obligation to uphold the propriety of the gentleman's sport. Similarly, *Chronicle* editors and journalists like Jamaicans Thaddeus Kitchener and Alfred Haughton were frequent distinguished guests at the social events of cricket clubs.

As the forerunner of social organizing in the West Indian communities of Boston, cricket clubs provided a foundation for the development of the island associations. Many of the founders and active members of the associations that were formed after the cricket clubs gained vital experience from organizing cricket in earlier years. Cricket as a bridge for community development crossed city and state lines. It was an effective vehicle for connecting West Indians in Boston with other West Indians in New Bedford, Massachusetts, Providence, Rhode Island, Connecticut, and New York. While the Massachusetts Cricket League competition was at the center of the existence of the teams, interstate friendly and exhibition games with other West Indians were crucial and drew some of the biggest crowds. The exhibition matches with visiting teams from New York to commemorate Memorial Day, July Fourth, and Labor Day were always much anticipated. Sometimes the matches were island-specific—for example, Jamaicans from New York playing Jamaicans from Boston or New York Jamaicans playing Barbadians from Boston and Cambridge.

Competitive and friendly exhibition games took West Indians out of Boston. Cricketers and their fans traveled to other parts of the Northeast for reciprocal national holiday games as well as to mark other occasions. Providence and New York were the most frequent destinations. The inter-city and interstate games were more than recreational sports; they provided opportunities for reunions, networking, and general socializing. As Elma Lewis, a prominent second-generation Barbadian, put it, "Cricket matches, whether here [in Boston], in New Bedford, Hartford, or New York, allowed my parents and other West Indian immigrants to connect and reconnect with family and friends; talk about news from the homeland; and report important changes that occurred in their lives in America."[23] Cricketers and their fans were encouraged to attend matches and accompanying events even when their teams did not play. In 1943, cricket was used as the medium, as the events announcements declared, for "entertaining and supporting Jamaican farm workers of the Connecticut Valley." On Labor Day of that year, the Joint Cricket League of New York played a friendly match in New York City with the Overseas Jamaica XI, which was made up of temporary Jamaican farmworkers in the U.S. Farm Security Administration program. The celebrations continued in Hartford, Connecticut, in October in a "Jamaican Field Day and Civic Farewell," headlined by a cricket match between a team of veteran West Indian players from New York and a combination of cricketers from the ten farm camps in Connecticut, at which the Jamaican temporary workers were stationed. The civic farewell ceremony to honor the departing farmworkers, who were returning after their six-month contract, was a pregame event that included cricketers and fans from all over the East Coast, including Boston and Cambridge. The *Chronicle* publicized these events, describing them as opportunities to "showcase West Indian and British cultures, as well as bring people of West Indian origin together." The paper encouraged cricketers to attend even though they had not been slated to play. The distinguished guests at the civic farewell ceremonies included the governor of Connecticut, the mayor of Hartford, the commissioner of agriculture, and the British consul general.[24]

Connections, such as those afforded by the farewell event for farmworkers, were useful for the sustainability of the cricket teams. They were fertile grounds for recruiting players. It was at such events that players and club officers learned about potential players who had just arrived on the East Coast, who were planning to emigrate from the West Indies, or who could be persuaded to move to Boston from other northeastern cities. Fielding a consistent full squad was one of the biggest problems the teams faced. There were numerous reports about matches with less than eleven players on one or both teams. Even more drastic, there were a few instances when matches were postponed or canceled because whole teams failed to show up or because they lacked sufficient players. The *Boston Advertiser* of September 5, 1926, reported that the Athletics forfeited points because the team did not show up for the match with University. Similarly, the *Globe* of August 3, 1942, lamented that Windsor lost against the Wanderers because it could not muster a full team. That year, Massachusetts Cricket League officials worried openly about too many game postponements, which they attributed to the fact that the players had to work on Saturdays, when the games were played. They advocated for moving game day to Sunday. Indeed, quite a few of the West Indian players were constrained by work obligations. Census records confirm that many of them worked as elevator operators, laborers, and bellhops. One of the best-known star players, Claudius Grant, was a laborer. Fortunately for the teams, Grant and many other star players competed for decades, making the rounds in the various West Indian teams. Along with this longevity of players, the teams also often relied on borrowing players from other sports, especially baseball.

Baseball, which occasionally helped alleviate the player-shortage problem, paradoxically, was one of the biggest impediments to the growth of cricket in Massachusetts and other parts of the country. By the 1930s, all hopes that cricket would be the national sport in America had evaporated, and countless newspaper sports columns in the United States simultaneously lamented the decline of cricket and extolled the ascendancy of baseball. Even the *Chronicle*, a staunch supporter of West Indian cricket in Boston, admitted in 1932, "Yes, Sir, there's only one national game—Baseball. Young and old, men and women, all can participate in this great game. No other sport has been able to displace it."[25]

A prevalent narrative at the time was that, simply put, cricket could never have overtaken baseball because baseball was American and cricket was not. Diverse commentators outlined the fundamental differences that set the two sports apart and underscored their "nationality." Baseball, they claimed, appealed to the core of the "American personality" in its liveliness and decisiveness. Cricket, with its opaque and cumbersome rules and protocols that dragged games tediously for hours and days, was off-putting to Americans.[26] The following assessments are representative of the baseball-versus-cricket narrative of the first half of the twentieth century:

Cricket is the sport of the leisurely. It is the best form to stop a cricket match for luncheon or for tea, and to quit for the day long before the sunset gun booms. The American wants quick, snappy contest, with a definite result in sight. Baseball measures up to his habits of thought and action, just as cricket fits with British customs and traditions.[27]

Cricket isn't a sport. It is a ceremony.[28]

To those who say, "why not establish cricket as the national sport?" I say baseball is the greatest game in the world and one of the noblest triumphs of American civilization. Cricket is infantile compared with it.[29]

Cricket was born as a British product, and over centuries the Britishness of that sport continued to solidify, even as it spread to diverse peoples in the British Empire. In 1878, American author Julian Hawthorne remarked, "Cricket is so British that the bats and balls should be quartered upon the British flag; and a wicket should be every true Englishmen's [sic] tombstone. Surely, all pious Britons must hope to enter paradise through the wicket gate."[30] This idea, that cricket is British to the core, was a crucial feature of West Indians' adaptation to their new lives in Boston and around America. While the Massachusetts Cricket League and proponents of cricket in America were lamenting the defeat of cricket by baseball because of the former's quirky foreignness, West Indian immigrants saw the exclusivity afforded by cricket as an efficacious tool at their disposal as Black people in Jim Crow America. Not only did that sport confer on them a potent identity that is associated with whiteness, but it also allowed them to navigate interracial spaces that baseball, notoriously at the time, did not afford the Black citizens of America.

Cricket was a major reason why West Indians in Boston and Cambridge in the early part of the twentieth century were viewed as the "other Blacks." At a time when African Americans were advancing in baseball and fighting for desegregation in that sport, it was conspicuously remarkable to see people of African descent who embraced a similar yet different and foreign sport. A Jewish American resident of a neighborhood in Dorchester that bordered the expanding Black neighborhood of Roxbury articulated the distinctiveness that cricket conferred on the Black foreigners: "I know very little about cricket, but I used to know this much—that it is a game of White Englishmen. But I saw Negroes from the British Colonies in West India [sic] play in Franklin Field on Saturdays better than any Englishman. And what is most admirable is their keeping to all the gentlemanly dictates of the game. They are Black Englishmen."[31]

The cricketers and other members of the West Indian communities of Boston and Cambridge savored the identity of "the other" conferred by cricket and endeavored to adhere to the expected decorum that came with the game. Cricket as the "gentleman's game" was a familiar premigration cultural phenomenon in their home nations that the immigrants continued to uphold in Boston. The players were reminded of this fundamental characteristic of cricket on the pitch, at their annual banquets, and in church. In his farewell speech at the election meeting, outgoing Massachusetts Cricket League president, attorney Cyril Butler, reiterated the principles of cricket: "harmony, friendly rivalry, and clean sportsmanship."[32] In his sermon at the 1935 annual end-season cricketers thanksgiving service, Reverend Leroy Fergusson described cricket as "the oldest and most skillful and cleanest of games." He admonished the cricketers to remember the noble traditions of the sport and keep up the standards—emulate character, patience, perseverance, and good comradeship. The *Chronicle* report on the event noted, "The rector was listened to with rapt attention by the assembled cricketers and as some of those conscience-stricken brethren recalled some of their misguided squabbles [on the cricket field], many squirmed in their seats and looked uncomfortable."[33] The misguided squabbles, notwithstanding the West Indian teams, were often applauded for their decorum. The *Boston Globe* of August 3, 1934, rated the Windsors as the "classiest team in the League."[34]

The projection of this genteel character of the sport at the center of the evolving Black immigrant community was timely. Many of the players, as well as their fans, saw this aspect of cricket as a tool to assert their difference from Southern migrants, who constituted the fastest-growing group of Boston's Blacks. Boston was not different from other northeastern cities, like Philadelphia, where the influx of Southerners met with backlash that maligned the newcomers as boisterous, uncouth, and prone to crime. While the *Chronicle* was never as blatant as the other Black publication, the African American–owned *Boston Guardian*, its deft coverage of West Indian propriety, as reflected in cricket and other West Indian institutions, contributed significantly to setting the West Indians apart from the other arriving Blacks.

The purported egalitarianism of cricket was another feature the Black immigrants found useful in their adaptation to pre–civil rights movement America. Although cricket was known as the sport of kings and lords, it enjoyed a parallel reputation as an inclusive sport that brought diverse races, peoples, and classes together. American poet and novelist Julian Hawthorne, as a tourist in England, marveled at this inclusiveness.[35] This reputation extended far beyond England to the outposts of the British Empire.[36] The British West Indies was one of those outposts. In a memoir by C. L. R. James—known as a classic on the history of cricket—the author recalls the composition of the school teams he remembers growing up in his native Trinidad: "As soon as we stepped on the cricket or football [soccer] field, more particularly the cricket field, all was changed. We were a motley crew. The children of some white officials and white business men, middle-class blacks, and mulattos, Chinese boys, some of whose parents could speak no English at all, and some black boys who had won exhibitions or whose parents had starved and toiled on plots of agricultural land and were spending their hard-earned money on giving the eldest boy an education."[37]

West Indians in Boston saw this inclusiveness in cricket in their new home and hoped that it would alleviate the racial divisions and racism that were evident in that northern city. The Black immigrants considered cricket a racially integrated sport. In 1938, in an upbeat article titled "Cricket Takes Sports Center," the *Chronicle* affirmed, "Unlike many other sports, cricket is both international and interracial." It continued (strangely, given that the perceived Englishness of the sport was still being touted), "Long ago its English accent disappeared and gave way to a cosmopolitanism that provides excellent teams among Negro, Indian, Portuguese, and native African and Māori players . . . and West Indian businessmen and laborers. The sport holds equal attraction and good sportsmanship for all."[38] The West Indian teams, which were the only "colored" teams, played in the Massachusetts Cricket League against white teams with which they exchanged home ground visits. A few West Indian players even served as umpires. Importantly, leadership of the league was open to both white and colored players and officials. By the 1930s, some West Indian players had been elected to the executive committee of the league, and two men of color had been elected president. Dr. Don F. Pinheiro of New Bedford, who was of Cape Verdean descent, was the first person of color to head the league. Although neither West Indian nor a cricket player, prominent African American attorney and avid advocate for Black advancement in Boston, Cyril F. Butler, was elected president of the league for the 1935–36 season. In his farewell speech, Butler invoked the inclusive character of cricket and hoped that under the leadership of his successor, John F. Dixon, who was white, "the same principles will prevail and so enable cricket in the Commonwealth to point the way to interracial amity and consistence."[39] Another president expressed similar expectations. Upon his election in 1940, D. E. Foote, a veteran player for Everett, a white team, who had been the manager of the West Indian Wanderers team for twenty-five years, pledged to use his position to develop the league further as an example and shaper of racial integration and equality.[40]

But was cricket in Massachusetts a flawless paragon of racial equality, enough to render West Indians immune to the challenges of racism and anti-Blackness? The league was not a fully nonracial entity. The racial composition of the teams was rigid, resulting in clear distinctions between colored and white teams. Up until the mid-1930s, although the teams played against each other, white and Black players did not play in racially integrated teams. In the first decade of the twentieth century, the capstone of each season was an all-star match between the white stars and the colored stars. While this friendly match and the competitive matches during the season suggested a type of "separate but equal" reality, the West Indian players exhibited a race consciousness that allowed them to detect racial "unevenness" within the integrated league and cricket in Massachusetts. According to *Chronicle* reports, both players and fans complained about the state of the home fields of the Black teams and about the resources to which they had access compared to those of white teams. The elite Ike Chambers annual benefit match also suggested a disparity along racial lines. The match, often touted as nostalgic and played at the prestigious Longwood Oval, consistently created the two competing teams exclusively from the white teams. This kind of marginalization reminded the West Indian players of their Blackness and prompted them and their fans to think of cricket affiliations along racial lines. The *Boston Traveler* of September 7, 1918, reporting on the end-of-season match between the Black and white teams, observed, "The game is attracting unusual interest among the West Indians, who love to see the teams of their color against strong white teams."[41] West Indian players may have begun to grasp the limitations of cricket as an inclusive sport before they emigrated. They may have known about the many undertones of racial inequality in cricket as it played out in their homelands. Even C. L. R. James, quoted earlier recalling the demographic diversity of his schoolboy days in cricket, knew firsthand of racial injustice within the sport. In his introduction to the fiftieth-anniversary edition of *Beyond a Boundary*, Robert Lipsyte noted, "When the great wicketkeeper Piggott was not included on an all-island team in favor of a lesser player who was white, James came to understand that even cricket was not always cricket."[42]

Race consciousness among West Indians in Boston went beyond cricket. They could never completely evade their Blackness, especially outside of the cricket boundary. The racialization of people of African descent arriving from the Caribbean in the nineteenth and early twentieth centuries started as soon as they set foot on American soil. When they were questioned by the examining immigration officials, invariably, they stated "British" as their citizenship, which, coming from British colonies, was appropriate. However, the immigration officials modified their response and entered their citizenship in the passenger list as "Black British" or "British Negro." In their American homes, including in Greater Boston, they experienced the reality of this modification, because ultimately, whether they played or embraced cricket or not, they were Black in America. A Barbadian domestic worker articulated her disappointment upon realizing that cricket could not override Blackness in her new home: "After the weekend I would always announce to my mistress [her employer] that I was at a cricket match. I would even tell the butcher standing behind the counter in the store on Blue Hill Avenue. I wanted them to know that I was somebody. But they were never really glad for me."[43]

West Indian immigrants and their children did not delude themselves about the power of cricket to mitigate the challenges of racism. Individually and collectively, they experienced subtle and blatant discrimination that stemmed from being Black even as they asserted that they were Jamaican, Barbadian, Montserratian, West Indian, or British. The resolve to erect what came to be the physical icon of the West Indian community, St. Cyprian's, was born out of their determination to respond to racism. Seeing that their house church had become too small for the number of Black Anglican worshippers, they worked out an agreement with the predominantly white Church of the Ascension to use designated areas of their facilities for church services.

Some of the white parishioners were uncomfortable with the arrangement, and the church adopted a policy of thoroughly cleaning and fumigating the areas used by the Black Episcopalians every Sunday after they left. Some of the Black guest parishioners were cricketers, most of the Black worshippers were fans of cricket, and this was happening at the end of the first decade of the twentieth century, when the ascendancy of West Indian cricket in Boston was undeniable. But all this did not matter. Outside the cricket field, in a white church in Boston, the cricket-loving immigrants were Black people to whom the prevailing stereotypes were attached.

Bigotry against the budding St. Cyprian's congregation was only one of a multitude of manifestations of anti-Blackness. As it covered news about cricket, high tea parties, classical music recitals, celebration of British holidays, and the visit of the Duke and Duchess of Windsor, the *Chronicle* ran exposés about the Jim Crow–style assaults that were being perpetrated on Boston's citizens of African descent. From stories about barber shops in Cambridge that refused to serve Black customers to physical attacks on Black people by police and civilians, the paper tackled issues related to anti-Blackness. It also paid extensive attention to racism in sports and recreation, declaring in its April 18, 1942, issue, "We will chase the racists and expose them in every boxing ring, football field, skating rink, and running track. At present, we should re-name Cambridge, Anniston, Alabama, for Jim Crow is here."[44] Nowhere else did the *Chronicle* demonstrate this passion for tackling injustice in sports as in its reporting on the 1930s campaign to integrate baseball. Nationally, the Black press and radical left-wing sportswriters were at the center of the sustained campaign for racial justice in baseball. *Chronicle* sportswriters and editors actively followed nationally prominent left-wing and civil rights journalists and activists. Eulogizing firebrand and self-proclaimed socialist journalist Heywood Broun in its December 30, 1939, issue, the *Chronicle* declared that to honor Broun, it would continue its fight for racial justice in baseball and all sports, and it was "proud to be among the so-called over-militant, radical Negro press."[45]

Indeed, with the motto "Fearless and Uncompromising—Advocate of Justice, Rights, and Opportunities," the *Chronicle* inspired and led the West Indian community in confronting racism in Boston and revisiting racial and other injustices in the homeland. By the 1930s and 1940s, the cricket-loving immigrants had also gained a reputation for being determined activists. The island associations served as platforms for educating their members about racial and other injustices and how to fight them. *Chronicle* editors and other West Indian men and women joined forces with American-born Blacks in organizations like the National Association for the Advancement of Colored People (NAACP), the Urban League, and the Boston branch of Marcus Garvey's Universal Negro Improvement Association (UNIA).[46]

Despite its pugnaciousness, the West Indian community could not halt the decline of cricket in the late 1940s. By that time, it was becoming obvious that the number of spectators at the games was declining. More devastating, there was an acute shortage of players. Veteran players hung on for decades, but nature took its course, and some died while others became too physically challenged to bowl or bat. With a huge hit on membership, the clubs atrophied. The women's auxiliaries, which were so crucial for providing practical resources for the teams, became defunct. Even the thanksgiving service at St. Cyprian's, which was a centerpiece of the social organization of the teams, experienced abysmal attendance. By 1950, many of the cricket teams were no more, and the few that lingered a few more years, like Windsor and University, were merely shells of what they had been. As Barbadian American Victor Bynoe lamented, "They simply went away, unceremoniously."[47] Why did this institution at the center of a thriving community decline? There were two major factors for the demise of cricket in the West Indian community: the seeming lack of interest of the second generation and the inability to procure replacement players from the homeland due to immigration restrictions.

By 1940, letters to the editor of the *Chronicle* lamented the absence of American-born West Indians in cricket. Many letters blamed parents and community leaders for not doing enough to capture the interest of young people in the "sports of their heritage." While the *Chronicle* accepted that argument, it also blamed the loss of young people on the lack of governmental and other institutional investments in the promotion of cricket in Massachusetts.[48] Whatever the reason, the reality was that the children of West Indian immigrants were more interested in American sports like baseball and basketball than in the British sport of their parents. Secondly, and more devastating, the McCarran-Walter Act of 1952 severely curbed immigration from the Caribbean. This was the final straw, ending all hopes of reviving the teams with newcomers from the islands. Cricket in Massachusetts went into a lull that continued until the 1980s. At that time, Boston and many other parts of the United States had begun to experience an influx of immigration from the Caribbean as a result of the 1965 Hart-Celler Act, which reopened avenues of immigration that had been closed by McCarran-Walter. Caribbean immigrants, far more diverse in island origin than the earlier wave, and South Asian immigrants, mainly from India and Pakistan, resurrected the Massachusetts Cricket League and resumed playing cricket in Franklin Park and other playgrounds. This new breed of cricketers and fans of color shares many of the features of cricket in the earlier era—interstate reciprocal matches, exhibition games on American national holidays, integrated cultural activities within their respective ethnic enclaves, and the affirmation of their cultural identities through cricket. Nevertheless, these new players and fans might know little or nothing about their West Indian predecessors, who were the first people of color to play cricket in Boston and the state of Massachusetts. The pioneering West Indians discussed in this essay crossed countless boundaries on the cricket field and challenged the boundaries of color and culture within the larger society. Their contributions deserve much greater recognition.

Notes

1. Stephen Hardy, *How Boston Played: Sport, Recreation, and Community, 1865–1915* (Knoxville: University of Tennessee Press, 1982), 4.
2. John Daniels, *In Freedom's Birthplace: A Study of Boston Negroes* (Boston: Houghton Mifflin, 1914), 170.
3. For more on the arrival and settlement of immigrants of African descent from the Caribbean and Central America, see Violet Showers Johnson, *The Other Black Bostonians: West Indians in Boston, 1900–1950* (Bloomington: Indiana University Press, 2006), 6–9.
4. Report of the British Embassy, Washington DC, to the foreign secretary, March 1934, Public Record Office, Kew (PRO) FO 598/15.
5. For more on the founding and growth of St. Cyprian's, see Robert C. Hayden, *Faith, Culture and Leadership: A History of the Black Church in Boston* (Boston: Boston Branch of the NAACP, 1983), 50–53.

6. For more on St Cyprian's, the associations, and the role of the *Boston Chronicle* in the vibrant Boston West Indian community of the first half of the twentieth century, see Showers Johnson, *Other Black Bostonians*, 48–71.

7. Cricket in America goes all the way back to colonial times. There is documentation of cricket being played in Philadelphia; New York; Hartford, Connecticut; and parts of Virginia since around 1710. By the nineteenth century, cricket was played widely beyond the northeastern states. There were cricket clubs in places as far south as New Orleans, Louisiana, and Savannah, Georgia. See P. David Sentence, *Cricket in America, 1710–2000* (Jefferson NC: McFarland, 2006). Chapter 1, "Cricket's Prologue in America," 5–13, is particularly useful for a background of cricket in America.

8. For more on the early history of the Longwood Cricket Club, see John Sedgwick, "Splendor on the Grass," *Town & Country Magazine* (August 1991), 105–7, http://johnsedgwick.biz/pdf/Town_Country_SplendorOnTheGrassFullWeb.pdf.

9. John Isaacs Chambers, fondly referred to as Ike, was also regarded as the "grand old man of Massachusetts cricket." Born in England, where he started playing cricket, he emigrated to America in 1883, and by 1890, he had become a most valuable member of the Longwood Cricket Club. The Wright brothers were icons in cricket and baseball in America. Their father, a professional cricketer in his native England, and the family emigrated to the United States when older brother, Harry, was three years old. Younger brother, George, was born in America. Like Chambers, they were fixtures in nineteenth-century cricket in Boston.

10. A. Newton Service, who was captain of one of the West Indian cricket teams, the Wanderers, gave a background of cricket among West Indian immigrants in Boston at the second annual election of the club. The proceedings of the meeting were reported in "Club Composed of West Indians," *Boston Herald*, November 26, 1903.

11. The other New England cricket leagues were the Bay State League and the Merrimac League.

12. C. L. R. James, who remains the all-time classic scholar of the history of cricket in the colonial West Indies, provides a vivid account of cricket among boys and young men in his native Trinidad and other West Indian locations. See C. L. R. James, *Beyond a Boundary* (London: Hutchinson, 1963).

13. Since the 1880s, major newspapers like the *Boston Globe*, the *Boston Herald*, and the *Boston Post* reported frequently on cricket matches at Franklin Field among the teams, which, at that time, were exclusively white.

14. "Cricket Notes," *Boston Globe*, August 25, 1935.

15. "Some Cricket Surprises," *Boston Globe*, May 19, 1905.

16. "Cricket News," *Boston Traveler*, February 9, 1920.

17. "West India C.C. Wins Heys Cup," *Boston Globe*, October 5, 1941.

18. "Claudius 'Cossy' Grant, Skipper for Windsor," *Boston Chronicle*, April 26, 1947. Sidney George Barnes, a first-rate, internationally acclaimed cricketer, was one of the

star members of the Australian cricket team of the 1940s, which was nicknamed The Invincibles, after its undefeated tour of England in 1948.

19. "We Are Shinning," *Boston Chronicle*, April 8, 1939.

20. "Club Composed of West Indians," *Boston Herald*, November 26, 1903.

21. "Cricket Drives," *Boston Globe*, August 31, 1920.

22. Interestingly, Reverend Leroy Fergusson, who can accurately be described as a leader of the Boston West Indian community of the early twentieth century, was not West Indian. He was a native of Raleigh, North Carolina.

23. Violet Showers Johnson, interview with Elma Lewis, Roxbury, Massachusetts, July 8, 1997.

24. "Jamaican Farm Workers to Be Entertained," *Boston Chronicle*, October 9, 1943.

25. "Baseball," *Boston Chronicle*, April 16, 1932.

26. For a useful explanation of the rules and protocols of cricket, see Harold R. H. Harris, "Race and Cricket: The West Indies and England at Lords, 1963" (PhD diss., University of Texas at Arlington, 2011), 100–135. With useful commentary on the cricket field, the ball, the bowler and bowling, the bat, batsmen and batting, the wicket, and the boundary, Harris deftly discusses the esoteric vocabulary of cricket, which, he states, "can cause stress to the uninformed," 122.

27. "Baseball in British Eyes," *Boston Transcript*, March 3, 1914.

28. From the letter of an American tourist in England to the *Boston Post*, October 9, 1912.

29. Letter responding to the article "Baseball Is Waning," *Boston Transcript*, March 16, 1932.

30. *Golden Rule*, February 20, 1878.

31. "Cricket," *Boston Chronicle*, February 25, 1933.

32. "Massachusetts State Cricket League Elects Dixon New President," *Boston Chronicle*, February 22, 1936.

33. "Rev. Ferguson Admonishes Cricketers in Stirring Sermon," *Boston Chronicle*, October 5, 1935.

34. "Wanderers Face Stiff Cricket Game," *Boston Globe*, August 3, 1934.

35. Hawthorne noted that rich and poor played cricket in the greens (the parks) provided for all to enjoy. He was particularly touched by the resourcefulness of the working class. He declared, "It does my heart good to see them roll up a couple of ragged jackets for a wicket, steal a bit of mouldy [sic] board from somebody's backyard for a bat, and make play." *Golden Rule*, February 20, 1878.

36. For a critical discussion of the extension of cricket, see Jason Kaufman and Orlando Patterson, "Cross-National Cultural Diffusion: The Global Spread of Cricket," *American Sociological Review* 70 (February 2005): 82–110.

37. C. L. R. James, *Beyond a Boundary*, 50th anniversary ed. (Durham NC: Duke University Press, 2013), 25.

38. "Cricket Takes Sports Center," *Boston Chronicle*, April 16, 1938.

39. "Massachusetts State Cricket League."

40. "State Cricket Head Is Inter-racial Exponent," *Boston Chronicle*, May 18, 1940.

41. "All-Star Cricket Elevens Will Clash," *Boston Traveler*, September 7, 1918.

42. James, *Beyond a Boundary* (2013), xix.

43. Violet Showers Johnson, interview with "C. M." [pseudonym], South End, Boston, Massachusetts, June 17, 1989.

44. Leroy Johnson, "The Cantabrigan," *Boston Chronicle*, April 18, 1942.

45. "Heywood Broun," *Boston Chronicle*, December 30, 1939. For an excellent study of the role of the media in the campaign to integrate baseball, see Chris Lamb, *Conspiracy of Silence: Sportswriters and the Long Campaign to Desegregate Baseball* (Lincoln: University of Nebraska Press, 2012).

46. For more on the activism of Boston's West Indians in the first half of the twentieth century, see Showers Johnson, *Other Black Bostonians*, chap. 4, "Militant Immigrants and Relentless Ex-colonials"; and Showers Johnson, "Pan-Africanism in Print: The *Boston Chronicle* and the Struggle for Black Liberation and Advancement, 1930–1950," in *Print Culture in a Diverse America*, ed. James Danky and Wayne Wiegand (Champaign: University of Illinois Press, 1998), 56–84.

47. Violet Showers Johnson, interview with Victor Bynoe, South End, Boston, Massachusetts, August 6, 1990.

48. *Boston Chronicle*, April 18, 1942.

6

Black Eyes

A History of Race in the Boston Prize Ring

ANDREW SMITH

Just fancy what mingled emotions
Would fill the Puritan heart
To learn what renown was won for his town
By means of the manly art!
Imagine a Winthrop or Adams
In front of a bulletin board,
Each flinging his hat at the statement that
The first blood was by Sullivan scored
Thy bards, henceforth, O Boston!
Of this triumph of triumphs will sing,
For a muscular stroke has added a spoke
To the Hub, which will strengthen the ring![1]

The Puritan leader John Winthrop, who anointed Boston as a "City upon a Hill" in 1630, probably did not envision it as a beacon for professional boxing. Yet the vibrant port city composed of many diverse communities would one day become a crucible for blood sports—even if many of those activities, like prizefighting, were expressly prohibited by law. In 1889, when white boxers John L. Sullivan and Jake Kilrain, two seasoned pugilists based in Boston, traveled to the less-regulated American South for the sole purpose of fighting each other for money, their bout captured the imagination of a young poet, Vachel Lindsay, as well as much of the sporting nation. The outcome of that contest not only dictated who could call himself a champion but also gave the victor an opportunity to set standards for the sport that would endure long after his reign. The poet Lindsay wrote, "Upon an emerald plain / John L. Sullivan / The strong boy / Of Boston / Fought seventy-five red rounds with Jake Kilrain."[2] In the wake of those "red rounds"—fought with bare knuckles before a large gathering on a Mississippi field—the new "undisputed" champion decreed that subsequent battles, at least those at the heavyweight championship level, would be less brutal and more "scientific" than the recent spectacle. In future contests, participants would wear padded gloves and compete in a series of timed rounds, establishing a new and less brutal norm. But Sullivan also codified a cultural standard that until then had not been universally applied: Black boxers would not be allowed to challenge white "heavyweight" champions. Just as Boston claims responsibility for transforming professional boxing into a more modern, organized sport, leading to its eventual legalization, it also introduced a "color line" in prizefighting that tainted its future.

This chapter traces a century of African American prizefighters in Boston, from the 1880s through the 1980s. Drawing on the relevant secondary literature on boxing history, the history of race and sport, Boston's history of race relations, and primary source evidence from Boston newspapers, these narratives support three broad conclusions. First, Bostonians created the rules of engagement for modern, professional prizefighting, which included the establishment of a racial hierarchy that limited opportunities for Black boxers. Second, despite that inequality, Boston attracted a vibrant Black boxing community that was largely composed of "outsiders" who migrated from other countries or other parts of the United States. Third, the complicated nature of race relations in Boston extended to the boxing ring: the city fomented both abolitionism and racism; it promoted desegregation but rioted against integration. The many talented Black boxers who lived and worked in Boston from the 1880s through the 1980s experienced subtle but systematic racial inequality. They were not adopted as "insiders" as quickly or completely as Boston accepted white sporting heroes during the same period.

"Boston's history of race relations is complex and, at times, contradictory," Russell T. Wiggington writes in *The Strange Career of the Black Athlete*. "Boston was a leader in providing opportunities for its Black citizens; yet on other occasions the city fought relentlessly to uphold racial discrimination."[3] This contradiction played out within Boston's sporting community as well. The

Boston Celtics was the first National Basketball Association (NBA) team to draft a Black player, and the Boston Bruins were the first National Hockey League (NHL) team to integrate, but racial divisions affected the teams—and their fans—for decades. The Boston Braves were among the first Major League Baseball (MLB) teams to integrate before the franchise relocated to Milwaukee, yet the Boston Red Sox were the last team in the league to roster a Black player. Even within Boston's African American communities, sports historian Stephen Hardy notes, the games people played reflected social fissures in the city. Economically mobile Black Bostonians played "elite" sports like tennis, while immigrants from the Caribbean islands preferred British sports like cricket. Black migrants from the American South or the Canadian Maritimes often had limited economic resources and opted for working-class sports like football and boxing—these folks were crucial to the vibrant boxing community in Boston.[4]

For much of the mid-nineteenth century, however, that community was largely ungloved and underground. Prizefighting under the London prize ring rules (adopted in Great Britain in 1838 and revised in 1853) was a bare-knuckle affair; gloves were for sparring. In the wake of a brutal contest on the eastern shore of Maryland between white fighters Tom Hyer and the Irish-born "Yankee" Sullivan (real name James Ambrose), news of Hyer's "mauling" of an opponent thirty pounds lighter reverberated around the nation. The state of Massachusetts prohibited such contests within the Commonwealth in 1849.[5] There were still fights and fighters in Boston but fewer prizes to be won. A disorganized lineup of typically self-appointed champions failed to generate enough public interest to openly flout the law. But the cultural exchange that occurred between North and South during the Civil War led to the proliferation of sports like baseball and boxing. In the 1870s, the advent of the Gilded Age, America's rising power as an industrial nation created a sports-centric bachelor subculture—especially in northern urban hubs like Boston.[6]

Two popular pugilists that could straddle class lines and attract larger followings arose from that environment, foreshadowing the future of boxing. Jake Kilrain was born in New York but moved to Somerville, Massachusetts, as a young man. Plying his fistic trade in the ring, he also taught boxing to Boston's middle- and upper-class males at notable venues like the Cribb Club.[7] Boxer John L. Sullivan was born in the house his parents shared with another couple on East Concord Street in the Roxbury district. Like Kilrain, he sought to monetize his fighting prowess as he crested into adulthood; the "strong boy" of Boston challenged other prizefighters in the area for fixed purses. Staked by backers with disposable income, he was also known to gamble on himself. However, he was not eager to risk the social capital of his whiteness by taking on a Black challenger. The Canadian-born George Godfrey, one of the most notable Black prizefighters in the nation, repeatedly offered to meet Sullivan in the ring. The two fighters eventually arranged a bout at the Hub City Gym, which was run by one of the foremost African American boxing instructors in the nation, "Professor" John Bailey. But Boston police—perhaps for Sullivan's benefit—intervened to stop the contest before it occurred.[8]

By 1882, Sullivan had made enough of a name for himself that the heavyweight champion, Paddy Ryan, accepted his challenge. Like all of Sullivan's opponents on record up to that point, Ryan also fell to Sullivan's bare fists. The victorious Boston strong boy took the opportunity to proclaim himself champion of the world—a title that did not generate much dispute. Neither did his resolution to accept challenges to his new title only from white boxers. Like professional baseball in America, boxing was not originally a segregated sport. It took a conscious decision by its leaders, and the tacit agreement of its followers, to codify its racism. Sullivan even refused to meet challengers like Mervine Thompson, fighting under the Irish name Patrick O'Donnell, because of rumors that he had a "mixed" racial heritage.[9]

The exclusion of Black fighters from the highest levels of the sport led the Black boxing community to establish a "colored heavyweight championship" in 1882. "Professor" Charles Hadley was the third Black boxer to claim that championship. But to legitimize his title, Hadley had to conquer George Godfrey, widely considered to be the best fighter in Boston and beyond—at least among those who had no interest in racial hierarchies. After coming to Boston from "The Bog," a poor area of his native Charlottetown, on Prince Edward Island (PEI), Godfrey became a fixture in Boston boxing. By today's standards a light heavyweight, Godfrey's estimated 175 pounds put him squarely in the heavyweight class by the standards of his time, and by most accounts, he hit considerably heavier. Godfrey and Hadley had already fought to a draw in New York just a month before Sullivan pummeled Ryan, so the two men agreed to a rematch that was now considered a title bout. Again, Hadley and Godfrey fought to a draw, so the principals agreed to raise the stakes. Sullivan himself, the white heavyweight champion, would referee a match to the finish between the two Black fighters at the Cribb Club in Boston. When it was over, the self-proclaimed "champion of the world" anointed Godfrey as the new "colored champion," celebrating Godfrey's skill yet knowing he would never test it.[10]

While Sullivan went on tour, offering exhibitions around the country, Godfrey regularly defended his title in competitive matches—fighting as often as he could in the Hub City. He had ongoing bouts with other top Black heavyweights such as Hadley and McHenry "Black Star" Johnson, telling the *Boston Globe* that he was most certain of fair decisions in "a club room in Boston." It was an opinion that questionable decisions made in the rings of New York and Denver only reinforced. Godfrey was aware that his earnings were limited by his inability to compete for a world championship. But it was Boston's own strong boy, John L. Sullivan, who had set that precedent. Separate, but in no way equal, "championships" became the national norm.[11]

Unlike Sullivan, Long Island–born Jake Kilrain had little concern about taking on Black boxers. He and Godfrey met twice in the early 1880s, both times in Boston, with one fight inconclusive and another interrupted by police. Kilrain had been granted a championship title by the *National Police Gazette's* Richard Kyle Fox, largely because of Fox's distaste for Sullivan. In 1889, Kilrain convinced Sullivan to meet in a "London Rules" bout, which offered a bare-fisted opportunity to challenge Sullivan's title. A win by Kilrain would also offer him a chance to erase the color line his opponent had drawn. But it was not to be. In the seventy-sixth round, Kilrain's second, Mike Donovan, threw in the towel to protect Kilrain from suffering irreversible damage. With his win, Sullivan cemented his status as world heavyweight champion, using his victory to make a monumental change. Sullivan announced that from that point on, he would only receive challenges under Marquis of Queensberry rules, which set standards for boxing that included gloved contests and timed rounds. He also reaffirmed his commitment never to defend his title against a Black challenger. As boxing in the United States became more modern, professional, and palatable to a broader audience, it also became, like other sports of the time, overtly racialized and deeply segregated. Elliott Gorn, a historian of American sports and popular culture, writes, "A curtain of racism now fell over the ring, just as it fell over other major sports such as baseball and bicycle racing."[12] Despite Massachusetts's abolition of slavery at the turn of the nineteenth century, racial segmentation, stratification, and de facto segregation were apparent in Boston. In 1831, Mayor Harrison Gray Otis described the city's Black residents as "a quiet, inoffensive, and in many respects a useful race" but continued, "The repugnance to intimate social relations with them is insurmountable."[13] Through the rest of the nineteenth century, more Black people moved to Boston, with many coming from the American South, the Canadian Maritimes, and the Caribbean islands. Despite their cultural diversity, they were restricted to living in just a few areas of the city. As wealthier white Bostonians flocked to the Back Bay, lower-income people of color and immigrants replaced them in the North End. By the 1900s, a cluster of Black residents settled on the northwest slope of Beacon Hill until congestion and political machinations forced them into neighborhoods like Roxbury in the South End, where working-class Irish immigrants such as the Sullivan family had settled a generation earlier.[14] To many Black men and women from other parts of the nation and beyond, Boston remained a land of promise—promise of work, wages, and upward mobility—even if it was not the promised land for racial integration.

In 1887, a teenaged George Dixon followed in the footsteps of George Godfrey, immigrating from "The Bog" on PEI to the Hub of Boston. A tremendous athlete despite a very small frame, Dixon was attracted to boxing, watching bouts when he could at the various club rooms in the city. Underage and weighing less than a hundred pounds, he was not allowed to participate in even quasi-legal amateur boxing. Fortunately, Dixon had other options. Smart, personable, and literate, Dixon found a job in Elmer Chickering's photography studio, which afforded him access to local celebrities who came to get their photos taken. This is likely where he met Godfrey, Professor

Bailey, and other prominent Black prizefighters, picking up tips and tactics for the ring, which he was finally able to enter by adding weights to his shoes.[15]

Once Dixon got started, there was no stopping him. His speed, power, and physique impressed mixed crowds in clubs across Beantown. As Godfrey, who was at least fifteen years older than Dixon, started to decline when Sullivan consolidated his power and reinforced the color line, the problematically nicknamed "Little Chocolate" Dixon gained a national following. Tom O'Rourke, a native Bostonian who managed and promoted prizefighters, sought out Dixon and convinced him to enter into a managerial agreement. While Godfrey lobbied for higher purses and, as a result, fought far less, O'Rourke arranged as many dates as Dixon could fulfill. The young fighter usually picked up the winner's share of the purse. But Dixon remained skeptical of Boston's racial climate. He took plenty of interracial fights, yet despite his popularity, when he competed against a white boxer, Boston fans hurled vicious epithets. Dixon told the *Boston Globe* that if Black boxers tried to beat a white fighter anywhere outside of a "club room," they were likely to be killed.[16]

O'Rourke may not have wanted Dixon killed, but he had no qualms about exploiting him. He set fights for Dixon while committing him to sparring daily with a former British champion during performances at Boston's Old Howard Theater. O'Rourke also agreed to a "catch weight" bout for Dixon with British featherweight champion Fred Johnson that greatly advantaged the larger Johnson over the still-growing Dixon. And in the prelude to their match, O'Rourke allowed physical culture specialists to visit Dixon, testing, measuring, poking, prodding, and otherwise scrutinizing him as he trained. Despite such distractions, Dixon defeated Johnson and retained his claim as a world champion in both the bantamweight and featherweight divisions. That success propelled him into the biggest event of his still young career—a slot in the Carnival of Champions slated for New Orleans in September of 1892.[17]

Godfrey, on the other hand, could not secure the $1,000 purse he felt he deserved, so he agreed to take on Kilrain again in San Francisco for $500. With nearly twenty pounds over Godfrey and the inherent advantage, the *Boston Globe* noted, of being the white fighter in an interracial bout, Kilrain won the match. A subsequent loss at the hands of white light heavyweight

Joe Choynski in Coney Island seemed to confirm that Godfrey was coming to the end of his run in the prize ring. If he wanted to go to New Orleans for the Carnival of Champions, he would have to buy his own train and bout tickets to watch Dixon defend his title or see Sullivan take on another white challenger in James J. Corbett.[18]

The Carnival of Champions was proof positive that the Boston strong boy had fundamentally altered the sport of boxing in America. Regardless of what occurred in the ring on September 7, 1892, a new era in prizefighting had arrived: a series of boxing matches would take place legally, under the Queensberry rules, not in a secret field but in a public arena, with the sponsorship of the Olympic Club, a bona fide athletic association.

The Carnival of Champions would also serve as a reckoning for the Boston strong boy. During their contest, "Gentleman Jim" Corbett bounced around Sullivan, battering the champion with sharp punches from gloved fists for twenty-one rounds. No one could deny that there was a new world champion. But would the changes introduced under Sullivan's reign outlast him? Corbett promised to continue defending the title under Queensberry rules. And although he fought at least one Black opponent, Peter Jackson, before capturing the title, he upheld Sullivan's ban on Black boxers in heavyweight title fights. The ban did not strictly apply to lighter weight categories. The day before Corbett took Sullivan's title, Dixon scored a definitive win against Jack Kelly, a white opponent from New York who was reportedly making his professional debut. The proven champ eviscerated Skelly; the bout was mercifully concluded after eight rounds. A Black man had legally dominated a white man in the ring before thousands of spectators—the unprecedented spectacle provoked a strong reaction—and may have influenced Corbett's decision to uphold the color line. Not only was Dixon threatened personally, but the entire notion of interracial fights came into question. The *New Orleans Times-Democrat* immediately stated, "It was a mistake to match a negro and a white man, a mistake to bring the races together on any terms of equality, even in the prize ring," while the Olympic Club suddenly issued a ban on interracial matches in the Crescent City that lasted well into the twentieth century.[19]

The peaceful transition of power from John L. Sullivan to "Gentleman" Jim Corbett maintained a status quo in American prizefighting that represented progress for the sport while inhibiting progress for its Black participants. Although Boston did not prohibit interracial matches, it had not yet legalized prizefighting. Black champions like Dixon were limited in where they could compete and who they could compete against, while Black heavyweights like Godfrey were unable to fight for a world title at all. Both Godfrey and Dixon stayed close to Boston, where another newcomer, Barbadian Joe Walcott, joined their fraternity of Black boxers. Born in what was then British Guiana, Walcott's family later moved to Barbados, where he spent his childhood before arriving in Boston as a teenager. Like his predecessors, he worked a variety of jobs around the city, from moving pianos to operating elevators as well as sweeping up in at least one of the many fight clubs around town. Standing barely over five feet, Walcott tipped the scales right in between the other two local Black headliners, Godfrey and Dixon, fighting as a light-weight or welterweight through most of his career. Within a couple of years, Walcott engaged in approximately forty prizefights, registering only one loss: a four-round affair decided on points in his opponent's native New York. Although these three Bostonians of different weight classes could never meet in a ring, they traveled in the same circles, and collectively—with Godfrey's reputation, Dixon's title, and Walcott's record—positioned Boston to rival New York as a center for Black prizefighters.

In the Commonwealth, however, the law was used strategically to prop up white privilege in the face of Black resistance. In 1894, Bobby Dobbs, a veteran Black middleweight from the American South who had fought from coast to coast since the late 1880s, had become entangled with an exploitative manager named Ben Benton during a midwestern stint. Benton marshaled Dobbs into low-paying fights in New England so that he would rack up debts to Benton for training and travel before arranging a bigger fight with a more lucrative purse; it was prizefighting's version of sharecropping. Dobbs recognized the ploy too late and sought to nullify the contract so he could make his own fights. Benton responded by having Dobbs arrested in Mas-sachusetts. Boston courts sided with the white manager, sending Dobbs to prison until he agreed to pay a $300 restitution fee. Though Dobbs later won the Massachusetts Middleweight Championship in 1895, he left the country by the turn of the century. He went to box in England and Europe, where he—like other Black boxers—anticipated receiving fairer treatment.

The court of popular opinion in Boston's boxing community agreed. The same year Dobbs lost in court, Godfrey was knocked out by the Irish champion Peter Maher at the Boston Casino, where white fans roared their approval, clearly privileging their ancestral heritage over civic pride in their hometown fighter. In the summer of 1895, Beantown promoted its three best-known Black boxers in a three-day prizefighting event like New Orleans' Carnival of Champions.

The event was to take place at the West Newton St. Armory with Dixon scheduled for Tuesday, Walcott for Wednesday, and Godfrey in a rematch against Joe Choynski on Thursday. Unlike New Orleans in 1892, all three of these Boston bouts were interracial. On the first night, Dixon won his match against Braintree native Johnny Griffin on points in a good match. The next day, Walcott pounded on white Canadian Dick O'Brien, knocking him down four times in a bloody first round. Before Godfrey and Choynski started the final bout, Boston police intervened, stopping the two heavyweights from fighting and earning their purse. Police also arrested Walcott and his opponent, citing the 1849 act, which was rarely enforced but never revoked. The two boxers were charged with being principals in a prizefight. Despite the evidence, both pleaded not guilty. The judge instructed the jury to consider the existing law and suggested they base their decision on whether the men had engaged in a fight. After a few hours of deliberation, the jury sided with the boxers. No one went to jail, yet prizefighting in Boston remained illegal. At the end of the nineteenth century, the fifty-one-year-old law could still be weaponized, particularly against Black boxers.[20]

The early years of the new century were not encouraging for Black boxers in Boston. Godfrey, who tried to make the transition from fighter to teacher, contracted tuberculosis and died at his home in Revere in 1901. The following year, Dixon set off on a long British tour. Walcott, the "Barbados Demon," rose through the ranks of boxing and Boston society, positioning himself as a champion of the people as well as a prizefighting champion. In 1904, he announced a run for mayor. But a month into his campaign,

Walcott accidentally discharged a new gun at a dance hall, killing an inno-cent bystander and damaging his hand. His political campaign came to an immediate end. Although he continued to compete, fighting as much as he was able, Walcott steadily declined.[21]

Amid the tragedies, another expat from the Canadian Maritimes, Nova Scotia's Sam Langford, arrived in Boston to pursue a prizefighting career. Like Godfrey and Dixon, Langford came from a predominantly Black community in Atlantic Canada. Weymouth Falls, slightly inland at the edge of the South Shore, rests on nearly the same longitudinal line as Bar Harbor, Maine. It was established by Black loyalists fleeing the colonies during the Ameri-can Revolution. Like PEI's "Bog," Weymouth Falls was an underresourced community whose Black residents struggled for social and economic equity. Langford left home in his early teens, working his way to Boston, where his many jobs included handling floor duties at an athletic club. Eventually, he stepped into the ring himself. In many ways, Langford was a larger version of Walcott, taller than the Barbadian Demon but shorter than most of the opponents he faced as a heavyweight in the early twentieth-century fight game. In fact, the young Langford fought to a draw against Walcott shortly before the latter's tragic gun accident. Although he didn't have a heavyweight's stature, Langford's ability and ambition propelled him into the highest ech-elons of the sport. He took on the best heavyweights of the era—at least, those who would meet him. While the heavyweight title changed hands many times, the color line held fast, excluding Black boxers like Langford from the highest ranks of the sport. With that avenue closed to him, Langford fought the most notable Black contenders of his time, including Joe Jeanette, Sam McVey, and the "Galveston Giant," Jack Johnson. For many years, Langford averaged a prizefight a month, competing at venues around the Hub.[22] Like his Black boxing contemporaries, he worked to compensate for the lower purses available to him by engaging in more fights. The popular boxer was known as the "Boston Bonecrusher," although some called him, more deri-sively, the "Boston Tar Baby." In the middle of Langford's career, a glimmer of hope for racial equity arose in the fight game. Noah Brusso, a Canadian who fought under the Irish-sounding nom de guerre Tommy Burns, wrested control of a transient world championship title.

Burns, who was more committed to a high purse than maintaining a racial hierarchy, agreed to defend his title against Black boxer Jack Johnson for $30,000. Johnson decisively beat him, becoming the first Black heavyweight to be recognized as a world champion. It seemed as if the color line had been erased, opening the door for other deserving Black heavyweights like Langford. Instead, Johnson chose to capitalize on his role of being not only a champion but a Black antihero, defending his title against "white hopes"—challengers who might not be as competitive but who drew more fans, sold more tickets, and attracted more bets than Black fighters like McVey, Jeanette, or Langford. Though he did not overtly support segregation in boxing, the first Black heavyweight champion held fast to Sullivan's color line until he was exiled from the United States. He only defended his title once against a Black challenger.[23]

The city of Boston similarly upheld its tradition of racial segregation. When Johnson fought former champion and foremost "white hope" Jim Jeffries on Independence Day in 1910, twentieth-century sporting fans wanted more than telegraphed updates or round-by-round newspaper reports. New technology made it possible to record live action that could be viewed at other times. Fight films became salable products—and a hotly contested part of contract negotiations in championship boxing. The "Fight of the Century," as the Johnson-Jeffries match was called, was the kind of event that folks around the nation would pay to watch. But in the Jim Crow American South, legislators moved quickly to ensure that images like that of the Johnson versus Jeffries fight, showing a Black man battering a white man, were prohibited. It was a repetition of the reaction that occurred two decades earlier when the Dixon-Skelly bout in New Orleans made waves around the nation. But like systemic racism in other areas of American society, such prohibitions were not confined to the South. Boston also banned films of "The Fight of the Century" for fear they would incite race riots in the subtly but systemically racialized city.

Langford continued to fight in venues around the nation through the Jack Johnson era, which ended when Johnson lost to "white hope" Jess Willard in 1915. He remained in the ring as the title passed from Willard to Jack Dempsey. But the predictable physical decline after a lifetime of boxing had begun to take its toll, complicated by a series of eye injuries that impaired his ability to see punches coming. Despite a lengthy and successful prizefighting career, Langford, in the end, was poor and blind, relying on charitable assistance to survive. As the first wave of the Great Migration and the creative revival of the Harlem Renaissance drew more African Americans out of the South and into urban centers like New York and Boston, cautionary tales like Langford's might have served as a warning to other aspiring Black boxers who believed they could succeed in Beantown.[24]

But the lesson didn't resonate. Despite continued racial boxing inequities in Boston and across the nation, more and more African Americans were attracted to the sport. In the 1920s, Boston promoters suggested a "colored championship of Lenox Street," pitting local Black fighters like Charlestown's Johnny Noyes and New Bedford's William "Battling" Thomas against each other in a series of contests. The bouts were reminiscent of the repeated matches between Langford and other contemporary Black heavyweights that took place in the early 1900s. Though neither fighter was well known outside of the city, and their lives before and after their time in the ring have not been chronicled in boxing history, Noyes and Thomas fought as many as ten bouts together at venues like the Commonwealth Athletic Club, Mechanics Hall, and at least once, right out on Tremont Street.[25]

North Carolina's Jim McCreary also competed for an interracial title in Boston. Known as "The Battling Preacher," McCreary built a reputation in the prize ring and at the pulpit, where he secured the support of Boston's Black Christian community as well as its fight fans. McCreary boxed professionally in the Boston area for nearly a decade, rarely venturing out of Massachusetts. In 1921, he traveled to Syracuse, where he lost a match to world champion contender Harry Wills. His last professional fight took place in 1926, when he fought Theodore "Tiger" Flowers in Flowers's hometown of Atlanta, losing again to a world-class African American boxer. At the peak of his career, McCreary lured "Kid Norfolk" (real name: William Ward) to Boston three times with an invitation to compete in a "colored lightweight championship." Though he won the first bout at the Grand Opera House, McCreary lost the next two, held in the Mechanics Building. The trio of fights represented the high tide of McCreary's fistic fortunes. Like other Black boxers in Boston and beyond, McCreary had to reckon with the fact that white champion Jack Dempsey, who maintained the color line by defending his title only against white challengers, could earn hundreds of thousands of dollars from his major events, while the best Black prizefighters were earning only four- and five-figure payouts—an extreme disparity that underscored the economic inequalities between Blacks and whites inherent in the sport.[26]

Like the looming Great Depression, which had begun to affect many rural and urban African Americans long before the market crash of 1929, boxing's impending "dark ages" were foreshadowed in Boston by mid-decade. The increasing influence of the gambling industry and declining popular trust in the legitimacy of the sport were reducing the public's interest and hurting competition. In 1926, a Pennsylvania-born Black heavyweight, Feab Sylvester Williams, who fought under the name "Big" George Godfrey to piggyback off the name of his pioneering predecessor, came to the Mechanics Building in Boston to challenge a new hometown hopeful, the white fighter Jack "Boston Gob" Sharkey, whose real name was Joseph Paul Zukauskas. Born in New York, Zukauskas moved to Boston with his Lithuanian parents as a child. After a stint in the navy, he returned to his adopted hometown and embarked on a prizefighting career, blending the names of heavyweight champion Jack Dempsey and a former fighter, "Sailor" Tom Sharkey, to create his boxing identity. He won a questionable decision against "Big" Godfrey, an unsurprising outcome considering that he was a white hometown fighter facing a Black boxer from out of town.[27]

The next year, a Black Nova Scotian, Roy Mitchell, brought an impressive light heavyweight record down to the Boston boxing scene. He was pushed up to heavyweight bouts by Boston promoters, but only as a foil to white fighters. Mitchell started taking and losing prizefights in Beantown—sometimes under questionable circumstances, such as a disqualification against Nando Tassi in 1928. Another Black Canadian, Toronto's Larry Gaines, flatly accused Boston promoters and matchmakers, such as Eddie Mack, of offering him fights with marquee opponents like Sharkey, but only if he agreed to "take a dive" (lose in a fixed match). Godfrey came back to Boston at the end of the decade, losing a match against a white opponent in a similarly disputable referee's decision. Mitchell did not stick around for more and returned to

Canada. Gaines followed Dixon's lead, moving to the United Kingdom, where he believed he could get better treatment and fairer purses.[28]

Boston's Sharkey stayed in the game, racking up wins and losses under questionable circumstances. At one of the sport's lowest points, Sharkey ascended to the championship, where he continued to win or lose title fights with debatable disqualifications or referees' decisions. He may have benefited from fixed matches and taken dives as well. In his last interracial bout in the city of Boston, against "Unknown" Eddie Winston, the fear of fixing was so high that when it appeared Sharkey had knocked out Winston in the first round, the crowd and referee insisted he get up and restart the bout. Sharkey's final prizefight, in 1936, was another interracial heavyweight match. Although it did not last much longer than Sharkey's match with Winston, no one questioned the legitimacy of the outcome: Joe "Brown Bomber" Louis knocked out the Boston Gob in three rounds at Yankee Stadium. It was one of many stepping stones on Louis's road to reintegrating prizefighting's heavyweight championship. The desperation of boxing promoters looking to revitalize a dying sport created an opportunity to challenge the color line Sullivan had drawn decades before. One year after brutalizing Sharkey, Louis dethroned James J. Braddock, avenged a prior loss to German Max Schmeling, and embarked on a championship reign that lasted more than ten years. During that span, Louis remained one of the most active champions in history, defending his title against all comers, regardless of race, in venues across the country. The quality of his challengers was sometimes the only contestable element of the fights. By the 1940s, his opponents were often satirized as the "Bum of the Month Club." One stop in the tour brought him to Boston, where Louis met a white light heavyweight from Maine, Al McCoy, in the Boston Garden. After five rounds, Louis had beaten his opponent so badly that McCoy could only see out one eye. Even with both eyes functioning, it was unlikely that he could have stopped the Brown Bomber's barrage.[29]

After six years of prizefighting, Louis had finally fought in Boston. Although he remained active for eleven more years, he never returned. The racially charged atmosphere, combined with one of the lowest purses of his title run, could not persuade him to come back to the Hub. However, the denouement to Louis's remarkable and historically significant career linked him back to

Boston: Rocco Marchegiano (later known as Rocky Marciano) was born and raised in the working-class community of Brockton, about an hour south of downtown. Boston boxing aficionados might have seen him in amateur contests, state championships, or regional Golden Gloves tournaments during the late 1940s, but most of Boston's casual prizefighting fans were likely not aware of him until the early 1950s. By that time, Marciano had won more than thirty consecutive bouts, the majority by knockout. His winning streak continued with a technical knockout of Louis that ultimately sent the Brown Bomber into retirement. Bostonians were quick to adopt Marciano as a son of the city, particularly after a match in 1952, when he knocked out the Black boxer Arnold Raymond Cream, who used the fighting name of "Jersey" Joe Walcott in homage to the Barbados Demon. That victory made Marciano the next heavyweight champion of the world, a title he solidified in a rematch with Walcott the following year. Although Boston claimed him as "one of theirs," Marciano only fought professionally in Beantown twice and never defended his title there. Legal issues, as well as concern over the appetite for interracial matches, which many of Marciano's title defenses were, inhibited his desire to come "home." After earning the championship, he maintained his perfect record before retiring unexpectedly in 1955.[30]

The city of Boston adopted Marciano as a hometown hero. Meanwhile, one of the most gifted featherweight fighters in history slipped out of the city. Black boxer Joseph "Sandy" Saddler was born in one of the rougher neighborhoods of Boston that generated much of its boxing culture. For Saddler, the fastest way of making it on his own was the prize ring. Oddly tall and thin, with fast feet and an even faster mind, the "skeletal" Saddler hit harder and more frequently than his opposition expected. He started fighting for money before he came of age and kept at it for more than a decade of professional boxing. Saddler, too, recognized the need to leave the Hub to get a fair shot. Even then, it took more than 90 official bouts for Saddler to get a title match against a white fighter, Connecticut native Willie Pep. Like Marciano, Pep had been born with a longer Italian name, Guglielmo Papaleo, that managers encouraged him to shorten. In the late 1940s and early 1950s, Pep and Saddler traded the title many times, with Saddler winning three out of their four meetings. But he was unhappy about the fact that

Pep seemed to be more popular than he was. Saddler lost his final match to another white contender from Connecticut, Larry Boardman, and after nearly 150 bouts and more than a hundred knockouts, he hung up his gloves and settled in New York City, where he had long preferred to fight. Saddler later became a reputable trainer, most notably for George Foreman, whom Saddler helped develop into a heavyweight champion. But he remained wary of structural racism in boxing and was not shy about expressing his concerns about equity for Black prizefighters.[31]

As Saddler transitioned from the principal inside the ring to a cornerman for another generation of Black prizefighters, Boston's underlying racial tensions boiled over. Race riots in 1967 were triggered by the police's reaction to public protests in African American enclaves like Roxbury. Despite the turmoil, Boston remained an attractive option for many. New Jersey native Marvin Hagler experienced the race riots in Newark during the "long hot summer" of 1967, spending some of those days on the floor of his family's apartment to avoid any stray bullets that might come through the window. Following another outbreak of rioting in 1969, Hagler's mother moved the family to Brockton because they had relatives there and it felt safer. Brockton, which had long been home to white, ethnic, working-class families like the Marchegianos, had begun to diversify. Having grown up in Newark, an environment marked by de facto segregation, Brockton represented Hagler's first experience with racial integration. The only white people he regularly encountered in Newark had been police officers.[32]

Like the long line of Black prizefighters who had moved into the Boston area a century earlier, Hagler's experience in a multiracial community was not without problems, and boxing appeared to be a solution. A target of discrimination and bullying in his new environment, he sought training to defend himself—or vent his pent-up rage. The thoughtful and methodical manner he would display in the ring was apparent before he put on a pair of gloves. Hagler visited two local gyms, watching silently every day at one operated by Vinnie Vecchione, then visiting another gym across the street that the Petronelli brothers had opened a few years earlier. Hagler gravitated more toward their style—and away from the clientele at Vecchione's, which included one of the locals who had given him a hard time. At Petronelli's, he threw himself into training. Goody Petronelli recalls Hagler declaring at their first meeting that he was going to be a world champion. It seemed unlikely for the undersized newcomer, whom they nicknamed "Short Stuff," but Hagler's commitment and work ethic, which included practicing combinations in front of a mirror at home after returning from school or the gym—enabled him to progress faster than many of the other aspiring boxers there.[33]

Hagler quickly became a favorite son of the Petronelli family, who hooked him up with a job in their construction business while grooming him for amateur tournaments. They sometimes even took off the "Short" in his nickname, calling him instead by the more contemporary moniker, Marvin "Stuff" Hagler. They also appeared to accept an obvious fudging of Hagler's birth year so that he could enter sanctioned tournaments. The teenaged Hagler had great success in both the super welterweight and middleweight divisions, fighting at a weight between 156 and 165 pounds but dominating the action in many of his contests. In the 1973 national Amateur Athletic Union (AAU) tournament, held at the Hynes Auditorium in Boston, Hagler not only won his division but also was named "Outstanding Boxer" for the whole tournament, a lineup that included a handful of future Olympic and professional champions like Michael and Leon Spinks and "Sugar Ray" Leonard. But in the Boston newspapers the following day, the name of the Hub's next great boxing champion was spelled incorrectly, and his hometown was listed as Newark. Whether it was a simple error or the result of honest confusion over the similarity of Hagler's name to that of well-known boxing writer Barney Nagler, it certainly seemed indicative of the Boston press's disinterest in him.[34]

Following the tournament, Hagler immediately turned professional rather than wait another three years for the Olympics, as some of his counterparts in the AAU tournament chose to do, but his reception was not any warmer. The Petronellis made an agreement with a well-known Massachusetts promoter, Sam Silverman, to generate more publicity for Hagler and arrange some lucrative matches. They started Hagler at a Brockton high school gymnasium, where he knocked out another local fighter, Terry Ryan, who was also making his debut. For Ryan, however, the two-round knockout would be his last prizefight. Hagler earned $40 for his performance. Although Silverman moved him up to other venues like the Boston Arena—where so many enterprising Black boxers had fought a century before, often under the auspices of exploitative white promoters—Hagler was again dismissed by the Boston newspapers. Even the *Brockton Enterprise* in his adopted home-town, with an office right beside the Petronellis' gym, wouldn't send anyone to cover his matches. Silverman gave impromptu press conferences in a café across the street from both the gym and the newspaper, yet two years into an undefeated career, Hagler still took matches in a high school gym with little press and low purses.[35]

In 1976, Boston experienced another outbreak of race riots, ostensibly in response to the forced busing of public school students. Whatever the catalyst, decades of interracial tension were boiling to the surface. If the riots in Newark had pulled Hagler toward Boston, the new round of violence in Beantown may have influenced his team to explore moving out of the Hub. Like many Black boxers in Boston's prizefighting history, including Dixon, Langford, and Saddler, Hagler never felt as though he was "from" Boston, so he began to look for greener pastures. He and the Petronellis left Silverman and began working with J. Russell Peltz, a former aspiring sportswriter who came to dominate the pro boxing scene in Philadelphia. Although Philly had a vibrant Black boxing community that was welcoming to outsiders like Joe Frazier, Hagler suffered his first two professional losses at the Philadelphia Spectrum on questionable decisions. He returned to New England, competing in many small venues where he accumulated wins but earned small purses.[36]

In 1977, when "Sugar Ray" Leonard finally turned professional, he secured $40,000 in his first prizefight, an amount close to Hagler's total career earn-ings after four years and thirty victories. Unlike Hagler, Leonard did not anchor himself to one location but instead fought nationally, occasionally competing in bouts in New England. With his style, charisma, and a bank of good publicity, Leonard won a world title after just two years and twenty-five pro bouts. Hagler, still struggling for coverage in Boston papers let alone the national press, needed fifty fights and some pressure from Massachusetts politicians like Ted Kennedy and Tip O'Neill to get his first crack at a title. Hagler's opportunity came on the *undercard* of Leonard's championship bout, for a purse that equaled Leonard's debut prize of $40,000 on a night when "Sugar Ray" pulled in a million. To make matters worse for the Newark-born,

Brockton-raised fighter without a home engaging in his first match at a Las Vegas casino, he lost in another contestable split decision.[37]

It wasn't until 1980 that Hagler won a world championship. He had to go all the way to the United Kingdom to do it, persevering through a barrage of beer bottles thrown by angry fans after he cut up British middleweight Alan Minter so badly that the referee stopped the fight. At least one friendly fan hung a banner in Wembley Stadium reading "Bring It Home to Brockton," and *Sports Illustrated* correctly identified Hagler with his adopted city. The new middleweight champion was determined to defend his title at home as often as possible, though it significantly limited his earnings. Boston was no longer a destination for big-time prizefights, so while other African American fighters, even in lighter weight classes like Leonard, earned seven-figure paydays for defending their titles in Las Vegas casinos or major sports arenas, Hagler kept brawling in Boston—more for love than money and receiving comparatively little of either.[38]

It took a full decade of professional boxing at the highest level of a marquee division before Hagler got a multimillion-dollar purse, taking on Roberto Duran at Caesars Palace in 1983. Finally realizing his value and the limits of his appeal in Boston, Hagler fought the last five fights over the final four years of his career in the new center of the boxing universe, Las Vegas, with another bout taking place in the traditional "Mecca" of prizefighting, New York's Madison Square Garden. Hagler retained his title until he met "Sugar Ray" in April of 1987, fourteen years after they shared a ring in different divisions of the AAU tournament. In a decision that has been debated for years, Leonard emerged the new middleweight champion, while Hagler was left in the ring, saying, "It's not fair"—a sentiment that summed up much of his career and the shared experience of many Black boxers in Boston's history.[39]

One hundred years after the "strong boy" of Boston John L. Sullivan drew the color line, interrupting the progress made by Black boxing trailblazers like "Professor" Hadley, "Old Chocolate" Godfrey, and "Little Chocolate" Dixon, the experience of African American prizefighters in the Hub remained largely the same. They could fight for themselves but not for the city. A premier sports town so quick to adopt white athletic heroes like Baltimore's Babe Ruth, Perry Sound's Bobby Orr, and French Lick's Larry Bird and to celebrate "their" white ethnic heavyweights like Sullivan and Marciano did not champion their Black prizefighters—forcing Hall of Famers like Langford, Saddler, and Hagler to leave the "City upon a Hill" for higher ground in the fight game.

Notes

1. Quoted in Michael T. Isenberg, *John L. Sullivan and His America* (Urbana: University of Illinois Press, 1994), 113.

2. Vachel Lindsay, "John L. Sullivan, the Strong Boy of Boston," *New Republic*, July 16, 1919, 357–58.

3. Russell T. Wigginton, *The Strange Career of the Black Athlete: African Americans and Sports* (Westport CT: Praeger, 2006), 21.

4. John M. Carroll, "The Year of the Yaz," in *The Rock, the Curse, and the Hub: A Random History of Boston Sports*, ed. Randy Roberts (Cambridge MA: Harvard University Press, 2005), 77–78; Stephen Hardy, *How Boston Played: Sport, Recreation, and Community, 1865–1915* (Boston: Northeastern University Press, 1982), 138.

5. Isenberg, *John L. Sullivan*, 77–78; *Boston Daily Advertiser*, September 28, 1895.

6. James Emmett Ryan, "Fight Club, 1880: Boxing, Class, and Literary Culture in John Boyle O'Reilly's Boston," *Journal of American Studies* 54, no. 4 (2020): 712–13; Randy Roberts and Andrew R. M. Smith, "The Report of My Death Was an Exaggeration: The Many Sordid Lives of America's Bloodiest Pastime," *International Journal of the History of Sport* 31, nos. 1–2 (2014): 74; Elliott J. Gorn, *The Manly Art: Bare-Knuckle Prize Fighting in America* (Ithaca NY: Cornell University Press, 1986), 181.

7. Kevin Smith, *Boston's Boxing Heritage: Prizefighting from 1882–1955* (Charleston SC: Arcadia, 2002), 18; Gorn, *Manly Art*, 199.

8. Colleen Aycock and Mark Scott, *The First Black Boxing Champions: Essays on Fighters of the 1800s to the 1920s* (Jefferson NC: McFarland, 2011), 23–25; *Boston Globe*, January 28, 1888, and October 10, 1900.

9. Isenberg, *John L. Sullivan*, 109–13; Louis Moore, *I Fight for a Living: Boxing and the Battle for Black Manhood, 1880–1915* (Urbana: University of Illinois Press, 2017), 93–94.

10. Aycock and Scott, *First Black Boxing Champions*, 22–24; Moore, *I Fight*, 96–97.

11. *Boston Globe*, January 28, 1888, and April 13, 1888; Moore, *I Fight*, 3.

12. Isenberg, *John L. Sullivan*, 257–80; Elliott Gorn, "The Champion of All Champions: John L. Sullivan," in Roberts, *Rock, the Curse*, 218. See also Guy Reel, *The National Police Gazette and the Making of the Modern American Man* (New York: Palgrave Macmillan, 2006); Ryan Swanson, *When Baseball Went White: Reconstruction, Reconciliation, and Dreams of a National Pastime (Lincoln: University of Nebraska Press, 2014)*; and Michael Kranish, *The World's Fastest Man: The Extraordinary Life of Cyclist Major Taylor, America's First Black Sports Hero* (New York: Scribner, 2019).

13. Wigginton, *Strange Career*, 20–21.

14. Hardy, *How Boston Played*, 30–32; Carroll, "Year of the Yaz," 86–87.

15. Jason Winders, *George Dixon: The Short Life of Boxing's First Black World Champion, 1870–1908* (Fayetteville: University of Arkansas Press, 2021), 34–36.

16. Winders, *George Dixon*, 32–34, 40–42; Moore, *I Fight*, 79.

17. *Boston Daily Advertiser*, September 5, 1891, and September 8, 1891; *Boston Globe*, June 6, 1892.

18. *Boston Globe*, March 13, 1892, March 14, 1892, and November 1, 1892.

19. *New Orleans Times-Democrat*, September 8, 1892, 4.

20. *Boston Globe*, August 26, 1895, and August 30, 1895; *Boston Daily Advertiser*, September 4, 10, and 28, 1895.

21. *Boston Globe*, October 18, 1901; Moore, *I Fight*, 57–58.

22. See Clay Moyle, *Sam Langford: Boxing's Greatest Uncrowned Champion* (Seattle: Bennet and Hastings, 2006).

23. Geoffrey C. Ward, *Unforgivable Blackness: The Rise and Fall of Jack Johnson* (New York: Random House, 2004), 353.

24. Moyle, *Sam Langford*, 392–94; Smith, *Boston's Boxing Heritage*, 120; Andrew R.M. Smith, "Under Wraps: The Life and Legacy of Sam Langford," in Boston's Black Athletes: Identify, Performance, and Activism, ed. Robert Cvornyek and Douglas Stark (Lanham MD: Lexington Books, 2024).

25. Smith, *Boston's Boxing Heritage*, 88.

26. Smith, *Boston's Boxing Heritage*, 84–87.

27. Smith, *Boston's Boxing Heritage*, 98–99, 110.

28. Smith, *Boston's Boxing Heritage*, 113–18.

29. David Margolick, *Beyond Glory: Joe Louis vs. Max Schmeling and a World on the Brink* (New York: Random House, 2005); Smith, *Boston's Boxing Heritage*, 123.

30. Russell Sullivan, "Rocky Marciano and the Curse of Al Weill," in Roberts, *Rock, the Curse*, 236–44.

31. Mike Casey, "Brilliant Sandy Saddler and the Long Road to Acceptance," Boxing247 .com, February 13, 2006, https://www.boxing247.com/weblog/archives/107219; Smith, *Boston's Boxing Heritage*, 124; Andrew R. M. Smith, *No Way but to Fight: George Foreman and the Business of Boxing* (Austin: University of Texas Press, 2020), 81; Gerald Eskenazi, "Sandy Saddler, Boxing Champion, Dies at 75," *New York Times*, September 22, 2001.

32. Jonathan Fuerbringer and Marvin Milbauer, "Roxbury, Quiet in the Past, Finally Breaks into Riot; Why Did Violence Occur?," *Harvard Crimson*, June 15, 1967; George Kimball, *Four Kings: Leonard, Hagler, Hearns, Duran and the Last Great Era of Boxing* (Ithaca NY: McBooks, 2009), 25–26; Damian Hughes and Brian Hughes, *Marvelous: The Marvin Hagler Story* (Durington: Pitch, 2013), 23–24.

33. Kimball, *Four Kings*, 23–25.

34. Hughes and Hughes, *Marvelous*, 26–28; Kimball, *Four Kings*, 3–6.

35. Kimball, *Four Kings*, 6, 26–28; Hughes and Hughes, *Marvelous*, 28–30.

36. Hughes and Hughes, *Marvelous*, 34–37; Andrew R. M. Smith, "Blood Stirs the Fight Crowd: Making and Marking Joe Frazier's Philadelphia," in *Philly Sports: Teams, Games, and Athletes from Rocky's Town*, ed. Ryan Swanson and David Wiggins (Fayette: University of Arkansas Press, 2016), 143–44. See also J. Russell Peltz, *Thirty Dollars and a Cute Eye: 50 Years in Boxing* (Philadelphia: Bernie Briscoe, 2021).

37. Kimball, *Four Kings*, 6, 52; Hughes and Hughes, *Marvelous*, 58–59.

38. Clive Gammon, "It Was Blood, Sweat, and Beers," *Sports Illustrated*, October 6, 1980.

39. Kimball, *Four Kings*, 158; Hughes and Hughes, *Marvelous*, 213–226; Eric Raskin, "Disputed: Hagler vs. Leonard," *Grantland*, October 4, 2011.

7

The Color of Baseball

Race and Boston's Sporting Community

ROBERT CVORNYEK

Oh for the good ole Boston Tigers days when ole Carter
Field was the haven of many a baseball classic. The field
where the Tigers were kings!
—William "Sheep" Jackson, *Boston Chronicle*, July 11, 1942

I have always believed, very firmly, that Boston colored
athletes of yesteryear are forgotten too easily.
—William "Sheep" Jackson, *Boston Chronicle*, July 22, 1944

On May 29, 1993, the Boston Red Sox celebrated the history of Negro League baseball in a pregame ceremony at Fenway Park. The Sox invited Mabray "Doc" Kountze, former sports editor for the *Boston Guardian*, and Francis "Fran" Matthews, a local Cambridge star who played for the Kansas City Monarchs and Newark Eagles of the Negro National League, to participate.[1] As Kountze caught the ceremonial first pitch tossed by Matthews, all thoughts should have turned to the legendary Negro League players and teams of the past. Instead, both men rekindled memories of Boston's amateur and semiprofessional teams. Although Boston never hosted a team in the modern professional Black leagues, it did showcase the finest amateur Black players throughout all of New England. Kountze recognized the significance of the local game and published the only book on Black sports in Boston.[2] Matthews played longer in the city's hub leagues and for the well-known Boston Colored Giants than he did for the Eagles. When Matthews's career finally ended, he enjoyed recognition as a member of the Boston Park League Hall of Fame's class of 1987.[3] The story of Black baseball in Boston is truly a local one.

African Americans participated at all levels of the local game. Black churches and fraternal organizations fielded makeshift nines to promote recreation and enhance brotherhood among their members. These teams played a casual schedule and often competed at weekend picnics, holiday celebrations, and other social gatherings during the summer. At the next level, the city's independent amateur Black teams played fixed schedules usually carded against white teams that belonged to the city's segregated amateur leagues. Black amateur clubs operated on a neighborhood level and rarely traveled beyond Greater Boston. The semiprofessional teams represented Boston's baseball aristocracy. Semipro players were paid for their efforts, and this remains the critical distinction between them and their amateur counterparts. These teams traveled extensively throughout New England and frequently into Canada. Semipro baseball was a money-making operation and, as such, represents one of the earliest forms of Black entrepreneurship. Semipro teams supported a front office, which commonly included the owner and promoter—both responsible for a payroll that needed to be met each week. Players could not survive solely on their baseball salaries, so most played the game to supplement their incomes. College students who spent their summers at home could make good money playing on these teams as well.

Charlie Lloyd, who played ball for the Highland Colored Giants, provided a rare and intimate glimpse of semiprofessional life. Lloyd, a hard-hitting outfielder who played between 1927 and 1935, stated that "life for a Black baseball player was not an easy one. There was no official league and the team played wherever it could book an opponent which meant hours and sometimes days of traveling in parked cars and sleeping in cheap, sometimes segregated motels for just one game." Lloyd recalled that he received between $32 and $37 per game, just enough to keep a bachelor going.[4]

Boston holds a long and proud tradition of amateur and semiprofessional Blackball. In the years following the American Civil War, baseball grew in popularity in Boston and around the nation.[5] Unfortunately, opportunities for Black players to participate in the city's amateur leagues narrowed, and in 1870, Boston outfitted its first "colored" team, the Resolutes. During the late nineteenth and early twentieth centuries, a colored team included anyone considered nonwhite, and these clubs often included African Americans,

Native Americans, Cubans, and Cape Verdeans. Black or "colored," Boston's nonwhite teams distinguished themselves as premier baseball clubs throughout New England.

For the most part, these teams and the men who played the game remain unnoticed, so whenever we break the silence of the past, there is cause for joy and celebration. For too long, the history of Black baseball in Boston has focused on racism at the Major League level and overlooked the players who represented the local game and their significant presence in the community. Boston, like most northern cities, was not exempt from the indignities of segregation during the Jim Crow era, but the success of its Black baseball teams provided a constant reminder of the strength and accomplishment that accompanied the skill and determination of the city's ballplayers. Boston fans found a dignity and consistency in their Black players that shaped racial identity and reinforced the notion that the struggle for racial equality can be found in several different arenas, including the baseball stadium.

Boston Black Baseball, 1870–1900

During the late nineteenth century, the Boston Resolutes successfully represented the city's African American baseball fraternity. The team dates to 1870, but little is known of the Resolutes' history during its inaugural decade. Like most Black ballclubs in the immediate post–Civil War era, the Resolutes were a local, or "stay at home," team and did not schedule traveling games beyond Greater Boston. The team played other Black clubs, most likely representing fraternal organizations and churches, but also scheduled games against established white semiprofessional teams. Games staged between the Resolutes and well-known white clubs offered baseball fans of both races an opportunity to see the city's best players, and gate receipts provided club owners with needed funds to keep the teams financially sound. Both teams shared a percentage of ticket revenue, and it is reasonable to conclude that local rivalries developed between Black and white ballclubs to stimulate sales. Rivalries fueled gate receipts, but interracial play before an integrated crowd also strengthened racial pride and identity during a time when African Americans struggled to achieve recognition and racial equality.[6]

According to historian Leslie Heaphy, the team procured its name in a most unusual way. The Black Resolutes scheduled a game with a local white team also known as the Resolutes. Both teams agreed that the winner of the game reserved the right to use the name, and the loser would relinquish its moniker. The Black team won by the score of 25–12 and retained the Resolutes name. Despite the number of runs scored, M. T. Gregory, the winning pitcher, received accolades from fans and the press.[7] High-scoring affairs were typical in the nineteenth-century amateur game, and pitchers with strength and stamina ruled the day.

At the end of the decade, the renowned Mutuals of Washington toured New England on their way to Rochester, New York, but did not play the Resolutes. At the time, the Resolutes may not yet have had the drawing power that the Mutuals were looking for in their opponents. The Mutuals were made up of young Black players, most of whom worked for the Freemen's Bureau in Washington DC, and featured Charles R. Douglass, son of abolitionist Frederick Douglass. Historian Ryan Swanson notes that Charles and Frederick frequently corresponded about the team and Black baseball in the District of Columbia. Frederick also donated money to help outfit the team and lent his name and support to several fundraising events to keep the team afloat. The Mutuals scheduled games throughout the Greater Boston area, with white teams representing the newly established New England Association, and eventually played three of them. On August 10, 1877, the Mutuals lost to Lowell 7–0 before a crowd of six hundred fans at the city's fairgrounds, and they lost again on August 20 to the Live Oaks from Lynn, 10–2. The Rhode Islands met and defeated the Mutuals in two games played in Providence's Adelaide Park. Prior to the games, the *Providence Journal* reported that the Mutuals had "unsuccessfully competed with seven New England clubs for the victory" and now "pitched their tents" in Providence to take on the Rhode Islands. On August 17 and 19, the Mutuals lost by scores of 6–0 and 10–2, respectively. Despite the losses, the *Journal* characterized the Black players as "a strong, hardy set of fellows," with several of the players "displaying remarkable skill and agility in handling the leather." In particular, James Talbot, the Mutuals second baseman, turned a double play that "met with prolonged applause from the 400 spectators."[8]

Our knowledge of the Resolutes expands considerably during the 1880s. By then, the club emerged as the best-organized and most skillful Black team in Greater Boston. According to the New York *Freeman*, the leading African American newspaper in the nation, the Resolutes were the "only colored team in the state which has demonstrated ability of no mean order" and has "aroused interest in the white baseball public." The paper concluded in 1887 that "there should be a corresponding interest and pride taken in the nine by all the colored people in the city."[9]

By the late 1880s, several other independent Black ballclubs of professional caliber existed throughout the country, and in an attempt to consolidate these teams into a viable professional league, Walter S. Brown, a Pittsburgh newspaper dealer, announced his intention to establish the National Colored League (NCL).[10] The popular magazine *Sporting Life* reported that "there have been prominent colored baseball clubs throughout the country for many years past, but this is their initiative year in launching forth on a league scale by forming a league . . . representing . . . leading cities in the country. Boston, one of the nation's leading cities . . . fielded one of the best Black teams in the country."[11] On February 3, 1887, Marshall Thompson, manager and promoter of the Resolutes, accepted Brown's invitation, and his team joined the newly created NCL. Thompson immersed himself in local politics and served as one of the few African Americans who worked at the Massachusetts State House. This position allowed him to function as a link between the state's politicians and Boston's Black community. He earned enough political clout to be named a featured guest at Boston's 1887 St. Patrick's Day Parade and garnered sufficient popularity to run the Black community's cherished cakewalk contest.[12] As one of his many responsibilities, Thompson's leadership of the Resolutes would prove his most difficult challenge.

During the NCL's preseason organizational phase, Brown announced that the Eastern Division would include teams in New York, Boston, and Philadelphia, and the Western Division would have teams in Pittsburgh, Baltimore, and Louisville. The Resolutes competed in a few warm-up games in anticipation of their professional debut. They easily defeated the region's other major Black team, the Providence Grays, in a game played at Union Grounds in Boston, by the lopsided score of 20–5. The NCL opened on May 5, 1887, but only a few games into the season, storm clouds gathered, and it appeared as if the league was headed for disaster. Scheduling snafus and inadequate financial backing left the Resolutes out of money and stranded in Louisville on May 8, 1887. The team folded two days later when it became evident that the club failed to meet its financial obligation to travel and play in Pittsburgh. The *Louisville Courier Journal* ran the following description of the team's opening game in the new league:

> The National Colored League season was formally opened yesterday at the Louisville Base Ball Park. The Falls City team comprised of the best ball-tossers of the city were defeated with ease by the Boston Resolutes. The game was witnessed by about 500 people. The Resolutes are all fine players, especially the dusky little twirler Selden. He struck out thirteen men, and held the Falls Citys down to six hits, two of which were bases on balls. [William] Selden has a most deceptive drop curve, and a most perfect control over the ball. But there are no flies on the other Boston players. Smith is an excellent left-hand throwing catcher, and hits the ball hard enough to burst the cover. [Daniel]Penno, [William] Walker and [Charles R.] Williams are all good infielders, and understand thoroughly the fine points of the game.[13]

Despite the club's stellar performance, insufficient financing, bad luck, and ineffective leadership by the league's front office contributed to the demise of the NCL on May 28. Some teams, like New York, Baltimore, and Pittsburgh, remained on the road and barnstormed the country for most of the summer. Others, like Boston, returned home and continued their season playing games against local teams. "At last accounts," noted the *Sporting News*, "most of the Colored Leaguers were working their way home doing little turns in barbershops and waiting on tables in hotels."[14]

Not all the Resolutes made it back to Boston. Several notable players joined professional Black teams operating in the New York metropolitan area. Dan Penno, a Portuguese and Cape Verdean infielder from East Greenwich, Rhode Island, left the Resolutes to play for the Cuban Giants, the nation's first truly professional Black baseball club. The team originated in 1885 under the leadership of Frank P. Thompson, a hotelman and head waiter by profession, who masterfully combined two accomplished ballclubs from Philadelphia, the Keystone Athletics and the Orions, and another from Washington DC, the Manhattans, into the Cuban Giants. The team played its opening season at the luxurious Argyle Hotel in Babylon, New York, on Long Island and then later moved to Trenton, New Jersey. During the late nineteenth and early twentieth centuries, the team traveled extensively throughout New England, engaging in single-game contests or an extended "championship" series with notable white clubs. There were, however, no Cubans on the Giants. The waiters agreed to adopt the name as a way of scheduling games with white teams who refused to play against African Americans. According to one observer, "If Cuban in the team name was part subterfuge, Giants was pure tribute." Another Resolutes player, William H. Selden, joined Penno to help bolster the Giants' starting pitching rotation. Others, like Windsor W. Terrill, found a home with the Cuban X Giants, a team composed mostly of defecting Cuban Giants.[15]

The loss of such key players weakened the Resolutes, and the team struggled to thrive in later years. In 1889, Marshall Thompson reported that he was "hard at work towards reorganizing the Resolutes" and had been "offered backing by several prominent men," but Thompson's efforts failed to fortify the team. Instead, he orchestrated a merger of his team with a rival west-end club, the Seasides. Thompson was attracted to this team because they played excellent ball and openly challenged the Resolutes for the city's Blackball bragging rights. Both teams, however, scrambled for funds. Hoping to resolve financial woes for both clubs, the teams officially consolidated in May 1889 and thereafter were known simply as the Seasides. The new team fell under the control of Theodore E. Roberts, who moved the front office to 93 Union Street and appointed William James, one of his own, as team manager. He reported that he intended to schedule home games at Presumpscot Park.[16]

The Seasides lasted only one year, and the former Resolute players, now playing under the name of the Resolute Reserves, struggled through the 1890s. Midway through 1890, the defection of several key players, including the team's crack battery of a pitcher Windsor Terrell and catcher Alfred Davis, to the original Cuban Giants left the team without two top-notch gate attractions. Recurring financial difficulties, most notably a lack of travel money, resulted in forfeited games. When opponents began labeling the Resolute Reserves as unreliable, word spread, and the team experienced greater difficulty in scheduling games. Charges of financial mismanagement also hounded the team. The club hit rock bottom following an incident involving W. W. Walker, manager of the Reserves, and E. J. Ellis, manager of the Beverly Athletic Association, who nearly came to blows over absent advanced payments, lost gate receipts, and a history of forfeited games.[17]

Growth and Expansion, 1900–1920

As the nineteenth century turned into the twentieth, several new "colored" ballclubs emerged to fill the void left by the legendary Resolutes. The number of teams steadily increased, and the level of competition intensified. Moreover, an old-fashioned rivalry developed between teams representing Boston and Cambridge. Fans witnessed firsthand the convergence of these trends in the opening game of the 1901 season staged between the Mentors of Cambridge and the Windsors of Boston. Promoters billed the game as a showdown between rival communities—one destined to ignite local fervor. As an added attraction, the contest featured celebrity George Dixon, ex-featherweight champion of the world, as home plate umpire. The Mentors, established in 1900, drew players from the Black employees of Harvard University who worked in Memorial Hall. According to the *Boston Daily Globe*, the Mentors fielded one of the classiest, best-organized, and well-financed Black teams in the state.[18]

By 1903, the requisite number of teams and talented ballplayers allowed for the creation of Boston's first organized race league, called the Greater Boston Colored League (GBCL). Robert Teamoh, an African American journalist, organized the association and served as its president. Teamoh, a dynamic figure in the Black community, displayed a passion for politics and sports. In 1894, he was elected on the Republican ticket to the Massachusetts State Legislature representing Boston's upscale Ninth District. The Ninth's constituency included both Black and white residents, and Teamoh moved comfortably between both races. At thirty years old, he became the youngest African American to hold elective office in the State House. Teamoh knew the city well. He was born and raised in Boston, where he attended

Boston Latin High School and later the Boston Industrial Drawing School. As a young man, he developed an interest in newspaper writing and landed a position with the *Boston Globe*. At the *Globe*, his success and ambition led to his notoriety as the first Black reporter chosen as a member of the Boston Press Club. He also served as the director of the *Globe*'s athletic club.[19]

Teamoh scouted the region's best ballclubs and invited the West Medford Independents, Boston Royal Giants, Cambridge Washingtons, Malden Riversides, West Newton Athletics, and Allstons to join the league. Each team enthusiastically agreed. Upon completion of the first season, the Independents won the championship and the Royal Giants placed second. Years later, Joel Lewis, a pitcher for the Allstons, recalled, "The type of ball played was high grade, and the players, themselves, were as fine a bunch of fellows I have ever played with. I am sorry the League is not going today, as I believe players trained in it would have, by now, won wide recognition and helped considerably in the recognition of Colored players."[20] Lewis would never see another league like the GBCL, although word did circulate in April 1935 that a similar Greater Boston League had been planned by local African American promoters.[21]

Following their championship season in 1903, the West Medford Independents continued to have great success. Originating in 1902 and outlasting any of its league opponents, the team included a combination of local talent and players recently arrived from the South as part of the Great Migration. The Independents drew the largest crowds recorded at the town's Playstead Park and attracted a large number of fans when they played in nearby Boston. The original Independents thrived from 1902 to 1912, reorganized in 1912, and lasted until 1917, when most of the players enlisted to fight in World War I. After the end of the war, the team regrouped, added more players, and remained organized until the early 1920s.[22]

The first incarnation of the team evoked the strongest memories and connection to the community, mostly because of its championship season in the GBCL. Local resident Hilton Parnham, whose family members either played for the team or demonstrated their support from the bleachers, states, "First Independents, the original team, well it was really great." He recalls the players with a bit of exaggeration when he concludes, "I'd say all of them were of Major League caliber. Roy Campanella was a great catcher, we all know. But I'd say [Jim] Gabriel was his equal; especially in throwing. Gabriel threw from the rocking chair crouch. He had a powerful arm." Parnham adds that

Art Ransome was another great star and first baseman. . . . He could hit, field with that stretch, and he was a brilliant base-runner with that slide. . . . Otis Parham Sr. was one of the best right-handers in the state, bar none. . . . His pitching team-mate, Dick Banks of Arlington, was right up there with him. So, his fast ball was partly a knuckle ball that did tricks to enemy batters. The early outfield of Waldron Furr, Arnold Benjamin, and Branch Russell, was a good one, all sluggers. . . . The club beat the Boston Tigers regularly, and the Tigers were among the best in the country. . . . Other players replaced the old-timers later to keep the club strong. . . . But I'd say that Art Ransome and, later, the club left hander pitching star, your brother, Hillard Kountze, were the two best first basemen the club ever had. . . . You know that Medford Mayor Lewis Lovering had a lot to do with the success, and progress, of the Independent Baseball Club. He helped to get the first uniforms for the team and was the team's "Number One" fan. . . . Mayor Lovering let people know that this Afro-American athletic group was bringing honor and prestige to the city, and this is what the club did as long as it existed and represented Medford.[23]

By 1905, fan attention shifted to the Dartmouth Athletic Giants, a powerhouse club listed as the precursors of the legendary Boston Giants of the 1920s and 1930s. The Athletic Giants carded games against teams in Greater Boston, including Boston, Cambridge, Malden, Winchester, Everett, Lynn, and Medford. Teams from these cities reportedly played "mostly among themselves" but not in an organized league structure.[24]

In the heart of Boston's South Side, another team began its rise to prominence during the early decades of the twentieth century. The history of the Boston Tigers reads like a storybook tale. The ballclub started as a sandlot team of grammar school boys who managed to stay together over the years and develop into the region's most admired ballclub. Bob Russell and Arthur "Fat" Johnson were the two men most responsible for the success of the

Tigers. Russell, an excellent ballplayer and manager, combined his talent with Johnson, a money man and enthusiastic promoter, to create the team.[25]

The two met in 1912 and shortly thereafter helped a struggling sandlot ballclub aptly named the Progress Team to become the renowned Tigers. The Progress players attended and represented Robert Gould Shaw House, a community home for African American boys, located on Hammond Street. As a youngster, Russell reportedly spent a great deal of time at the Shaw House and played for the Progress club. In 1910, he entered English High School, where he became a stellar athlete and later attended Colby Academy in Maine. Russell's reputation as a power pitcher earned him a spot in the East Coast "Hotel Circuit," where he played each summer in Rhode Island and each winter for the hotel teams in Florida. He finally settled back in Boston, and by 1915, both he and Johnson succeeded in transforming the Progress club into the Tigers.[26]

When Johnson met Russell, he worked for the 20th Century Limited and spent most of his free time playing ball at Columbus Avenue Park. Johnson later partnered with Bertie Davis and operated a successful laundry business in the heart of Harvard Square. He became a popular figure in the square and cultivated friendships with the neighborhood's wealthy clientele. Johnson's business experience and connections made him the perfect spokesman and promoter for the up-and-coming Tigers.[27]

Prior to World War I, the team had come into its own and possessed enough moxie to challenge the St. John's team from Cambridge, an aggregation regarded as the "toast of the colored baseball fans and top attraction of this area." A spirited rivalry developed between the teams, but the onset of war interrupted the contests. On August 1, 1918, several members of the Tigers—including Arthur Carrington, William "Bullet" Campbell, James Moore, John "Southy" Thomas, and owner "Fats" Johnson—reported for military service at Fort Devens in Massachusetts.[28] When the Tigers ballplayers returned at war's end, they reestablished themselves, dominating Blackball in the Greater Boston area during the entire 1920s. Russell and Johnson had rejuvenated the team, which now enjoyed unparalleled success and admiration.[29]

The Pilgrims and the Tigers: The 1920s

In the years preceding and during World War I, African Americans left the South and relocated to the North as part of the nation's Great Migration. Black communities flourished and so did baseball. Ballparks that serviced Black neighborhoods—including Carter Field and Lincoln Park in Boston's South End, Russell Field and Hoyt Field in Cambridge, Playstead Park in Medford, and Dorchester's Town Field—remained busy with games through the 1920s and 1930s.[30] The Tigers opened the 1920s in glorious fashion and prompted the *Boston Globe* to report that they were "one of the best semi-professional teams in the state" regardless of color, and the team easily claimed the title as the "champion colored nine of New England." All season long, William "Bullet" Campbell provided excellent pitching while John "Southy" Thomas and Mose Sisco added the fine fielding and clutch hitting that defined a well-balanced team. Given the ballclub's success, the *Globe* expected the Tigers to eventually "travel over the country and play the strongest teams they could book."[31]

The paper's prediction came true but with an interesting twist when several Tiger players were asked to join a newly formed professional baseball league in 1921. On December 31, 1920, George Herman "Andy" Lawson, a Boston-area sports promoter, announced the creation of the new league as a rival to Major League Baseball's American and National Leagues. Lawson's Continental League, sometimes referred to as the Continental Baseball Association, captured the attention of the African American community after Lawson hinted that his new league intended to include Black ball-clubs. This was a bold move on Lawson's part, since the "gentlemen's agreement" to ban Blacks from professional baseball was still in effect. Lawson sought to include a Black team from Boston, and the obvious choice was the city's champion Tigers.[32] The Tigers changed their name to the Pilgrims for the move to pro baseball, highlighting the team's regional identity. But the ill-fated Continental League lasted only a few weeks, and the Pilgrims changed their name back to the Tigers before returning to the ranks of semipro ball. Years later, in 1943, William "Sheep" Jackson, a sportswriter for the *Boston Chronicle*, reminded his readers that in 1921, the Pilgrims were the "best negro baseball team that ever put on a pair of skates in this community . . . a club that compared favorably with any A.A. minor league club." Jackson recalled that the team "played its home games at the Everett High School Field on Chelsea Street." He continued, "It played weekdays and Saturday afternoons and I am glad to report played before several thousands at all times."[33]

Before the Pilgrims again became the Tigers, they played in a Continental League game against an opponent that significantly impacted the landscape of Black baseball in New England. The Pilgrims met the Cleveland Colored Giants in a doubleheader at Everett High School Park to open the season. The Pilgrims defeated the Colored Giants by scores of 10–2 and 12–2.[34] Not long after these games, the league folded, and the Colored Giants found themselves stranded in New England without scheduled games and a guaranteed income. Fortunately, James Gibbons, owner of the Gibbons Express Trucking Company in Providence, Rhode Island, rescued the team. Gibbons financed the team and promoted games with regional semiprofessional clubs. In so doing, he turned the Cleveland Giants into one of the premiere traveling ballclubs in Greater Boston and throughout southern New England.[35]

As fate would have it, the Pilgrims, now once more the Tigers, and the Cleveland Colored Giants clashed again, this time in 1923, to determine the regional Black baseball championship. The Black press touted the game as the principal athletic event of the Emancipation Day celebration held at Rocky Point Park in Rhode Island. African Americans in Rhode Island and throughout New England celebrated West Indian emancipation on August 1 instead of the traditional January 1 festival honoring President Lincoln's Emancipation Proclamation.[36] Emancipation Day drew thousands of celebrants, and the game served as the principal entertainment for all in attendance. The Colored Giants defeated the Tigers by a score of 4–3 in a ten-inning thriller. Southy Thomas, Mose Sisco, and Zeke Crudup received special praise for their efforts in a losing cause.[37]

Throughout the 1920s, the Tigers continued to play outstanding baseball. The team engaged in several championship games with ballclubs like the Philadelphia Giants and the Colored All-Stars from Providence, Rhode Island. The team even made sports history when it took part in the first baseball-football doubleheader. In the opening game, the Tigers played the Providence Colored All-Stars for the "colored baseball title" of New England, and later that day, the Providence Steam Roller football team met the Newport Torpedo Station in a gridiron classic.[38] But the Tigers remained fixed in the hearts of their fans for other reasons. They played most of their games nearby at Columbus Avenue Park, and most of the players hailed from places like Boston, Cambridge, Everett, Malden, and West Newton. Boston fans identified with these local men, knowing that the ballplayers experienced the same challenges and hardships off the field that they did. The fans also knew that baseball provided an opportunity to demonstrate Black talent and identity, especially in contests against white opponents.

Long after their careers ended, many former Tigers participated in a series of memorable Old-Timers' games that reunited them with their fans and reaffirmed their respected standing in the community. Billed as the "must-see game of the year," these contests featured former stars representing Boston and Cambridge. The tradition originated in 1937 under the sponsorship of the Cambridge Works Progress Administration (wpa) Recreation Committee and the guiding hand of its supervisor, ex-Tiger Ralph "Stody" Ward. The initial exhibition game quickly turned into a sizzling intercity rivalry that became a best-of-seven series between the teams. Games scheduled in Cambridge were played at the Russell E. Hoyt Playground field located on Western Avenue, and games held in Boston were at William E. Carter Playground on Columbus Avenue. In 1938, the opening contest between the teams played at Carter Field attracted over ten thousand fans, the most to attend a game in over a decade. The ensuing game played in Cambridge featured the town's mayor, John W. Lyons, who tossed the ceremonial first pitch, and the wpa Band of Medford, whose musicians entertained the crowd at Hoyt Field before and during the game.[39]

By 1940, the *Boston Chronicle* reported that the Old-Timers' games became a "magnet that draws people who, at one time, were rabid, dyed-in-wool fans" of the Tigers. The 1941 game, for example, featured most of the past Tigers. According to one observer, "The Boston Old-Timers' club will stir rosy memories as veteran ball fans gaze . . . on Big Jim Moore, the veteran and ex-Tiger first baseman; the famed pitcher 'Bullet' Campbell; and the popular player and pilot, Bob Russell, all ex–Boston Tigers, who need no introduction anywhere in New England." Fans attended the games to recall an important time in their lives when the Tigers showcased their remarkable talent and proved that they were the best semipro team, Black or white, in New England. They also attended to support the community, beginning in 1939. The financial proceeds of that year's game were donated to cover the medical expenses for beloved former Tiger center fielder Mose Sisco, and throughout subsequent years, gate receipts were collected for the North Cambridge Community Club.[40]

William "Sheep" Jackson and the Tigers

Before the opening of the 1945 baseball season, William "Sheep" Jackson, sports editor for the *Boston Chronicle*, found himself caught somewhere between memory and history as he recounted the triumphs and achievements of several ballplayers of the city's own Boston Tigers. Black fans enthusiastically supported the national pastime through the local men who played the game. During the 1920s, the Tigers emerged as the Black community's most beloved and successful semiprofessional ballclub. Decades later, Jackson ensured that the team's memory would never languish in the shadows. He passionately reminded his readers how their neighborhood ballplayers once illuminated the diamonds situated at Carter Park and Columbus Avenue Playground. Jackson made every effort to recognize and recount the history of Boston's Tigers to keep the team's memory alive.

Jackson enjoyed a lifelong relationship with amateur sport in Greater Boston. Born and raised in Malden, he excelled in baseball, football, basketball, and track at Malden High School. He later attended Cushing Academy on a football scholarship and Lincoln University in Pennsylvania, where he displayed his athletic versatility and demonstrated his academic talent. He accepted a part-time sports reporter position at the *Boston Chronicle* while still a student at Lincoln. Upon graduation from college, he married his girlfriend, Lydia, and relocated to a home on Broadway in Cambridge. In 1934, he served as the athletic director of the Cambridge Community Center and began his graduate studies at the Boston University School of Social Service and Religious Education. Despite his busy schedule, he managed to continue writing his sports column, "Sports Shots," for the *Chronicle*. In 1940, he became the paper's sports editor and strengthened his broader community connections as a field representative for the National Youth Association. Jackson answered his country's call for duty in July 1943, when he entered the U.S. Army. After a distinguished career in the military, he returned home, where he and his wife became the proud parents of a son, William Daniel Jackson. By 1945, Jackson had returned to his familiar role as a sportswriter. One of his first tasks combined his love of baseball, the Tigers, and his community. The result was a series of biographical sketches that reconnected the Boston Tigers to their fans and the community they both shared.[41]

Jackson epitomized the capacity of sportswriters to connect past sports events to the social and cultural outlook of the present. In the years between the publication of Sol White's monumental *History of Colored Baseball* in 1907 and Mabray "Doc" Kountze's *50 Sports Years along Memory Lane: Afro-American Sports History; Hometown, Local, National* in 1979, preserving the history of Boston's race teams fell mainly to local Black sportswriters who kept the public memory of the game intact. During the first half of the twentieth century, these chroniclers approached their subject in numerous ways, but always to make baseball's past part of a public transcript that clearly defined the Black community's collective memory. Sportswriters who recalled and interpreted the long and honored history of colored baseball occupied the ambiguous and oftentimes conflicted position of writing between memory and history.

Scholars have recently focused their attention on the relationship between the Black press and the integration of professional Major League Baseball during and immediately after World War II. Jackson elected to examine the sportswriter's role in explicating the proud heritage of local Black baseball, identifying neighborhood heroes to emulate and celebrating the game's contributions to Black cultural expression. Jackson, with his potential to reach broad segments of Boston's African American population, provides a strong example of how Black sportswriters exercised their right to interpret and make use of their community's baseball past.

Sports reporters enjoyed their widest readership in city newspapers, and in Boston, the *Chronicle* was the place for Black sports. The paper served as a lifeline to the city's baseball enthusiasts, often capturing the personalities and highlights of past years and their impact on Black cultural identity. In Jackson's series, he entwined the game's history with feature stories on former player's careers. He covered special occasions like retirements, managerial and front-office appointments, and neighborhood commemorations of local sports heroes to familiarize his readers with players whose past accomplishments proved worthy of consideration. Sometimes, newspaper coverage of the death of Black ballplayers evoked an outpouring of stories and memories that turned otherwise private mourning ceremonies into public expressions of the history and meaning of Black baseball. Jackson operated as a middleman somewhere between history and memory and fashioned a usable baseball past, albeit selective and incomplete.

Jackson also examined traditions in progress to further influence the community's collective identity. One such tradition, Old-Timers' Days, made the game's historic past and racial identity part of contemporary social life. During the mid-1930s and early 1940s, long after most of the Tigers had retired from baseball, the community clamored for their return in a series of Old-Timers' games that often pitted former players who hailed from Cambridge against their teammates from Boston. These contests, often benefiting local charities, were played at Hoyt Field in front of fans where "everybody knows everybody else." Children accompanied parents and grandparents to get their first look at the men whom their elders considered legends in the community. As one observer noted, "Baseball is the game we love," and the Old-Timers' game "will present a galaxy of some of the greatest diamond stars in New England's progressive history even though many of the boys will be long past their prime." Jackson and any other sportswriter in the city would agree but add that in their prime, a number of these men were good enough to play in the Major Leagues. These celebrations encouraged Jackson to reflect on the game's history and the accomplishments of former players.[42]

Golden Age of Black Baseball, 1931–46

As the 1920s ended, no one could have predicted the economic devastation that awaited most Americans during the Great Depression. The duration and severity of this economic collapse affected most aspects of life, including Black baseball. By 1931, the professional Negro National League crumbled under the weight of the Depression and the recent death of its founder, Andrew Rube Foster. Many players found themselves without a team and a paycheck. This unfortunate situation led many players to seek tryouts with local semiprofessional teams. Boston, like many other cities, benefited from this influx of talent.

In 1932, the Black press reported that "Lincoln Park and the William E. Carter Playground ought to be scenes of a large number of good baseball games . . . since there are three exceptionally good colored ball clubs with enough talent and ability to make games interesting anywhere." The Boston Tigers, the Philadelphia Giants, and the Boston Royal Giants contained comparable talent and remained competitive with one another and the strongest semipro white teams in the state.[43] The Providence Colored Giants, another regional team that included exceptional talent, petitioned to play in Boston's Twilight League and became the fourth powerhouse semipro team playing in Boston.

In addition to the Philly Giants, Tigers, and the Colored Giants, numerous other ballclubs represented Boston's Black neighborhoods. Clem Mack's Boston ABC team attracted many professional Black barnstorming teams to Boston's Lincoln Park. Prior to his arrival in Boston in 1935, Mack managed the Colored House of David and scheduled games with teams around the country. He used his contacts to card games in Boston with teams like the New York Colored Giants and the Homestead Grays. The ABCs probably traveled farther than any Boston-based team, as evidenced by its preseason trip to the South during its inaugural season in 1935. Reports from Henderson, North Carolina, affirmed that the "Boston ABC baseball club which gained national publicity in its first trip here in southern training quarters is now ready to pack up and depart for New England. The new team has been here since the middle of March whipping into shape for what is expected to be the most strenuous baseball season in Boston and which may result in that city securing a franchise in the Negro National League by next year." Mack's efforts, however, did not result in a professional franchise, and his tenure in the city lasted only one year.[44]

Black teams also participated in the city's amateur leagues. The city's Park League, for instance, hosted several African American teams in the late 1930s. These teams included the Rangers, Mohawks, and Wolverines. Ike Bailey's Rangers included a mix of veterans and youngsters, and manager Edward Hill of the Mohawks joined the Park League in 1938 after winning the championship of the Sunset League the year before. Fans, however, favored the Wolverines and their star player, Eugene Wood, a former outstanding athlete at Memorial High School.[45] The Wolverines originated in 1934 and served as the athletic counterpart to the civic-minded Wolverine Club located at 558 Massachusetts Avenue.[46]

West Newton fielded one of the most competitive teams in Greater Boston during the 1920s and 1930s. The team originated as the Colored Town Nine and came from an area known as the Colored Village. Since the turn of the twentieth century, African American families had established a community there centered on the Myrtle Baptist Church. Baseball quickly became a passion among the residents. The Colored Town Nine operated in the 1920s, sometimes under the name of the Galloping Dominoes, and played an informal and independent schedule with nearby white teams. In 1932, a former star with the Boston Tigers, Earl Lomax, reorganized the team as the West Newton Colored Tigers and coaxed several of his Tiger teammates to join the club. Former Tigers who accepted Lomax's invitation included Gus Gadsen, Fleet Taylor, Zing Rice, and Stody Ward. The addition of these "outsiders" helped transform the club into a truly semiprofessional outfit. In 1932, the team emerged as a strong regional contender with a record of eighteen games won against twelve losses. The following year, the West Newton Tigers compiled a 22-12 record, and in 1934 the team reached a high point by going 34-5. The Tigers grew in popularity as the team continued to excel on the field. According to one observer, the fans "hustled through their suppers, converged on the local ballpark, filled up the small grandstands, stood two and three-deep along the sidelines, and around the fifth inning tossed their nickels, dimes, and (sometimes) quarters into the baseball caps that were passed around." In 1935, the team ceased playing as a semipro team and joined the Newton Twilight League. A year later, the seasoned veterans disbanded the team and ended a memorable era in West Newton sports history.[47]

The 1930s and 1940s, however, belonged to the Philly Giants, Boston Colored Giants, and Providence Giants. By the early 1930s, the Boston Tigers no longer stood atop the city's Black baseball world. The team opened the 1932 season by defeating a strong opponent in the Lincoln Athletic Club of Harlem. Yet the Tigers, which included former Providence Giants standouts Oliver Marcelle at third base and Peter "Tubby" Johnson in the outfield, failed to perform as expected.

This was the last year the team would remain competitive, and the press declared that the end of the Tigers represented both "confusion and possibilities" for Boston's Black baseball future. Confusion in that the familiar Tigers had lost their combative edge and possibility in the form of the Boston Giants, a new team destined to capture the attention and support of the former Tiger fans.[48]

The Tigers did maintain their presence in the following years. In 1934, the team defeated the Harvard All-Stars, a team composed of current and past Harvard baseball players, by a score of 9–4 in a benefit game for St. Monica's Home. An aging Jim Moore hit a grand slam to win the game. Baseball legend George Herman "Babe" Ruth had agreed to toss the ceremonial first pitch of the game but was unable to attend because he experienced a hard afternoon against the Red Sox and wasn't feeling well. More important than the presence of the "Bambino" was the meaning behind the game, expressed eloquently in the *Boston Chronicle*: "The contest was simply another example of the inter-racial friendship bond which is slowly being revealed at Harvard and also to the ability of 'Fats' Johnson as a promoter." By 1935, the Tigers rarely played in the city, but in subsequent years, many of the players returned to thrill their followers in a series of Old-Timers' games played at Carter Field.[49]

For a moment, the Providence Giants helped fill the void left by the Tigers. The Giants name had been popular among Black teams since the nineteenth century, and all three Greater Boston teams adopted the same title. The Providence Giants opened the 1930s in strong fashion. Arthur "Daddy" Black, the owner of the team, assembled a championship team in 1931 that included several professional players looking for work after the demise of the Negro National League. Black, an African American, had been involved in owning and promoting sports teams since the mid-1920s, when he managed the all-white Providence Monarchs Baseball Club. Black made his livelihood as the "Numbers King" of Black Providence. He operated his illegal numbers racket from his home on Cranston Street in Providence's Hoyle Square neighborhood. His operation took in an estimated $5,000 a day during the height of the Depression in 1932.[50]

In 1931, Black acquired the Providence Colored Giants from Daniel White-head, his friend and fellow sports promoter. Black had the financial resources and sports connections to acquire the finest Black players to play for his team. He acquired, for example, Oliver "Ghost" Marcelle, an outstanding third baseman who previously played for the championship Baltimore Black Sox. Marcelle was approaching the end of his career when he signed with Providence, but Black managed to attract younger players on their way up. Pitchers Luther Farrell and Jesse Hubbard, both former Providence Giants, played for the Bacharach Giants and, between them, defeated the mighty Pittsburgh Crawfords twice in a doubleheader in 1934. Likewise, out-fielder "Tubby" Johnson joined the New York Black Yankees after departing Providence. Other players with professional experience included Elmore "Scrappy" Brown and Robert "Highpockets" Hudspeth.[51]

Rhode Island's semiprofessional and amateur leagues refused admission to the powerhouse Giants, and local clubs declined to play them. Black took his team to Boston and found a home in the city's Twilight League, where his team captured the league title in 1931. Black's Giants opened the season in grand fashion by assisting in the dedication of Boston's newest ballpark, Lincoln Park, located at Massachusetts Avenue and Island Street. The stadium operated as the Hub's first sports venue owned and operated by an African American, John H. Prioleau.[52] During the season, Black arranged for his team to travel to New York to play the Harlem Stars, owned by entertainer Bill "Bojangles" Robinson. Robinson's Stars, later to become the New York Black Yankees, defeated the Giants in a doubleheader played at the Polo

Grounds by scores of 6–4 and 8–1.[53] In the postseason, Providence challenged the Philadelphia Giants for New England's "Grand Title." The Providence Giants entered the contest as heavy favorites but lost to the Philly Giants in a hotly contested nine-game contest.[54]

Black believed the team failed to play professional-level ball. The Providence Giants never achieved its full potential or merited its hefty payroll. Black's financial investment did not produce a favorable return, and his interest in Blackball decreased. Moreover, the likelihood of the team becoming an independent and professional traveling team diminished as players weighed their options for the upcoming year. Black turned the team back to Whitehead with disastrous results. During the opening game of the 1932 season, several players on the team mutinied and left the field under rumor that Whitehead did not have the money to pay them. Whitehead replaced his high-priced talent with local players and successfully managed to complete the season. Black, however, met a more disastrous fate. He was murdered, gangland style, at his home in Providence by rival mobsters looking to muscle in on his territory.[55]

Following the demise of the Providence ballclub, the Philly Giants and the Boston Colored Giants became the city's major Black baseball attractions. There has been some confusion, mostly because of inconsistent reporting in the press, over the history and names of both these clubs. As sport historian Dick Thompson correctly explains, the name Philadelphia Giants had been used by many squads over the years, but the team originated in 1902 under the leadership of Sol White, a member of the Baseball Hall of Fame for his playing and managing accomplishments. In 1905, the team toured New England, where it generated excitement and enjoyed an enthusiastic following. The New England bookings, especially Boston, were so successful that the team returned each summer. The city's supportive fans made an impression on one of the Giants, pitcher Danny McClellan. He recalled the loyal fans in Boston when he took control of the team in 1923 and relocated the historic franchise there during each summer. McClellan's Phillies made an impressive showing in their first Boston-based year by defeating several of the region's most talented white teams, including the Providence Steam

Roller and ballclubs from Salem, North Cambridge, Dilboy, and Fitchburg and additional teams from the Bay State Twilight League.[56]

When the Giants made their customary entrance into Greater Boston in June 1925, baseball authorities rated them as one of the best Black semiprofessional teams in the nation. The team satisfied these expectations by defeating the Pennsylvania Red Caps of New York in a thrilling six-game series played in ballparks throughout Greater Boston. The series, billed as the "Colored World Championship," was really the semiprofessional championship, which featured two East Coast traveling teams in their quest for regional supremacy. The Red Caps hailed from New York City and derived their name from Pennsylvania Station in Manhattan. The Boston press described the Red Caps as "thumpers" capable of hitting the long ball and more serious than the Philly Giants in their desire to win. William Reavis managed and promoted the Red Caps, and Julius Thomas served as team captain.[57]

The Philadelphia Giants prevailed in the series, defeating the Red Caps in four games, losing one, and tying another. The first game, played at Fore River Stadium in Quincy before a crowd that "packed every part of the field," featured the Giants' premier pitcher Will Jackman. The Giants won behind Jackman's shutout performance, 1–0. The Giants triumphed in their second game, played at Walk-Over Park in Brockton, by a score of 4–2 but experienced their only defeat a day later at Ridge Hill Grove, 7–2. Jackman picked up another win in Game Four at the Walpole Grounds in Boston, 4–2, but the Giants ended up tying their rivals in Game Five at Memorial Park in Rockland, 4–4. In the sixth and deciding game, with Jackman resting, the Giants won an impressive victory behind the stellar pitching of Bill Pierce, 7–0. The games provided a "tonic" of excitement for Philly supporters who recorded an average attendance of 2,500 fans at each game. In Brockton, the women's Charitable Club held a celebratory dinner for both clubs that featured dancing until midnight and musical selections from "Tootsie" Jackman, "playboy of the diamond."[58]

The series featured several of the finest Black players in baseball. The Giants fielded New England's most potent African American battery in Will Jackman and Burlin White. The team also acquired the talented Bill Yancy for the 1925 season. Yancy would later have a successful professional baseball career, playing fourteen seasons in the Negro Leagues. He ended his career as a manager in Latin America, where he helped introduce baseball to Panama. Yancy also played for New York's legendary Harlem Renaissance basketball team and was inducted into the National Basketball Hall of Fame in Springfield, Massachusetts, in 1963. The Red Caps featured a young and rising star in Dick Seay. He too would enjoy a long career as a player and manager in the Negro Leagues, especially with the Newark Eagles, where he played shortstop and second base for the team's "million-dollar" infield.[59]

The series delighted local fans and prompted one enthusiast to pen the following poem after the final game:

Just a game at twilight.
On the park Schwab built,
I saw the Philly Giants
Win a little tilt.
They beat the Pennsy Red Caps
Seven runs to none.
Then the gathering gloom
On the horizon did loom.
And the day's work was done.
—*Philadelphia Tribune*, September 26, 1925

In 1926, the Phillies enjoyed another successful season and, in the midst of a ten-game winning streak, defeated their New England rivals, the Providence Giants, in the first game of a three-team doubleheader at Providence's Kinsley Park. In the second game, the Providence Giants were carded to play their major competition in the state's Suburban League, the Cromptons. Both the Giants and the Cromptons were vying for first place in the league. What made this afternoon particularly interesting was the fact that the Phillies substituted themselves for the Providence Giants and "played under their colors." According to Providence's owner and promoter Daniel Whitehead, "The Quakers [Philadelphia Giants] are to represent his club, the Providence Giants, in the nightcap and the result will count in the Suburban standing." At a time when free agency ran wild among the players and owners and players wore the uniforms of several clubs during the same season, this was the first time a team completely transformed itself into another. The Providence Giants secured a 7–3 victory over Crompton, but all the players were Philly Giants.[60]

Although based in Boston, the team toured extensively throughout New England, Upstate New York, and Canada. McClellan's Phillies did, however, enter into an agreement with the town of New Bedford to play an increased number of home games at the town's Sargent Field. The team secured permission to use the field, and it became their base of operations. By 1931, the press reported that John H. Prioleau, a young businessman from Roxbury, intended to purchase the Giants from McClellan and rename the team the Boston Giants. Prioleau promised Boston a team that would rank with the best semiprofessional teams in the country and the chance to see this team play against the strongest Black teams and leading white teams.

McClellan refused to relinquish control of the team and remained a Philly Giant until the team disbanded in 1935. In fact, 1934 proved a transitional year as "Smilin'" Dan McClellan attempted to pull a Connie Mack, which meant bringing in new, younger players to replace the old. The pivotal transition failed to materialize, and the team ended its historic run in Boston the following year.[61]

The Boston Giants entered the fray in 1932 and joined the Phillies and Tigers as one of the city's top three Black teams. The local newspapers remarked that the team had "not been organized long" and had been "placed in the field by the owner of Lincoln Park"—namely, John Prioleau. Oliver Marcelle served as the team's first manager. The Boston Giants were soon replaced by Burlin White's Greater Boston Royal Giants. White had starred with the Philadelphia Giants for over a decade before he and owner Danny McClellan had a falling out in 1934 over McClellan's decision to restructure the team with younger players. Baseball enthusiasts touted White's Royal Giants as the city's leading team and intended to go places. Sports reporters perceived the new club as outclassing the Philly Giants and other potential African American competitors, including the Malden Giants, Rangers, and Cleveland Colored Giants, but not as formidable as the old Tigers or Providence Giants. A proven master promoter of his team, White booked games as far away as Ohio. He purchased the team its own bus and outfitted them in the finest uniforms. According to one report, "The Royal Giants have their own bus, and attired in neat blue-grey uniforms with dark caps and red, white, and blue stockings, they make a very attractive appearance on the field."[62]

During the late 1930s, the press referred to the team by a few different names. Some reports listed the team as the Boston Giants, others called them the Royal Giants, and still others termed them the Royal Colored Giants. Regardless of the name, the team became the only Black club to represent the city by the early 1940s. With the Philadelphia Giants losing momentum in Boston, Burlin White, manager of the Boston Giants, sensed that Black baseball competition "may become a thing of the past." In response, White issued a "challenge to the Philadelphia Giants to play a grand baseball fest" at Lincoln Park to start the 1936 baseball season. The Boston Giants had dominated area play by compiling a record of eighty-seven wins, twenty-two losses, and five ties. The Phillies had been on a steady slide and could not match their nearby rivals. The Phillies declined the offer and headed for the road. White was surely disappointed in the outcome, since he hoped that the city's support of the contest with the Phillies would "encourage the players and tend to keep good teams in Boston instead of on the road."[63] With the Philadelphia Giants out of town for most of the season and the Boston Giants making their customary trips throughout New England and Canada, the Wolverines and Rangers supplied local fans with a steady diet of baseball.[64]

In an attempt to stimulate broader interest in local Black baseball, "Lefty" Brown and Fran Matthews, both local youngsters who made it to the professional Negro Leagues, beckoned their amateur and semipro counterparts to "get in line and stack their talent against that of boys from other sections." By the early 1940s, sportswriters lamented the Black community's loss of attention to baseball and labeled it the "low point" in the city's rich historical tradition of Blackball. Veteran reporter Mabe Kountze sadly observed that Blackball was "dead as a door-knob" and added that "the old-timers take their tattered uniforms out of moth balls again, sepia Boston will dream of the once famous Boston Tigers." For Kountze, the answer to the dilemma rested in the hands of those former players, who needed to "take off their coats, grab a ball and bat, and show the kids how the game should be played."[65]

Fortunately, in 1942, the Boston Royal Giants made an impressive come-back and ensured that Black baseball remained alive and well in the city. Team manager Burlin White enlisted the services of his famous batterymate, William "Cannonball" Jackman, who left the Philadelphia Giants to play for White. Jackman's reunion with White finally gave the city something to savor. In addition, the team received a gracious request to represent the city in the ranks of professional Black baseball.

According to baseball historian Todd Peterson, sports promoter Abe Saperstein decided to create a rival Black professional baseball league in 1942 to keep his hand in the lucrative promotions game. Saperstein gained notoriety as the creative force behind basketball's Harlem Globetrotters but also played a powerful, but controversial, role as a promoter of Negro League baseball contests. Saperstein believed that Negro League owners intended to maximize their interests by restricting him from scheduling and publicizing games, especially the popular East-West All-Star Game in Chicago. In response, he formed the Negro Major Baseball League of Amer-ica (NMBLA) and requested the Boston Colored Giants to join him in his venture. In addition to Burlin White's Giants, the league consisted of Bingo De Moss's Chicago Brown Bombers, Bunny Down's Cincinnati Clowns, Bill Casey's Baltimore Black Eagles, Charlie Henry's Detroit Red Sox, and Jimmy Brown's Minneapolis–St. Paul Gophers. League president Robert Jackson slated May 17 as opening day.[66] Peterson noted that despite the reported support and involvement of such notable African American figures as Jackson, who formerly served as commissioner of the Negro American League; sportswriter Russell Cowens; and professional football star Fritz Pollard, the league was little more than a shadow operation.[67]

On May 2, 1942, the *Boston Chronicle* reported that the new NMBLA had already started spring training and that Boston was well represented by White's Boston Royal Giants.[68] Local fans supported the Giants' decision to join the new league and welcomed the chance to watch some of the nation's better Black teams. "Sheep" Jackson, writing for the *Chronicle*, stated that "the bean town has been hungry for good Negro baseball. Not since the days of Bob Russell's Boston Tigers, the Boston Giants, and the original Lincoln Stars has the city been treated to their first sport here—baseball."

Jackson believed that the Black fans of Greater Boston and Providence, Rhode Island, would support the team and ask only in return that their team play aggressively and intelligently.[69]

White assembled an outstanding group of players. He mixed seasoned veterans like "Cannon" Jackman with rookie stars like Boston University baseball captain Charles Thomas. His roster included former Tigers' pitching ace Elmer Munroe and Fran Matthews, who recently played professionally with the Newark Eagles. On the eve of opening day, White challenged the conventional wisdom that the Cincinnati Clowns had the championship wrapped up even before the season started and predicted that his team also possessed championship mettle. There is no evidence to support White's statement, since there exists no record of the Giants playing any games in the new league. "Sheep" Jackson asked, "What's happened to the new Boston team, the Royal Giants?" By opening day, three teams, including the Giants, left the NMBLA and returned to independent play. Only a few games were played under league auspices. The Royal Giants took to the road for most of the summer, leaving Jackson to wonder in July why "they seem to have dropped out of existence."[70]

During the mid-1940s the team traveled extensively, playing fewer and fewer games in the Hub. In 1944, however, the team embraced the name Boston Colored Giants and later maximized its presence in the city as a member of the city's Park League and City League. Under the watchful eyes of owners Bob Russell and "Fats" Johnson, former owners of the Boston Tigers, the team had "certainly given the fans of Bean City something to talk about." The team added professional sensation Jesse "Lefty" Brown to the pitching rotation and helped desegregate Boston's Fenway Park by playing a game there against the New York Cuban All-Stars. In the following year, 1945, the Boston Colored Giants traveled to Yankee Stadium in New York to participate in a four-team doubleheader. In the opening game, the Colored Giants defeated another African American team, the Miami Giants, by a score of 10–0. Boston's Colored Giants continued to play successful baseball in 1946, but in that year, Jackie Robinson had already broken the color line in professional baseball as a member of the Montreal Royals, the Brooklyn Dodger affiliate in the International League. Support for Black baseball shifted to Black players in the white professional leagues, and local Black teams suffered a decline in attendance. Fan support, especially financial support through ticket sales, dwindled in 1946 and 1947, leaving one sportswriter to comment that "a ballclub cannot run on cheering, it takes money to keep the club on the road." In 1947, William "Bullet" Campbell assumed the reins of team manager, but no one could replace the style and promotional expertise of Burlin White. The integration of modern Major League Baseball in 1947 through the persons of Jackie Robinson and Larry Doby signaled a dream come true for most Black baseball fans, but it also prefigured the end of Boston's Black teams. The city's African American fans had experienced their most bittersweet moment.[71]

During the 1930s and 1940s, Boston was home to two of the most legendary players in all New England Black baseball, pitcher Will "Cannonball" Jackman and his batterymate, Burlin White. Born on October 7, 1897, in the small town of Carta, Texas, Jackman began his semiprofessional baseball career in 1918 playing on teams in the Houston and San Antonio region before barnstorming his way through Oklahoma, Maryland, New Jersey, and New York. He settled in Boston sometime in 1924, when he opened the baseball season with the Boston Monarchs but finished with the city's Philadelphia Giants.[72] He spent the remainder of his career in Greater Boston, except for the year 1935, when he played professionally for the Brooklyn Eagles of the Negro National League.[73] He dominated his opponents from the mid-1920s through the late 1940s and pitched his last game in 1953 at the age of fifty-six.[74] Although Jackman's career statistics remain incomplete, existing records indicate that he compiled a record of two hundred wins against eighty-six losses in a career that included games against professional and semiprofessional teams, both Black and white. He struck out 1,354 batters and posted a 2.89 earned run average.[75] Jackman recalled pitching in nearly 1,200 games during his lifetime.[76] One measure of his greatness involves a spectacular performance in one of the nation's most beloved baseball cathedrals. On July 8, 1945, Jackman took the mound at Yankee Stadium and shut down his opponent, the Miami Giants, allowing only one infield hit through seven innings and eventually winning the game on a three-hit shutout. By this time, he had perfected his underarm motion, which bewildered Miami's batters throughout the afternoon. The *Chicago Defender* captured the moment and reported, "Bill Jackman a white-haired submarine specialist, turned in a three-hit shutout versus Miami. He struck out ten batters and aided his own cause by accounting for five runs, with four hits in five trips to the plate."[77] Sportswriter Glen Stout reported that Jackman, at his peak, commanded a fee of $175 per game and an additional $10 for each strikeout. "If I was young today," Jackman said in 1971, "I'd probably be worth a million."[78]

The community paid its tribute to Jackman in two commemorative events. One was held on August 24, 1944, at Fenway Park, the other on July 14, 1971, at Carter Field, where he played many games as a member of the Philadelphia Giants and Boston Colored Giants. The 1944 tribute was not well attended, and sportswriter "Sheep" Jackson chastised Black fans by writing, "It was a sad gathering. . . . It was to be Will Jackman Day . . . a player whose hurling has thrilled thousands in this section for the past twenty years. It was to be a tribute to Will and the colored fans were to honor this great pitcher—one of their own. But alas, Ole Joe and his friends stayed at home."[79] Prior to the game, Mayor Maurice J. Tobin presented Jackman with a billfold, but the token did not provide Jackman with luck, as he lost the game.[80] The 1971 event had a much different outcome. Ralph "Stody" Ward, longtime friend and fellow teammate, not only introduced Jackman and regaled the crowd with stories of his accomplishments but also placed the event in a broader historical context: "This affair for Will Jackman will close out an era of good baseball by Black players," Ward commented. "It is amazing to note the intestinal fortitude of these Black ballplayers. They continued to play day after day and year after year with the knowledge that fate had decreed that they could never enter the Big Leagues, Minor Leagues, or even Little Leagues during this particular era." Jackman, often referred to as "Baseball's Great Unknown" or the "Best Ballplayer You Have Never Heard Of," came along too soon to play in the white Major Leagues, but he was clearly not unknown or unappreciated by the city's Black fans, who regarded him as the region's greatest pitcher and top baseball attraction.[81]

In the twilight of his career, Jackman grew to depend on his batterymate, Burlin White. In 1948, Taunton's local newspaper, the *Gazette*, remarked that "despite their age, these two timeless baseball stars are still the greatest drawing cards in New England."[82] Burlin White was born on February 5, 1895, in Richmond, Indiana. In 1914, he began his playing days in West Baden Springs, one of Indiana's most popular mineral water resorts, with a team called the Sprudels.[83] More than thirty years later, he ended his career in Boston's Carter Field as the catcher and manager of the city's Royal Giants. Nearly three thousand fans attended a testimonial game in his honor on July 19, 1946, recognizing the years he spent playing the game, a dozen of which he spent in the Boston City League. White enjoyed a long and fruitful baseball career, alternating between independent professional Black teams and semiprofessional clubs between 1915 and 1942. A lifelong catcher, he played for Rube Foster's Chicago American Giants in 1916 and 1917. Foster would later establish the first professional Black league, the Negro National League, in 1920 and earn the name "Father of Negro League Baseball." White also played alongside Henry "Pop" Lloyd with the Atlantic City Bacharach Giants. Lloyd, considered by many baseball historians as the greatest ball-player, Black or white, mentored White in the fine points of the game and honed his leadership skills. White became the manager for two Boston-based teams, the Philadelphia Giants and the Boston Royal Giants.[84]

Known as the "Dean of Colored Baseballers," White scheduled games for his Colored Giants in cities throughout the United States and Canada and even booked and played a Fourth of July game at Yankee Stadium.[85] Although White achieved great success as a player-manager for an African American team, he consistently championed the cause of integration, especially in Boston. In an interview given in 1938, White expressed this belief: "The combined colored support of fans from Rhode Island and Massachusetts would be sufficient to show both of Boston's major league club owners that our people when once interested are quite capable of making a true major league attendance representation."[86]

At the end of the 1934 baseball season, Deedy Crosson, former stellar player for the Boston Tigers, penned a column for the *Boston Chronicle* that drew fan attention to the finest ballplayers in the region. Crosson listed Burlin White of the Boston Colored Giants as the best Black catcher in New England. According to Crosson, "There are very few fast baseball players who can steal bases on the throwing arm of Whitey." More importantly, White's ability to catch a game from behind the plate helped young pitchers improve their craft. Crosson credited White with developing the skills of Will "Cannonball" Jackman when both played together as members of the Philadelphia Giants. The standout pitchers included Jackman of the Philadelphia Giants and Elmer Monroe of the Boston Tigers. Both men reportedly "can make the ball hum across the plate." Moreover, they "defeated the strongest teams in New Hampshire, Vermont, Maine, and Massachusetts."[87] Several years later, in 1942, the *Boston Guardian* recalled these same men in a prophetic editorial that stated that the "probable elimination of the Major League Color Ban will serve to revive many memories of Boston players who might have made the grade . . . include[ing] pitchers Big Bill Jackman and Elmer Monroe . . . [and] catcher Burlin White."[88]

Ever mindful of Greater Boston's other star players, journalist William "Sheep" Jackson reminded his readers of the local men who thrilled the city's neighborhood fans. Jackson penned his "All-Colored Team" with the following players. He listed Elmer Monroe, Everett and Sam McClellan, and Newton and Al Dupree (Mechanics Arts) as pitchers; Buster Reddick (Rindge Tech) as catcher; Fran Matthews (Rindge Tech) as first base; Dodo Fraser (Lynn English) as second base; Reddie Hilliard (Cambridge Latin) as shortstop; Leon Furr (Medford) as third base; Zing Rice (Medford) as center field; Bob Russell (Boston English) as left field; and Jit Taylor (Everett) as right field. In the semiprofessional ranks, Jackson selected Mose Sisco as the most gifted ballplayer.[89] Sportswriter Mabe Kountze compiled a list too. He asked Stody Ward, former Boston Tiger and keen observer of the city's Black baseball scene, to list the players who had the potential to compete at the Major League level. Ward responded with the following list:

First Base: Pappy Ricks, Jim Moore, Fran Matthews
Second Base: Deedy Crosson, Rabbit Tucker
Third Base: Marcelle, Gus Gadsden (and the author adds the name of Stody Ward, he overlooked)
Centerfield: Mose Cisco, Sheriff Blake
Leftfield: Zing Rice, Lem Roach, Tubby Johnson
Rightfield: Ceph Cephus, Jesse Hubbard

Catchers: Burlin White, Bust Reddick, Bob Russell

Pitchers: Bill Jackman, Al Dupree, Bullet Campbell, Elmer Monroe, Lefty Brown, Windshield Willie Robinson, and others[90]

Although Boston's top Black ballplayers were denied admission to the white Major Leagues, several played professionally in the Negro Leagues. One team, the Newark Eagles of the Negro National League, expressed special interest in local Boston talent. According to sportswriter Mabe Kountze, Abe Manley and his wife, Effa, co-owners of the Eagles, were "sweet" on the baseball talent in Greater Boston, and their club led all others in signing New England players. Kountze reported that "the Eagles, formerly of Brooklyn, first began with Bill Jackman of Boston . . . since then Newark has given trials to Bus Reddick, catcher . . . Honey Green, outfielder and pitcher . . . and Fran Matthews, first baseman." In June 1938, Kountze added the name of pitcher Jesse "Dizzy" Brown to the list of Newark players.[91]

The Boston Blues and the United States League, 1946

In 1945, the color line in modern baseball was truly erased when Jackie Robinson signed a contract with the Brooklyn Dodgers baseball organization on October 23. Earlier that year, however, Branch Rickey, the same person who signed Robinson, launched one last attempt to create a segregated league of professional Black ballplayers called the United States League (USL). Rickey announced the formation of the USL on May 7, 1945, and introduced its president, John Shackelford, an African American lawyer from Cleveland, Ohio. Rickey designed the League as an alternative to the Negro National and American Leagues and a potential farm system for Major League Baseball teams that opted to eventually sign Black ballplayers.[92] It was during the 1946 season, the league's second year in operation, that President Shackelford offered a franchise to the Boston Blues.[93] No one in Boston seemed familiar with the team. Allen Johnson, the team owner, ran a nightclub in Mounds, Illinois, and none of the players hailed from Boston. Sportswriter William "Sheep" Jackson understood the tenuous connection to the city and wondered, "In this new colored league there is an entry known as the Boston Blues. Have you heard of them?" He further noted that "the funny part of the set-up is that the club is playing all of their games in the west and New York. How come, Boston?"[94] In a recent interview with Robert Scott, a former pitcher and first baseman for the Blues, Scott confessed that he did not remember playing a single game in Boston. The USL folded midway through the 1946 season and the Blues disbanded.[95]

Dreams and Lost Opportunities: Integration, 1946

Long before Jackie Robinson signed a contract with the Brooklyn Dodgers and integrated modern professional baseball, Boston's local clubs experienced interracial baseball. Robinson's heroic accomplishment may have signaled the end and not the beginning of a process that occurred earlier at the local level. Baseball, after all, was the local pastime long before it became the national one. Unlike many places where the color line in semiprofessional and amateur had been drawn indelibly by the middle of the twentieth century, Boston experienced a long history of integrated team and league play. One team, the Library Bureau of Cambridge, provides a good example of an amateur integrated team that achieved widespread acclaim during the early 1920s. Backstop Buster Williams and outfielder Clarence (first name unknown), both African American, led the team to a championship season in 1920 and a trip to Chicago to play the Bureau's midwestern champs in Chicago.[96] During the 1920s and 1930s, African American teams slowly integrated the previously all-white amateur and semiprofessional leagues. These leagues usually admitted only one team composed of all African American players. The Providence Colored Giants achieved the distinction of being the only Black team to win a league championship. In 1931, the team captured the title of Boston's Twilight League. The legendary Tigers would play in the newly established Boston City League in 1932. The City League, led by former president of the New England League Claude Davidson, promised to "give to the youth of Boston a fine chance for athletic development and to the interested baseball fan a long list of carefully scheduled baseball games."[97]

On occasion, Boston's semiprofessional teams fielded an integrated roster. A few months after Jackie Robinson's ill-fated tryout with the Boston Red Sox, he returned to Boston as a player for the Kansas City Monarchs. The Monarchs scheduled a game against the Boston Navy Yard Athletic

Club on August 13, 1945, at Braves Field. Robinson's return captured most of the attention. Lost in the story, however, is the Naval Yard team, which included an impressive array of Black and white players. The Navy Yarders were managed by Curt Fullerton, former Red Sox and Yankee pitcher, and included several of the finest white players in the city. The team also posted two African American starting players. Second baseman Billie Burke, a former standout with the Boston Tigers, and catcher Buster Reddick, who played professionally for the Newark Eagles, represented the Navy Yard club. Both men played at Rindge Tech and were local favorites.[98]

The integration of Major League Baseball stimulated interest in eliminating the color line in Boston amateur baseball. In 1946, Jesse "Lefty" Brown, one of the top sinker ball pitchers in the professional Negro Leagues, playing for teams like the Newark Eagles, Baltimore Elite Giants, and New York Black Yankees, organized the New England Black and White Stars. This team, the city's first truly integrated ballclub, played its home games at Carter Field. According to the *Boston Chronicle*, "The Stars utilized some of the best players of both races who have become famous in recent years on the local sandlots." In 1946, the team compiled an impressive record against several of New England's top semipro teams and then traveled down South and out West to play against many professional minor league teams.[99]

The story of Brown's Black and White Stars was replicated in other cities around the region. In Providence, Rhode Island, the Circle Athletic Club (AC), led by pitcher Charles Butler, became the city's first truly integrated team in 1949. Ernest "Biffo" Duarte, prizefighter and sports promoter from Providence's Fox Point neighborhood, acted as the inspiration behind the city's first integrated team. He personally scouted the players, Black and white, because he wanted a mixed-race team of only the best players. He struggled to land his ballclub in the Tim O'Neil Amateur League, and only after relentless requests for a franchise did his dream come true. By season's end, the Circle AC had conquered all its divisional opponents in the Independent National League and then set its sights on the American League victors for the local amateur championship. The Circle players subsequently won the city championship and, in the process, made history as the first integrated team in the city to do so.[100]

It is important to recognize that there were alternatives to the model of integration utilized by the Brooklyn Dodgers in hiring Jackie Robinson. Major League teams had several options, including signing multiple Black players at once to create a genuinely integrated team like Boston's Black and White Stars or Providence's Circle AC. They might have also expanded the league to include the top African American professional teams. In Boston, fans gathered to watch the Black and White Stars compete against their local and regional opponents in a bid for racial equality. The baseball diamond served as a vital arena in the struggle for freedom, and the game reflected the city's racial flexibility and spirit.

Postscript

In 1946, most African American baseball fans in Boston turned their attention to Jackie Robinson and future Dodger teammates Roy Campanella and Don Newcombe. Both Campanella and Newcombe attracted regional attention as they helped desegregate the New England League by playing for Brooklyn's affiliate in nearby Nashua, New Hampshire. The promise of integration, accentuated by America's Cold War role as the self-described leader of the free world, became a reality, and baseball played an integral role in the nation's racial transformation.

Closer to home, a former member of the city's renowned Boston Tigers affirmed the reassuring role of baseball in the local Black community. William "Bullet" Campbell, no longer able to play the game, returned home to where it all started so many years before. He joined Fran Matthews and Buster Riddick of the Boston Colored Giants and Herman "Bud" Tyrance of the Philly Giants on the Robert Gould Shaw House's baseball diamond to teach the youngsters how to play the nation's pastime. These former and current players established the first annual Shaw House baseball school for youngsters aged twelve to fifteen years old.

Thirty years earlier, Shaw House offered young men of the same age the chance to play and combine their talents as the Tigers. Campbell knew the important role baseball had played in his life. He also understood how the game created a sense of solidarity between the players and those who supported them. It was a relationship worth preserving.[101]

Notes

1. *Boston Globe*, May 30, 1993, 50; September 30, 1994, 57.

2. Mabray Kountze, *50 Sports Years along Memory Lane: Afro-American Sports History; Hometown, Local, National* (Medford MA: Mystic Valley, 1979).

3. *Boston Globe*, May 30, 1993, 50. Matthews played for the Boston-based Philadelphia Giants from 1934 to 1935 and the Boston Royal Giants from 1935 to 1937, 1942, and 1946 to 1949. He played professionally for the Newark Eagles in 1938, 1940–42, and 1945 and briefly with the Kansas City Monarchs in 1942 and with the Philadelphia Stars in 1945.

4. David Ortiz, "Negro Leagues Remembered," *Cambridgetab* 29, no. 42 (July 26, 2000): n.p., located in the Negro League File: Boston, National Baseball Hall of Fame Library, Cooperstown, New York.

5. On the early game in Boston, see Troy Soos, *Before the Curse: The Glory Days of New England Baseball, 1858–1918* (Jefferson NC: McFarland, 2006), 1–100.

6. For information on the early history of Black baseball, see Michael E. Lomax, *Black Baseball Entrepreneurs, 1860–1901: Operating by Any Means Necessary* (Syracuse NY: Syracuse University Press, 2003), 14–60.

7. Leslie Heaphy, *The Negro Leagues, 1869–1960* (Jefferson NC: McFarland, 2003), 24. The roster for the 1870 team is located in Dick Clark and Larry Lester, eds., *The Negro Leagues Book* (Cleveland: Society for American Baseball Research, 1994), 52.

8. Charlie Bevis, *The New England League: A Baseball History, 1885–1949* (Jefferson NC: McFarland, 2008), 20; *Providence Journal*, August 18, 1877, 1; Ryan Swanson, "Bases Loaded: Race, Reconstruction, and Baseball in Washington, D.C., 1865–1876," in *The Cooperstown Symposium on Baseball and American Culture, 2003–2004*, ed. William Simons (Jefferson NC: McFarland, 2005), 59.

9. *New York Freeman*, February 19, 1887, https://agatetype.typepad.com/. The roster for the team included A. A. Selden (manager), Marshall Thompson (manager), Robert Brown, Bunnie Cross, Ambrose Davis, Joseph Harris, Lewis, Dan Penno, Plunto, William H. Selden, Ed Smith, H. C. Taylor, Windsor W. Terrill, R. A. Walker, George Waters, and Charles Williams.

10. Lomax, *Black Baseball Entrepreneurs*, 63–70; Heaphy, *Negro Leagues*, 24.

11. *Sporting Life*, April 13, 1887, quoted in Lomax, *Black Baseball Entrepreneurs*, 66.

12. *Boston Daily Globe*, March 20, 1887, 2; March 25, 1887, 4; September 5, 1896, 5; February 5, 1904, 5.

13. "The Colored League Opening Day in Louisville," *Louisville Courier Journal*, May 8, 1887, in Dean A. Sullivan, *Early Innings: A Documentary History of Baseball, 1825–1908* (Lincoln: University of Nebraska Press, 1997), 148.

14. Jerry Malloy, ed., *Sol White's History of Colored Baseball with Other Documents on the Early Black Game, 1886–1936* (Lincoln: University of Nebraska Press, 1995), xxiv. For additional information, see Lomax, *Black Baseball Entrepreneurs*, 63–70; and Heaphy, *Negro Leagues*, 24.

15. Malloy, *Sol White's History*, 16, 20, 143, 145, 150; James Overmyer, "Early Days," in *Shades of Glory: The Negro Leagues and the Story of African American Baseball*, ed. Lawrence Hogan (Washington DC: National Geographic, 2006), 21–24; John Thorn, *Baseball in the Garden of Eden: The Secret History of the Early Game* (New York: Simon and Schuster, 2011), 188–89; Clark and Lester, *Negro Leagues Book*, 52–54; Brian Carroll, *When to Stop the Cheering? The Black Press, the Black Community, and the Integration of Professional Baseball* (New York: Routledge, 2007), 9.

16. *Boston Sunday Globe*, January 5, 1889, 5; *Boston Daily Globe*, May 14, 1889, 3.

17. *Boston Daily Globe*, May 7, 1890, 6; May 13, 1891, 9; July 20, 1891, 3; April 6, 1896, 9; *Boston Sunday Globe*, August 15, 1897, 6.

18. *Boston Daily Globe*, May 27, 1901, 6; June 30, 1902, 8; August 11, 1902, 6; March 27, 1903, 2. According to the *Globe*, the following players appeared on the Windsors' roster: "Oliver, C; Belden and Eppa, P; Bankis, SS; Williams, 1B; Walker, 2B; Allen, 3B; Ray, RF; Brown, CF; and Charley Oliver, LF."

19. I am indebted to Lorenz Finison for sharing his resources on Teamoh, especially as it relates to his interest in cycling. See "Mr. Robert T. Teamoh, Reporter, *Boston Globe*," in *The Afro-American Press and Its Editors*, ed. Irvine Garland Penn (Springfield: Willey, 1891), 360–64; *Black Legislators in the Massachusetts General Court, 1867–Present* (Boston: State Library of Massachusetts, 2010), 1; Nell Painter, "Black Journalism: The First Hundred Years," *Harvard Journal of African American Affairs* 2, no. 2 (1971): 39; and *Freeman*, June 7, 1890, 6.

20. *Boston Daily Globe*, March 6, 1903, 9; *Boston Chronicle*, March 5, 1938, 6.

21. *Boston Chronicle*, April 27, 1935, 7. The list of promoters included "From Malden, Moe Ashton; 'Sheep' Jackson from Medford; Pat Parnham from Cambridge; Wyman Lee from Newton; the Messrs Lomax and Grey from Everett; the Messrs Collins and Taylor from Lynn; Dodo Frazier from Boston; rep of the Tigers or Highlands, from Roxbury rep of the Rangers."

22. *Boston Daily Globe*, June 21, 1915, 3; August 23, 1915, 4.

23. Kountze, *50 Sports Years*, 28–29.

24. *Boston Globe*, August 3, 1905, 5.

25. *Boston Chronicle*, April 28, 1945, 7.

26. *Boston Chronicle*, April 28, 1945, 7.

27. *Boston Chronicle*, April 28, 1945, 7.

28. *Boston Chronicle*, April 3, 1943, 1, 3.

29. *Boston Chronicle*, April 28, 1945, 7.

30. Glenn Sout, "Diamonds Aren't Forever," *Boston Magazine* (September 1986): 94–95.

31. *Boston Globe*, September 22, 1920, 9.

32. For information on Lawson and the Continental League, see Jerry Kuntz, "George H. Lawson: The Rogue Who Tried to Reform Baseball," *Baseball Research Journal* 37 (2008): 46–48.

33. *Boston Chronicle*, January 23, 1943, 7.

34. *Boston Globe,* May 25, 1921, 4.
35. *Providence Journal,* July 19, 1921, 7; July 24, 1921, 5.
36. *Providence Evening Bulletin,* July 31, 1923, 6.
37. *Providence Journal* August 2, 1923, 7.
38. *Nashua Telegraph,* August 4, 1921; *Providence Evening Bulletin,* September 30, 1922; *Providence News* September 30, 1922; *Providence Evening Bulletin,* July 31, 1929.
39. *Boston Chronicle,* August 27, 1938, 6; September 3, 1938, 6, 7; September 10, 1938, 6.
40. *Boston Chronicle,* August 5, 1939, 6; August 19, 1939, 6, 7; July 13, 1940, 6; July 20, 1940, 6; July 27, 1940, 6, 7; August 3, 1940, 6, 7; September 7, 1940, 7, 8; July 5, 1941, 6; July 12, 1941, 7; July 19, 1941, 6; July 26, 1941, 6; August 16, 1941, 6; August 23, 1941, 7; August 30, 1941, 7; September 6, 1941, 6; September 11, 1943, 7; September 18, 1943, 5, 7.
41. For biographical information on William "Sheep" Jackson, see *Boston Chronicle,* July 3, 1943, 7; July 24, 1943, 7; October 30, 1943, 7; March 11, 1944, 7; August 27, 1944, 7.
42. On the critical role played by sportswriters in recording the history of the Black baseball, see Lawrence Hogan and Robert Cvornyek, "Black Sportswriters and the (Re)construction of Negro League Baseball," in Simons, *Cooperstown Symposium,* 68–79.
43. *Boston Chronicle,* June 11, 1932, 6.
44. *Boston Chronicle,* April 27, 1935, 6; May 18, 1935, 6; June 8, 1935, 6; *Lewiston Daily Sun,* June 22, 1935, 11.
45. *Boston Chronicle,* April 27, 1938, 5.
46. *Boston Chronicle,* April 6, 1940, 7.
47. Frank Ryan, "The Colored Village Nine: Barnstorming with a Black Ball Team from West Newton," *Boston Herald American/Beacon,* April 3, 1977, 24–25; 27, located in the West Newton File, National Baseball Hall of Fame Library, Cooperstown, New York.
48. *Boston Chronicle,* April 9, 1932, 7; April 23, 1932, 7; April 30, 1932, 7; May 14, 1932, 7; May 28, 1932, 7; June 25, 1932, 7.
49. *Boston Chronicle,* June 2, 1934, 6; June 9, 1934, 6; July 14, 1934, 6.
50. *Boston Chronicle,* October 1, 1932, 1–2; *Providence Journal,* July 12, 1926, 5.
51. *Boston Chronicle,* August 19, 1933, 6; August 18, 1934, 6; James A. Riley, *The Biographical Encyclopedia of the Negro Baseball Leagues* (New York: Carroll and Graf, 2002), 199, 274, 397–99, 511. Located in the Dick Thompson Papers is a *Philadelphia Tribune* newspaper clipping dated May 14, 1931, that lists the following players on the Providence Giants: "The P.G.'s are carrying 15 men on their squad. They are Spencer Jones (Hilldale), Tom Dixon (Philly boy), Dixie Matthews (Providence College), catchers; Luther Farrell (Bacharachs), Bullet Campbell (Hilldale), Cliff Carter (Hilldale) and Edward Dudley, pitchers. The infield consists of Highpockets Hudspeth at first; Decker (an Indiana boy) at second; Elmore 'Scrappy' Brown at short; and Ollie Marcelle at third. The outfield includes Jess Hubbard, Tubby Johnson, and Babe Melton." Miscellaneous Newspaper file, Dick Thompson Papers, Museum of African American History, Boston, Massachusetts (hereafter cited as Thompson Papers).

52. *Providence Journal*, June 18, 1931, 11; June 20, 1931, 8; June 21, 1931, 6; *Baltimore Afro-American*, June 30, 1931, 15.

53. *New York Age*, July 25, 1931, 6; *New York Amsterdam News*, July 7, 1931, 13; *Providence Journal*, July 16, 1931, 9.

54. *Philadelphia Tribune*, August 13, 1931; *New Bedford Evening Standard*, August 26, 1931, clippings located in the Thompson Papers.

55. *Boston Chronicle*, April 30, 1932, 7; October 1, 1932, 1.

56. For an early biographical sketch of McClellan, see *New York Age*, June 3, 1939, 8. See also Dick Thompson, "Cannonball Bill Jackman: Baseball's Great Unknown," *National Pastime: A Review of Baseball History* 27 (2007): 43; *Providence Evening Bulletin* July 2, 1923, 7; July 17, 1923, 6; July 20, 1923, 4; July 23, 1923, 6; August 11, 1923, 11; August 13, 1923, 7; and August 25, 1923, 7.

57. *Philadelphia Tribune*, July 4, 1925; *Quincy Patriot Ledger*, August 10, 1925. Newspapers located in the Thompson Papers.

58. *Brockton Times Enterprise*, September 9, 1925; September 10, 1925; September 11, 1925; September 12, 1925; September 15, 1925; *Philadelphia Tribune*, September 26, 1925; *Quincy Patriot Ledger*, September 14, 1925; September 15, 1925; and September 16, 1925. Newspapers located in the Thompson Papers.

59. *Philadelphia Tribune*, July 25, 1925; and *Quincy Patriot Ledger*, September 15, 1925. Newspapers located in the Thompson Papers. For biographical information on Yancy and Seay, see Riley, *Biographical Encyclopedia*, 706–7, 888–89. For the complete 1925 rosters of each team, see Clark and Lester, *Negro Leagues Book*, 91.

60. *Providence Journal*, August 1, 1926, section B, 3; August 2, 1926, 7; August 9, 1926, 7.

61. *Philadelphia Tribune*, March 19, 1931, clipping located in the Thompson Papers; *Boston Chronicle*, April 28, 1934, 6.

62. *Boston Chronicle*, June 11, 1932, 6; May 12, 1934, 6; June 9, 1934, 6; August 24, 1935, 6; April 25, 1936, 6; March 26, 1938, 6.

63. *Boston Chronicle*, April 25, 1936, 6.

64. *Boston Chronicle*, May 16, 1936, 6.

65. *Boston Chronicle*, April 6, 1940, 7; *Boston Guardian*, March 8, 1941, 6.

66. *Boston Chronicle*, May 2, 1942, 7.

67. Todd Peterson, *Early Black Baseball in Minnesota* (Jefferson: McFarland, 2010), 196–97; Neil Lanctot, *Negro League Baseball: The Rise and Ruin of a Black Institution* (Philadelphia: University of Pennsylvania Press, 2004), 112–14; Rebecca Alpert, *Out of Left Field: Jews and Black Baseball* (New York: Oxford University Press, 2011), 79–81.

68. *Boston Chronicle*, May 2, 1942, 7.

69. *Boston Chronicle*, May 9, 1942, 7; May 16, 1942, 7.

70. *Boston Chronicle*, June 27, 1942, 7; July 11, 1942, 7.

71. *New York Age*, July 14, 1945, 11; *Boston Chronicle*, July 29, 1944, 5; August 15, 1944, 7; September 2, 1944, 7; July 14, 1945, 11; August 11, 1945, 7; March 30, 1946, 7; April 27,

1946, 7; May 8, 1946, 7; May 11, 1946, 7; May 25, 1946, 7; June 15, 1946, 7; August 31, 1946, 7; May 13, 1947, 7.

72. Thompson, "Cannonball Bill Jackman," 43. One of the earliest accounts of Jackman pitching in Boston for the Monarchs is located in the *North Adams Evening Transcript*, May 16, 1924, 3. His teammates were listed as Pryor, third base; Clark, shortstop; Thompson, first base; Perry, second base; Flemming, right field; Phillips, left field; Sisco, center field; Fuller, Catcher; Ballis, Catcher; Evans, pitcher; and Dillon, pitcher.

73. Thom Loverro, *The Encyclopedia of Negro League Baseball* (New York: Checkmark, 2003), 149.

74. See William Jackman, "Application Form for the National Baseball Hall of Fame, 1972," Thompson Papers.

75. Thompson, "Cannonball Bill Jackman," 45.

76. "Sports in the News," *Newport Daily News*, July 14, 1971, 21.

77. *New York Age*, July 7, 1945, 11; *Chicago Defender*, August 11, 1945.

78. Stout, "Diamonds Aren't Forever," 98.

79. Quoted in Thompson, "Cannonball Bill Jackman," 50.

80. *Boston Chronicle*, September 2, 1944, 7.

81. Ralph "Stottie" Ward, "Will Jackman Nite Program, Carter Field, July 14, 1971: Highlights and Background of Will Jackman," Thompson Papers; *Newport Daily News*, July 14, 1971, 21.

82. Thompson, "Cannonball Bill Jackman," 52.

83. *Boston Chronicle*, April 30, 1938, 6.

84. Riley, *Biographical Encyclopedia*, 833.

85. *Boston Chronicle*, July 20, 1946, 6.

86. *Boston Chronicle*, March 12, 1938, 6.

87. *Boston Chronicle*, September 29, 1934, 6.

88. *Boston Guardian*, August 8, 1942, 4.

89. *Boston Chronicle*, May 22, 1943, 7; June 5, 1943, 7.

90. Kountze, *50 Sports Years*, 46–47.

91. *Boston Chronicle*, June 11, 1938, 6.

92. *New York Times*, May 8, 1945, 22.

93. Lanctot, *Negro League Baseball*, 263–70, 289–91.

94. *Boston Chronicle*, June 15, 1946, 7.

95. Robert Cvornyek, interview with Robert Scott, Atlantic City, New Jersey, October, 2011.

96. *Boston Globe*, September 2, 1920, 9.

97. *Boston Chronicle*, April 2, 1932, 7.

98. *Boston Chronicle*, August 4, 1945, 7; August 11, 1945, 7; August 18, 1945, 7.

99. *Boston Chronicle*, July 20, 1946, 7.

100. Robert Cvornyek, "Integrating Providence Baseball," *Providence Journal*, July 18, 2010, 22.

101. *Boston Chronicle*, June 22, 1946, 7.

8

Covering Race and Sports in Boston

The Pioneering Work of Mabray "Doc" Kountze

DONNA L. HALPER

If you searched the pages of Boston's most influential newspapers during the 1930s and 1940s, you would seldom have seen the name of Mabray "Doc" Kountze—even if you tried the various misspellings or variants of his first name. Neither the *Boston Globe* nor the *Boston Herald* quoted him, nor did the majority of the other white-owned publications in the city, despite the fact that he was a prolific sportswriter and commentator who would later be described as "perhaps the preeminent black reporter" in Greater Boston as well as a "pioneer in Boston's black press."[1] Kountze (whose last name is pronounced like "counts") spent several decades writing for Boston's two Black newspapers—ten years with the *Boston Chronicle* and then nearly seventeen years with the *Boston Guardian*. He also reported for the Associated Negro Press, and that meant his coverage of sports (with a focus on the accomplishments of Black athletes) could be read in Black newspapers nationwide, including the *Chicago Defender*, the *Pittsburgh Courier*, the *Indianapolis Recorder*, and the *Baltimore Afro-American*. In addition, he was the first Black sportswriter to receive a press pass to cover the Boston Red Sox and the Boston Braves.[2] But if you were an average white sports fan in Boston, there was a good chance you had no idea who he was.

One reason he was not more widely known was demographics: compared to other cities, Boston still had a very small Black community. In the 1940 census, Boston's population was close to 771,000, but only 23,000 were Black—about 3 percent. And while the public schools were integrated, as were many of the city's businesses, opportunities for Boston's Black residents were limited—if not by law, then certainly by custom. Nowhere was this more evident than where Bostonians lived. Boston was a city of neighborhoods, where the white residents generally lived among "their own." Black residents of Boston lived among "their own" too, but it was not by choice: while white Bostonians had many different locations where they could seek housing, there were only two areas of the city where landlords would rent to Black tenants.[3] And while some white Bostonians might have a Black colleague at work or see a local Black entertainer at one of the city's nightclubs, it is doubtful that the vast majority of Boston's white residents knew much about Boston's Black community. They also were unfamiliar with the hardworking Black journalists who covered it; since Boston was only 3 percent Black, the community's newspapers were not as influential or widely known as the newspapers in cities with larger Black populations. (Interestingly, when I began my research on Doc Kountze a few years ago, I was disappointed to find that the Boston Public Library did not have complete runs of either the *Guardian* or the *Chronicle* on microfilm. And as I write this article, neither of these two seminal resources has been digitized.)

Yet despite working in their own separate spheres, that didn't mean all the members of the Black press were unknown to their white colleagues. Perhaps the best example of someone who was very well known was William Monroe Trotter, the owner and publisher of the *Boston Guardian*. Trotter, a tireless and outspoken advocate for equality and "easily the most familiar face on the streets of Boston's black community," was frequently quoted by the mainstream Boston press.[4] A few of the city's Black sportswriters were also well known to the public: several had previously been successful high school or college athletes whose exploits were described in Boston's sports pages. One example was William "Sheep" Jackson, a star football player for Malden High School, who went on to become a social worker in Cambridge, Massachusetts, as well as a reporter at the *Chronicle* before moving to Cleveland and writing for the *Call & Post*.[5]

But Kountze was not a star athlete, although he did play some schoolboy sports. Unfortunately, recurring childhood illnesses (which relatives believe may have been related to asthma) prevented him from playing regularly.[6] When he first began reporting, circa 1930, his name was probably not familiar to many people. And at that time, he was more likely to be called Mabe rather than Doc. Some of his relatives have surmised that he eventually became known as Doc because of his passion for learning and his knowledge of Black history. He developed a reputation in the community as an expert on a wide range of topics and was perceived as a wise and trustworthy authority—"something of a guru."[7]

In the early 1930s, Boston's mainstream sportswriting community probably did not see Mabe Kountze as an expert—he was barely out of his teens when he began writing for the *Chronicle*, encouraged by Sheep Jackson to give sports reporting a try. He had done some sports cartooning in high school and thought about becoming a professional cartoonist, but there were few openings in Boston for that. Sportswriting turned out to be a much better choice. He quickly focused on Boston's Black semipro teams; his beat was "whatever and whoever the *Boston Globe, Boston Herald,* or *Boston Post* didn't write about."[8] He also covered college sports, especially those schools that had Black athletes or Black coaches. Before long, the white sportswriters at least knew who he was, having encountered him at a local sporting event or seen him at Fenway Park as early as 1934.[9] At least one white sportswriter became familiar enough with his work to occasionally ask for his opinion: Bill Cunningham of the *Boston Post* quoted him about boxer Joe Louis several times and even referred to one of Kountze's columns in the *Chronicle*.[10] (That, of course, was the exception. Other than sometimes referring to a comment William Monroe Trotter had made, few of the mainstream reporters quoted what the writers at the *Chronicle* or *Guardian* had to say.)

As time passed, more of Boston's white reporters, along with their editors, came to know Kountze's name because he was a frequent letter writer. Sending letters and postcards was a common practice in that age before the internet; it was often a social activity, used for keeping in touch with people in distant locations. But for Kountze, letter writing was not just a way of saying hello. As a Black journalist in a segregated country, where most mainstream newsrooms were all white, he felt a duty to try to correct the record if he read something that misrepresented or ignored the contributions of Black Americans. So he wrote letters—to "friends, foes, editorial pages"—sharing information he believed people needed to see.[11] Eventually, a few Boston newspapers began publishing some of the letters he sent to the editors. For example, some were printed in the *Boston Globe*, beginning in the 1950s; up until then, his name had not appeared in their newspaper. And throughout the '50s, '60s, and '70s, his letters on a variety of topics got published. Some offered praise to a columnist or reporter; others offered his critique of something he disagreed with. And sometimes he wrote because he saw what he felt was an omission: In one letter, he encouraged the newspaper to include more stories about Black history.[12] In another, he mentioned two local Black marines who had died in Vietnam but were not part of a story about local members of the military who had given their lives during the war.[13]

Mabray Kountze was born in 1910, one of ten children of Hillard and Madeline Mabray Kountze. His father had been born into slavery in Virginia, circa 1862. His mother was born after the Civil War, in 1868, and was the free daughter of former Virginia slaves. The Kountze family eventually settled in West Medford, Massachusetts; historians consider this part of Medford (a city about seven miles north of Boston) among the oldest continuously African American communities in the United States, outside the South.[14] He attended Medford High School, but due to his ongoing health issues, he graduated later than some of his classmates, in 1932. Unlike some of his siblings, he did not attend college, although he took some adult education courses at Harvard.[15] He was what we today would call a lifelong learner—an avid reader who eagerly soaked up as much knowledge as he could find. One thing he noticed in school was how little Black history was taught, including the history of Medford's Black community. He decided to do his part to rectify what he saw as a serious omission, and as time passed, he carved out a niche for himself as Medford's local Black historian. Over a thirty-year period, he researched and ultimately published a six-hundred-page book, *This Is Your Heritage*, which included a long section devoted to the history of Medford's Black community.[16]

His love of sports, especially baseball, was inspired by two of his brothers, Al and Hillard. Al was a hard-hitting outfielder, Hillard was a pitcher with an outstanding curveball, and both played semipro ball. He was not only among their biggest fans, but he also helped them with their workouts, including sometimes serving as the catcher.[17] He sincerely believed each was good enough for the Major Leagues—Hillard, for example, pitched at least two no-hitters while a member of the Boston Colored Tigers.[18] But of course, neither of his brothers would get the chance to even play in the minor leagues, let alone the majors. And while his connection to his brothers was personal, he witnessed so many other Black players who had Major League potential but never received the recognition—or the pay—that they deserved. And speaking of pay, writing for the Black press was not especially lucrative either; Kountze supported himself by working at the West Medford post office.

Although Boston's Black population was not large enough to support a team in the Negro Leagues, there was a thriving semipro circuit, which, at one time or other during the 1930s and 1940s, included the Boston Colored Tigers, the Boston Royal Giants, and the Roxbury Wolverines. The *Chronicle* and the *Guardian* were among the only newspapers that regularly covered Black semipro baseball, and Mabe Kountze was one of the sportswriters who went to the games, writing about players who might otherwise have been ignored. Like other Black sportswriters of his era, he continued to be frustrated by the policies of Major League Baseball (MLB) as he watched outstanding Black players who should have been given a chance but never were. In his writings, he cited players like veteran catcher Burlin White, a "smooth, efficient machine behind the plate," who could easily throw out any batter trying to steal. White had played in the Negro Leagues before coming to Boston as the Royal Giants' player-manager, and Kountze felt privileged to interview him about his twenty-four-year career.[19] Burlin White's frequent batterymate was equally well known by Black fans (and some white ones as well). Bill "Cannonball" Jackman was a successful Negro Leagues pitcher who also joined the Royal Giants at times as they barnstormed through New England. Some Major League managers who had watched Jackman pitch said he was the equal of successful white pitchers like Walter Johnson and Bob Feller.[20] If he couldn't get Jackman a Major League tryout, Kountze was determined to at least make sure he received good coverage in the Black press; but somehow, that didn't seem to be enough.

Rather than just sitting around being frustrated by how unfairly Black athletes were treated, Kountze decided to take some action. Individual sportswriters like Frank "Fay" Young of the *Chicago Defender*, Wendell Smith of the *Pittsburgh Courier*, and Sam Lacy—then with the *Washington (DC) Tribune* but later with the *Baltimore Afro-American*—were speaking out in their columns about why Major League Baseball needed to change; so in 1933, Kountze came up with the idea of creating a new advocacy organization. He called it the National Negro Newspaper All-American Association of Sports Editors (NNNAAA), and though it had an awkward name, it had a noble purpose: to advocate for Black athletes and to make the mainstream press more aware of them.[21] By the mid-1930s, he had worked his way up to the *Chronicle's* sports editor position. Even though he was working for a comparatively small newspaper, he contacted the sports editors at the major Black publications, inviting them to work with him to promote the accomplishments of Black athletes to white publications. The new organization was directed by Kountze and covered various sports, including baseball, football, and track and field.[22] Focusing on historically Black colleges and the conferences they played in, the NNNAAA even made news by naming its own All-Americans and selecting its own All-Star teams.[23] Thanks to the fact that Kountze wrote for the Associated Negro Press, the new organization's selections got printed in numerous Black publications.[24] Unfortunately, the editors at many white publications continued to believe their readers weren't interested in what Black college teams and Negro Leagues players were doing. (Perhaps these editors should have observed the crowds at many Negro Leagues games. White fans regularly attended the games in several cities; the annual All-Star Game was especially popular with fans of both races.[25]) Meanwhile, the members of the NNNAAA, individually and as a group, continued to work tirelessly to persuade MLB executives to abandon their policy of segregation. Baseball historian Glenn Stout, who has written extensively about Kountze, believes the organization's efforts have long been underappreciated: "The seminal role of Kountze and the other members of the NNNAAA in the eventual breakdown of the color line has never been adequately acknowledged. A version that anoints [Branch] Rickey and [Jackie] Robinson as singular heroes is both more palatable and more easily told."[26]

And speaking of his seminal role, not enough has been said about Kountze's advocacy for local Black athletes; he saw sports as a good way to keep young people out of trouble. He also advocated for their coaches and managers: many had been former players, and he made sure they still got some attention, even after their playing days ended. It is thanks to his articles, including the obituaries he wrote when some of them died, that modern researchers know about these people who were so important in the Black community of their day. For example, his obituary for Mose Sisco was widely reprinted. Sisco, a popular semipro baseball player for two decades and another alumnus of the Boston Tigers, was "one of the best center-fielders in the country" and became the athletic trainer at Boston University, working with all their teams. He even coached schoolboy hockey, one of the few Black men of that time to be a trainer for a predominantly white school or to coach hockey. He also helped train the U.S. Olympic hockey team in both 1932 and 1936. All but forgotten today, Sisco lives on in the words of tribute that Kountze paid to him when he died too young, at age forty-five.[27]

As a Black reporter who saw firsthand the many indignities and slights that were part of being a person of color in America (in his Mose Sisco obit, Kountze could not help but mention that despite being an outstanding player, Sisco played for a team with no Major League affiliation and thus never received the recognition he deserved), Kountze somehow managed to remain optimistic about the future of race relations. Of course, he was realistic about it: someone who knew him years ago told a reporter in 2021, "[Doc] was keenly aware that he was a Black man in America. . . . He knew that because of his intelligence, he would have access to certain things. But because of his skin, there is certain access he wouldn't have."[28] In spite of the challenges, he continued to believe in integration, and he also believed that sports, especially baseball, could lead the way in bringing about positive change. He refused to give up on the idea.[29] So sometime in 1935, he arranged a meeting with the management of Boston's National League baseball team, the Braves, to propose that the Braves consider breaking the color line and signing some Black players. He contacted Phil Troy, the Red Sox club secretary, and Ed Cunningham, who held a similar role with the Boston Braves. As Kountze recalled the meeting years later, both men agreed that there were indeed talented Black players, and both agreed the color barrier should be removed. Troy, whom Kountze called "a fine gentleman," then pointed to the front office as the reason why the Sox would not be making any changes. Kountze perceived that Cunningham was "more hopeful" about changes eventually being made, but the meeting concluded without either baseball executive committing to take any action.[30]

Kountze waited to hear something further, but nobody got in touch. So at some point in 1938, he decided to revisit his previous efforts to persuade Boston's baseball executives to integrate. He arranged another meeting, this time with Bob Quinn Sr., president and part owner of the National League's Boston Braves, who were now known as the Boston Bees. Kountze suggested bringing Black baseball to Braves Field. He talked about some of the great Negro Leagues and semipro players who would surely attract a crowd. And reprising his deep respect for Boston's history, he referred to Boston's role in securing America's independence as well as its role in the abolitionist movement. He discussed how fitting it would be for segregation in baseball to end in Boston. Kountze wrote later that his meeting with Quinn was very cordial and that Quinn personally knew many Black ballplayers as well as several Negro Leagues team owners. He also seemed to agree that Black players should be signed and that bringing Black teams to Braves Field would be a good idea. But Quinn then told Kountze that he was just one owner, and as much as he might be sympathetic to Kountze's suggestions, the other owners would vote him down. He did predict, however, that not only would baseball integrate but the National League would have Black players before the American League did.[31]

By the early 1940s, even the generally optimistic Kountze had grown increasingly frustrated by the lack of movement in integrating Major League Baseball; he especially felt the Boston teams were stalling. On April 8, 1942, there was an exhibition game played at Fenway Park between the Baltimore Elite Giants and the Philadelphia Stars; it was the first time Negro Leagues teams had played there.[32] Other cities had held Negro Leagues games at their Major League parks, but Boston was one of the last to do so. Kountze saw it as a largely symbolic "goodwill gesture" that might entertain the fans, but it didn't bring the players any closer to getting their chance at the big leagues. Meanwhile, World War II was raging, and some Black sportswriters had decided this was not the right time to be pushing to integrate baseball, but Kountze disagreed. He remarked on the Black troops fighting bravely overseas and noted they were not "fighting for a 'separate' democracy." He said this was not the time to back down, and he encouraged his sportswriting colleagues to keep up the pressure on baseball executives.[33]

Some of the reporters did exactly that. Kountze was there at Fenway in early April 1945 when the Red Sox gave a tryout to three Black players: Sam Jethro, Jackie Robinson, and Marvin Williams. By many accounts, it was Sam Lacy of the *Baltimore Afro-American*, along with Wendell Smith of the *Pittsburgh Courier*, who were the prime forces behind the tryout, and locally, at least one of the white reporters, Dave Egan of the *Boston Daily Record*, was also supportive. So was a local politician—Boston city councillor Isadore "Izzy" Muchnick. Muchnick was a strong believer in integration, and he wanted to see Black players get a fair chance. But the tryout, like that 1942 exhibition game, turned out to be just more symbolism. The Red Sox executives, like Sox vice president and general manager Eddie Collins, did not seem enthusiastic (or serious) about it; in fact, they seemed like they were just going through the motions.[34] The three players did various fielding and throwing and hitting drills, and then it was over. Nothing came of it. Kountze was bitterly disappointed and irritated that the players were not shown more respect: Robinson had been in the army fighting for his country, yet when he entered Fenway Park, "many saw him as just another Colored boy," Kountze recalled. He had worked hard to persuade Boston's baseball teams to sign Black players, and it still didn't seem that there was a genuine interest in doing so. "In Boston, we all expected a fair trial," he wrote.[35] But fairness was not in the cards that day. Kountze also mused that while he thought the three players did a good job, it was a shame that some of the talented local players—like Bill Jackman—never got a tryout even though they deserved one.[36] And Kountze recalled the prediction that Bob Quinn of the Braves had made to him in 1938. But it would take several more years before that prediction finally came true, when Jackie Robinson was signed by the then Brooklyn Dodgers and took the field in April 1947. And in Boston, the Braves (who had returned to using their original name) had their first Black player, Sam Jethro, in April 1950, nine years before the Red Sox's Pumpsie Green finally took the field in August 1959. Before that occurred, Kountze continued to believe that the Red Sox were taking their time—they were, as it turned out, the last Major League team to integrate. And he did not hesitate to take the Sox management to task in the pages of the *Guardian*; he also wrote to the *Boston Globe* in 1956, saying that it had been eleven years since the three Black players had their (alleged) tryout, and while several members of the front office seemed sincere about making a change, nothing was happening, and the time for making excuses had long since passed.[37]

Although he earned a reputation over the years as one of the sportswriters who spoke out about the need for integration of the Major Leagues, Kountze was never just a baseball writer. During the 1930s and 1940s, he covered a wide range of sports: as mentioned earlier, he frequently wrote about big-name athletes like boxing champ Joe Louis, but he also wrote a lot about college football and basketball, with a focus on the players from Black colleges. And he never missed an opportunity to promote the NNNAAA, making sure that the annual All-Star and All-American selections were publicized and the reporters who voted for the players were acknowledged.[38] He also began publishing some commentaries that appeared in newspapers like the *Chicago Defender* (whose editor felt the need on several occasions to issue a disclaimer that Kountze's views didn't necessarily represent the views of the newspaper). In one 1935 article, he took the Black press to task for focusing on Joe Louis to the exclusion of other stories that affected Black people far more than what a celebrity boxer was doing. He referred to "our beloved but over-publicized Joe Louis" and stated that the writers as well as many Black leaders who obsessed over every Louis victory were being distracted from more urgent matters in the news, like the unjust prosecution of nine Black teenagers in Scottsboro, Alabama. He wrote, "The white man would rather have us put all our dough and energy on a man like Joe than to have the same valuable assets directed in an important issue like the Scottsboro case."[39] It would not be the last time Kountze would use sports as a vehicle for expressing his views about current events.

Like other Black sportswriters (and NNNAAA members), Kountze frequently weighed in when he saw injustice toward Black athletes in college sports, especially if the incident occurred in Greater Boston. To cite one of many examples, a controversy occurred in late 1939 involving a gifted (and very popular) college football player named Lou Montgomery. The young fullback had almost single-handedly elevated the fortunes of the Boston College (BC) team, leading them to a winning season and an ultimate bowl invitation. But whenever BC traveled to play a southern team, Montgomery had to sit on the bench. Black sportswriters (and a few white ones) were outraged about that, but to make matters worse, Montgomery was also not allowed to play in a November 4, 1939, game in Boston because BC's opponent, then called Alabama Polytechnic (today known as Auburn), insisted the southern rules apply up north too. Kountze was one of numerous Black reporters who spoke out. He wrote for the Associated Negro Press that Boston College had "cater[ed] to southern prejudice" by going along with Alabama's demand for segregation even in Boston. Kountze noted the irony of Montgomery having to sit on the bench in Boston, which was "once known as the Cradle of Liberty." The dual meaning was clear: once, long ago, Boston was the home of the patriots who fought the Revolutionary War, and once upon a time, Boston was known as a city that stood up for freedom . . . but not anymore. Kountze also quoted *Chicago Defender* sports editor Frank "Fay" Young, whose column had taken Boston College to task: BC was a Christian college, yet by allowing Lou Montgomery to endure discrimination, the school was being hypocritical. Kountze agreed and remarked on the irony of a school from the south getting its way up north: "The sons of those who fought to enslave us [have] won a victory."[40] And the fact that BC lost the game seemed like some sort of divine justice.

By the late 1930s, Kountze had begun putting more time into his other passion—Black history. He was a firm believer in what would later be called "Black pride," and he was teaching an adult education course in Boston, focusing on the stories of Black accomplishment he believed had been omitted. Some of his talks became columns, picked up by the Associated Negro Press. Among the topics he wrote about was whether "Negroes" (as they were then called) should go back to Africa. While noting that some Black leaders like Marcus Garvey had advocated for that, the younger generation today saw America as their homeland, and thus, they were focused on achieving full citizenship and equality in America. He observed that some southern, racist members of Congress wanted Black people to go back to Africa, but very few modern Blacks shared that sentiment. Rather, while they had left a great heritage in Africa, they were in the process of building a great heritage in America—one that Kountze believed would someday outdo whatever had been left behind.[41]

He also used his columns to set the record straight on historical figures he believed had been misinterpreted, such as Booker T. Washington. Having reread *Up from Slavery* thoroughly, he encouraged people to do the same—to look at what Washington had written rather than what some people claimed he had written (advice that is still valid even today). Among the assertions that Kountze said were misinterpreted was Washington's statement criticizing the efforts many Southerners made to prevent Black people from voting. Washington said about this, "The wrong to the Negro is temporary, but to the morals of the white man is permanent." As Kountze understood it, Washington was not saying that the wrong inflicted upon southern Blacks should be minimized, nor was he saying Black people did not deserve the right to vote. Rather, Kountze wrote, Washington was warning southern whites that there would be a lasting negative impact because of what they had done. Kountze explained, "The denial of Negro suffrage in the South has hurt the South. As Booker once said, you can't hold a man down in the gutter without staying there yourself."[42]

It is worth keeping in mind when we read Kountze's historical columns, as well as his previously mentioned six-hundred-page book on Black history, that he was self-taught, and he lived in an era when even microfilm was still not widely available, making it a challenge to locate and access source material. Kountze was undeterred; he read as many books as he could find on a wide range of subjects and corresponded with the authors, seeking additional information. Books, along with sports, were his life: he never married, and he devoted his time to his work as a reporter and a researcher (and he was still working well into his early eighties). Kountze was asked in a 1990 interview why he had spent thirty years working on *This Is Your Heritage*. He said, "It took a long time to finish it, because it is difficult being a black historian. So much of our history has been destroyed and lied about. Everything is so hidden."[43] Many of the people in Medford who read it were grateful for all the effort he put into it and impressed with all the research, but some questioned whether everything in it was factual, as did some people who heard him speak. For example, he made assertions about certain famous people being secretly Black or having Black ancestry (baseball slugger Babe Ruth, for example) that were difficult to prove or probably untrue (though widely believed by some). He also asserted that Hannibal Hamlin, Abraham Lincoln's first vice president, was Black, citing two newspapers. However, Hamlin's relatives have always denied it, and in an early 2022 conversation I had with the archivist at his memorial library in Paris, Maine, it was suggested that this story was spread by anti-Lincoln partisans rather than being historically accurate.[44] But errors or questionable assertions aside, it is undeniable that Kountze was a repository of interesting facts—especially about Black athletes, past and present. His 1979 book *50 Sports Years along Memory Lane* contains a wealth of information about the Negro Leagues as well as stories about the players he saw and wrote about and his observations about the eventual integration of baseball. The book is especially useful for its coverage of Black semipro baseball—information not widely available anywhere else.

Kountze was an eyewitness to so much sports history, yet he preferred to work behind the scenes and seldom called attention to himself, according to Glenn Stout, with whom he corresponded. He was even reticent to be interviewed in person, although he finally relented.[45] In the late 1950s, he retired from the *Boston Guardian* but continued as a freelancer for another Black newspaper, the *Bay State Banner*, well into the late 1970s. He also did some freelancing for several Medford newspapers. And even though he did not want the limelight, some of the new generation of writers and researchers wanted to recognize his work. So did the Boston Red Sox: on May 29, 1993, he took part in a tribute to the Negro Leagues, held at Fenway Park, in which Sam Jethro, Minnie Minoso, and Ernie Banks were among the honorees. Kountze was an honoree too: he caught the ceremonial first ball, which was thrown by former Negro Leagues player Fran Mathews. The Red Sox, in recognition of Kountze's long career as a sportswriter, gave him a permanent pass to Fenway Park, and when he spoke to the crowd at the ballpark, he said the tribute was "a great victory for the Negro Leagues." He also stated that the memory of the league—through former players who made it to the Major Leagues—would "live on forever." And he encouraged the kids in the crowd to "stay out of courts, get into sports."[46]

Mabray "Doc" Kountze died the following year, on September 26, 1994; he was eighty-four years old. Since then, a few people have written about his amazing life, recognizing his achievements, but much of his work remains unavailable to researchers because most of the publications for which he wrote are still not digitized, and other information (including correspondence between him and William Monroe Trotter of the *Boston Guardian*) resides in the Boston University Archives, where it too is not digitized. Still, every now and then, people find out about Kountze—perhaps from an online article by Glenn Stout, perhaps by trying to research Black baseball in Boston. But everyone who delves into his life comes away convinced that he was a uniquely talented person who spent many years advocating for Black athletes. Author and Boston television reporter Ted Reinstein wrote a 2021 book about the long struggle to integrate Major League Baseball, and Kountze became a key part of the story. As Reinstein told a reviewer, "I begin and end [my] book with Doc Kountze. . . . He strikes me, in many ways, as the quintessential unsung hero in the story, essentially unknown, later relatively anonymous. He was not a celebrity, not powerful, not wealthy. He was really, really dedicated to do something to abolish segregation in baseball. By collaborating with other people, he was able to help do this. He's the perfect example of an unsung hero."[47]

Notes

1. Howard Bryant, *Shut Out: A Story of Race and Baseball in Boston* (Boston: Beacon Press, 2002), 26; Bob Hayden, "Boston's Black History: Mabray 'Doc' Kountze," *Bay State Banner* (Boston), March 2, 1978, 6.
2. Glenn Stout, "Doc's Cause: Curing Baseball of Bigotry," *Middlesex News* (Framingham MA), July 28, 1987, 1D, 5D.
3. Catherine Elton, "How Has Boston Gotten Away with Being Segregated for So Long?," *Boston Magazine*, December 8, 2020, https://www.bostonmagazine.com/news/2020/12/08/boston-segregation/.
4. Hayden, "Boston's Black History," 6.
5. "Malden Wallops Somerville, 28–0," *Boston Herald*, October 19, 1924, B15.
6. Eugene A. Sylvester, "The Conscience of the Community Is Laid to Rest," *Medford (MA) Transcript*, October 5, 1994, 1, 8; Mabray "Doc" Kountze, *50 Sports Years along*

Memory Lane: Afro-American Sports History; Hometown, Local, National (Medford MA: Mystic Valley, 1979), 22.

7. Ted Reinstein, *Before Brooklyn: The Unsung Heroes Who Helped Break Baseball's Color Barrier* (Guilford CT: Lyons, 2021), xi–xii.

8. Glenn Stout, "Letters from Doc," in *Best American Sports Writing 1995*, ed. Dan Jenkins and Glenn Stout (Boston: Houghton Mifflin Harcourt, 1995), x.

9. Long, "Mabray Kountze, 84; Historian, Former Negro League Spokesman," *Boston Globe*, September 30, 1994, 57.

10. Mabe Kountze, "Says Louis-Schmeling Bout 'Powderhouse,'" *Indianapolis Recorder*, May 14, 1938, 12.

11. Reinstein, *Before Brooklyn*, xiv–xv.

12. Doc Kountze, "They Too Shared Toil, Sacrifice," *Boston Globe*, July 1, 1970, 16.

13. M. "Doc" Kountze, "Afro-American Veterans," *Boston Globe*, February 10, 1973, 6.

14. Jordana Hart, "Medford Enclave of Blacks Endures," *Boston Globe*, April 8, 1990, NW1.

15. Long, "Mabray Kountze, 84," 57. The author attempted to verify which courses he took, but the archivist found no record of his enrollment, and said records for noncredit/nondegree adult education courses from that era may not have been preserved. The author has also found other examples of broadcasters and journalists who took adult education courses, often as "special students" who were not enrolled in a degree program.

16. Hart, "Medford Enclave," NW1.

17. Stout, "Doc's Cause," 1D, 5D.

18. "Not a Hit Made of Kountze," *Boston Globe*, August 26, 1917, 14.

19. Kountze, *50 Sports Years*, 22–23.

20. Dick Thompson, "Cannonball Bill Jackman: Baseball's Great Unknown," *National Pastime: A Review of Baseball History* 27 (2007), available at https://sabr.org/journal/article/cannonball-bill-jackman/.

21. Stout, "Letters from Doc," xiii.

22. Kountze, *50 Sports Years*, 24.

23. Stout, "Letters from Doc," xiii.

24. "Sports Writers Release Ratings," *California Eagle* (Los Angeles), July 26, 1935, 8.

25. Ursula McTaggart, "Writing Baseball into History: The Pittsburgh Courier, Integration, and Baseball in a War of Position," *American Studies* 47, no. 1 (Spring 2006): 116–17.

26. Stout, "Letters from Doc," xiii.

27. Mabe Kountze, "Sisco, Trainer of U.S. Hockey Teams, Dies," *Chicago Defender*, January 27, 1940, 24.

28. Reinstein, *Before Brooklyn*, xv.

29. Bryant, *Shut Out*, 26.

30. Kountze, *50 Sports Years*, 24.

31. Kountze, *50 Sports Years*, 24–25.

32. "Star Negro League Nines at Fenway Next Tuesday," *Boston Globe*, September 3, 1942, 21.

33. Mabray Kountze, "Are Big Leagues Fooling Us? Writers Should Demand Truth," *Detroit Tribune*, September 19, 1942, 12.
34. Bryant, *Shut Out*, 30–31.
35. Kountze, *50 Sports Years*, 46.
36. Kountze, *50 Sports Years*, 48.
37. Mabe Kountze, "Colored Athletes and the Red Sox," *Boston Globe*, July 20, 1956, 8.
38. "William Green on All-U.S. Five," *Pittsburgh Courier*, May 12, 1934, 15.
39. Mabe Kountze, "New England Scribe Has a Bit to Say," *Chicago Defender*, July 6, 1935, 15.
40. Mabe Kountze, "Boston College Bows to Rebels," *Chicago Defender*, November 11, 1939, 24.
41. Mabe Kountze, "Know about Yourself: Should Negroes Return to Africa?," *Chicago Defender*, January 13, 1940, 13, 15.
42. Kountze, "Know about Yourself," 15.
43. Hart, "Medford Enclave," NW1.
44. "Ask the Globe," *Boston Globe*, July 12, 1983, 28.
45. Stout, "Letters from Doc," xi.
46. Richard Thorpe, "Red Sox Play Host to Negro Leagues Tribute," *Bay State Banner* (Boston), June 3, 1993, 3.
47. Rich Tenorio, "Review of Before Brooklyn: The Secret Heroes Who Helped Break Baseball's Color Barrier," *Guardian*, February 21, 2022, https://www.theguardian.com/sport/2022/feb/21/before-brooklyn-the-secret-heroes-who-helped-break-baseballs-color-barrier.

Fig. 1. Black students arrive by bus with a police escort at South Boston High School during the court-ordered desegregation crisis. Courtesy of Spencer Grant.

Two-thirds mile, class A—Final heat—O. M. Ertz, New York, 1; U. S. Paige, Brooklyn, 2; Louis Hunter, N. J. A.

)2⅗ to
came
:erson,
tchen,
encer,

itional
iald in
) beat
second
ce for
; final
; lead
:alized
; beat
ipping
it was
'olum-
here it
e how
s meet
pe car-
[t is a

Kitty Knox, the Colored League Member.

C., 3; time, 1:50. Time limit of 1:50 placed on heats, two

Fig. 2 Katherine T. "Kitty" Knox integrated the League of American Wheelmen (LAW) in 1893. When the LAW barred African Americans from cycling in competitions the following year, she successfully battled to retain her affiliation and initiated a movement to eliminate discrimination against Black cyclists. Courtesy of Smithsonian Libraries and Archives, Washington DC.

Fig. 3. Charles Titus's legacy of leadership on the basketball court and in the community remains unparalleled. He started his career at UMass Boston in 1974 and retired in 2020. During that time he served as the men's basketball coach for twenty-nine years and was named athletic director in 1980. He was instrumental in creating the university's Sport Leadership and Administration Program. He retired as the university's vice chancellor of athletics and recreation, special projects, and programs. His service as a leader and mentor in the community included participation in the Boston School Sports Partnership and the Titus Foundation. Courtesy of UMass Boston Athletics.

Fig. 4. The Pawtucket Free Wanderers pose with trophies won during the 1892–93 season. As the Watson brothers were growing up, the Wanderers were the dominant team in Rhode Island. Courtesy of Brian Bunk.

Fig. 5. Beginning in the early twentieth century, cricket emerged as a popular sport among the Afro-Caribbean community. Courtesy of *Boston Herald-Traveler* Photo Morgue, Boston Public Library.

Fig. 6. George Godfrey, nicknamed "Old Chocolate," arrived in Boston at an early age and trained at the famous Professor Bailey's Hub City Gym. Godfrey fought as a middleweight by today's rules, but he often found himself in the ring with much heavier opponents. His success against fellow Black boxers earned him the title Colored Champion of America. White boxers, especially champion John L. Sullivan, refused to fight him. During a career that started in the 1870s and lasted nearly three decades, Godfrey invested his money wisely in real estate. He died in his home in Revere, Massachusetts, on October 18, 1901, at age forty-eight. Wikimedia Commons.

Fig. 7. The Boston Colored Giants, a semiprofessional barnstorming club, was the city's premier Black team. During the late 1940s, pitcher Will Jackman (*top row, center*) reunited with catcher Burlin White (*top row, left*) and re-created the region's most celebrated African American battery. Courtesy of James E. Spencer.

Fig. 8. Mabray "Doc" Kountze devoted his life to writing about African American sports in local Black newspapers, including the *Boston Chronicle* and *Boston Guardian*. He was the first African American reporter to receive a press pass to cover the Boston Red Sox, the Braves, and the Bruins. Courtesy of the Kountze Family Collection / *Medford Transcript*.

Fig. 9. Ralph Dawkins Sr. participated in the United Golf Association Championship held in Canton, Massachusetts, under the auspices of the Bay State Golf Association in 1941. The tournament, regarded as a turning point in professional Black golf, featured golfers from around the country. Dawkins hailed from Jacksonville, Florida. The first national championship for African American golfers, the Negro National Open, took place in Stow, Massachusetts, in 1926. Courtesy of Marvin Dawkins.

BILL RUSSELL   6:09   215 lbs.

Fig. 10. Bill Russell symbolized the intersection of race and sport in Boston. He led the Boston Celtics to eleven National Basketball Association (NBA) championships during his thirteen-year career with the team. In 1966 Russell made history when the Celtics elevated him to head coach, the first African American to hold the position in the NBA. Russell distinguished himself off the basketball court as an activist for civil rights and racial freedom in the United States and throughout the world. Courtesy of Boston Herald-Traveler Photo Morgue, Boston Public Library.

Fig. 11. Willie O'Ree shattered the color line in the National Hockey League in 1958 when he skated onto the ice at the Montreal Forum as a member of the Boston Bruins. He was inducted into the Hockey Hall of Fame in 2018. Courtesy of Boston Herald-Traveler Photo Morgue, Boston Public Library.

Fig. 12. Arthur Ashe offers free instructional lessons to neighborhood youngsters at the Sportsmen's Tennis Club's Courts in Franklin Field in Dorchester on August 3, 1971. Ashe distinguished himself as a champion tennis player, author, and fearless proponent of the Black freedom movement. Photo by Ed Farrand / *Boston Globe*, courtesy of Getty Images.

Fig. 13. Jason Collins made history as the first openly gay male athlete in major professional sports. After completing the 2012–13 basketball season with the Boston Celtics, he declared his sexual orientation in an essay for *Sport Illustrated*. His announcement received positive endorsement from former teammates and the press. Courtesy of Bruce Bennett / Getty Images.

Fig. 14. Michael Holley confronted Boston's racial consciousness as a sportswriter and media personality. He wrote for the *Boston Globe* and later cohosted the city's midday sports program on radio station, WEEI. He left radio in 2018 to accept a television position with NBC Sports Boston. He currently cohosts the program *Brother from Another* and serves as an adjunct professor of communication at Boston University. He is a *New York Times* best-selling author and recipient of the Pulitzer Prize for Meritorious Public Service for his work with the *Akron Beacon Journal* in 1994. Courtesy of D. Dipasupil / Getty Images.

Fig. 15. Allison Feaster serves as vice president of team operations and organizational growth for the Boston Celtics. Before entering the Women's National Basketball Association as a first-round pick, she excelled on the court for Harvard University, where she earned Ivy League Player of the Year three times. Courtesy of *Boston Globe* / Getty Images.

Fig. 16. The Marshall W. "Major" Taylor memorial resides at the entrance to the Worcester Public Library in Salem Square. The bronze statue commemorates the life of Major Taylor, a civil rights advocate who fought to integrate cycling during the late nineteenth and early twentieth centuries. Taylor held many world records during his professional cycling career. He became known as the "World's Fastest Man." He endured racial discrimination throughout his lifetime, but his talent, determination, and courage successfully challenged racism in cycling. Courtesy of Toby Mendez / Major Taylor Association.

9

Pioneers of African American Golf at the Crossroads

The 1941 Negro National Open Golf Championship Tournament

MARVIN P. DAWKINS AND JOMILLS H. BRADDOCK II

In 1941, the city of Boston hosted an African American golf tournament, the United Golfers Association (UGA) Negro National Open Golf Championship Tournament, which made a much-needed contribution to the historical record of the early pioneers of African American golf. This tournament marked the last time that the UGA's earliest Black champions of golf would meet in mass competition on a national scale. The post–World War II UGA Negro National Open champions and the successful Black golfers who played in the Professional Golfers' Association (PGA) after the Caucasians-only clause was removed have received the lion's share of recognition as pioneers of Black golf. But their predecessors—Black golfers who competed exclusively behind the veil of segregation in venues organized by Blacks themselves—deserve greater recognition than they have received. The Negro National Open Golf Championship Tournament was a milestone event that delineated early Black golfers from those who came later and serves as a historical corrective regarding the early pioneers of African American golf.

Rise of Black Golf in the Modern Era

The modern history of golf in America can be traced to the 1870s, when the first golf courses were constructed by English and Scottish immigrants. Increasing interest in the sport led to the establishment of the United States Golf Association (USGA) in 1894. The game grew in popularity during the early twentieth century, especially among wealthy whites.[1]

Until recently, however, less attention has focused on the fact that African Americans have been a part of golf's history in the United States from the outset.[2] The game of golf was introduced to America during the postslavery period after the Civil War. Following the years of Reconstruction (1865–77), the brief progress that African Americans had experienced came to an end. This was replaced by a growing pattern of extreme racial segregation and discrimination that became woven into the fabric of American culture and daily life. Across all sectors of society, Blacks were excluded from participation in mainstream white America, including sports. By the final decade of the nineteenth century, worsening racial conditions led historian Rayford Logan to characterize this period as the "nadir" (lowest point) of Black American life.[3] Negative treatment of the Black population and their relegation to subservient roles provided the sociohistorical context that led to their introduction to the game of golf.

During this highly racialized period of American history, nowhere was the display of white supremacy more evident than on the golf course—a bastion of privilege and status. Golf was clearly a "white sport," and Blacks were to be its "servants" rather than "players." African Americans served as caddies for wealthy white golf patrons at elite golf courses in country club settings around the nation. Black caddies did not have equal access to opportunities to climb the ladder that led to a professional golf career.

This is not to suggest that only African Americans served as caddies. Some of the legendary white figures in golf's earlier days in America, such as Italian American Gene Sarazen and German American Walter Hagen, were from poor families and caddied in their youth. Unlike their Black counterparts, they did not have to cross the color barrier that most Black caddies faced. As a result of his own caddying background and his interaction with African American caddies, Hagen had high regard for them. He reflected, "If anyone gets the idea that the colored caddie doesn't know the game he is soon disabused. These boys know golf from A to Z, and they quickly learn all there is to learn about any player's game. They usually hand out the right clubs, and their judgment is just as good, if not better than that of the average boys in the North. . . . These boys are experienced bag-toters but that is not all. They can give advice and at times their humor is refreshing."[4]

Except for their roles as caddies, African Americans were largely excluded from mainstream golf during the first half of the twentieth century, and much of their story is still missing from the historical record. Despite that exclusion, they developed as golfers, organized their own activities behind the veil of segregation, and gained public notice largely through the Black press. The advancement of golf in cities and smaller communities during segregation was spearheaded by the Black elite, who took the lead in creating organizations that "paralleled" those established by whites, with one significant difference. The Black elite promoted golf across all social classes in African American communities, unlike their white counterparts.[5] Even with this strong, connected presence, the history of Black golf in specific cities and communities in America has been poorly chronicled in the literature on golf's beginnings in the United States.[6]

Black caddies increasingly gained respect as athletes, and saw some positive progression in their entrance to professional golf, albeit nonlinearly and without full recognition. Remarkably, in 1896, seventeen-year-old African American caddie John Shippen and fellow caddie Oscar Bunn, a Native American of the Shinnecock tribe, gained entry to play in the USGA National Golf Championship Tournament over the objections of white entrants.[7] It was only the second USGA National Golf Tournament Championship. Also in 1896, the U.S. Supreme Court established the principle of "separate but equal" (*Plessy v. Ferguson*), which legalized racial segregation.[8] While the story of Bunn's and Shippen's USGA "racial breakthrough" in golf at the height of Jim Crowism is significant, they have not received the recognition they deserved. Modern golf history recognizes Shippen as one of golf's "pioneering personalities," a demarcation that underscores the fact that these achievements were an aberration.

Despite the examples of Bunn and Shippen in 1896, a significant national racial breakthrough did not occur again until the mid-twentieth century. A 1955 U.S. Supreme Court ruling, *Holmes v. Atlanta*, outlawed segregation at public golf courses.[9] Nearly a decade later, in 1964, Charlie Sifford gained membership in the PGA. The private organization had removed its "Caucasians-only" bylaw in 1961.[10] Still, the floodgates of acceptance did not suddenly open for African Americans in mainstream American golf.[11] In fact, the rising popularity of golf in America during the early twentieth century was accompanied by the erection of formal and informal racial barriers. The widespread destruction of these barriers only happened in the latter half of the twentieth and early twenty-first centuries under pressure for reform.

Organized Black Golf in America: The UGA

Boston was among the leading cities in the sport's early days, when major organizations were established that laid the foundation for African American participation in golf. Through the 1920s, evidence of substantial Black golf activity could be found in cities located in the Northeast, South, and Midwest. Among the Black golf clubs during this period were Shady Rest (Scotch Plains, New Jersey), Mapledale (Stow, Massachusetts), Saint Nicholas (New York City), Fairview (Philadelphia, Pennsylvania), Bunker (Pittsburgh, Pennsylvania), Wilson Park (Baltimore, Maryland), and Riverside-Citizens-Capital City clubs, which evolved into the Royal Golf Club (Washington DC). Noted Black golf clubs in the Midwest and Deep South included Windy City (Chicago, Illinois), Acorn (Richmond, Virginia), and Lincoln (Jacksonville, Florida).[12]

The UGA was an organization created by Blacks in 1926 to advance interest in golf in the African American community and holds a particularly important connection to Boston. The UGA paralleled the whites-only PGA, which had been established ten years earlier.[13] Although short-lived, the Mapledale Golf Club in Stow (near Boston) deserves special note as the site where the UGA—the national "umbrella" organization for Black golf—was established. Scholars agree, "The UGA was organized when Robert Hawkins hosted a tournament at his newly opened, 9-hole Mapledale golf course in Stow, Massachusetts, which was attended by golfers, mostly from the east coast. . . . Although Hawkins was elected president of the UGA at the organizing meeting in 1926, Dr. George Adams of Washington DC became the UGA's first official president when the organization was formally chartered in 1927."[14]

The annual premier event of the UGA was the Negro National Open Golf Championship Tournament, which was played annually to crown a national Black golf champion. Except for the World War II years between 1942 and 1945, the UGA's Negro National Open took place annually from 1926 to

1976, when dwindling participation led to the end of the UGA.[15] Despite its demise, the role of the UGA in African American golf remains significant.

National Negro Open Golf Tournaments

The signature event of the UGA was the staging of a national golf championship tournament, planned to be an annual affair after the first tournament was held in 1926 and where the first annual meeting of the UGA was held at its founding. The "National," as it became known, established the recognized "national champion" annually among Black golfers. Before the UGA was founded, a few local Black golf clubs had held tournaments identified as being "national." For example, Walter Speedy, a member of Chicago's Alpha Golf Club, organized what was termed a "national championship" golf tournament in 1915.[16] Ten years later, the Shady Rest Country Club, a Black resort in Westfield (Scotch Plains), New Jersey, held the International Golf Championship Tournament and called it "the first colored open golf championship" in America.[17] However, since these events were staged by local golf clubs before a nationally organized body (the UGA) was created, they did not carry the prestige and recognition accorded the winner of the UGA's Negro National Open Golf Championship. In addition to being the site for this "umbrella" organization's first national golf championship, Stow (about thirty miles west of Boston) was also the place where the "best Black golfer in America" title would be bestowed for the first time. The Mapledale Golf Club in Stow hosted the first three UGA Negro National Open championship golf tournaments (1926, 1927, and 1928) before closing in 1929 under the weight of the Great Depression.[18]

Except for the World War II years, the Negro National Open Golf Championship Tournaments were held at various locations for six and a half decades. A list of the specific UGA Negro National Open Golf Championship Tournaments by year, location, and winner (men's professional and women's) can be seen in table 1.

1941 Open: Early Pioneers' Last Stand

The UGA and participants in its championship tournament, the National Negro Open, can provide a useful gauge in identifying "early" and "later"

DAWKINS AND BRADDOCK

Table 1. UGA Negro National Open championships, 1926–76

Year	Location	Winner: Men	Winner: Women
1926	Stow MA	Harry Jackson	
1927	Stow MA	Pat Ball	
1928	Stow MA	Porter Washington	
1929	Westfield NJ	Pat Ball	
1930	Casa Loma WI	Edison Marshall	Marie Thompson
1931	Kankakee IL	Edison Marshall	Marie Thompson
1932	Indianapolis IN	John Dendy	Lucy Williams
1933	Kankakee IL	Howard Wheeler	Julia Siler
1934	Detroit MI	Pat Ball	Ella C. Able
1935	Yorktown Heights NY	Solomon Hughes	Ella C. Able
1936	Philadelphia PA	John Dendy	Lucy Williams
1937	Cleveland OH	John Dendy	Lucy Williams
1938	Kankakee IL	Howard Wheeler	Melnee Moye
1939	Los Angeles CA	Cliff Strickland	Geneva Wilson
1940	Chicago IL	Hugh Smith	Melnee Moye
1941	Canton MA	Pat Ball	Cleo Ball
1942–45 (no competitions)	—	—	—
1946	Pittsburgh PA	Howard Wheeler	Lucy Williams
1947	Philadelphia PA	Howard Wheeler	Thelma Cowan
1948	Indianapolis IN	Howard Wheeler	Mary Brown
1949	Detroit MI	Ted Rhodes	Thelma Cowan
1950	Washington DC	Ted Rhodes	Ann Gregory
1951	Cleveland OH	Ted Rhodes	Edline Thornton
1952	Pittsburgh PA	Charles Sifford	Alice Stewart
1953	Kansas City MO	Charles Sifford	Ann Gregory
1954	Dallas TX	Charles Sifford	Thelma Cowan
1955	Detroit MI	Charles Sifford	Thelma Cowan
1956	Philadelphia PA	Charles Sifford	No competition
1957	Washington DC	Ted Rhodes	Ann Gregory
1958	Pittsburgh PA	Howard Wheeler	Vernice Turner

194

Year	Location	Winner: Men	Winner: Women
1959	Washington DC	Richard Thomas	Ethel Funches
1960	Chicago IL	Charles Sifford	Ethel Funches
1961	Canton MA	Pete Brown	Vernice Turner
1962	Memphis TN	Pete Brown	Carrie Jones
1963	Washington DC	Lee Elder	Ethel Funches
1964	Indianapolis IN	Lee Elder	Renee Powell
1965	Detroit MI	Cliff Brown	Ann Gregory
1966	Chicago IL	Lee Elder	Ann Gregory
1967	Miami FL	Lee Elder	Ethel Funches
1968	Washington DC	James Black	Ethel Funches
1969	Sicklerville NJ	Jim Dent	Ethel Funches
1970	New Haven CT	James Walker	Exie O'Chier
1971	Pittsburgh PA	Jack Price	Exie O'Chier
1972	Chevy Chase MD	James Black	Mary Truitt
1973	Sicklerville NJ	not found	Ethel Funches
1974	Braintree MA	Charlie Owens	Clara Kellnudi
1975	Baltimore MD	Charlie Owens	Laurie Stokien
1976	San Diego CA	Lou Harve	Debra Bennett

Sources: Dawkins and Kinloch, *African American Golfers*, 41; Demas, *Game of Privilege*, 89–91.

pioneers of Black golf. Early UGA National Open champions from the 1920s, 1930s, and early 1940s gave way to a new generation of players in the postwar era, when the tournament resumed in 1946. None of the entrants in the 1941 professional division would hold the UGA National Championship title again after the war. Thus, the 1941 Negro National Open was the last in which winners from the earliest Negro National Open in 1926 would emerge victorious.

Interest in the 1941 Negro National Open was also sparked by an announcement that world heavyweight boxing champion Joe Louis would launch his own national golf tournament that same year. The inaugural "Joe Louis Open Golf Tournament" was planned to take place in Detroit and would feature a larger purse than the UGA National, making it the richest Black golf tournament ever held. Given Louis's national popularity, this announcement not only shed a national spotlight on Black golf in America but also generated widespread interest among Black golfers to enter and play in both the Joe Louis and UGA national tournaments. The promoters of the Joe Louis Open strategically planned the tournament to end four days before the start of the UGA National to permit travel to Detroit and Boston on consecutive weekends. Compared to previous UGA Negro National Open championships, the level of excitement about the UGA tournament in 1941 was greater than usual. Joe Louis also planned to enter both tournaments as an amateur, even though his "golf hobby" was often viewed as a distraction by his boxing promoters and handlers.[19]

Boston's selection as the site of the 1941 UGA Negro National Open championship also represented a return to the city where the last of the three initial UGA championships took place in 1928 (see table 2 for tournaments held in Boston).

The actual location of the three earliest UGA Negro National Open championship tournaments (in 1926, 1927, and 1928) was the Black-operated Mapledale Golf Course and Resort in Stow, Massachusetts. The site of the 1941 tournament was the Ponkapoag Golf Course in Canton, Massachusetts, a town, like Stow, that was considered part of Greater Boston.[20] The Ponkapoag Golf Course was completed as an eighteen-hole course in 1938 under the Works Progress Administration (WPA), a major program of the Great Depression–era New Deal administration of President Franklin Delano Roosevelt.[21] Interestingly, in 1939, a year after the completion of the Ponkapoag course, the WPA completed a similar project, the now historic Langston Golf Course, built for the Black golfing community in Washington DC. Although

Table 2. UGA championships held in Boston, 1926–76

Year	Location
1926	Stow MA
1927	Stow MA
1928	Stow MA
1941	Canton MA
1961	Canton MA
1962–76	Braintree MA

construction on Langston had begun before Ponkapoag, its completion was preceded by a long battle by African Americans in the nation's capital seeking greater access to golfing for Black people considering the Jim Crow laws that prevented them from playing on public courses in the city. Ironically, despite its celebrated status today as a historical landmark, when Langston was completed in 1939, it was built as a nine-hole course even though the original plan called for eighteen holes. Unlike Ponkapoag, Langston was unable to host a UGA national tournament until it was expanded to eighteen holes in the 1950s.[22]

Scholars Marvin Dawkins and Graham Kinloch describe the events leading up to the sixteenth UGA Negro National Open championship tournament in Boston:

The 1941 UGA Negro National Open tournament attracted 200 golfers, which set a record for the event. Participants came from all regions of the country, and, except for the conspicuous absence of Joe Louis and Howard Wheeler, they comprised a "star-studded" array of African American golfers, described by A. L. Miller, who covered the event for the *Atlanta Daily World* sports department, as the "fastest field of professionals ever assembled."[23] Many golfers came directly from Detroit after competing in the first Joe Louis Open tournament, which finished only four days earlier. Even though Louis had already sent in his entry, made reservations, and asked for the assignment of a caddie, his recent reconciliation with his wife, Marva, led him to alter his plans by remaining in Michigan to spend a second honeymoon. However, he donated the leg trophy for the women's championship with the men's trophy provided by the *Chicago Defender*. The reason for Howard Wheeler's absence was unclear. According to sportswriter, Ric Roberts, Wheeler, who won the UGA National in 1933 and 1937, was expected to lead a contingent of entrants from the deep South which would also include the 1934, 1935 and 1936 UGA champion, John Brooks Dendy, along with Atlanta-based Lincoln Golf Club members Clarence Chandler, Eddie Roby, Hugh Smith, Honey Smith and others.[24] Among the golfers participating in this tournament in the professional and amateur divisions were some who had played in the first UGA Negro National Open Championship in 1926, including Robert "Pat" Ball, Porter Washington, Cliff Edmonds, Beltran Barker and Dr. George Adams of Washington DC, who served as the first official president of the United Golfers Association.[25]

On the first day of the tournament, a huge rainstorm interrupted play, which made the Ponkapoag course much slower for the rest of the three-day event. However, the rainstorm on the first day did not appear to dampen the spirited competition and enthusiasm of the golfers. Clyde Martin, the teaching pro to Joe Louis and recent winner of the inaugural Joe Louis Open tournament a week earlier at Detroit's Rackham Golf Course, was the favorite to win the UGA National in Boston. Calvin Searles and Zeke Hartsfield, co-runners-up at the Joe Louis event, expected to be among the top competitors. Although Zeke Hartsfield led by three strokes after the first thirty-six holes, he would falter in the second round with a pair of 79s. The drive toward the championship became a duel between Pat Ball, the veteran pro at the Palos Park course in Chicago, and Clyde Martin, who in 1940 had become personal golf tutor to boxing champion Joe Louis and moved to Detroit after being named the initial golf pro at Langston when it opened in Washington DC in 1939. Robert "Pat" Ball won the tournament by one stroke over Clyde Martin in the professional division. Possibly more exciting than the final scores were reports of the amount of cash received by golfers who finished in the money (see table 3).

Ball, who finished first, was one of the top money winners in the tournament and one of the most accomplished early pioneers of Black golf. Ball won UGA Negro National Open championship titles in 1927, 1929, 1934, and 1941. Although the championship in Boston would be the last for him, Ball became the first four-time UGA Negro National Open winner. Ball had moved to Chicago from Atlanta at the age of sixteen to pursue a golf career after caddying for famed golfer Bob Jones at the East Lake Golf and Country Club in Atlanta. He was also among a small group of "colored" golfers to compete in the National Public Links Golf Tournaments. Ball was granted a court injunction that allowed him to play in the National Public Links Championship of 1932 in Philadelphia after attempts to exclude him on

Table 3. UGA Negro National Open championship finishers, 1941

Final thirty-six holes	Score	Prize money
Pat Ball	302	$275.00
Clyde Martin	303	$150.00
Zeke Hartsfield	307	$110.00
Solomon Hughes	309	$90.00
James Clark	310	$75.00
Eddie Jackson	311	$60.00
Calvin Searles	312	$45.00
Hugh Smith	315	$32.50
Eddie Roby	315	$32.50
Joe Roach	316	$20.00
Cecil Shamwell	318	$15.00
Edison Marshall	318	$15.00
James Adams	320	—
Porter Washington	324	—
Ralph Dawkins	324	—
Oscar Clisby	324	—
Hugh Shippen	328	—
Beltran Barker	330	—
Ted Jones	337	—
John Thompson	338	—
Preston Knowles	342	—
Ernest Hill	342	—
Tom Pearson	349	—
Benny Robinson	359	—
Rudolph Johnson	371	—
C. R. Clark	373	

Source: Dawkins and Kinloch, *African American Golfers,* 54–55. For details of the story of the entry and participation by Shippen and Bunn in the second USGA golf championship tournament held in 1896, see Sinnette, *Forbidden Fairways,* 17–19; Dawkins and Kinloch, *African American Golfers,* 17–20; and Demas, *Game of Privilege,* 34–37.

racial grounds. In 1938, Pat Ball became the first Black golfer to be named a teaching pro at Palos Park, a public golf course near Chicago.

Some of the other outstanding early Black pioneers who finished among the top twenty-five scorers at the 1941 UGA championship were widely known nationally. They included Porter Washington, Calvin Searles, Edison Marshall, Solomon Hughes, Clyde Martin, and Zeke Hartsfield. Many other leading golfers like Ralph Dawkins (Jacksonville, Florida), Eddie Jackson (Detroit, Michigan), and Eddie Roby (Atlanta, Georgia) were better known for their performances at regional and local Black golf tournaments. The local favorite at the 1941 UGA championship was Porter Washington, who had won the UGA Negro National Open championship in 1928, when it had last been played in Boston. Washington had also served as teaching pro at the Mapledale Golf and Country Club in Stow, the site of the first UGA championship in 1926.[26] Calvin Searles, a then up-and-coming phenom, had his greatest performance several years after participating in the 1941 event. He competed against top white pros in the 1944 All-American and World Championship Golf Tournament organized by George May, the flamboyant president of the Tam O'Shanter Golf and Country Club near Chicago. These tournaments were first played during World War II and provided one of the few opportunities for Black golfers to enter and compete directly against some of the best white golfers in the country. As golf historian Lane Demas describes, "Calvin Searles in 1944 [challenged] the world's best white player, Byron Nelson, for the lead in the final round before a late quadruple bogey left him in twenty-second place. Searles' fine play in [the Tam O'Shanter] tournament dedicated to servicemen was quite poignant: within months he was killed in action in France, a promising golf career cut short by both racial segregation and war."[27]

The consecutive tournament weeks of 1941 offered Black golfers what may have been the largest payouts of prize money ever up to that time. The winner of the Joe Louis Open, Clyde Martin, received $500, earning another $150 as runner-up in the UGA Negro National Open for a total of $650 in prize money across the two tournaments. However, for most participants, there was no payout, and some struggled financially to make the trips from their hometowns to Detroit to play in the Joe Louis tournament and then to Boston for the UGA National. Whether this explains the conspicuous absence of noted professional and early Black golf pioneer Howard Wheeler from the Boston event is unclear.[28] Wheeler had teamed with Clyde Martin to compete in an exhibition match against two white professional golfers, brothers Emerick and Chuck Kocsis, to demonstrate how well African American golfers perform in direct competition with white pro golfers. Emerick was the current state PGA champion, and Chuck was a former American Walker Cup star. Wheeler was a three-time UGA National Negro Open champion and a gallery favorite known for his colorful play, which included an unorthodox, cross-handed grip and a habit of hitting drives from a tee made of paper matchboxes.[29] Martin and Wheeler defeated the Kocsis brothers (3–2) in this thrilling exhibition of interracial golf play.[30] If Wheeler had entered the UGA national tournament in Boston the following week, he would have been an exception to the "changing of the guard" thesis as the only early Black golfer to continue to win UGA Negro National Open Golf Championships after 1941. In total, Howard Wheeler, who mentored Charlie Sifford and other later Black golf pioneers, won six UGA Nationals, becoming the only golfer to win this event across three decades (1933, 1938, 1946, 1947, 1948, and 1958).[31]

Among women who played in the 1941 UGA National Open Championship in Boston, Cleo Ball, wife of Pat Ball, won the championship, defeating Geneva Wilson, the defending UGA women's champion, in the semifinal round and Vivian Pitts in the final round. Therefore, for the first and only time, a husband and wife held the men's professional title and the women's amateur title. Although not the primary focus of this examination, early Black golf pioneers among women did not experience their last stand at the 1941 UGA championship in Boston. For example, Lucy Williams, who had previously won the UGA Nationals in the women's division in 1932, 1936, and 1937, would go on to win the championship again in 1946 when the tournament resumed.[32]

There were other unique outcomes of the 1941 UGA Negro National Open Golf Championship at the Ponkapoag Golf Course in Canton, Massachusetts. First, men who participated in the professional division included six previous winners (including three multiple winners) of UGA Negro National

Open championships between 1926 and 1941. Pat Ball (1927, 1929, 1934, and 1941), Porter Washington (1928), Edison Marshall (1930 and 1931), John Brooks Dendy (1932, 1936, and 1937), Solomon Hughes (1935), and Hugh Smith (1940) were all previous UGA National Negro Open Champions.[33] Second, the 1941 championship in Boston would be Pat Ball's fourth and last time winning the UGA Negro National Open championship. In fact, none of the previous winners participating in the 1941 National Open would ever hold this title again.

Thus, this tournament should be recognized in the history of Black golf in America as representing a "changing of the guard" and a clear demarcation between "early" pioneers of Black golf and those who came later. Later pioneers of Black golf, who emerged after the Negro National Open championship resumed in 1946, included many up-and-coming Black golfers, some of whom won multiple UGA Negro National Open championships and became widely known. Among them were Ted Rhodes (1949, 1950, 1951, and 1957), Charlie Sifford (1952, 1953, 1954, 1955, 1956, and 1960), Lee Elder (1963, 1964, 1966, and 1967), Pete Brown (1961 and 1962), James Black (1968 and 1972,) and Charlie Owens (1974 and 1975).[34] These later pioneers of Black golf were those whom golf historian Calvin Sinnette referred to as "modern" Black professional golfers who competed in UGA tournaments while also crossing over into the mainstream after the PGA dropped its "Caucasians-only" clause in 1961. The first Black PGA golfer was Charlie Sifford, who joined the organization in 1964. Finally, during the 1941 UGA annual meeting held in conjunction with the Negro National Open Golf Championship Tournament, a "changing of the guard" also occurred in UGA leadership, ironically reflecting a return to the past, as Dr. George Adams, the first "official" UGA president (1927), and Robert Hawkins, the first "unofficial" UGA president (1926), were elected UGA president and first vice president, respectively.[35]

Boston was the site of a significant event in Black golf history, the 1941 staging of the UGA Negro National Open Golf Championship Tournament. The importance of this event is that it assembled the largest gathering of previous UGA National Champions; it included Black golfers who had played as far back as the first UGA National Golf Championship in 1926, also held in Boston (Stow); and it was the last UGA National Championship held before play was suspended due to World War II. The UGA Negro National Open Golf Championship resumed in 1946, one year after the war ended, but none of the golfers who had played in 1941, including the tournament winner, Robert "Pat" Ball, would ever again hold the official title of "best Black golfer in America." A new generation of UGA Negro National Open champions had emerged.

This "changing of the guard" would relegate early Black golf pioneers to near obscurity. For example, when Tiger Woods won his first of five Master's Golf Championships in 1997, he paid homage to Black golf pioneers, but the three "pioneers" he referenced were "later" pioneers in the history of Black golf in America. As authors Marvin Dawkins and A. C. Tellison note, "Woods specifically recognized the efforts of black golfers Lee Elder (in 1975, the first black to play in the Master's), Charlie Sifford (in 1964, the first black to gain full PGA membership), and Ted Rhodes. Although Rhodes is regarded by some as the greatest black golfer before Tiger Woods, he was probably unknown to millions of television viewers who heard Woods' tribute."[36] While Elder, Sifford, and Rhodes won multiple UGA Negro National Open championships and are, indeed, well deserving of Tiger Woods' tribute as Black golf pioneers, an earlier generation of Black golf champions, many of whom took their last major stance at the 1941 UGA National in Boston, are equally deserving of recognition.

This chapter also has implications for recent efforts by the golf establishment in America to recognize the accomplishments of African American golfers of the past. For example, in 2004 Charlie Sifford was inducted into the prestigious World Golf Hall of Fame—the first African American golfer to receive this honor. Sifford, who in 1964 became the first Black golfer to gain full membership in the PGA, expressed the hope that he would not be the only Black golfer to receive this honor.[37] In 2009, the PGA granted posthumous membership to later Black golf pioneers Ted Rhodes and Bill Spiller and early pioneer John Shippen. The PGA also recognized the contributions of heavyweight champion Joe Louis to the advancement of golf by granting him an honorary PGA membership.[38] This long-overdue recognition of the contributions of Black golfers has continued: the USGA Golf Museum and

Library is collecting and preserving artifacts and documents related to African American golf history and staging exhibitions. They have joined forces with the PGA to establish a permanent mural honoring America's Black golfers at the World Golf Village in St. Augustine, Florida. In these tributes by the golf "establishment," it is important to shed greater light on early pioneers of Black golf. The 1941 UGA Negro National Open Golf Championship in Boston serves as a distinct historical marker identifying the last time the earliest pioneers of Black golf in America came together on a mass scale for a national competition.

Historian Dr. Carter G. Woodson, often called the "Father of Black History," saw corrective scholarship as a means of acquainting the larger public with accurate information about the positive contributions of African Americans to all areas of American life. In the case of Black golf, we suggest that making a distinction between "early" and "later" Black golf pioneers can be best viewed as a "clarification" rather than a correction. The history of African Americans in Boston sports and in American sports in general would be incomplete without this recognition of the role and significance of the sixteenth annual UGA Negro National Open Golf Championship Tournament of 1941 in advancing the development of African American golf.

Notes

1. Some often-cited books covering the modern history of golf in America include Herbert Warren Wind, *The Story of American Golf* (New York: Simon and Schuster, 1956); H. B. Martin, *Fifty Years of American Golf* (New York: Argosy-Antiquarian, 1966); Herbert B. Graffis, *The PGA: The Official History of the Professional Golfers' Association of America* (New York: Thomas Y. Crowell, 1975); Al Barkow, *The Golden Era of Golf* (New York: St. Martin's, 2000); Mark Frost, *The Grand Slams: Bobby Jones, America, and the Story of Golf* (New York: Hyperion, 2004); and George Kirsch, *Golf in America* (Urbana: University of Illinois Press, 2009).

2. See Calvin H. Sinnette, *Forbidden Fairways: African Americans and the Game of Golf* (Chelsea MI: Sleeping Bear, 1998); Marvin P. Dawkins and Graham C. Kinloch, *African American Golfers during the Jim Crow Era* (Westport CT: Praeger, 2000); Pete McDaniel, *Uneven Lies: The Heroic Story of African Americans in Golf* (Greenwich CT: American Golfer, 2000); and Lane Demas, *Game of Privilege: An African American History of Golf* (Chapel Hill: University of North Carolina Press, 2017).

3. Rayford W. Logan, *The Betrayal of the Negro: From Rutherford B. Hayes to Woodrow Wilson* (London: Collier-Macmillan, 1969).

4. "Hagen Puts O. K. on Race Caddies," *Baltimore Afro-American*, November 16, 1929, 7.
5. See Dawkins and Kinloch, *African American Golfers*, 21–34; Marvin P. Dawkins, Jomills H. Braddock II, and Shelby Gilbert, "African American Golf Clubs in the Early Development of Black Golf," *Western Journal of Black Studies* 42 (2018): 3–14.
6. See Dawkins and Kinloch, *African American Golfers*, 21–34.
7. Dawkins, Braddock, and Gilbert, "African American Golf Clubs."
8. For details of the *Holmes v. Atlanta* decision, see Demas, *Game of Privilege*, 149–59.
9. C. Sifford and J. Gullo, *Just Let Me Play: The Story of Charlie Sifford, the First Black PGA Golfer* (Latham NY: British American, 1992).
10. Graffis, PGA. Also see Dawkins, "African American Golfers."
11. Dawkins and Kinloch, *African American Golfers*, 22–25.
12. For details of the story of the entry and participation by Shippen and Bunn in the second USGA golf championship tournament held in 1896, see Sinnette, *Forbidden Fairways*, 17–19; Dawkins and Kinloch, *African American Golfers*, 17–20; and Demas, *Game of Privilege*, 34–37.
13. Dawkins, Braddock, and Gilbert, "African American Golf Clubs," 7–8. Also see "Golf Pioneer Honored," *Florida Star*, September 5, 1959, 7.
14. Dawkins and Kinloch, *African American Golfers*, 41; Demas, *Game of Privilege*, 89–91.
15. Dawkins and Kinloch, *African American Golfers*, 22–25.
16. "Colored Golf Players," *New York Age*, October 14, 1915, 6.
17. "Golf Tournament," *Baltimore Afro-American*, June 20, 1925, 7.
18. "Mapledale Country Club," Freedom's Way National Heritage Area, accessed April 12, 2022, https://freedomsway.org/story/mapledale-country-club/.
19. Lane Demas, "The 'Color-Blind' Golf Tournament That Brought Joe Louis, Bing Crosby, and Charlie Sifford to the Same Greens," a national conversation hosted by the Smithsonian and Arizona State University, March 7, 2019, https://www.whatitmeanstobeamerican.org/ideas/the-color-blind-golf-tournament-that-brought-joe-louis-bing-crosby-and-charlie-sifford-to-the-same-greens/.
20. For details, see Marvin P. Dawkins and Walter C. Farrell, "Joe Louis and the Struggle of African American Golfers for Visibility and Access," *Challenge: A Journal of Research on African American Men* 14 (2008): 72–90.
21. "Canton, Massachusetts," Wikipedia, accessed April 9, 2022, https://en.wikipedia.org/wiki/Canton,_Massachusetts.
22. "Ponkapoag Golf Course Development-Canton MA," Living New Deal, accessed April 9, 2022, https://livingnewdeal.org/projects/ponkapoag-golf-course-canton-ma/.
23. For an exception, see Marvin P. Dawkins and Jomills Henry Braddock II, "Teeing Off against Jim Crow: Black Golf and Its Early Development in Washington, DC," in *DC Sports: The Nation's Capital at Play*, ed. Chris Elzey and David K. Wiggins (Fayetteville: University of Arkansas Press, 2015), 57–72.
24. Dawkins and Kinloch, *African American Golfers*, 54, 57.
25. Dawkins and Kinloch, *African American Golfers*, 53.

26. "Louis Lures Golfers," *Baltimore Afro-American*, August 16, 1941, 21.

27. Dawkins and Kinloch, *African American Golfers*, 44.

28. Dawkins and Kinloch, *African American Golfers*, 156.

29. Demas, *Game of Privilege*, 105.

30. Dawkins and Farrell, "Joe Louis and the Struggle," 77.

31. Dawkins and Kinloch, *African American Golfers*, 73.

32. "Two Birdies Paved Way for Victory," *Baltimore Afro-American*, August 23, 1941, 22.

33. Marvin P. Dawkins and A. C. Tellison Jr., "Golf," in *African Americans and Popular Culture*, vol. 2, *Sports*, ed. Todd Boyd (Westport CT: Praeger, 2008), 56.

34. For more detailed examination of the experiences of Black women golfers, see M. Mikell Johnson, *The African American Woman Golfer: Her Legacy* (Westport CT: Praeger, 2007); M. Mikell Johnson, *Heroines of African American Golf: The Past, the Present, and the Future* (Bloomington IN: Trafford, 2010).

35. See Sinnette, *Forbidden Fairways*; Dawkins and Kinloch, *African American Golfers*; McDaniel, *Uneven Lies*; and Demas, *Game of Privilege*.

36. Dawkins and Tellison, "Golf," 56.

37. "Charlie Sifford Hall of Fame Induction 2004," PGA of America, accessed August 7, 2024, https://www.pga.com/story/remembering-the-legendary-charlie-sifford.

38. "PGA Bestows Membership on African-American Pioneers," pga.com, February 4, 2011, https://www.pga.com/archive/pga-america-bestows-membership-african-american-pioneers.

PART 3

Power and Performance in the
Freedom Movement

10

Center of Controversy

Bill Russell and Boston

ARAM GOUDSOUZIAN

"Boston has been wonderful," Bill Russell proclaimed in April of 1957, a few months after his arrival in the city. "I feel as if I'm home." The rookie center for the Boston Celtics had every reason to exude optimism. He had arrived in Boston four months earlier, midway through the Celtics' professional season, after leading the University of San Francisco to a fifty-five-game winning streak and two consecutive National Collegiate Athletic Association (NCAA) titles, then driving the United States to the gold medal at the Olympic Games in Melbourne. News of his joining the Celtics initially spurred great anticipation: "Bill Russell's Buildup Rivals That of Ted Williams," touted a headline in the Boston Globe. His dynamic shot blocking and extraordinary rebounding proved the perfect complement to the Celtics' cast of dynamic offensive stars, and after an incredible double-overtime Game Seven, Boston beat the St. Louis Hawks for its first National Basketball Association (NBA) championship.[1]

On a personal level, Russell seemed to be living a 1950s middle-class ideal. He soon bought a ranch-style home on Main Street in suburban Reading. On the day he moved in, his wife, Rose, gave birth to their first child, Bill Jr. Two more children, Jacob and Karen, followed. Russell signed lucrative contracts with the Celtics, built a huge record collection, and drove a Chrysler Imperial with a built-in hi-fi and the license plate "Celtics 6." As a poor child in West Monroe, Louisiana, he had begged his mother for an electric train set. Now he could afford an elaborate one, with assorted bridges, switches, and stations. Those clattering, whistling toy trains brought him satisfaction, suggesting contentment with his larger situation.[2]

But sixteen years later, in June of 1973, Russell called his time in Boston a "traumatic experience." Boston, he said, "is probably the most rigidly segregated city in the country." He blasted the "code of conduct" expected of Black athletes. In thirteen seasons, he had led the Celtics to eleven NBA titles—for the last two titles, he was the player-coach, the first Black head coach in NBA history. He also won five most valuable player awards and took twelve trips to the All-Star Game. He earned the widespread respect of his peers and the popular acknowledgment that his defense had revolutionized basketball. Yet Russell claimed, "After the last championship all I could hear was that there were too many Black guys on the team." Two years later, the warm feelings he'd once felt about Boston were entirely gone. "I don't care if I ever go to Boston again," he said.[3] What happened?

At first glance Russell seems an integrationist hero in the mold of Joe Louis, Jesse Owens, or Jackie Robinson. Though he did not desegregate professional basketball, he did integrate it. Russell was the first Black superstar in the NBA—the first to garner abundant publicity, the first to change the nature of the sport, the first to spearhead his team's championship success. His Celtics served as basketball's archetype of successful racial integration. As Boston won title after title, Russell exchanged public praise and private loyalty with his white teammates and coach, and more Black players became critical contributors to the Celtics' dynasty. Russell further embodied the sport's cherished values of selflessness, integrity, and intelligence. He established an unrivaled standard of excellence and deserves his reputation as the greatest winner in the history of American team sports.[4]

Yet Russell defied any easy political characterization. He challenged the liberal pieties that historically governed Black sports icons. In 1964, he attacked the sport's racial double standards. When he identified the NBA's unofficial quota system that restricted African American players to four or five roster spots, he also rejected the prevalent assumption that Black celebrities should be deferential, as evidenced by his refusal to sign autographs or to act friendly with fans. He even defended the principles of Malcolm X and the Nation of Islam while questioning the nonviolent strategy of Martin Luther King Jr.: "We have got to make the white population uncomfortable and keep it uncomfortable," he told the *Saturday Evening Post* in 1964, "because that is the only way to get their attention." By the late 1960s, Russell was a touchstone figure for young athletes of the Black Power generation.[5]

Russell's politics were shaped by his contentious relationship with the city of Boston. The liberal optimism infusing his 1957 pronouncement crumbled into cynicism. That disenchantment stemmed from multiple, related sources: the place of basketball in the region's sporting fabric, the insular Boston media, the white majority's traditional expectations of Black athletes, the city's marginalized Black community, the surging Black activism of the 1960s, and the tenacious conservatism of Boston's white ethnics. Russell, moreover, mixed fierce intelligence and admirable principles with a complex, sensitive personality. His intense convictions only deepened the gulf between the man and the city he represented.[6]

Before setting foot in the Boston Garden, Russell faced a unique set of expectations and doubts. His aerial shot blocking contradicted prevailing wisdom about how to play defense, and few East Coast observers had ever seen this phenomenon. Many figured that the bulky, crafty pivotmen of the NBA would dominate the heralded rookie. "We've all heard about Russell's greatness," said George Yardley of the Fort Wayne Pistons, "but I'm not so sure that he'll be the sensation that a lot of people predict." These forecasts stung the thin-skinned Russell, who had found much meaning and self-worth in his success as a basketball player.[7]

Russell's anxieties were magnified upon arriving in Boston. On his first day in the city, he and his wife were taking a cab to the Registry of Motor Vehicles to complete the paperwork on their new Chrysler. Harold Furash, an insurance executive and season ticket holder, accompanied them. During the ride, the cab driver lectured Russell. With a paternalistic tone, he instructed Russell to treat people politely and avoid an inflated ego. Russell was a grown man with an international reputation, yet the white taxi driver assumed a condescending authority over him.[8]

"I would never be a legitimate sports hero in Boston or anywhere else," he told Rose after his first press conference. In his early years with the Celtics, Russell maintained a surface graciousness, but in private, he bristled at the Boston media. A small-minded provincialism tainted the city's sports pages.

In the late 1950s, the city still had five daily newspapers as well as countless papers in the suburbs and surrounding cities such as Worcester, Lowell, and Providence. Yet reporters ignored events outside Boston, and they obsessed over local figures. Unlike in New York or Los Angeles, sports provided most of the city's celebrities, focusing the microscope on stars from the Red Sox, Celtics, and Bruins. Influential columnists had an enormous influence on public opinion. For example, "Colonel" Dave Egan of the *Boston Record* famously feuded with Ted Williams, shaping many fans' perception of the Red Sox slugger.[9]

Racism further polluted Boston sports. Many whites expected Black athletes to act with deference and good humor. When Russell expressed intelligence or anger, he contradicted those expectations. The Celtic players often spoke to community groups to drum up support. One time during his early career, Russell recalled, "I went to one where the people were so insulting that I just left. You know? My mother always said, 'Don't let anyone do anything to you.' And I wouldn't." Boston's most prominent team, the Red Sox, was the last professional baseball team to integrate. Before the franchise finally promoted Elijah "Pumpsie" Green in 1959, few reporters had pressed the team about its continued segregation. Russell interpreted public doubts or resentment about him in the context of this culture.[10]

Bostonians also exhibited indifference to basketball. Though the average attendance at Boston Garden spiked during Russell's rookie season, it plummeted the next year. The Celtics played an exciting brand of up-tempo basketball, featuring not only the magnificent Russell but also the playmaking wizardry of Bob Cousy, the sharpshooting of Bill Sharman and Tom Heinsohn, and a deep bench that came to include Sam Jones, Frank Ramsey, and John Havlicek. The Celtics lost to the St. Louis Hawks in the 1958 NBA Finals and then began a string of consecutive championships from 1959 to 1966. Yet after the 1957 championship, attendance at Boston Garden never averaged over ten thousand fans.[11]

Meanwhile, the Bruins of the National Hockey League (NHL) sold out the building. The Bruins owned a loyal, passionate fan base because previous generations had woven hockey into the New England sports fabric. Stars such as defenseman Eddie Shore and the "Kraut Line" of Woody Dumart,

Milt Schmidt, and Bobby Bauer had led the Bruins to Stanley Cups in 1929, 1939, and 1941. Basketball possessed a weaker grip on the area's sports fans. Boston's city schools did not even have basketball teams from the mid-1920s to the mid-1940s. Holy Cross, in Worcester, won the 1947 NCAA title, but the region had no other college basketball powerhouses. The Bruins thus received the prime dates at Boston Garden. The Celtics struggled to fill seats.[12]

In the 1950s, the Celtics tried to overcome this apathy through the energetic outreach of publicist Howie McHugh, the dramatic calls of radio announcer Johnny Most, and exhibition games and clinics all around New England. But Boston reporters still begrudged coach Red Auerbach, a man devoid of tact. They howled when Auerbach picked Charley Share in the 1950 NBA Draft, snubbing Holy Cross star Bob Cousy. "Look," barked Auerbach, "am I supposed to win or worry about the local yokels?"[13]

Ironically, the Celtics got Cousy anyway—the Chicago Stags picked him and then folded, so Cousy arrived in Boston via a dispersal draft. He then emerged as one of the NBA's signature superstars. His game possessed imagination, daring, and flair. He dribbled at breakneck speed, possessed impressive peripheral vision, and carved delicate passes through swarms of defenders. He passed behind his back, over his head, and through his legs. He flipped in floaters, hook shots, and one-hand sets. Cousy was also articulate and honest. Reporters flocked to him. National magazines marveled at his abilities: *Sports Illustrated* even published step-by-step illustrations of his fancy moves.[14]

Cousy was six foot one, so the average fan could easily relate to him—especially as a popular anxiety spread that "Frankensteins" dominated basketball. By the late 1950s, as Russell was joining Cousy in Boston, sportswriters were mourning that the small guard was a vanishing breed. Amid such conversations, Russell seemed a big Black menace driving out the little white man. He attracted fewer emulators and fewer admirers. Russell was six foot nine, with long arms and bouncy legs. He focused on the underappreciated arts of defense and rebounding. And he was a Black man in a predominantly white sports culture. Russell admired and respected Cousy, but it annoyed him when a fan approached him after a game to say, "I've just shaken the hand of the greatest basketball player in the world, Bob Cousy.

Now I want to shake the hand of the second greatest." Over the 1960s, Russell earned more and more respect, but he never shook off the sensibility of the lone Black outsider, looming in the shadow of the spotlight.[15] "I'll never be another Ted Williams or a Bob Cousy," he said. "Not in this town."[16]

"There's a team over there in Boston Garden made up of blacks and whites, Catholics and Protestants, coached by a Jew, and they've been world champions for a long time now," marveled Dick O'Connell, general manager of the Red Sox, during a fellowship breakfast at Fenway Park. "Everyone's running around looking for theories and searching into history for explanations. If you want a perfect example of what we've been talking about, just look at the Celtics." Indeed, the perennial NBA champions showcased an impressive team chemistry built around swarming defense, crisp passing, and poise in high-pressure situations. The players often referred to their "pride," and the press wrote of the "Celtic mystique."[17]

In the early 1960s, as the civil rights movement spotlighted the nation's enduring inequalities, the Celtics looked like racial integration in action. Other teams suffered from tensions between Black and white players, but the Celtics trumpeted their respect for one another as men. During a 1961 preseason tour, when Black Celtics encountered racist treatment at restaurants in Indiana and Kentucky, their white teammates stood in solidarity. As the local press often noted, the players' wives developed friendships across race lines as well. This spirit continued as Blacks assumed a larger identity on the team. When Russell had joined the Celtics, he was the only Black player. The team steadily added contributors such as Sam Jones, K. C. Jones, Satch Sanders, and Willie Naulls. In the mid-1960s, the Celtics became the first franchise to start five African Americans.[18]

Russell loved his team's ethic of interracial cooperation. "We were always going somewhere together—different guys in groups of three or four at different times," he remembered. "I once went to four different shows on four straight days with a different set of guys each time." This culture fed the Celtics' winning ways, and it reflected some objectives of the Black freedom movement. For Russell, it also acquired deep personal meaning. Though the Celtics rarely had introspective, emotional, touchy-feely discussions, they forged strong personal bonds. Russell tended to keep people at arm's length. But once he trusted them, he sought to be a good friend. His family hosted an annual Christmas party, where he got each player a gift. When a teammate needed a favor or a gesture of kindness, Russell was there. "I know Frank Ramsey is drunk because he just invited me down to Kentucky during the off-season," he said during one celebratory banquet after a title, referring to his white teammate from the South. "I know I'm not drunk because I didn't accept the invitation."[19]

But Russell drew a sharp line between the Celtics and the city of Boston. Outside the bubble of his team, he grew increasingly disenchanted with the racism he encountered. He endured such indignities as getting questioned by police while idling in a parking lot—just because he was a Black man in a luxury car. "Hey, nigger, how many crap games did it take you to win that car?" he once heard while rolling down the street. When Pumpsie Green joined the Red Sox in 1959, Russell served as his city tour guide. On late-night drives, Russell spilled his anger and anxiety. He told Green which writers were trustworthy and which were prejudiced. He also highlighted the city's racial segregation. He pointed out not only Black hot spots such as Connolly's and the Hi-Hat but also the places where whites made African Americans feel unwelcome. When they zipped through Irish Catholic enclaves such as South Boston and Charlestown, he warned Green about the "brick-throwing racists."[20]

For such reasons, Russell drew sustenance from a community of Black athletes. He assumed a leadership role among those in the Boston area. He mentored numerous young African American players, taking special interest in local college stars such as Jim Hadnot of Providence and high school players such as Bill Hewitt, who attended Cambridge Rindge and Latin School. His fellow Black teammates also depended on his leadership. Both Sam and K. C. Jones stayed with the Russells until they found their own homes. The African American players tended to bond over jokes, jazz music, and common experiences. Russell was their beacon. "I always felt safe around Russell as a black person," said backup center John Thompson, an African American man of both great intelligence and size who would go on to become a celebrated, outspoken coach at Georgetown University, "and I felt very much unsafe with him not around."[21]

Part of Russell's disillusion stemmed from his experiences in suburban Reading. When he moved to Massachusetts, he had first considered buying a large nineteenth-century home on Summer Avenue, where old farmhouses sat back from the street. As he toured with the real estate agent, neighborhood kids crowded for a glimpse of the Celtics star. But some parents objected. According to rumor, they considered raising money to buy the home first. After their objections reached Russell, he bought a more modest ranch house on Main Street, a busier section of town with a nearby gas station and grocery store. Twice in one month in 1958, burglars ransacked his home in broad daylight while his wife was attending social functions. No neighbors reported any suspicious activity. Russell also noticed cars following his Chrysler through the town center late at night. His family had come to Reading to seek a comfortable middle-class life. Instead, he felt he was under surveillance, a tall Black outsider amid white suburbanites.[22]

In 1962 Reading held a "Bill Russell Day," honoring the athlete with a testimonial dinner at the local country club. Five hundred people came. The town leaders gave his wife, Rose, a charm bracelet. Russell's teammates spoke on his behalf. They had never seen him so emotional. "One of the greatest achievements a man can attain is to be called a friend," said Russell, getting teary-eyed. "You said this to me tonight. I appreciate it. I really do." Russell had always sought after a sense of belonging: his mother had died when he was young, and he was an insecure teenager. He had found fulfillment through basketball and the opportunities it offered. The Reading ceremony seemed to signal his true arrival in a new hometown.[23]

Soon after, however, "Bill Russell Day" seemed like a cruel joke. When the Russells looked for a new home in the quieter, leafier west side of Reading, a petition protested that a Black family was moving in. As a result, the Russells instead bought a large brick home on the east side of town. Still, the bigotry persisted. When Russell left on road trips, vandals tipped over his garbage cans. Once, upon returning from a long weekend away, the Russells found their home in disarray. Beer had been poured on the pool table, trophies were smashed, "NIGGA" was spray-painted on walls, and their bed was soiled with feces.[24]

In the mid-1960s, Russell was foreshadowing important developments in Black politics and culture that would surface across the nation: the focus on institutional racism and structural inequality that characterized the post–civil rights era and the emphasis on pride and self-determination associated with Black Power. "I dislike most white people because they are people. I like most black people because I am black," he told *Sports Illustrated* in 1964. That same year, in the *Saturday Evening Post*, he castigated other Black athletes who saw their public statements as part of a "popularity contest." Russell thus refused to operate within the constraints that guided most Black culture icons. He would not parrot liberal pieties or pretend to be apolitical.[25]

In the winter of 1964, he even quit signing autographs as a matter of principle. In his mind, when fans were seeking an autograph, they were treating him more like a commodity than a real person. As a young adult during the civil rights revolution, that type of interaction made him increasingly uncomfortable. "I refuse to smile and be nice to the kiddies," he said. "I don't think it's incumbent upon me to set a good example to anybody's kids but my own." The public often expected popular Black athletes to express gratitude and humility because they had more fame and money than other African Americans. Russell rejected that supposition. His *Saturday Evening Post* profile was entitled, "I Owe the Public Nothing."[26]

That defiance kindled the resentment of many in the Boston media. Most white reporters from the city's newspapers were accustomed to Black athletes who projected humility and good cheer, reassuring the public of racial progress. Russell's anger shocked and disquieted them. "I felt betrayed," wrote Jerry Nason of the *Globe*. "The answers Bill offered seemed to lead nowhere but deeper into that wasteland." A writer for the *Record-American* opined that Russell "should count his blessings once in a while." Tim Horgan of the *Traveler* thought that if Russell smiled more, he would foster more racial progress. Confusing whites' sentiments and Blacks' needs, he wrote, "Russell strikes me as the type who's going to keep this race trouble alive and festering much longer than necessary."[27]

Russell had his own resentments. "He considered some of us fools, and he didn't suffer us so gladly," remembered Bud Collins, who sometimes covered basketball in his early years with the *Herald* and then the *Globe*. Russell knew that some reporters, such as Clif Keane of the *Globe*, sprinkled racial slurs into their conversations. He would never win the same heroic coverage as star white athletes. His wariness with the press, even amid the incredible Celtics dynasty of the 1960s, meant that sports reporters caught only glimpses of the genuine, thoughtful, cackling Russell that his friends and teammates knew well.[28]

Even if Russell liked some reporters, he saw the press as unwilling to address the larger patterns of racial inequality in Boston. While sharing a cab, he told George Sullivan of the *Traveler* that they lived in the nation's most racist city. Sullivan asked if that statement was on the record. Russell responded, "Your paper hasn't got the guts to run that story!" Sullivan wrote it up. His editor killed it, just as Russell had predicted. The next day, Sullivan walked into Boston Garden to find Russell brandishing a copy of the *Traveler*. "I've been reading this back and forth," he said with a cackle. "I can't find the story."[29]

Russell associated himself with a new, aggressive generation of Black leadership in Boston. African Americans had historically composed only about 3 percent of Boston's population, remaining confined to the South End and Lower Roxbury. The Black community exercised little political power beyond the scraps that came through ward boss "Shag" Taylor, a lieutenant of Mayor James Curley's political machine. Other middle-class professionals assumed community leadership positions in the postwar years. Between 1940 and 1970, a huge influx of Southern migrants roughly tripled the Black population, increasing their proportion of the city to 16 percent. Black neighborhoods swelled and pushed into neighboring communities, and Blacks suffered from substandard schools, inflated rents, inferior health care, and few outlets of political expression. Thus, amid the national civil rights movement, a new class of community activists challenged racial discrimination within such institutions as the Boston School Committee and the Boston Redevelopment Authority.[30]

These activists targeted the de facto segregation of Boston schools. By 1960 the Boston branch of the National Association for the Advancement of Colored People (NAACP) had formed an education committee headed by Ruth Batson, a mother shocked by the decrepit schools with predominantly Black enrollments. By May 1963, as the Birmingham campaign was capturing international attention and mobilizing America's conscience about Southern racial injustice, the NAACP and other public policy groups had compiled damning evidence and demanded a public hearing. The all-white Boston School Committee, led by Louise Day Hicks of South Boston, refused to acknowledge any form of segregation, whether de facto or de jure. Now more militant activists emerged, including Reverend James Breeden. Mel King unsuccessfully ran for the school committee.[31]

Russell participated directly in the city's movement. In May 1963, he led a march from Roxbury to Boston Common, where ten thousand people rallied for human rights and many speakers made connections between the Birmingham campaign and Boston's own racial struggle. The next month, a coalition of organizations staged a "Stay Out for Freedom Day," a one-day boycott of Boston schools. Russell supported the protest by touring nine "freedom centers" at churches and social centers, where children participated in political workshops and sang freedom songs. Russell captivated his young audience. "Wear your color as a badge," he implored, appealing to them to embrace not only their education but also their Black identity.[32]

To many whites, Boston was exempt from charges of racism. In truth, cities such as Boston professed racial enlightenment while maintaining racial segregation. In response, Black activists engaged in vigorous grassroots politics, including another school boycott in February 1964 and a march featuring Martin Luther King Jr. in April 1965. These protests helped stimulate the passage of the Racial Imbalance Act of 1965, which recognized and outlawed de facto segregation in Massachusetts schools. Yet the new community leaders, including Russell, maintained a consistent frustration with the second-class status of Blacks.[33]

Despite the passage of the Racial Imbalance Act, the Boston School Committee refused to compel racial integration. In June of 1966, Boston School Committee member Louise Day Hicks, an opponent of busing and desegregation of Boston's public schools, tried to speak at graduation ceremonies for Patrick T. Campbell Junior High School in Roxbury. She was booed off the stage, and civil rights leader Virgil Wood called her the "Hitler of Boston." Media coverage of the incident placed all the blame on Black activists and students. One television report was even narrated by Hicks.[34]

In the aftermath, Russell communicated the frustrations of Black Boston while serving as an important liaison to powerful whites. After signing a telegram on behalf of the city's African American leaders that protested biased news coverage, he hosted a meeting of forty media editors and executives, where they heard demands for more Black reporters and more perspectives from Black Bostonians. The meeting led to the formation of a new Boston Community Media Committee, which helped bring more African Americans into the city's television newsrooms.[35]

Russell also replaced Hicks as the commencement speaker for the students at Campbell Junior High. The school held an alternate "Freedom Graduation" in the basement of a Catholic church, since the Boston School Committee prohibited the use of school grounds. There, the Celtics star told a sweating, clapping, stomping audience of seven hundred people that "a poisoned atmosphere hangs over this city. It is an atmosphere of hate, distrust, and ignorance." He decried the inferior facilities of Black schools, and he warned about the perils of neglecting people's rage and pain: "There's a fire here in Roxbury and nobody is listening, and the fire that consumes Roxbury will also consume Boston. The fire will spread."[36]

In 1964, Russell bought Slade's, a barbecue restaurant on Tremont Street, in the heart of the South End. The restaurant, an institution among Black Bostonians since the 1930s, had added live music in the 1950s. Although Russell's celebrity further boosted patronage, he was a terrible business owner, losing $60,000 when he sold the restaurant in 1968. In the interim, however, Russell learned more lessons about who held power in the city as he interacted with inspectors looking for bribes, police officers looking for favors, and gangsters looking for protection money. Thanks to Slade's, Russell kept his finger on the pulse of the Black community. In 1968, as one reflection of his commitment to the city's freedom movement, he used Slade's to feed

Black activists who had established a tent city in a South End parking lot to protest the lack of affordable housing.[37]

By that time, Russell stood as a key figure in the Revolt of the Black Athlete, a movement that highlighted racism in sports while placing athletes as advocates of Black freedom. In 1966 Russell published a groundbreaking autobiography, *Go Up for Glory*, which bitterly recounted the racism that he had endured while articulating a human rights agenda. In 1967, when Muhammad Ali refused his induction into the Vietnam War, Russell attended the "draft summit" organized by football star Jim Brown and then penned an essay in *Sports Illustrated* expressing admiration for the stand Ali had taken. In 1968 he supported the Olympic Project for Human Rights (OPHR), a movement to boycott the Mexico City Olympics. The new generation of militant Black athletes looked to Russell as a touchstone. Harry Edwards, the controversial leader of the OPHR, depended on Russell for advice. He admired Russell's moral and intellectual clarity: "He was the person that I looked to, to understand not just the principle, but the price."[38]

Yet while most athletes espousing Black Power ideals were treated with derision from the mainstream press, Russell earned great respect. At the end of a tumultuous 1968, *Sports Illustrated* named him Sportsman of the Year. The smarter sportswriters recognized that he called for unity across racial lines in both his language and his example. Most remarkably, in 1966, Russell became the player-coach of the Boston Celtics. He was the first African American head coach of a major team sport. In 1968 and then again in 1969, he led aging, underdog Celtic squads to improbable championships. In thirteen seasons in Boston, he won eleven NBA titles, making him, without question, the greatest winner in American team sports history.[39]

"I am not a Russell fan—as a man," wrote Al Hirshberg of the *Herald-Traveler* after the 1968 title. He had doubted that Russell could be an effective player-coach, and he thought Russell was a racist. But now, Hirshberg wrote, he had to admit that he admired "the heart and the ability and the savvy and the will." Russell was not beloved in Boston, like Bobby Orr of the Bruins. But he forced Bostonians of all kinds to respect him—not only as an athlete but as a leader, as a Black person speaking his truth, as a man.[40]

* * *

In 1969, Russell retired from pro basketball. He moved to Los Angeles and worked as an actor, talk show host, college campus lecturer, and color commentator for NBA games on ABC. He kept his distance from the people of Boston. In 1972, when the Celtics retired his number, Russell insisted that it take place in an empty Boston Garden, with only a few old teammates in attendance. "I thought of myself as playing for the Celtics, not for Boston," he reflected. "The fans could do and think whatever they wanted. If they liked what they saw, fine; if not, the hell with it."[41]

In 1973, when Russell joined the Seattle Supersonics as coach and general manager, his comments about Boston's racial segregation and bigoted culture triggered gripes from the Boston media. "I am not a racist sportswriter," protested Larry Claflin of the *Herald American*. "I suspect Russell is the racist." Russell had attributed the city's lack of enthusiasm for the Celtics to the team's racial composition, and he had a point. When the Celtics again rose to prominence in the mid-1970s, the team revolved around two white stars, Dave Cowens and John Havlicek. From 1969 to 1975, average attendance at Boston Garden jumped by more than 50 percent.[42]

In this same era, Boston acquired a notorious reputation for its race relations. White neighborhoods such as South Boston and Charlestown mixed Irish American pride, working-class identity, and political frustration. Like other white ethnics in the city, residents in these enclaves already resented the white Anglo-Saxon Protestant dominance of financial institutions and major corporations. Now Black activism infiltrated their worlds. In 1974, when a court-ordered busing program began to desegregate Boston schools, white mobs greeted buses of Black children with racist slurs and calls for resistance. South Boston and Charlestown became symbols of American racism, not unlike Selma or Birmingham in the 1960s.[43]

"I expected what's happening in Boston," said Russell. He had long pointed to the city's patterns of political exclusion, geographic segregation, and cultural bigotry. If anyone cared to consider it, he now seemed less like a troublemaker and more like a prophet. He remained a persistent critic of the city. In his 1979 memoir *Second Wind*, he wrote that "if Paul Revere were riding today, it would be for racism: 'The niggers are coming! The niggers are coming!' he'd yell as he galloped through town to warn neighborhoods of busing and black homeowners." In 1988, during his brief stint as coach of the Sacramento Kings, he joked, "I would rather be in jail in Sacramento than mayor of Boston." When he did join an official Celtics ceremony, such as Auerbach's retirement in 1985 or a farewell to Boston Garden in 1995, he ignored any public ovations.[44]

In the past few decades, that resentment has melted. Near the close of the twentieth century, his daughter Karen Russell and business adviser Alan Hilburg started encouraging Russell's participation in public life, which reaped financial rewards and supported his favorite causes. As part of this effort, Russell again became a presence in Boston. In May 1999, the Fleet Center hosted a celebrity-studded tribute that benefited organizations that promoted youth mentoring; when Russell hoisted his number six to the rafters, a huge crowd roared its cheers, and his eyes welled with tears. In the twenty-first century, Russell consulted with the Celtics, threw out first pitches at Fenway Park, and accepted various awards from Boston institutions.[45]

In 2013, a statue of Russell was unveiled in the plaza outside Boston City Hall. The monument speaks to his impact on the city as well as his intelligence and activism. But it is worth remembering that this scenario would have seemed implausible during Russell's heyday as the Celtics center. Bill Russell may be a Boston sports legend now, but during the 1960s, he was the most visible critic of the city's racism.[46]

Notes

1. Unpublished article in Bill Mokray Scrapbook, 1956–57, Basketball Hall of Fame, Springfield, Massachusetts; *Boston Globe*, December 19, 1956.

2. Jeremiah Tax, "The Man Who Must Be Different," *Sports Illustrated*, February 3, 1958, 32; Bill Russell as told to Al Hirshberg, "I Was a 6'9" Babe in the Woods," *Saturday Evening Post*, January 18, 1958, 68; Irv Goodman, "Cousy, Sharman, Russell & Co.," *Sport*, March 1958, 60; *Washington Post and Times Herald*, September 1, 1957. On African Americans and postwar consumer culture, see Lizabeth Cohen, *A Consumers' Republic: The Politics of Mass Consumption in Postwar America* (New York: Alfred A. Knopf, 2003), 166–91.

3. *Boston Herald American*, June 6, 1973; *Springfield Union*, June 6, 1973; *Washington Post*, June 6, 1973; *Los Angeles Times*, June 6, 1973; *Chicago Defender*, June 6, 1973; *Baltimore Afro-American*, June 12, 1973; *Boston Globe*, April 12, 2005.

4. On Russell's career, see Thomas J. Whalen, *Dynasty's End: Bill Russell and the 1968–69 World Champion Boston Celtics* (Boston: Northeastern University Press, 2004). On his rivalry with Chamberlain, see John Taylor, *The Rivalry: Bill Russell, Wilt Chamberlain, and the Golden Age of Basketball* (New York: Random House, 2005). On the Celtics dynasty, see Jeff Greenfield, *The World's Greatest Team: A Portrait of the Boston Celtics, 1957–1969* (New York: Random House, 1976); Joe Fitzgerald, *That Championship Feeling: The Story of the Boston Celtics* (New York: Charles Scribner's Sons, 1975); and Dan Shaughnessy, *Ever Green: The Boston Celtics; A History in the Words of Their Players, Coaches, Fans and Foes, from 1946 to the Present* (New York: St. Martin's, 1990).

5. Edward Linn, "I Owe the Public Nothing," *Saturday Evening Post*, January 18, 1964. On Russell's ideology and persona in the 1960s, see also Gilbert Rogin, "We Are Grown Men Playing a Child's Game," *Sports Illustrated*, November 18, 1963; Bill Russell with Bob Ottum, "The Psych . . . and My Other Tricks," *Sports Illustrated*, October 25, 1965; Bill Russell as told to William McSweeney, *Go Up for Glory* (New York: Berkley Medallion, 1966); and William F. Russell, "I'm Not Involved Anymore," *Sports Illustrated*, August 4, 1969.

6. Most of the material and ideas in this essay are drawn from Aram Goudsouzian, *King of the Court: Bill Russell and the Basketball Revolution* (Berkeley: University of California Press, 2010). See also Aram Goudsouzian, "Bill Russell and the Basketball Revolution," *American Studies* 47, nos. 3–4 (Fall–Winter 2006): 61–85.

7. See *Los Angeles Times*, August 23, 1956; *Boston Globe*, December 6, 1956; March 25, 1965; *New York Times*, December 20, 1956; *Chicago Defender*, January 5, 1957; and *San Francisco Chronicle*, January 7, 1957.

8. Harold Furash, interview with the author, March 19, 2007.

9. Russell, *Go Up for Glory*, 55; Leigh Montville, *Ted Williams: The Biography of an American Hero* (New York: Doubleday, 2004), 67–72.

10. *Boston Globe*, November 12, 2000; Howard Bryant, *Shut Out: A Story of Race and Baseball in Boston* (Boston: Beacon Press, 2002), 1–12, 31–36, 43–48.

11. Peter C. Bjarkman, *Boston Celtics Encyclopedia* (Champaign IL: Sports Publishing, 2002), 117.

12. *Boston Herald*, January 28, 1958; February 11, 1959; *Boston Globe*, January 29, 1958; March 10, 1958; March 19, 1958; March 22, 1958; January 20, 1960; March 7, 1960.

13. Mike Carey with Jamie Most, *High above Courtside: The Lost Memoirs of Johnny Most* (Champaign IL: Sports Publishing, 2003), 49–54, 386–87, 402; Red Auerbach and Joe Fitzgerald, *Red Auerbach: An Autobiography* (New York: G. P. Putnam's Sons, 1977), 63–66, 106–8, 201–3.

14. "The Cousy Circus," *Newsweek*, January 21, 1952, 80–81; Al Hirshberg, "Cousy Shoots like Crazy," *Sport*, March 1953, 28–31, 82–83; "Basketball's Little Big Shot," *Time*, December 28, 1953, 37; Stanley Frank, "Basketball's Amazing Showboat," *Saturday Evening Post*, December 18, 1954, 25, 58–59; Al Hirshberg, "Roommate: Bob Cousy," *Sport*, March 1956, 48–56; Herbert Warren Wind, "Bob Cousy: Basketball's Creative Genius," *Sports Illustrated*, January 9, 1956, 42–58; Herbert Warren Wind, "Bob Cousy: The Man and

the Game," *Sports Illustrated*, January 16, 1956, 28–32, 56–58; "Celtics Climb on Cousy's Clever Coups," *Life*, February 11, 1957, 77–80; Al Hirshberg, "A Visit with Bob Cousy," *Sport*, December 12, 1959, 30, 91–92; Ed Linn, "The Wonderful Wizard of Boston," *Sport*, January 1960, 52–60.

15. *Boston Globe*, March 6, 1957; December 23, 1960; *Sporting News*, January 7, 1959; January 14, 1959; *New York Post*, January 15, 1959; *Chicago Defender*, January 10, 1960; November 5, 1962; Hirshberg, "Visit with Bob Cousy," 91; Russell, *Go Up for Glory*, 57.

16. *Boston Record-American*, March 28, 1964. On Cousy and Russell, see also Gary Pomerantz, *The Last Pass: Cousy, Russell, the Celtics, and What Matters in the End* (New York: Penguin Press, 2018), 71–150.

17. Auerbach and Fitzgerald, *Red Auerbach*, 234–35; *Boston Globe*, February 16, 1960; February 21, 1961; March 24, 1963; December 27, 1963; *Boston Herald*, March 17, 1964.

18. Tommy Heinsohn with Leonard Lewin, *Heinsohn, Don't You Ever Smile? The Life and Times of Tommy Heinsohn and the Boston Celtics* (Garden City NY: Doubleday, 1976), 82–83; Russell, *Go Up for Glory*, 115; Ray Fitzgerald, *Champions Remembered: Choice Picks from a Boston Sports Desk* (Brattleboro VT: Stephen Greene, 1982), 66–67; Bill Russell with Alan Steinberg, *Red and Me: My Coach, My Lifelong Friend* (New York: Collins, 2009), 79–84; Bob Cousy with Ed Linn, *The Last Loud Roar* (Englewood Cliffs NJ: Prentice-Hall, 1964), 99.

19. Blaine Johnson, *What's Happenin'? A Revealing Journey through the World of Professional Basketball* (Englewood Cliffs NJ: Prentice-Hall, 1978), 115; Bob Cousy, interview with the author, April 23, 2007; Gene Conley, interview with the author, April 10, 2007; Gene Guarilia, interview with the author, January 14, 2008; Mel Counts, interview with the author, January 10, 2008; Tom "Satch" Sanders, interview with the author, August 25, 2008; Ed Linn, "Bill Russell's Private World," *Sport*, February 1963, 62.

20. Bill Russell and Taylor Branch, *Second Wind: The Memoirs of an Opinionated Man* (New York: Random House, 1979), 193–94; Whalen, *Dynasty's End*, 52–53; Sharon O'Brien, "'We Want a Pennant, Not a White Team': How Boston's Ethnic and Racial History Shaped the Red Sox," in *Sports Matters: Race, Recreation, and Culture*, ed. John Bloom and Michael Nevin Willard (New York: New York University Press, 2002), 176–81; Bryant, *Shut Out*, 55–59, 81–86.

21. Earl Lloyd, interview with the author, March 16, 2007; Al Attles, interview with the author, August 5, 2008; Wayne Embry with Mary Schmitt Boyer, *The Inside Game: Race, Power, and Politics in the NBA* (Akron: Ohio University Press, 2004), 108; Sanders, interview with the author; K. C. Jones with Jack Warner, *Rebound* (Boston: Quinlan, 1986), 79–86; Leonard Shapiro, *Big Man on Campus: John Thompson and the Georgetown Hoyas* (New York: Henry Holt, 1991), 37–38; *Los Angeles Times*, January 18, 1966; Tony Kornheiser, "Bill Russell: Nothing but a Man," in *ESPN Sportscentury*, ed. Michael MacCambridge (New York: Hyperion, 1999), 187.

22. Peggy White, interview with the author, March 15, 2007; *New York Times*, April 6, 1958; *Chicago Defender*, April 21, 1958; Russell, *Go Up for Glory*, 134–35.

23. *Reading Chronicle*, May 16, 1963; May 23, 1963; Heinsohn and Lewin, *Don't You Ever Smile?*, 86–87; Harold Furash, telephone interview with the author, March 19, 2007.

24. Fred Katz, "The Unknown Side of Bill Russell," *Sport*, March 1966, 79; White, interview with the author; Karen K. Russell, "Growing Up with Pride and Prejudice," *New York Times Magazine*, June 14, 1987, 26.

25. Rogin, "We Are Grown Men," 82; Linn, "I Owe the Public Nothing," 60–63.

26. Jerry Izenberg, "The Unpopular Star: How Much Does He Really Owe the Fans?," *Sport*, August 1966, 44–47, 81–82; Linn, "I Owe the Public Nothing."

27. *Boston Globe*, March 24, 1964; *Boston Record-American*, March 28, 1964; *Boston Traveler*, January 14, 1964.

28. Bud Collins, telephone interview with the author, February 20, 2008; Tim Horgan, telephone interview with the author, February 21, 2008; Leigh Montville, telephone interview with the author, August 5, 2008; Leigh Montville, *Tall Men, Short Shorts: The 1969 NBA Finals; Wilt, Russ, Lakers, Celtics, and a Very Young Sports Reporter* (New York: Doubleday, 2021), 51–54, 264–70.

29. Ron Thomas, *They Cleared the Lane: The NBA's Black Pioneers* (Lincoln: University of Nebraska Press, 2002), 177.

30. Thomas H. O'Connor, *Building a New Boston: Politics and Urban Renewal 1950–1970* (Boston: Northeastern University Press, 1993), 59–62, 225–39; Stephen Thernstrom, *The Other Bostonians: Poverty and Progress in the American Metropolis, 1880–1970* (Cambridge MA: Harvard University Press, 1973), 178–83, 197–219; Barry Bluestone and Mary Huff Stevenson, *The Boston Renaissance: Race, Space, and Economic Change in an American Metropolis* (New York: Russell Sage, 2000), 25–26, 40, 87; Phillip L. Clay, ed., *The Emerging Black Community in Boston* (Boston: Institute for the Study of Black Culture, University of Massachusetts at Boston, 1985), 117–19; Mel King, *Chain of Change: Struggles for Black Community Development* (Boston: South End, 1981), 27–149; Alan Lupo, *Liberty's Chosen Home: The Politics of Violence in Boston* (Boston: Beacon, 1988; orig. 1977), 133–42.

31. Reels 5 and 12, *Papers of the NAACP*, part 3, "The Campaign for Educational Equality," series D: Central Office Records, 1956–1965, microfilm, University of Memphis Library; Ronald P. Formisano, *Boston against Busing: Race, Class, and Ethnicity in the 1960s and 1970s* (Chapel Hill: University of North Carolina Press, 1991), 22–47; Jon Hillson, *The Battle of Boston* (New York: Pathfinder, 1977), 52–57; Mel King, "Three Stages of Black Politics in Boston, 1950–1980," in *From Access to Power: Black Politics in Boston*, ed. James Jennings and Mel King (Cambridge MA: Schenkman, 1986), 23–38.

32. *Harvard Crimson*, May 9, 1963; *New York Times*, June 16, 1963; June 18, 1963; June 19, 1963; June 23, 1963; *Boston Globe*, June 18, 1963; June 19, 1963; *Boston Herald*, June 18, 1963; June 19, 1963; *Chicago Defender*, May 13, 1963; June 19, 1963.

33. Jason Sokol, *All Eyes Are upon Us: Race and Politics from Boston to Brooklyn* (New York: Basic, 2014), ix–xxvi, 99–100.

34. *Boston Herald*, June 17, 1966; June 19, 1966; *Boston Globe*, June 17, 1966; *Bay State Banner*, June 25, 1966.

35. *Los Angeles Times*, July 29, 1966; *Bay State Banner*, July 2, 1966; J. Anthony Lukas, *Common Ground: A Turbulent Decade in the Lives of Three American Families* (New York: Vintage, 1986), 496–97; Mel King, telephone interview with the author, January 25, 2008.

36. *Boston Globe*, June 22, 1966; June 23, 1966; *Bay State Banner*, July 2, 1966.

37. *New York Post*, August 19, 1964; *Washington Post*, June 9, 1973; Harold Furash, interview with the author, March 19, 2007; Russell and Branch, *Second Wind*, 205–7; *Sporting News*, March 5, 1966; March 1, 1969; *Boston Globe*, November 7, 1968.

38. Russell, *Go Up for Glory*; Bill Russell with Tex Maule, "I Am Not Worried about Ali," *Sports Illustrated*, June 19, 1967, 18–21; *Los Angeles Times*, December 1, 1967; Harry Edwards, *The Revolt of the Black Athlete* (New York: Free Press, 1970), 39–40, 120; John Underwood, "The Non-trial Trials," *Sports Illustrated*, July 8, 1968, 11–13; Harry Edwards, interview with the author, May 23, 2007. On the draft summit, see also Jonathan Eig, *Ali: A Life* (Boston: Houghton Mifflin Harcourt, 2017), 245–48.

39. George Plimpton, "Reflections in a Diary," *Sports Illustrated*, December 23, 1968, 40–44; Frank Deford, "Two Seconds Stretch for First," *Sports Illustrated*, April 29, 1968, 25–26; Whalen, *Dynasty's End*; Montville, *Tall Men, Short Shorts*.

40. *Boston Herald-Traveler*, April 24, 1968.

41. *Boston Globe*, March 13, 1972; Russell and Branch, *Second Wind*, 202–3.

42. *Boston Herald American*, June 6, 1973, June 8, 1973; Bjarkman, *Boston Celtics Encyclopedia*, 117. On the great Celtics' teams of the 1970s, see Bob Ryan, *Celtics Pride: The Rebuilding of Boston's World Championship Basketball Team* (Boston: Little, Brown, 1975); Michael Connolly, *Rebound! Basketball, Busing, Larry Bird, and the Rebirth of Boston* (Minneapolis MN: Voyageur, 2008).

43. Formisano, *Boston against Busing*, 1–21, 75–80, 108–37; Lupo, *Liberty's Chosen Home*, 15, 79, 85–88; Thomas H. O'Connor, *Bibles, Brahmins, and Bosses: A Short History of Boston*, 3rd ed. (Boston: Trustees of the Public Library of the City of Boston, 1991), 198–220. See also Jeanne Theoharis, *A More Beautiful and Terrible History: The Uses and Misuses of Civil Rights History* (Boston: Beacon Press, 2018), 49–54; D. Garth Taylor, *Public Opinion and Collective Action: The Boston School Desegregation Conflict* (Chicago: University of Chicago Press, 1986), 44–91; and Louis P. Masur, *The Soiling of Old Glory: The Story of a Photograph That Shocked America* (New York: Bloomsbury, 2008).

44. *Seattle Times*, November 24, 1974; Russell and Branch, *Second Wind*, 183; *Sacramento Bee*, January 16, 1988; January 17, 1988; Frank Deford, "No. 2 in the Rafters, No. 1 in Their Hearts," *Sports Illustrated*, January 14, 1985, 40–44, 79–81; *Boston Globe*, January 16, 1988; January 15, 1995; January 22, 1995; *Boston Herald*, April 22, 1995.

45. *New York Times*, June 16, 2000; *Boston Globe*, May 27, 1999; October 8, 1999; May 12, 2000; November 8, 2000; April 12, 2005; *Boston Herald*, May 27, 1999; *Jet*, June 14, 1999; Dan Pearson, "A Green Giant," *Boston*, December 2000, 240.

46. Chris Forsberg, "Bill Russell's Statue Unveiled," ESPN.com, November 1, 2013, https://www.espn.com/boston/nba/story/_/id/9914066/statue-boston-celtics-great-bill-russell-unveiled-boston.

11

Willie O'Ree

The Sky's the Limit

GEORGE FOSTY

Born at the height of the Great Depression to a family of modest means, Willie O'Ree's rise in the sport of ice hockey is one of the great chapters in North American sports history. The first Black man to play in the National Hockey League (NHL), O'Ree's story is an inspiration for all who aspire to achieve their goals and dreams. O'Ree inherited a long family legacy of Black liberation. While it would be years before O'Ree learned the details of his family history, he is the direct descendant of a slave who escaped to Canada from South Carolina and fought for the British during the American Revolution in return for his freedom. His parents continued this legacy, continually pushing the envelope of the freedoms they believed America afforded them. Historians have more recently discovered the significance of O'Ree's entry into the NHL, much of which was previously unknown or underappreciated. Tracing and recording the history of early Black hockey across North America provides a better understanding of the historical importance of O'Ree and how he fits into the Black Canadian hockey tradition. Often described as the "Jackie Robinson of hockey," O'Ree cannot be judged simply by his achievements in breaking the color barrier in the NHL. Instead, his story must be seen in the context of the history of hockey and how it connects the sport's past with its present and future.

The youngest of thirteen children, O'Ree was born on October 15, 1935, in Fredericton, New Brunswick, Canada, to freedom fighters in their own right, Rosebud Wright and Harry Douglas O'Ree. When they arrived in Fredericton, the O'Rees were one of only two Black families living there. Both of O'Ree's parents were raised in Gagetown, a Black loyalist community on the outskirts of the city that served as a military outpost and the home of many Black families who fought on the side of the British during the American Revolution. Strategically important, Gagetown would later become an important stop for ships traveling the St. Lawrence River during the 1800s. Today, it is home to Canadian Forces Base Gagetown. The story is featured in the 2019 documentary *Willie: How the Descendant of Escaped Slaves Changed Hockey Forever.*

O'Ree learned to skate in 1938 at the age of three and developed his passion and craft with his family by his side. His father flooded the backyard of their family home to create a rink and strapped a pair of double-blade wood-block skates over his child's winter shoes. The experience stayed with O'Ree. He later recounted how skating on the ice made him feel like he was flying. On skates, he was in his very own element.[1] From the start, his father and eldest brother, Richard, served as his mentors. They watched over the lad and patiently taught him the finer points of skating and the game of ice hockey. The loving family attention had an impact, driving O'Ree to feel the thrill of hockey and how it was part of his life—the air that he breathed.[2]

In his autobiography, published in 2000, O'Ree writes that racism was not a visible part of his early childhood. Even though all his childhood friends were white, he does not recall being treated differently. By the time he was in his teens, however, he seemed to have gained a sense of societal limitations.[3] Just when this awareness of racism and the color barrier first became apparent to the young O'Ree has never been clear. However, he notes in his autobiography that he did not date white girls and that his parents told him to "stay with his own kind."[4]

O'Ree attended two elementary schools in Fredericton. From grades one through six, he went to Smythe Street School, two and a half blocks from his house. Later, he attended the York Street School for grades seven and eight. His family attended St. Anne's Anglican Church, where he was an altar boy and sang in the choir.[5] In the winter, he spent hours skating on the ice of nearby Island Lake. The experience had a lasting effect on him. At night, while skating on the lake, he looked to the sky and saw all the stars. For O'Ree, the world seemed limitless, not only in terms of the universe, but also in terms of his young dreams of being a professional hockey player.[6]

When he was not skating on Island Lake, O'Ree could be found at nearby Wilmont Park playing organized hockey. All the hours he spent skating as a young child paid substantial dividends. By the time he was a young teenager, he started playing pickup games with his older brother and his friends, who were in their twenties and often played a rougher style of hockey.[7] Playing with older kids and adults taught young O'Ree how to give and take a hit. In high school, however, this style of play became problematic. He bodychecked the coach's son during a tryout for his local high school team, breaking the young man's collarbone. He was immediately dropped from the team.[8]

O'Ree claimed on more than one occasion that if he had not pursued a career in hockey, he would have strived to become a professional baseball player. His father had been a big baseball fan. When not playing hockey, a young O'Ree was active in several sports, including rugby, swimming, and soccer. Baseball, however, became his other passion in addition to his love for hockey.[9] In 1949, at the age of thirteen, he played for the Fredericton West Enders baseball team, which won the city league bantam title. As part of the prize, the team won a trip to New York City to watch the Brooklyn Dodgers play the New York Yankees at Ebbets Field. There he met Jackie Robinson, the first Black man to play Major League Baseball.[10]

A year later, in 1950, O'Ree refocused his attention on hockey in what became the start of his professional career. He played two games for the Fredericton Falcons, members of the New Brunswick Amateur Hockey Association (NBAHA). They played both games during a Falcons playoff run, and O'Ree did not impress. In the two contests, he registered zero goals and zero assists while posting four minutes in penalties. The following season he played six regular games for the Fredericton Merchants, members of the York County Hockey League (YCHL). He scored ten goals while adding four assists, with only two minutes in penalties. During the playoffs, O'Ree participated in eight games for the Merchants, scoring an impressive ten goals and five assists with only eighteen penalty minutes. In the fourteen games he played with the Fredericton Merchants, he recorded twenty goals and nine assists: more than a two-point game average. A season later, at the age of seventeen, O'Ree moved up to the Fredericton Junior Capitals, members of the New Brunswick Junior Hockey League (NBJHL). He played three games and scored two goals. The next year, he played a total of nineteen regular season and playoff games with the Capitals, scoring a total of twenty goals with three assists. A season later, O'Ree played only two games with the Capitals, registering zero goals and assists.

Despite the spotty statistics, the 1953–54 hockey season marked a crucial moment in his young career. That season he played a total of forty-eight regular and playoff games, posting an impressive twenty-two goals and twenty-one assists. Though his game percentage numbers were not as high as they had been during his time with the Merchants in 1951–52 or during his second season with the Capitals (1952–53), he posted twenty-five points (fifteen goals, ten assists) for the Capitals during their impressive twenty-five-game playoff run. That cemented his scoring reputation, demonstrating that when given the chance, he could be a solid scoring leader and a threat on the ice.

In 1954 he moved to the Quebec Frontenacs of the Quebec Junior Hockey League (QJHL), which paved his way to becoming the first Black hockey player in the NHL. He scored twenty-seven goals and fourteen assists in forty-three games for the Frontenacs. During the playoffs, he suited up for seventeen games, scoring seven goals and six assists. It was while playing for the Quebec Frontenacs under coach Phil Watson that the prospect of eventually playing in the NHL became a possibility. Watson was a former thirteen-year veteran of the NHL, having spent his career playing for the New York Rangers and Montreal Canadiens. Watson was the first to see O'Ree's potential, telling him that he could be the first Black man to play in the NHL. He also cautioned the young man, telling O'Ree that because of his skin color, he would face a great deal of animosity and harassment from other players and fans. He advised him to keep a cool head and remain focused.[11] Two short years later, after achieving success in the minor leagues, Watson's vision became reality for O'Ree.

The 1955–56 season became one of the most productive of his career. He signed with the Kitchener Canucks of the Ontario Hockey Association (OHA) and played in forty-one games, scoring thirty goals and twenty-eight assists. He scored an additional four goals and three assists in the team's eight playoff games. Though he did not know it, his time with Kitchener ultimately strengthened his resolve on the ice. O'Ree, a young twenty-year-old professional, played under the direction of Jack Stewart, another former NHL player. Stewart was a defenseman who played twelve seasons in the NHL with the Detroit Red Wings and later the Chicago Black Hawks. While with Detroit, Stewart was on two Stanley Cup–winning teams. He was also named to the NHL All-Star Team on five occasions. In 1964 he was inducted into the Hockey Hall of Fame.

O'Ree incurred an injury that led to the loss of sight in his right eye while playing for the Junior Canucks. During a game in Guelph, Ontario, he skated in front of the opponent's net to screen the goaltender, only to be hit above the right eye by a deflected puck that was fired by his defenseman from the blue line. The damage was immense. The puck shattered the retina at the back of his right eye. He also sustained a broken nose, broken cheekbone, and several facial cuts.[12] For the next eight weeks, he remained at home recovering from his injuries. Only his doctor knew he was blind in one eye. Ignoring the doctor's advice, O'Ree returned to hockey as if nothing had happened, all while trying to adjust to playing with a potentially career-ending handicap.[13]

By 1956, O'Ree joined the storied Quebec Aces of the Quebec Hockey League. Coach George "Punch" Imlach went to O'Ree's home in Fredericton during the summer and offered him a one-year contract totaling $4,000 (a $3,500 one-year contract with a $500 signing bonus). It seemed a good offer at the time, given that the average yearly salary in 1956 was $4,800. This would be the equivalent of $43,570 in 2022. O'Ree was not satisfied, however. He told Imlach that he also wanted a $300 bonus if the Aces reached the playoffs as well as additional money if he scored more than twenty goals in a season. Imlach begrudgingly agreed.[14] O'Ree played fifteen games for the Quebec Aces, scoring three goals and three assists.

O'Ree experienced some of the worst racial incidents of his career while at the Quebec Aces, and he began to fight back. He refused to accept the bullying and name-calling. As a result, he received eighty minutes in penalties in sixty-eight games during his just first year with the Aces, making him the third-most penalized player on the team. O'Ree has always maintained that if he had not fought back, he would have been "run out of the league."[15]

Of all the teams O'Ree played against, his most bitter Quebec League memories are associated with the Chicoutimi Sagueneens and their fans.

When the Aces played that team, O'Ree was subjected to name-calling and harassment. Fans threw things at him, poured drinks on him, spat at him, and hurled racist epithets.[16] On one occasion, O'Ree was attacked by a fan while skating off the ice and into the penalty box. The incident produced a bench-clearing brawl as O'Ree's teammates attempted to come to his aid.[17]

In the 1950s, part of Canadian hockey's success was the sport's ability to promote cultural tensions between Canada's French- and English-speaking societies. Quebec teams were seen as representative of the province and its culture. This form of racism was at the core of the sport and was often reflected in the actions of team officials, players, and fans. The more rural the French Canadian or English Canadian team, the greater the animosity toward visiting clubs or individuals, each seeing the other as different. Unsurprisingly, O'Ree and other players of color experienced racial hatred directed toward them by some Quebecois fans.[18]

O'Ree was not the only Black player to play for the Aces during the 1956–57 season. Stan Maxwell, a native of Truro, Nova Scotia, joined him. The two bonded immediately and became close friends. The second of fifteen children, Stan "Chook" Maxwell was born to a Black family on March 24, 1935. He excelled in sports as a child and spent hours playing hockey and baseball with his siblings. Unable to afford a simple goal net, he scored his first five hundred hockey goals between goalposts made of rocks.

After signing his first professional hockey contract with the Quebec Aces, Maxwell embarked on a fifteen-year professional career that included his debut into the NHL. He skated for the Kingston Frontenacs of the Eastern Professional Hockey League, Los Angeles Blades of the Western Hockey League, and Toledo Blades of the International Hockey League.[19] Then on January 18, 1958, the Boston Bruins called up O'Ree to play against the Montreal Canadiens. In this game, he became the first Black man to play in the NHL regular season. O'Ree's official NHL debut was more about the Bruins' desire to overcome a losing slump and fill their injury-prone and trade-shortened roster than any interest in making a political or historic statement. In fact, the club initially downplayed the historic importance of the event.

Ironically, this was not the first time O'Ree had dawned a Bruins jersey. On September 21, 1957, both O'Ree and Stan Maxwell represented the club in an exhibition game between the Bruins and their farm club, the Springfield Indians, at Boston Gardens. Both were impressive, as O'Ree and Maxwell each drew assists in a 4–2 Bruins victory with 6,711 fans on hand to witness the historic event. Because the game was considered an exhibition and not a regular season NHL contest, both O'Ree and Maxwell were never recognized by the NHL, the Boston Bruins Hockey Club, or the Hockey Hall of Fame for their joint accomplishment in that game.

O'Ree played only two games for the Boston Bruins, producing zero goals and zero assists, which resulted in a demotion back to the minor leagues. This time he landed with the American Hockey League's Springfield Indians. At the time, the Springfield Indians were coached and co-owned by former NHL player Eddie Shore, who had a reputation as one of the toughest and dirtiest competitors ever to play in the NHL. The low point in Shore's career occurred in January 1930, when he attacked the Toronto Maple Leafs' Ace Bailey from behind. Bailey's head hit the ice, knocking him out and causing him to suffer a series of convulsions. The injury was so serious that it ended Bailey's career. While at Springfield under Coach Shore, O'Ree dressed for only six games, playing less than six minutes in total. Shore never gave an explanation for limiting O'Ree's playing time.[20]

Though the 1957–58 season began on a high note, O'Ree's relegation to Springfield, his treatment by Shore, and his resulting lack of scoring when finally given an opportunity were disastrous. He had failed to impress during his break into the NHL. Surely O'Ree and those around him thought his future in professional and senior hockey was, at best, quite limited.[21]

After his six games at Springfield, O'Ree returned to the Quebec Aces, where his performance was mediocre for the next two years. In 122 games with the Aces, he scored only twenty-six goals with forty-two assists. In 1959, he was traded to the Kingston Frontenacs, part of the newly formed six-team Eastern Professional Hockey League, where he skated in fifty games, registering twenty-two goals and twenty-five assists. After four seasons of mediocre play, O'Ree appeared to have rediscovered his earlier scoring form with Kitchener.

O'Ree got a rare second chance to perform and impress in the NHL, an experience that brought great racial strife for him. The Boston Bruins invited him to return for the 1960–61 NHL season. He played in forty-three games, scoring four goals and registering ten assists. While on road games to Detroit, New York, and Chicago, O'Ree was often the recipient of racist name-calling and on-ice cheap shots from opposing players.

Things got out of hand during one game in Chicago. The game was less than two minutes old when Chicago's Eric Nesterenko skated to O'Ree and called him the N-word. Before O'Ree could respond, Nesterenko butt-ended O'Ree in the mouth with his stick, knocking out two of O'Ree's front teeth, splitting his lip, and breaking his nose. O'Ree responded by hitting Nesterenko on the head with his stick. The cut to Nesterenko was so severe that it required more than a dozen stitches to close. The incident resulted in a bench-clearing brawl between their two teams. O'Ree and Nesterenko were given five-minute penalties each for fighting. However, both players were forced to leave the ice to address their injuries. Chicago officials did not allow O'Ree to return to the game, since they couldn't guarantee they could keep O'Ree safe from either the opposing team's players or the local fans. He stayed locked inside the Bruins' dressing room with security guards placed at the door for his own protection. Following the game, the Bruins required a police escort out of the arena. It was the worst racist incident of O'Ree's career and one that he never forgot.

The Bruins traded O'Ree to the Montreal Canadiens after the 1960–61 season. Because of the talent that Montreal possessed, they transferred O'Ree down to the Eastern Professional Hockey League (EPHL). There he played sixteen games for the Canadiens farm team, the Hull-Ottawa Canadiens. While with Hull-Ottawa, he scored ten goals and registered nine assists. The Hull-Ottawa Canadiens ended their season as the EPHL champions. During the 1961–62 season, O'Ree played twelve games for the Hull-Ottawa Canadiens before he was traded once again. This time, he went to the Los Angeles Blades of the Western Hockey League.

His move to Los Angeles proved fruitful, both professionally and personally. O'Ree scored twenty-eight goals and twenty-six assists in his first season with Los Angeles. A year later, he registered twenty-five goals and twenty-six assists. During his third year, the 1964–65 season, he registered thirty-eight goals and twenty-one assists. While with the Los Angeles Blades,

O'Ree met Bernadine Plummer, a young university student from Portland, Oregon, who became his first wife. Within two years of their marriage, the couple welcomed two boys, Kevin (1963) and Darren (1965). Constantly on the road, O'Ree relied on Bernadine to raise their family in his absence. Within four years, their marriage was on the rocks. Bernadine eventually moved with the two boys to Texas, leaving him to continue his playing career in California on his own. Six seasons into his tenure with Los Angeles, O'Ree signed with the San Diego Gulls for the start of the 1967–68 season.

Professional hockey's six-team expansion in 1967 became a ripe opportunity for O'Ree to return to the NHL. The NHL added the Los Angeles Kings, Oakland Seals, St. Louis Blues, Pittsburgh Penguins, Philadelphia Flyers, and Minnesota North Stars. O'Ree thought it was only a matter of time before he would be called up to play in the NHL once again. That call never came. People in hockey circles discovered he was blind in his right eye, and simply because of that factor alone, no NHL team wanted to take the risk. O'Ree was also thirty-two years of age, old age by NHL standards. After signing with San Diego, O'Ree played seven seasons with the Gulls (1967–74), scoring 153 goals and 159 assists.

In 1972, O'Ree met his second wife, Deljeet Kaur Manak, an Indo-Canadian student at the University of Victoria. They were introduced through her brother, a sports reporter. One year later the two were living together in San Diego. Following their marriage, Deljeet gave birth to the couple's daughter, Chandra, in 1979.

In addition, during the 1972–73 season, O'Ree also played for the American Hockey League's New Haven Hawks, scoring twenty-one goals and twenty-four assists in fifty games. In 1974, O'Ree played his last season with the San Diego Gulls. He went on to play hockey for the California Senior League's San Diego Charms. He ended his playing career in 1979, following a season with the Pacific Hockey League's San Diego Hawks. In total, he played in 785 professional games, scoring 328 goals and 311 assists. After O'Ree's three years in the NHL, from 1958 to 1961, no Black man would play for the league until 1974, when Mike Marson was drafted by the Washington Capitals.

O'Ree was not an exception as a Black man who played hockey but rather the product of a long-forgotten Black New Brunswick hockey tradition.

Therefore, to claim that he is the "Jackie Robinson of hockey" is to fail to fully recognize his unique accomplishments and historic significance. Beyond the professional arena, he is his own story—living proof of a Black hockey tradition that once existed and has yet to be fully recognized or documented.

Prior to World War I, Black hockey traditions were well established in Eastern Canada. Evidence exists of established Black hockey leagues—most notably, the Colored Hockey League of the Maritimes and teams in the New Brunswick region.[22] O'Ree's autobiography, cowritten with historian Michael McKinley in 2000, references the Black hockey traditions that existed prior to O'Ree's entry into the NHL.[23]

In fact, O'Ree and McKinley refer to "Black hockey leagues" (meaning more than one) existing at the beginning of the twentieth century. This revelation is important, as the book, *The Autobiography of Willie O'Ree: Hockey's Black Pioneer*, was published four years before the release of George and Darril Fosty's book *Black Ice: The Lost History of the Colored Hockey League of the Maritimes, 1895–1925*. To this day, *Black Ice* remains the only book detailing the history of the Colored Hockey League of the Maritimes. Follow-up research in the eighteen years since the book's publication has uncovered evidence of Black teams existing in New Brunswick around the same time as the Halifax-based Colored Hockey League. This discovery is important.[24]

A lack of historical documentation on Black communities in New Brunswick is a major obstacle in the efforts to rediscover the history of Black hockey traditions in New Brunswick and to pinpoint how O'Ree and his story fit into this narrative. In 1972, the historian W. A. Spray attempted to document that history in his book *The Blacks of New Brunswick*, which contained place names and information on New Brunswick's Black communities. Unfortunately, at the time of his writing, very little evidence of the region's Black history remained. The book's seventy-two pages (with an additional twenty-one pages of illustrations) contained no reference to Black hockey history or any detailed discussion of Black provincial sports teams or leagues.

The Spray book was heavily criticized upon its release. Not only did critics attack the abbreviated length of the book, but they also attempted to dismiss the role of Blacks in the shaping of New Brunswick's early history. Claiming that fewer than 2 percent of New Brunswick's early population was Black (as late as 1974, fewer than two thousand Blacks were living in the province), these critics argued that historian W. S. MacNutt had devoted less than 2 of the 339 pages of his highly praised 1963 book *New Brunswick, a History: 1784–1867* to the contributions of Black pioneers, loyalists, and Black communities. As a result, Spray's critics concluded that if MacNutt did not mention it, then it could not have existed or been important.[25]

In the years since MacNutt's and Spray's works, the lack of information on the history of Blacks in New Brunswick, as well as their hockey traditions, resulted from racism and cultural arrogance precipitated by accepted narratives. Following the release of O'Ree's autobiography in 2000 and the 2004 publication of *Black Ice*, more of New Brunswick's lost Black hockey legacy has come to light, making it possible to put O'Ree's achievements in proper historical context.

During the 1920s, one of O'Ree's uncles was said to have been known for his hockey skills and was a star in the Fredericton Leagues. We also know of references to other Blacks playing hockey in the Fredericton and Moncton, New Brunswick, areas. O'Ree himself implies that his own father was a hockey player or had a love and familiarity for the game, having introduced his son to skating and hockey when the child was only three. O'Ree also refers to his older brother Richard (thirteen years his senior) as having been a hockey player. O'Ree makes additional reference to three prominent Black communities that existed in and around Fredericton (Barker's Point, Spring Hill, and Gagetown), which were likely areas where Black hockey was being played.

The rediscovery of Black Canadian hockey history also provides context for O'Ree's tenure with the Boston Bruins. Of all the cities in the United States, Boston has the greatest Black hockey tradition. Following the influx of job-seeking Black Canadians to the Boston region in the 1920s, teams composed of former players and families from the Colored Hockey League of the Maritimes (1895–1930) were now playing in and around Boston.

On February 13, 1929, a *Boston Daily Advertiser* article titled "Colored Panthers on Arena Hockey Bill Tomorrow" reported,

The Colored Panthers, the comedy hockey team who created so much fun in the Arena last season, are on the bill at the St. Botolph Street rink tomorrow. The Negro team will play the St. Joe's of East Boston. . . . This will be the first appearance of the Colored Panthers in the Arena this season. They have won five out of six games this season and hope to get revenge for the defeat suffered in a game with St. Joe's last season. The Negro team has a new defense player who weighs more than 200 pounds. Talbert, States, Mills, Gibson and other players, who were favorites last season, are with the team again.[26]

The history and eventual fate of the Colored Panthers is unknown. From some of the surnames listed, there is little doubt that the team had historical and/or family links to both Nova Scotia and the Bog of Charlottetown, Prince Edward Island.

Between 1901 and 1930, racism and harsh economic conditions forced many African Canadian families to leave Canada for a better life in the United States. So prevalent was the exodus that many long-established African Canadian communities witnessed a 20 to 70 percent population decline. Effectively "starved out of Canada," many of these families resettled in the Boston area. It was in the Boston region that these Canadian families helped establish a small, but competitive, Black hockey tradition.

The earliest reference to hockey-playing Blacks in the Boston area occurs in 1911. That year, during a game between two local boys' school teams played on a frozen pond near Framingham, Massachusetts (a community twenty miles east of Boston), the ice broke. Six youths drowned as a result. The local newspapers reported on the tragedy, naming five of the players and sending condolences to their families. A sixth player was simply referred to as "a negro boy." Unlike the respect afforded to the white victims, the local press did not feel any obligation to give the name of the Black child or express condolences to his family. To this day, this young Black child's identity remains a mystery. Historically, his death is important, as he remains the first and only Black hockey player known to have died during a hockey game. He also holds the distinction of being the first Black player to be mentioned in the annals of early American and Boston-area hockey history.[27]

During the 1920s and 1930s, at least six all-Black senior semipro teams were formed in the Boston area. Three of the teams—the West Medford Ramblers, the Wellington Maroons, and the Spring Green Hockey Club—included local Black hockey players who honed their skills playing alongside white counterparts on area ponds or in the white-dominated Boston school leagues. Though the names of many of these Black players remain lost to history, of the few identified to date, most appear to share the same surnames as those of well-known African Canadian families who had been active in the Colored Hockey League. Among the most common are those of Talbot and Johnson.

By 1933, four Black players were recognized as rising stars in the New England high school leagues. On January 14, 1933, the local *Boston Guardian* newspaper wrote,

> Hockey, which is considered to be the fastest of all sports, found four of our boys around the ice. At Technical High, Horace Robinson gained the distinction of being the first colored boy to represent that school in hockey in over 20 years. Robinson played a wing post, being a fast skater and a dangerous shooter, once within the blue line. Kenneth Perry, the other lad, saw plenty of action with the Lake AC sextette of Spring Green, a semi-pro outfit. Both of these lads were fancy handlers of the stick, and hard checking players, with Perry playing a defensive position. At the East Providence High, Leroy and Vernon Beaubian, wing and defense man, aided materially in the success of the town out-fit. Vernon is at present matriculating at the Kent Hill Prep School in Maine, was also a hard checking man who proved a tower of strength in holding opposing wingmen while the older brother was a flashy speedster in the art of securing rebounds and firing powerful shots at opposing goalies.[28]

Young African American players were rising through the scholastic ranks in Boston and surrounding communities.

O'Ree played only forty-five games in the NHL before being returned to the Senior Leagues. In the years that followed, neither O'Ree nor his fellow Black hockey player, Stan Maxwell, both consummate professionals, ever complained publicly about their treatment by the NHL or the lack of opportunities they were afforded. The two men were later teammates with the Los Angeles Blades, distinguishing themselves as two of the Western Hockey League's marquee players.

Following his professional hockey career, O'Ree took a security officer job with the San Diego Chargers of the National Football League (NFL). He eventually worked his way into a supervisory position. He later left the Chargers organization to take a position as security manager at the exclusive Hotel Del Coronado in San Diego.

Maxwell, in the final years of his life, worked tirelessly to promote amateur sports programs in his native Nova Scotia, where he also became active in the Truro Baptist Church. In his youth, Stan Maxwell's mother and father raised their son to be humble and religious. His mother, Naomi, was of the Parris clan, one of the original families of the Colored Hockey League. She often told her son, "You shouldn't have to talk about yourself, let other people do it if it is deserving."[29] As a result, Stan never boasted about his hockey skills or compared himself with others. Stan "Chook" Maxwell died in 2001 at the age of sixty-six. To this day, people who knew him or witnessed his career still talk of the man with great affection, appreciation, and respect.[30]

Much of O'Ree's recognition came later in his life. The NHL rediscovered him in the 1990s, inviting him to work as a hockey ambassador in their newly established diversity program. In 1998, O'Ree was named to the position of NHL director of youth development while promoting hockey diversity. Five years later, he was awarded the Lester Patrick Trophy for outstanding service to hockey in the United States. In 2005, he received the Order of New Brunswick and was inducted into the New Brunswick Sports Hall of Fame. In 2007, he was inducted into the Black Ice Hockey and Sports Hall of Fame in Nova Scotia. Eleven years later, in 2018, he was inducted into the Hockey Hall of Fame, becoming the first Black man to achieve the honor. A year later, he was also inducted into the Canadian Sports Hall of Fame.[31] In 2022, the Boston Bruins honored O'Ree as the first Black player to compete in the NHL, retiring his number twenty-two jersey. In 2022, he was awarded the U.S. Congressional Gold Medal for his lifetime achievements.

Notes

1. Willie O'Ree and Michael McKinley, *The Autobiography of Willie O'Ree* (Toronto: Somerville House, 2000), 7.
2. O'Ree and McKinley, *Autobiography of Willie O'Ree*, 9–10; Nicole Mortillaro, *Willie O'Ree: The Story of the First Black Player in the* NHL (Toronto: James Lorimer, 2012), 21.
3. O'Ree and McKinley, *Autobiography of Willie O'Ree*, 10, 16.
4. O'Ree and McKinley, *Autobiography of Willie O'Ree*, 22.
5. O'Ree and McKinley, *Autobiography of Willie O'Ree*, 25.
6. O'Ree and McKinley, *Autobiography of Willie O'Ree*, 27.
7. O'Ree and McKinley, *Autobiography of Willie O'Ree*, 28.
8. O'Ree and McKinley, *Autobiography of Willie O'Ree*, 29.
9. O'Ree and McKinley, *Autobiography of Willie O'Ree*, 29, 30.
10. O'Ree and McKinley, *Autobiography of Willie O'Ree*, 38.
11. Willie O'Ree and Michael McKinley, *Willie: The Game-Changing Story of the* NHL's *First Black Player* (Toronto: Penguin Random House, 2020), 49–51.
12. O'Ree and McKinley, *Willie*, 53–55.
13. O'Ree and McKinley, *Willie*, 56–57.
14. O'Ree and McKinley, *Autobiography of Willie O'Ree*, 36–37.
15. O'Ree and McKinley, *Autobiography of Willie O'Ree*, 51.
16. O'Ree and McKinley, *Autobiography of Willie O'Ree*, 50, 51.
17. O'Ree and McKinley, *Autobiography of Willie O'Ree*, 52.
18. George Fosty and Darril Fosty, *Splendid Is the Sun: The 5,000 Year History of Hockey* (New York: Stryker-Indigo, 2004), 181.
19. George Fosty and Darril Fosty, *Tribes: An International Hockey History* (New York: Stryker-Indigo, 2013), 178–81.
20. O'Ree and McKinley, *Autobiography of Willie O'Ree*, 59.
21. Fosty and Fosty, *Splendid Is the Sun*, 128–29.
22. George Fosty and Darril Fosty, *Black Ice: The Lost History of the Colored Hockey League of the Maritimes, 1895–1925* (New York: Stryker-Indigo, 2004).
23. Fosty and Fosty, *Splendid Is the Sun*, 197.
24. Fosty and Fosty, *Tribes*, 178–81; O'Ree and McKinley, *Willie*, 7–9. For a complete accounting of the history of the Colored Hockey League, see Fosty and Fosty, *Black Ice*. For a complete accounting of ancient Black or minority hockey traditions worldwide, see Fosty and Fosty, *Splendid Is the Sun*.
25. William A. Spray, *The Blacks of New Brunswick* (Fredericton: Brunswick, 1972). Unfairly criticized at the time of its publication for its lack of detailed information, Spray's work is an important starting point for historians interested in documenting the early history of Blacks in New Brunswick. Without Spray's efforts, almost nothing would be known of Black New Brunswick history.

26. O'Ree and McKinley, *Autobiography of Willie O'Ree*, 16, 28, 29.

27. Fosty and Fosty, *Tribes*, 96, 97.

28. Fosty and Fosty, *Tribes*, 97.

29. Fosty and Fosty, *Tribes*, 97, 98.

30. Fosty and Fosty, *Tribes*, 180; O'Ree and McKinley, *Autobiography of Willie O'Ree*, 11.

31. Daryl Bell, "The NHL's First Black Player, Willie O'Ree, Had a Short but Pathbreaking Stint with the Boston Bruins," *Andscape*, February 14, 2017, https://andscape.com/features/nhl-first-black-player-willie-oree/. See also Steve Simmons, "Don't Compare Hall of Famer Willie O'Ree to Jackie Robinson," *Toronto Sun*, June 30, 2018, https://torontosun.com/sports/hockey/nhl/simmons-dont-compare-hall-of-famer-willie-oree-to-jackie-robinson.

12

Zero Love

The Intersection of Race and Class in Boston Tennis

SUNDIATA DJATA

The game of tennis was introduced to the United States in 1874, not long after the end of slavery. In Boston and throughout the nation, it was a sport identified with the upper classes. Its organizers embraced the social and political norms of racial segregation, and as late as the 1890s, tennis held little appeal for the working classes, Black or white. There were no public courts, and private courts at country clubs were reserved for the elite. Arthur Ashe, the first Black male player to win a grand slam title in 1968, called tennis the "sport of kings," which aptly describes the elitism of the sport.[1] In 1881, a group of tennis club members from the Northeast established the United States National Lawn Tennis Association (USNLTA), a racially segregated governing body formed to standardize the rules and regulations of the game. By 1880, the sport had become so popular among the upper classes that private clubs were finding it difficult to accommodate the demand, and the first public courts were established. These courts were largely in white neighborhoods and inaccessible to Blacks. Despite elitism and white supremacist exclusionary practices, Black Bostonians have been playing tennis at least since the 1890s.

The Roots of Black Tennis

Responding to their exclusion from the USNLTA, Black players on the East Coast formed the American Tennis Association (ATA) in 1916. During a tournament in New York City between the Association Tennis Club of Washington DC and the Monumental Tennis Club of Baltimore, team members contacted and enlisted the support of known Black tennis clubs to help establish the association. Prior to the creation of the ATA, faculty members at Tuskegee Institute, a historically Black college in Alabama, introduced the

244

game to its students. Subsequently, Tuskegee hosted the first Black college tennis tournament in 1895.[2]

The ATA created a national tournament with affiliated clubs and organizations to host their own local tournaments, most of which took place east of the Mississippi. The ATA provided competitive tennis opportunities for Black players but also admitted players from other racial backgrounds, especially at the national level. Although both associations had names that suggest that they were national in scope, only the ATA offered memberships to any player regardless of race or religion.

Racial discrimination in the USNLTA became explicit in 1929, when the organization excluded two Black players, Gerald L. Norman Jr. and Reginald Weir, from the National Junior Indoor Championships in New York City. Claiming that the USNLTA was experiencing a decline in memberships "because of race," the USNLTA said there was "a need for separate tournaments administered by the USNLTA for white players, and the ATA for Black players."[3] In a letter to Edward B. Moss, executive secretary of the USNLTA, Robert W. Bagall of the "colored people's organization" (the National Association for the Advancement of Colored People [NAACP]) charged that "class and caste snobbery" was the reason for USNLTA's refusal to accept the entries from Norman and Weir. Norman's father was a tennis coach at Bryant High School in Queens, New York, where he coached white boys. The letter from Bagall read, in part, "If the facts are as stated, the action of the United States Lawn Tennis Association constitutes an action unfair, unsportsmanlike, and calculated to degrade the sport you protest to cultivate and against which we as well as many other Americans, white and colored, wish to protest in the strongest terms." He added that members of the USNLTA "were un-American, and class snobs," fearful of competition from Black players.[4] Moss replied, "In pursuing this policy we make no reflection upon the colored race, but we believe that as a practical matter, the present method of separate associations for the administration of the affairs and championships of colored and white players should be continued."[5] The incident exemplified the racial attitude of the USNLTA administration, since Moss defended racial segregation in writing, exposing the practice by the organization and confirming that the

USNLTA should continue it. Moreover, there was the sense that whites feared competing with Blacks in various sports.

Black Tennis in Boston

Most of the tennis clubs at the turn of the century did not allow Blacks or Jews, including those in the Boston area. One of the first and most prominent of these exclusionary clubs in Boston was the West Side Tennis Club, founded on April 22, 1892. When it opened on June 10 of that same year, the club had thirteen members. By the end of its first season, membership had risen to forty-three.[6] At that time, the only "stated requirements" for joining the West Side Tennis Club were that members had to be older than sixteen, be endorsed by a current member, pay a ten-dollar initiation fee, and demonstrate the ability to play a good game of tennis. There was no explicit statement that Blacks were excluded.[7]

Continuing discrimination at white tennis facilities led members of the Jewish and Black communities in Weston, Massachusetts, to establish a private tennis club, the Wightman Center, in 1966. Jerome Rosen, a Boston attorney, received a call from Sidney Cohen, the senior partner of an accounting firm, asking Rosen to become the director of a new tennis facility he was organizing along with Summer "Sonny" Rodman, Harrison "Rosie" Rowbotham, and Bernard "Bill" Pearson. They were all avid tennis players who believed there was a need for an indoor tennis facility accessible to the Black community. At the time, such a facility was unavailable in Boston. The Badminton and Tennis Club existed and had an indoor court, but it was only open to the Boston elite. Rosen agreed, and together they founded the Hazel Hotchkiss Wightman Tennis Center.[8] Rosen's written historical account does not include any mention of race or religion. However, Arthur Worth "Bud" Collins Jr., a sports journalist, wrote about Black members of the club. In 1969, he called it "an athletic club for all peoples," adding, "Color, race, religion, politics have nothing to do with entrance requirements." Assessing the regional club situation, Collins wrote,

> As centers of sportsmanship, most of New England and America's private athletic clubs are a fraud. Sportsmanship, to be genuine, has to go

beyond games, and extend to life outside the toy department. Almost without exception, these clubs—the pillars of tennis, golf, swimming, boating, riding—are bigoted and restrictive in their admission policies. The people raising the handsome Wightman Center in Weston will not go that way. Among the 300 family memberships are Negroes, Jews, people of all faiths and convictions. "It is a private club," says a prime mover, the president, Harrison Rowbotham, "but not in the usual sense. We are taking people on the basis of their being acceptable citizens—and, of course, for their ability to pay the bills."[9]

The current general manager affirms that the club was founded by Jews because Jews were not permitted in other Boston-area clubs. Although Wightman maintained an open-door policy of admitting anyone to club membership, it is unknown how many Blacks have been members or joined the staff over the years, making it difficult to determine just how racially diverse the membership has been.[10]

Racial issues at the Longwood Cricket Club have long impacted Black national players because the club hosted national and international tournaments from 1917 to 1999, including the National Doubles, U.S. Nationals, and Davis Cup. There was some hope of racial change "by degrees" in 1948, when the *Boston Globe* reported, "Prejudice against Negro athletes is giving way, the current instance being the admission of one of the race to the indoor national championship now being held by the United States Lawn Tennis Association in New York City." Until Dr. Reginald Weir became the first Black to play in "such a tournament" in 1948, the USNLTA had "opened its events to all shades except one," the *Globe* noted, adding, "Apparently intolerance is on the wane." Baseball great Jackie Robinson "integrated" into Major League Baseball the previous year. Two years before that, Yale University let Levi Jackson carry the ball, following a long-established tradition of athletic racial tolerance set by Harvard and Dartmouth. "The time may come when the aristocratic turf at the Longwood may be trod by the extreme swift feet of Negro competitors," the *Globe* wrote. "Then the play will be really open."[11]

Longwood and Integration: Althea Gibson

Women's tennis champion Althea Gibson broke the color barrier at clubs like Longwood in the 1950s. News reports noted that Gibson was to play "for the first time" in the women's National Doubles at the Longwood Cricket Club in Chestnut Hills, Massachusetts. "Gibson was the first Negro to play in the big-league tennis circuit. She has three times played in the National Singles at Forest Hills" but had never played in the National Doubles at Longwood.[12] By 1956, sports journalist Bud Collins was working at the *Boston Herald*, where he was the lone reporter with any interest in tennis. One day, his editor rattled off a surprising series of questions: "How good is the colored girl? Could she win at Forest Hills? [She'd] be the first of her kind to win, if she does, wouldn't she?" The editor did not know Gibson's name, but he knew that a Black woman winning the U.S. Nationals was a story.[13]

The conversation continued in 1957, when Boston newspapers reported that Gibson, who had just won Wimbledon, might make her first appearance in the National Doubles at Longwood. Previously, she had entered in the doubles draw but didn't participate because it conflicted with the "Negro national championship" (ATA), which she had won nine or ten times. According to Gibson, the ATA stopped asking her to play their national tournament so that they could develop new champions, and she could play USNLTA tournaments without a conflict.[14] The ATA top officials, Bertram Baker and Arthur Francis, decided to push for Blacks to play in the USNLTA events.[15]

Longwood was particularly eager to have Gibson play that year because the men's tournament had lost its major attraction, Lew Hoad, who turned professional after winning at Wimbledon for the second year in a row. Gibson was reputed to be the best amateur woman player in the world in 1957, although not yet in a class with Helen Wills, Suzanne Lenglen, Anna Margrethe "Molla" Bjurstedt Mallory, Helen Jacobs, Alice Marble, and other more recent USNLTA champions. Nevertheless, Collins noted, she was considered "a formidable performer" and one who had "done in tennis what Jackie Robinson did in baseball, and what no one has yet done in golf."[16] The following week, the *Boston Globe* announced that Gibson, the "Cinderella of the tennis world," would play in Boston at the National Doubles, teaming with Darlene Hard;

the ATA had given Gibson the "green light" to play at Longwood.[17] Despite the proclamation that Gibson "broke the color barrier" at Longwood and their eagerness to have her compete at their club, her play in the championships did not persuade Longwood to extend membership to Blacks.

Longwood and Freedom: Arthur Ashe

In 1968, Arthur Ashe won the amateur national championship at Long-wood.[18] In the decades that followed, he often referred to Longwood in conversations about racial issues in national and international tennis. The year 1968 was a pivotal one in civil rights history: Reverend Martin Luther King Jr., a major leader in the civil rights movement, was murdered in Memphis while supporting a strike by the city's garbage collectors, and in Los Angeles, presidential candidate and civil rights supporter Bobby Kennedy Jr. was murdered after a campaign rally.

In Ashe's hometown of Richmond, Virginia, the tennis champion defeated two Black Jamaicans, Lance Lumsden and Richard Russell, in the 1968 Davis Cup match at Byrd Parks. This was a monumental occurrence because Byrd Parks was racially segregated; most Blacks played at Battery Park, on Richmond's north side. Louis C. Einwick Jr., general chairman of the Richmond Tennis Patrons Tournament Committee, which brought the Davis Cup to the city, later noted, "Blacks, including Ashe, were outlawed from playing at Byrd Park until the mid-1960s . . . the 1968 Davis Cup was probably the first time Ashe played, at least competitively, at Byrd Park."[19] As the only Black player in the upper echelon of tennis, Ashe thought of himself as "the black lining in the ivory-white cloud of tennis." Collins wrote, "So now Sunday he was on the hallowed grass of the Longwood Cricket Club in Chestnut Hill—oldest tennis club in the country. This was a place where they shook hands with Arthur Ashe, but a club which would never continence [sic] his kind as a member." Ashe understood that an effective way to combat the institutional racism prevalent in tennis rested on his performance ability. "I know this," Ashe said, "but I can't shut myself away from it all by withdrawing. Maybe in 300 years everything will be straightened out. And I'll work for it. But now tennis is what I do best, the way I'll earn my living, so I'll have to play."[20]

Ashe held little hope of immediate change. When he was asked how it felt to win a national title at a club that would never have him as a member, Ashe responded, "I don't like the situation in these clubs."[21] In that summer, Ashe and Collins discussed racial issues in tennis during an interview with Boston's public TV station, WGBH. With no commercial constraints, they talked at length about race relations in the United States (Jim Crow), the future of South Africa (apartheid), and what it was like for Ashe to play at clubs that refused to admit him as a member. "I hope I see changes," Ashe said.[22] "I guess seven-eighths of the clubs I play at exclude Negroes from membership. . . . I can't force clubs to admit Negroes, even though I might think it's morally wrong, to have rules against them."[23] Later, after Ashe won the U.S. Open, Collins rushed to Ashe, hoping to continue their Long-wood conversation for a larger audience on CBS, a commercial station. Collins reported a directive that came from the producer: "Don't get into all that black stuff—just tennis." After all, CBS had ads to run.[24]

In the Longwood final against Robert "Bob" Lutz, the fans supported Lutz. Some argued that racism had nothing to do with the fans' support of the white player, claiming that it didn't confirm the conclusion of the Kerner report on racism.[25] Ashe had always been popular at Longwood, "but the 20-year-old Lutz, with his bold and often showy shot-making, was a vibrant kid in scattering the seeds en route to the final," Collins wrote, noting that the crowd expressed enthusiasm for both players. He wrote, "The gathering of 5000 hailed both men with prolonged excited applause for what they had accomplished."[26] Although both players were underdogs, Lutz was the "sentimental favorite."[27] One fan, John Gray of Dover, proclaimed, "I'm for Lutz, he's never won anything big." Another, Steve Lofchie of Chestnut Hill, said, "I'm for Lutz. He fits the American image, the player who comes from nowhere to win." Why didn't Ashe fit the American image? He was a "Negro in the purest of the white man's worlds—the exclusive tennis club set."[28]

Oddly, Ashe made a great issue of being excluded from playing in apart-heid South Africa all while he was still unable to join private clubs in the United States.[29] During the U.S. Pro Tournament at Longwood in August 1971, Ashe was fighting to get a visa to play in South Africa.[30] When white South African Frew McMillan and Australian John Newcombe took the court at Longwood, McMillan received an uncomfortable welcome. The local NAACP chapter protested South Africa's refusal to grant Ashe a visa to play in the South African Open. "Paint him black and send him back," members yelled at McMillan, who "largely tuned them out," but Newcombe, "Ashe's friend and ally," begged them to stop because "they threw off his concentration. Ashe was unsympathetic." Ashe told the *Baltimore Afro-American*, "I have nothing against the South African players who I meet, travel with and play with almost every day. This thing is bigger than tennis." The paper defended Ashe against his critics—most of whom were his fellow players who had to endure the noise. "Arthur Ashe has become aware that he will be a man much longer than he will be a tennis player," Collins wrote.[31]

Many believed that Ashe should have boycotted the match against white South African Cliff Drysdale, but Ashe believed he could do more for Blacks by showing his skill on a tennis court. He also knew that Drysdale was against apartheid. "I've talked about tennis with a lot of black leaders, well known and others," Ashe told an interviewer. "There was talk about my not playing Davis Cup. I considered not playing Davis Cup as my personal protest against South Africa's being in the competition. I talked to Bob Kelleher [USNLTA president] about this four hours one day." He added, "I know that I make money for clubs that wouldn't allow me or other blacks to be members. This is immoral, I believe, but if I don't play—if I withdraw—then there is no black man in tennis, and I have no chance of trying to change the situation."[32]

Autonomy and Self-Definition: Sportsmen's Tennis Center

Still excluded from the country club scene, David Alvs, Jim Smith, and several friends founded the Sportsmen's Tennis Center (STC) in 1961 (the name was later changed to the Sportsmen's Tennis and Enrichment Center [STEC]). This was the first indoor nonprofit tennis club built by and for the Black community. Their goal was to provide a place where Black youths could learn and play the game with the advantage of having indoor courts to use in the winter.[33] At that time, most existing indoor courts were still located in private clubs where Blacks either were entirely unwelcome or could not afford the annual dues.

New England's ATA chapter issued Smith a charter. In 1965 the Committee for Greater Tennis Activity was formed to involve people from other sections of the city in the sport. By 1967, the Internal Revenue Service granted the STC its nonprofit status.[34] According to Alveta Haynes, a former executive director of the club, "David and Jim were visionaries, but they were also visionaries with no money. But that didn't stop them, nothing ever did."[35] Their dream intrigued Collins, who wrote, "[Tennis] had become stagnant and needed to update its stodgy image by extending beyond the country-club set and reaching into minority communities." Ten years later, the center had seven courts.[36]

Smith greatly influenced both young Black players and the expansion of Black tennis in the Boston area. A former businessman and an Air Force veteran of World War II, Smith became the club's first tennis coach, holding tennis lessons on the playground and at the former Franklin Field. Recruiting a few volunteers, Smith began teaching the game to seven children from the Bromley-Heath public housing project, enrolling them in junior classes in the Cabot Street Gymnasium in Roxbury in 1962. Later tournaments were held at the William Carter Courts in Roxbury.

Without the full support of the city, the STC had to use whatever space could be found, which encouraged Smith to advocate for the young tennis players. The facilities were modest; they "played around the grass growing out of the asphalt and swept away the cracked glass, and volunteers carried a net in the trucks of their cars." Smith brought in tennis legends like Billie Jean King and Arthur Ashe to convince the city government to approve the Sportsmen's building license. "Tennis is not a traditional sport in the inner city and many of the schools either don't have tennis or have a very short rotation for tennis," Smith argued, "so we are allowing kids to learn a sport that can provide a college scholarship and a lifelong sport."[37] In 1968, the STC moved its program to Franklin Field in Dorchester, which was owned by the city of Boston but was not well kept. In 1970, the city approved the license for the Sportsmen's building in Dorchester's Harambee Park and construction began. The junior training program became a year-round activity with the expansion of the Franklin Field Center in 1973.[38]

In 1983, *Tennis* magazine reported, "Many tennis people thought that Jim Smith and his staff were the best teaching pros in Boston. Certainly, they are the busiest." At the time, they gave about ninety lessons a week to almost three hundred people. In addition, "they handle the junior program with 2,000 kids in it." Nearly 3,000 new players were introduced to the game annually through the STC.[39]

In 1984, parents of students enrolled in the tennis program decided to honor Smith. "Our children expand the idea of excellence into their school and other activities," one parent noted. "Jim deserves credit for inspiring our youth."[40] In 1993, the United States Tennis Association (USTA) New England executive director, Bruce Greenspan, selected Smith for induction into the organization's Hall of Fame.[41] Smith also worked with the sportswriter Bud Collins to organize matches featuring tennis professionals from Australia competing against U.S. amateurs at Harvard University. During the 1970s and 1980s, well-known personalities visited the club, including Andrew Young, Dinah Shore, Gordon Parks, and Bob Lobel. Professional players like Ashe, Gibson, Leslie Allen, Zina Garrison, Lori McNeil, and Tim Mayotte also made appearances at the club. In 1989, Smith and his wife, Gloria, organized a goodwill tennis tour to the Soviet Union with Reebok sponsorship.

Leslie "Les" Smith, son of the founder and chairman of the board, became the manager in September 1990 after serving as assistant manager, teacher, and director of the summer camp.[42] By 2002, the center was annually providing low-cost tennis instruction to more than 1,200 youths between the ages of four and eighteen. Today, the club also offers after-school programs, which emphasize academics and community spirit.

In 2007, when club finances were faltering from years of poor management, Toni Wiley joined Sportsmen's as a consultant. Wiley, who had grown up down the street from the club, stayed with the organization, eventually becoming a board member, executive director, and CEO. As a former corporate leader, she quickly saw the cracks in the organization's operations. Despite its long history of providing low-cost tennis and academic programming, Sportsmen's finances were in disarray. Wiley developed a new funding plan, reworking its branding and messaging to attract grants and donations. The organization also gradually increased membership prices and expanded its adult program to fill up the courts while students were in school. In 2021, Sportsmen's budget had increased fourfold, and the organization is presently engaged in a $9 million capital campaign.[43]

Several program participants have made headlines. Ullian Fassitt was the top-ranked junior in New England. Roxbury's Stephanie Loatman was one of only a few New England players in the 1973 ATA Nationals. Chip Wilder played for the University of Massachusetts varsity team. Billy Busiek won a scholarship to Tennessee State. And two women from the program played on the old Virginia Slims Circuit.[44]

For decades, it was common to praise any Black player with promise as the next Gibson or Ashe, praise that fell upon the shoulders of a particular young Black male tennis player. In 1975, New York City's thirteen-year-old Doug Henderson landed a berth in the fourteen-and-under division at the Wightman Tennis Tournament in Weston. Despite his 6–1, 6–3 loss to the number-two seed, people were convinced that he was good enough to win on the junior circuit, where he won an upset victory in an invitational meet in Hingham the previous December. "Because he is black and a tennis player to boot, the next Arthur Ashe can't be too far away. Why, it could even be Doug Henderson! Nobody wants to label Doug Henderson at age thirteen. Things are tough enough at his age."[45]

Ashe's legacy was a heavy one for a young athlete to carry. "It is unfair to compare Doug with an Ashe," said Jim Smith, one of the teachers who coached Henderson on wooden floors at the old Williams Building on Shawmut Avenue.[46] Henderson had a difficult task ahead of him, Smith said: "And even if he gets into a tournament, there's no guarantee that he'll have it easy. It may be politics, or it may be just because he's Black. But every time he gets into a big tournament, he winds up playing the No. 1 or No. 2 seed in the first rounds. It should happen once in a while. But nobody should be that unlucky all the time." This complaint was common for Black players competing on all levels. In winning the Old Colony Tournament, Henderson defeated the top seed in the first round. After that, he reached the semifinals of another South Shore tournament, again having to defeat the top seed. "But we are worried that having to play so many seeded players will turn him off. We want him to meet the best. But we don't want to kill his spirits, either," Smith said.[47]

Sportsmen's Tennis Center and the Black Community

By the 1980s, Smith and the STC staff had accomplished a great deal, but they dreamed of doing more. Under Smith's guidance, the young players had learned to take their tennis seriously and become competitive. Their instructors used tennis as a tool for learning basic skills for success in life. The STC closed out its 1982–83 season with fifteen juniors ranked in the New England Lawn Tennis Association (NELTA). Its twelve-and-under team was the winner of the five-state Penn League organized by NELTA, and its fourteen-year-old team placed third. Also, one of their former juniors made the National Collegiate Athletic Association (NCAA). Their success was celebrated in a half-hour documentary that aired on prime-time television.[48] That year, the STC sent juniors to ten USTA sectional tournaments, where they won seven tournaments and were runners-up four times for an incredible club record.[49] In addition, the club enjoyed success in the ATA Nationals (seven wins and seven runners-ups out of seventeen events).[50] In 1984, the USTA joined the NELTA in honoring the STC as the Most Outstanding Club of the Northeast.[51] At the time, the club had fifteen juniors among the rankings in the NELTA in various age categories, and some were ranked in both singles and doubles. Moreover, the club fielded five adult teams in the Michelob Light League, with two of the teams making the playoffs. The club also had three teams in the Working Women's League and teams in the Men's A League. The Greater Boston high school and private school tennis teams were also well represented among Sportsmen's juniors.

Three talented brothers, Scott, Shaun, and Troy Crichlow, also came out of the program. Shaun, who at age five loved basketball, was "beside himself" when his mother signed him up for tennis lessons one summer. He had no interest in tennis because it was not the sport that other children in his neighborhood played—one of the major reasons given for why fewer Blacks participated in tennis.[52] Despite his initial reluctance, Shaun was hooked after one lesson and began to go to the club daily. As a teenager, he became one of the top-ranked youths in New England, traveling to the then Soviet Union to play exhibition matches. He later won a tennis scholarship to Ohio State University and Hampton State University.[53] His older brother, Scott, who began playing at age six, landed a college scholarship and a slot on the professional tour, later becoming a coach. The youngest, Troy, discusses his time at STC:

> I was lucky to grow up at Sportsmen's Tennis & Enrichment Center. At Sportsmen's I saw a lot of people with my background loving the game, having success in the game, and making a career to provide for their families through the game of tennis. Seeing Jim and Gloria Smith own a tennis club in Boston and impact so many lives in a positive way inspired me to do more in tennis then just be a great player. I have a lot of pride in being part of the continuance of their excellence and will hopefully inspire other young African Americans to do the same.[54]

Allan Curtis, a pro at the Franklin Center and an old friend of Ashe, had a theory on why it was taking so long for young Black players to develop. While he was pleased that more Blacks were coming into tennis, he believed that there was a need for additional individual instruction. "You need to do much more," says Curtis, also a USNLTA umpire in the area. "I've been around this game for twenty years, both as a player and a teacher, and there are two distinct brands of tennis. I call one Black playground tennis, which means basically getting the ball over the net. There can be a hundred different styles of strokes, no real quality. It's more for recreation than preparing for playing a tournament competition. The other kind is what I call 'white competitive brand tennis,' and it is more demanding of a player."[55] *Demanding*, often used as a code word for *discipline*, indicated a fundamental misreading of the powerful and innovative style that African Americans displayed in playground tennis.

The ATA remained strong in New England. The STC hosted the ATA's national tournament in 1971, 1972, 1983, and 1992.[56] At the fifty-fifth ATA Nationals in 1972, Horace Reid won the Men's Singles title, while Lorraine Bryant won the women's singles championship. The finals match between Reid and Art Carrington was the first time an ATA match was televised. Headquarters for the 1983 tournament was at the Franklin Field Tennis Center complex, with its seven indoor and eight outdoor courts, a spacious lobby, and lounge area. The adult events were held at the Harvard University courts. The STC, with the assistance of a public relations firm, Sky Productions, made the nationals a memorable event.[57]

After the ATA agreed to hold the 1992 nationals at the STC club, it had to have the six existing courts resurfaced with Plexipave. They used eight courts at the University of Massachusetts Boston and twelve courts at Milton Academy, one of the private schools located just ten minutes from the club. Longwood provided eight courts for the seniors, while the STC sought the use of ten courts at the Massachusetts Institute of Technology.[58] STC held a fundraiser to boost its number of indoor courts. Five courts were donated by Reebok in the name of Charles E. Hardison, one of the juniors, who was tragically killed in April of 1990.[59]

As late as the 1992 tournament, however, one sportswriter maintained that anyone who had "ever swung a tennis racket" more than likely knew about the USNLTA but were "probably not aware of the American Tennis Association," although they "should" have been, since it is the "oldest African-American sports organization." Not only were players expected from "all over the country" that year, but, as Les Smith noted, he also fielded calls from African players who wanted to play in the tournament. "The USNLTA is mostly concerned with private clubs and the pros," Smith insisted. "The ATA is for grassroots tournaments. We want to give the lower ranked players a chance to be big man on campus." Those "big men" would come out of Saturday's finals.[60]

Besides the STC's players, there have been some other remarkable individuals in Boston's Black tennis history. According to *Boston Globe* reporter Nancy Bradley, one of the earliest was Celestine Jean Richards (Bayne), who received little recognition but was "a truly talented racquet wielder who holds that title among New England's colored tennis players" in the 1930s. She seldom entered open competition; nevertheless, she held "complete dominance over players of her race." She played at the Columbus-AV municipal courts for the Boston Tennis Club (BTC), which had produced many fine tennis players. The teams of the BTC and the Balrac Tennis Club have always done well in dual matches. Richards was the number-one player of the BTC, while the Balracs have a pair of capable representatives in Marion Kerr and Odessa Barrows.[61]

Richards also competed against the ATA Nationals queen, Ora Washington, eight-time ATA singles champion. According to Richards's sister, Doris Jones, Richards felt that Washington was "too strong." Among Richards's accomplishments, she was runner-up in the 1935 New England Tennis Association (NETA) and winner of the women's doubles in 1937 with tennis partner Adassa Barrows. Richards also joined Washington in an Eastern doubles final. She won the NETA 1933 Loving Cup and at the New York State Open mixed doubles was runner-up. She was also a finalist in the 1934 NETA women's doubles and the 1937 Pennsylvania Open women's doubles runner-up. She played recreationally into her sixties or seventies, mostly on Martha's Vineyard, where she had an island cottage. Many Roxbury natives who eschewed tennis during their youth played the sport every day on Martha's Vineyard in the late 1960s and 1970s. Through much of the 1980s, the Mary Tucker Invitational Tournament was held annually on the island before Labor Day weekend.[62]

One of New England's mainstays in tennis has been Art Carrington, the compiler of *Black Tennis: An Archival Collection; 1890–1962.* "Tennis has been my life," Carrington says, "as a player, teacher, coach, and historian . . . for more than six decades." His mother introduced him to tennis at age ten, and he learned to play at the all-Black North End Tennis Club in Elizabeth, New Jersey, in the 1950s and 1960s. In 1972, he gave a New England TV audience a glimpse of Black tennis when he lost the final of the ATA Championships to Horace Reid in five sets. The match was broadcast by WGBH. Carrington won the title the following year, but unlike Ashe, he felt uncomfortable in the white tennis milieu of that time and chose to apply his expertise in the game to teaching. In 1980, he opened the Carrington Tennis Academy at Hampshire College in Massachusetts, where he taught more than two thousand players for over forty years, developing a unique brand of instruction based on "whole body integration."[63] During his career, Carrington has been honored as Coach of the Year and received many community service awards.[64]

As with Black tennis players, the achievements of Black coaches outside traditionally Black tennis circles have also been overlooked. It was considered a major breakthrough in 1981 when Benny Sims was hired as a teaching professional at Longwood. Simms had been the star of the 1975 Texas

Southern University tennis team, where he received the Beefeater Trophy of Excellence and won the ATA Nationals.[65] Ashe recruited Sims to serve as a national coach for the USTA player development program, the first Black to hold that position. As the head pro at Longwood, Sims said, "I am the closest vantage point some of these members have to a black person." Being the pro at an all-white tennis club failed to faze Sims, but he conceded that some people had to adjust to the idea of a Black pro. "Tennis has always been a sport dominated by whites. Longwood is no exception," he said.[66] Jack Crawford, chairman of the committee that selected Sims, argued, "I'll probably get some flack once some people realize that the new pro is black, but who cares? He was the most qualified of nearly fifty applicants, a likeable guy with a fine record. So, we hired him."[67]

Although the club reached a milestone in tennis when it hired a Black pro, the club received few, if any, applications for membership from Blacks. According to Sims, Black people hadn't forgotten how exclusive clubs like Longwood used to be or the reality of discrimination. According to Bud Collins, no Black had ever applied to Longwood. "The place is a lot broader than it was," said one club member. "We have quite a few Jews, even though there was a time when Boston Pops Orchestra conductor Arthur Fiedler had a difficult time getting in. I feel certain blacks could be accepted now. Technically, we did have one black, an infant that was adopted by a member."[68] Reportedly, during Sims's tenure, Longwood had a diverse membership and would have welcomed even more diversity given the chance. However, it is unclear how the club defined *diversity* and to what degree it existed there. The fact that a member can only recall one Black member (who had been adopted as an infant) raises questions about the club's commitment to diversity.

Sometimes, silence on an issue speaks loudly. Few Blacks have played on college tennis teams at predominantly white colleges in Boston. It is difficult to obtain information about the number of Blacks in playing and coaching positions at the colleges and universities in Boston. The numbers are not readily available. For example, the University of Massachusetts Boston women's team for the 2021–22 season features one Black player, Tanya Kibiy.[69]

259

Slightly more information is available about Harvard. Cheryl Alexis was Harvard women's tennis's first Black player, but the dates of her time on the team are not available.[70] Harvard also recruited brothers Thomas and James Blake. Thomas was a four-year letter winner from 1995 to 1998 and a three-time All–Ivy League singles and two-time All–Ivy League doubles honoree. Thomas became the first Black player to be named the men's tennis Ivy League Player of the Year in 1997.[71] James followed Tom to Harvard. Although initially unsure about Harvard, partly because he knew that his brother had the number-one spot, he worried about the challenge of combining both academics and tennis at high levels. James entered the Ivy League school as the number-one-ranked eighteen-and-under player in the country. He teamed with Tom to win collegiate tournaments in singles and doubles and became Harvard's first-ever freshman All-American. In his sophomore year, he was named the Intercollegiate Tennis Association (ITA) Collegiate Player of the Year.[72] He also became the first Ivy League player ever to win both the singles and doubles tournament at the ITA All-American tournament, a collegiate grand slam event.[73]

As it is with Black players, there have been few Black tennis coaches at the college level. Currently, Jovan Jordan-Whitter is the assistant men's and women's tennis coach at the University of Massachusetts Boston, joining the team in 2021. However, Harvard University made some major hires on July 1, 2007. Traci Green became the first Black head tennis coach hired at Harvard. Under her guidance, the team completed the biggest turnaround in thirty-five years of Harvard women's tennis. Green became the first Black coach at Harvard to win an Ivy League title, coaching five All-Ivy selections in 2009.[74] Sims served as an assistant coach at Harvard University during the 1979–80 season, becoming the first Black tennis coach in the Ivy League when he was hired. Ironically, Sims coached an all-white team. In an interview, he said, "Growing up in a project complex that bordered a neighboring town that had one of the largest KKK presences in the South, I never knew why I couldn't sit in the front of a bus or sit downstairs in a movie studio; or why my mother could not try on a dress in a department store like I witnessed White ladies doing? It was only much later that after getting older did I realize the underlying reasons for these things."[75]

*   *   *

It is impossible to measure how much the history of racial segregation in tennis affected the development of the sport in Black communities and limited opportunities for Black players. The ugliness of racial segregation created Black institutions like the ATA and the STC so that Blacks could have some level of tennis training and competition. The open-door policies of these organizations illustrate what the USNLTA could have been. The ATA was more national in scope, allowing Black players from various regions to compete against each other. Unlike the Negro Leagues and some other Black organizations, which also were established due to racial segregation, the ATA continues to offer competitive tennis and now works with the USTA.

The history of Black tennis in Boston reflects the impact of racial, cultural, and social segregation and discrimination. Blacks who were attracted to the sport responded to that racism by creating their own opportunities for play, including their participation in the ATA. Historically Black colleges advanced the sport in Black communities by building courts and hosting tournaments. Even after Gibson and Ashe were able to play in national tournaments and private clubs in Boston and elsewhere, they and other Blacks were not welcome as members. The exclusion of Black players from private clubs inspired Alvs and Smith to form the STC, a club where Black people could play tennis on indoor courts. Boston has been fortunate to have a club like the STC, which has created opportunities for junior development as well as community tennis, allowing Black people to participate outside of the private-club arena.

Over the years, Jim Smith's staff produced competitive players who successfully challenged the idea that tennis is a "white sport." Jim and Gloria Smith died in the 1990s, leaving a legacy reflected in the support that the STC has received. Dr. Clyde Green, whose grandfather helped start the ATA, said, "The Sportsmen's Club has played a significant role in the development of Boston's black tennis players."[76] At the STC, Black tennis professionals like Sims volunteered to teach the game to Black youths. Before working at STC, Sims and a couple of friends created a similar program to teach young people the game. During his tenure at the STC, seven of his students played on the national junior circuit. Later, he broke the color barrier by becoming a coach at Longwood, the club where, decades earlier, Gibson and Ashe were excluded from membership. The achievements of these players, coaches, and supporters illustrate the Black contribution to tennis in New England, which is deserving of a prominent place in tennis history. The potential for greater development of tennis in Black communities lies ahead.

Notes

1. Arthur R. Ashe Jr., *A Hard Road to Glory: A History of the African-American Athlete 1919–1945* (New York: Amistad, 1993), 59.
2. For information, see Sundiata Djata, "Game, Set, and Separatism: The American Tennis Association, a Tennis Vanguard," in *Separate Games: African American Sport behind the Walls of Segregation,* ed. David K. Wiggins and Ryan A. Swanson (Fayetteville: University of Arkansas Press, 2016), 165.
3. "Protest Follows Barring Colored Tennis Players," *Boston Globe,* December 25, 1929.
4. "Protest Follows"; Greg Ruth, *Tennis: A History from American Amateurs to Global Professionals* (Urbana: University of Illinois Press, 2021), 39. The NAACP argued that the USNLTA "were un-American, and class snobs," fearful of competition from Black players. Racism was more striking on the East Coast than on the West Coast; see Ruth, *Tennis,* 141.
5. "Why U.S.L.T.A. Bars Negroes," *Boston Globe,* December 27, 1929.
6. "The West Side Tennis Club History," West Side Tennis Club, accessed April 12, 2024, https://thewestsidetennisclub.com/About_Us/Our_History#:~:text='Ihe%20courts %20opened%20on%20June,dressing%20rooms%20and%20cold%20showers.
7. Ruth, *Tennis,* 12.
8. Jerome Rosen, "The Early History of Wightman Tennis Center: A Test of Memory," Wightman Tennis Center, 2024, https://www.wightmantennis.org/early-history.html. Sonny and Rosie later were named to the New England Tennis Hall of Fame. On December 1, 1967, the corporate name was changed to the Hazel Hotchkiss Wightman Tennis Center Inc. Pamela W. Fox, "Wightman Tennis Center Celebrates 40 Years," *Weston Historical Society Bulletin* 41, no. 2 (Fall 2010): 24.
9. Bud Collins, "A Private Club—for All," *Boston Globe,* June 18, 1969.
10. Interview with the general manager (name omitted), March 1, 2022.
11. "Open Competition," *Boston Globe,* March 13, 1948. Note that the "extreme swift feet" of Blacks is stated, focusing on the athleticism of Black tennis players, another racial issue of commentators. See Sundiata Djata, *Blacks at the Net: Black Achievement in the History of Tennis,* vol. 1 (Syracuse NY: Syracuse University Press, 2006), 183–91.
12. "Althea Gibson Makes Longwood Bow in Nationals," *Boston Globe,* August 5, 1953.

13. Steve Tignor, "The Arthur and Arthur Show: Ashe, Collins and the 1968 US Open," *Tennis*, August 26, 2018, https://www.tennis.com/news/articles/the-arthur-and-arthur-show-ashe-collins-and-the-1968-us-open.

14. Althea Gibson, *I Always Wanted to Be Somebody* (New York: New Chapter, 2021), 50.

15. Gibson, *I Always Wanted*, 51.

16. Harold Kaese, "Mrs. Wrightman Wires Congratulations Longwood Expects," *Boston Globe*, July 11, 1957.

17. "Miss Gibson Will Play at Longwood; Wimbledon Queen in U.S. Doubles," *Boston Globe*, July 16, 1957.

18. Neil Amdur, "Ashe Beats Lutz in 5 Sets for U.S. Amateur Title," *New York Times*, August 26, 1968.

19. Fred Jeter, "Hometown Hero Ashe Conquers Richmond 50 Years Ago in Local Davis Cup Match," *Richmond Free Press*, November 8, 2018.

20. Bud Collins, "Ashe Outslugs Lutz for U.S. Net Title," *Boston Globe*, August 26, 1968.

21. Tignor, "Arthur and Arthur Show."

22. Tignor, "Arthur and Arthur Show."

23. Collins, "Ashe Outslugs Lutz."

24. Tignor, "Arthur and Arthur Show."

25. Tignor, "Arthur and Arthur Show."

26. Collins, "Ashe Outslugs Lutz."

27. See "Tiny Bob Tiptoes through the Amateurs," *Sports Illustrated*, September 2, 1968.

28. Collins, "Ashe Outslugs Lutz."

29. Collins, "Ashe Outslugs Lutz."

30. "South Africa Denies Visa to Arthur Ashe," *New York Times*, January 29, 1970. For a discussion of tennis and apartheid, see Djata, *Blacks at the Net*, 52–84.

31. Michael Widmer, "Protests Hit South Africa Stars," *Baltimore Afro-American*, August 7, 1971; Eric Hall, *Arthur Ashe: Tennis and Justice in the Civil Rights Era* (Baltimore: Johns Hopkins University Press, 2014), 119, 155; Adrian Brune, "Boston . . . before the Marathon, a Hub of Tennis: Longwood Cricket Club, B&T and the Common Courts Are Just a Few Hotspots That Hosted Tennis before Running Became the Official Sport," Baseline Report, November 9, 2020, https://therallyreport.substack.com/p/boston-before-the-marathon-a-hub.

32. Michael Widmer, "Protests Hit South Africa Stars," *Baltimore Afro-American*, August 7, 1971; Hall, *Arthur Ashe*, 119, 155; Brune, "Boston . . . before the Marathon."

33. There are different versions circulating about the founders of the club. Some sources argue that it was the married couple, Jim and Gloria Smith. Hannah Green, "How Toni Wiley Brought Boston's Black-Led Tennis Club Back from Brink," *Business Journal*, August 10, 2021, https://sportsmenstennis.org/about/our-history/.

34. Marilyn April Dorn, "Sportsman's Tennis Camp Big Winner," *Boston Globe*, August 16, 1973.

35. Jonathan Whitbourne, "Sportsmen's Tennis Club," *Tennis Week*, March 7, 2002, 20.

36. Hannah Green, "Toni Wiley," *Business Journal*, August 10, 2021, https://www.bizjournals .com/charlotte/bizwomen/news/profiles-strategies/2021/08/how-toni-wiley-lead -sportsmens-to-60-years.html?page=all.

37. Green, "Toni Wiley."

38. "Tennis Is Only One of the Important Things Kids Learn in the Sportsmen's Tennis Club," *Black Tennis*, Summer 1983, 10.

39. "Sectional News: Boston," *Black Tennis*, Summer 1983, 9.

40. "Parents to Honor Jim Smith for Help to Young Tennis Players," *Black Tennis*, Spring 1984, 13.

41. Also honored was Titus Sparrow, awarded posthumously. After thirty-five years of officiating matches in the predominantly Black American Tennis Association, Sparrow in 1956 became the first Black official in the USTA. He went on to umpire the David Cup and at Forest Hills and Longwood. Jim Greenidge, "The Hall Calls This Top 10 List," *Boston Globe*, May 14, 1993.

42. Geri Hamlin, "Interview with Director of the '92 ATA Nationals in Boston," *Black Tennis*, Spring 1992, 25.

43. Green, "Toni Wiley."

44. "Tennis Is Only One," 9.

45. Larry Whiteside, "Black Youth, 13, Seeks Tennis Breakthrough," *Boston Globe*, July 2, 1975.

46. Whiteside, "Black Youth."

47. Whiteside, "Black Youth."

48. "Sportsmen's T. C. in Review," *Black Tennis*, Spring 1984, 13.

49. "Tennis Is Only One," 9.

50. "Sectional News: Boston," *Black Tennis*, Spring 1984, 12.

51. "Sportsmen's T. C. in Review," *Black Tennis*, Spring 1984, 13.

52. See Djata, *Blacks at the Net*, 187–92.

53. Whitbourne, "Sportsmen's Tennis Club."

54. "USTA.com Black History Month Profile Spotlights STEC Coach Troy Crichlow," usta.com, February 26, 2019, https://www.usta.com/en/home/stay-current/newengland/troy-crichlow -black-history-month.html; Chantal Roche, "Crichlow Brothers—in Their Own Words," U.S. Tennis Association of New England, February 10, 2021, https://www.facebook.com/ USTANewEngland/videos/crichlow-brothers-in-their-own-words/141810861099149/. He has served as a coach on various levels and was the 2016 recipient of USTA New England's William Freedman Award for his outstanding contribution to junior development.

55. Whiteside, "Black Youth."

56. There is a photo of ATA players playing at the Springfield (Massachusetts) Tennis Club in 1922 with this article. Adrian Brune, "Breaking Barriers: Beyond Tennis' Color Line,"

Baseline Report, February 22, 2022, https://www.tennis.com/baseline/articles/hall
-of-fame-unveils-new-exhibit-breaking-barriers.

57. "Tennis Is Only One."

58. Hamlin, "Interview with Director." Plexipave is a cushioned hard court that is similar to Deco Turf.

59. Jim Greenidge, "ATA's 76th Bash in Boston 1,500 Players Expected for 6-Day Tennis Tournament," *Boston Globe*, August 4, 1992. Hardison was killed at age sixteen in Milton. "Charles had the personality that every man in the world would like to have," said Jim Smith, who coached Hardison in tennis for the past eight years. "If you could bottle it, you could make a million dollars. He was destined to be a leader." He was found in the basement of his home with four gunshot wounds. "Milton Youth, 16, Found Slain in Home," *Boston Globe*, April 13, 1990; Diane Bartz, "High School Tennis Star Slain in Quiet Suburb," AP News, April 13, 1990.

60. Greenidge, "ATA's 76th Bash."

61. Nancy Bradlee, "Women's Sports," *Boston Globe*, June 13, 1934.

62. Bijan Bayne, interview with the author, August 13, 2022. Vineyard native and teenager Johnny Rogers won at least once (men's singles) before playing on an NCAA Division I championship team at Hampton Institute in 1976.

63. Steve Tignor, "Art Carrington Is Still Making Black Tennis History Matter," *Tennis*, July 30, 2020, https://www.tennis.com/news/articles/art-carrington-is-still-making
-black-tennis-history-matter.

64. "Art Carrington," American Tennis Association, accessed April 3, 2024, https://www
.yourata.org/team/art-carrington-.

65. *The Tiger* (Texas Southern University) 27 (1975): 280–84.

66. "Men's Tennis Celebrates Black History Month, Honors Former Assistant Coach Benny Sims," Harvard University, February 16, 2021, https://gocrimson.com/news/2021/2/16/mens
-tennis-celebrates-black-history-month-honors-former-assistant-coach-benny-sims.aspx.

67. "Men's Tennis Celebrates."

68. Bud Collins, "Longwood Has New Pro: From Broken Glass to Bent Grass," *World Tennis*, June 1982.

69. Darin Wong, interview with the author, March 21, 2022. Most staff members at area colleges did not respond to informational requests.

70. Wong, interview.

71. "Men's Tennis Honors Tom Blake '98 for Black History Month," gocrimson.com, February 23, 2021, https://gocrimson.com/news/2021/2/23/mens-tennis-honors-tom
-blake-98-for-black-history-month.aspx. See also "Tennis—Hall of Fame Class of 2013: Thomas Blake '98," Harvard University Club, accessed March 21, 2022, https://harvardvarsityclub.org/sport/tennis/.

72. Meredith Rainey-Valmon, "Celebrating Black History Month Profiles from the Ivy League's Back History: James Blake," Ivy@50, 2007, http://ivy50.com/blackhistory/story.aspx?sid=4/12/2007.

73. David Freed and Samantha Lin, "The Road Less Traveled," The Crimson, December 3, 2013, https://www.thecrimson.com/article/2013/12/3/harvard-tennis-james-blake-road-less-traveled/.
74. The Philadelphia native came to Harvard after three years as head coach at Temple, where she orchestrated a complete turnaround of the program.
75. "Men's Tennis Celebrates."
76. "Sectional News" (Spring 1984), 12.

13

The Darling and the Dyke

Differing Receptions of the Comings Out of Jason Collins and Brittney Griner

JAIME LOKE

In a short two-week span in April 2013, two African American basketball players, Brittney Griner and Jason Collins, publicly swung open the doors of the closet and stepped out. Brittney Griner is a former star basketball player at Baylor University and, at the time, had just joined the Phoenix Mercury of the Women's National Basketball Association (WNBA). Jason Collins, a former Boston Celtics basketball player who spent thirteen seasons with the National Basketball Association (NBA), became the first male athlete in history to unveil his same-sex preference while still a professional player. While Collins decided to pen an article in *Sports Illustrated*, Griner chose to nonchalantly mention her homosexuality during an interview with the same media outlet. Evidence shows that the media's reception of the two basketball players' declarations vastly differed. Collins's coming-out statement was described with terms such as *historic, landmark,* and *monumental.*[1] Griner's coming-out announcement was greeted with far less fanfare by the media, who mostly treated her acknowledgment as a minor news event. Even Maggie Gray, the interviewer who spoke with Griner, regarded the topic of lesbians in sports as normal.[2]

Unparalleled Visibility and Acceptance

Both Griner's and Collins's announcements unfolded against a backdrop of unprecedented progressive social leaps. Instead of shying away from the topic, both news and entertainment media have increased public attention to gay civil rights issues since 2013.[3] This has taken place as a wave of acceptance of LGBTQIA+ community members swept the nation during the 2010s, indicating a pivotal time in the move for equality and LGBTQIA+ rights. In 2000, not a single state in the United States allowed gay marriage. When Proposition 8, a ballot measure to ban gay marriage, was proposed in California in 2008, fewer than five businesses publicly came forward to support same-sex marriage rights.[4] Only two years later, in 2010, the Obama administration banned discrimination based on gender identity in federal workplaces. In May 2012, both then president Obama and vice president Biden publicly declared their support for same-sex marriage.[5] The following month, the Pentagon celebrated LGBTQIA+ Pride Month for the first time. In 2013, hundreds of major corporations signed a brief in favor of overturning the Defense of Marriage Act.[6] At best, gay marriage at the time was neither legal nor banned.[7] In 2015, the U.S. Supreme Court legalized same-sex marriage nationwide. According to recent data from Pew Research Center, a majority of Americans (61 percent) now favor same-sex marriage—a statistic that hovered at a mere 37 percent in 2009.[8]

Homophobia in Sports

Despite this wave of acceptance, which could in part explain the burgeoning number of athletes who have felt more comfortable stepping out of the closet, sports still remain a unique domain when it comes to sexual orientation. Sports have been called the "last bastion of male domination."[9] Sports scholars have noted that "the confines of the closet have long been institutionalized in the world of professional sports, and the politics of coming out remain contentious."[10] Sports remain a stronghold for homophobia, though recent research has started to show that it is on the decline.

In the changing landscape of the United States' acceptance of LGBTQIA+ individuals, the sports arena seems like a reluctant, petulant child who has refused to join the crowd—or at least wrestled with its decision to join the majority of the nation. David Plummer has stated that a deep, "almost palpable" ambivalence about homophobia has continued to persist in sports.[11] Recent examples indicate that homophobia has not been eradicated completely. In 2002, Mike Piazza, a baseball player for the New York Mets, held a press conference just to quell circulating rumors that he was gay and to reaffirm his heterosexuality.[12] In 2008, NBC broadcasters failed to acknowledge gold medalist Matthew Mitchan's sexual orientation, and cameras did not show his family or same-sex partner, who were supporting Mitchan from the stands.[13] In 2013, Nick Casa, a football player at the University of Colorado, claimed that a scouting crew had asked him a series of what Casa called "weird" questions. In an interview on ESPN Denver, Casa said, "They ask you like, 'Do you have a girlfriend? Are you married? Do you like girls?'"[14]

Homophobia in male and female team sports manifests itself. Mary Kane and Helen Lenskyj state that the "ubiquitous but invisible lesbian" in women's sports (as sports is always positioned as a masculine domain) can only be understood through women who defy stereotypical feminine attributes.[15] Heavy physical contact team sports such as football and basketball have served as an "endlessly renewed symbol of masculinity."[16] Male athletes are always assumed to be heterosexual because traditional sports prowess is understood to be inherently a male quality, and anything other would be a contradiction.

Women present a paradox to the maintenance of male hegemony in sport. On the one hand, to accept that women are participating in sports, the hegemonic explanation is that all women in sports must be lesbians—demonstrating a deviation from heteronormative identity. On the other hand, lesbians are still women, and women in sports are seen as invading a space of male dominance and thus targeted through heterosexism as well. Ultimately, it is a complex task to balance any acceptance of women, heterosexual or lesbian, in a heavily male-dominated field such as the world of sports.

Even so, it is important to note that the acceptance of female homosexuality in sports has increased since research was conducted on lesbian athletes in the mid-1990s. Nicole Melton and George Cunningham's research has also found instances of lesbian athletes of color being supported by their teammates.[17] Their work was an exploration of audiences' reactions via readers' comments sections and centers on how society, during what is seemingly exceptional progress for all LGBTQIA+ members, received these two prominent basketball players after the revelations of their homosexuality. More specifically, this chapter explores patterns in the differences and commonalities between the reception of Griner, a female athlete, and Collins, a male athlete. Both Griner's and Collins's cases present an interesting opportunity to investigate the different public receptions of a gay (male) athlete versus a lesbian (female) athlete.

Sports and Black Homophobia

Legions of studies have concluded that organized sports are, overall, a highly homophobic institution. Back in 1992, veteran sports researcher Michael Messner established, "The extent of homophobia in the sports world is staggering. Boys [in sports] learn early that to be gay, to be suspected of being gay, or even to be unable to prove one's heterosexual status is not acceptable."[18] Echoing Messner's sentiments, in 1998 Gert Hekma penned, "Gay men who are seen as queer and effeminate are granted no space whatsoever in what is generally considered to be a masculine pre-serve and a macho enterprise."[19]

Black male athletes are normally associated with highly competitive and combative team sports such as football and basketball. Unlike the power and strength tied to Black athleticism, participation for gay male athletes is instead associated with feminized sports (sports that are either traditionally accepted as feminine endeavors such as ice-skating, cheerleading, gymnastics, and/or other nonaggressive sports such as swimming, running, and diving, which are perceived as nondisruptive to feminine ideals). According to Anderson and McCormack, "Black athletes sweat, fuck and fight, while gay men are concerned with the aesthetics of their form."[20] The dominant discourse pertaining to Black and gay athletes holds homosexuality and Blackness to be culturally incompatible categories.[21] For many, it is unimaginable that Black men could even be gay, and this is particularly prevalent for Black gay athletes.

The web of oppression intensifies when race, class, gender, and sexuality are combined.[22] Black gay athletes not only struggle to deal with racism and homophobia in the dominant culture but also fear the backlash of discrimination within their own communities. Gay Black athletes could find themselves excluded from both their racial community *and* their sexual community.[23]

Awareness of Black homophobia was brought to the forefront through California's Proposition 8. It was widely reported that Blacks voted disproportionally against gay marriage. Most studies find that Black men maintain elevated rates of homophobia compared to white men. Part of this stems from the denial of homosexuality in Black communities. Black Americans make up a disproportionately large percentage of people in the lower economic classes, and for an already marginalized group, homophobia serves as a way for Black boys and men to "elevate" their position by saying, "At least I am not gay."[24] Economically disadvantaged Black gay athletes might be pressured to remain the closet so as to not jeopardize their chances of escaping poverty.

Triple Threat for Black Lesbian Athletes

While there has been a plethora of research surrounding Black gay athletes, there has been a dearth of research regarding *Black lesbian athletes*. According to Sara Bridges, Mary Selvidge, and Connie Matthews, "All lesbian women of color share a common element in that they personally are confronted with living in a society that sustains racism, sexism, and heterosexism."[25] Homosexuality is often viewed as a whites-only disease among those in the Black community.[26] Many believe that gays and lesbians threaten the stability and continuation of Black families and communities.[27] As a result, Black lesbians are thrust into the spheres of racism and heterosexism both in the greater public and in their personal communities.[28] Author bell hooks claims that the Black community "may be perceived as more homophobic than other communities because there is a tendency for individuals in black communities to verbally express in an outspoken way anti-gay sentiments."[29]

Black churches have been identified as central spaces in fostering homophobia; they play an important role in its roots, legitimation, and constant reinforcement.[30] During and after slavery, the Black church sustained and supported Black people physically, mentally, and socially.[31] The church's influence among Blacks is strong across all socioeconomic levels and is often a dominant element in the social networks of the Black community, even among Black people who do not attend church.[32] Blacks continue to be profoundly influenced by the religious ideologies and imageries in which they were raised, and this influence continues to affect mature beliefs and practices.[33]

Black lesbians are framed as either masculinized or sexualized women in ways that mirror the stereotypes of Black women everywhere (Greene argues that Black heterosexual women *and* Black lesbians are perceived as "defective females who want to be or act like men and are sexually promiscuous").[34] According to Cornel West, "The subculture of black lesbians is fluid and the boundaries are less policed, precisely because black female sexuality in general is more devalued hence more marginal in white and black America."[35] Black lesbians are marginalized due to not only their race but also their sexuality—edging them further onto the margins as deviant women.

According to Pat Griffin, the differences in how homophobia and sexism are manifested in both women's and men's sports need much more attention.[36] To understand discrimination against lesbians in sports, one must also understand sexism against women. When legendary tennis player Martina Navratilova was interviewed in 2010, she was asked why, after thirty years since she came out, there are still so few open lesbians.[37] Navratilova said, "There is a kind of reverse homophobia with women because they must almost prove they are straight. They are seen as dykes just because they play sports. A journalist would never dare ask a male athlete, a football player or a softball player: 'Are you gay?' unless they were a figure skater but it is OK to ask a female tennis player."[38] Darcy Plymire and Pamela Forman suggest, "An open discussion of lesbians in sport is rarely, if ever, undertaken in the traditional mainstream media. Media discussions of lesbianism usually bemoan the unfair lesbian stigma that confronts heterosexual women in sport. Alternately, the media make a spectacle of lesbianism when an athlete comes out or is outed. In either case, lesbians are marginalized and the code of silence is reinforced."[39]

In the past, women in sports have endured intense abuse over their perceived sexuality. Women have been dropped from teams or found themselves benched or suddenly ostracized by coaches and teammates.[40] Victoria Brownworth finds that coaches impose informal quotas on the number of lesbians, or at least the number of athletes they think *look* like lesbians, on their teams.[41] Young female athletes in college and high school have endured verbal abuse from male athletes, heterosexual teammates, opposing teams, spectators, classmates, and at times, even their own teammates.[42] According to Griffin, "Negative recruiting is perhaps the most self-serving of all attacks on lesbians in sports."[43] *Negative recruiting* is defined as reassuring prospective athletes and their parents that there are no lesbians in a certain program while characterizing players in a rival school's program as lecherous lesbians.[44] This scare tactic takes advantage of parents' and athletes' lack of information, suggesting that young women will be safe in the recruiting program but not in a rival school, where "bull dykes stalk the locker room in search of fresh young conquests."[45] This not only illustrates the pervasiveness of societal concerns about lesbians in sports compared to gay athletes (as gay men are not seen as masculine enough to occupy the world of sports) but also reinforces the notion that women are weak and need protecting from deviant and predatory women (i.e., lesbians).

Sexual Citizens

Brittney Griner, a professional basketball player with the Phoenix Mercury, nonchalantly came out during an interview with *Sports Illustrated* reporter Maggie Gray. Griner, then the star player of Baylor University's women's basketball, led her team to an undefeated 2011–12 season. Griner led Baylor to win their second national championship. She revealed that at Baylor, a conservative Christian college, her coach requested she not discuss her sexuality while still enrolled. After graduating and authoring a memoir, Griner decided to publicly come out.

Jason Collins's coming-out announcement as the first openly gay athlete in a major sport was through a column he penned for *Sports Illustrated.* He notes that he "didn't set out to be the first openly gay athlete playing a major American team sport." He continues, "But since I am, I'm happy to start the conversation."[46]

The self-revelations of these two athletes are more than just stories that highlight their sexual preferences. Iannotta and Kane explain that "stories about sexuality are more than simple individual, human-interest stories; they are instead cultural narratives with social and political implications."[47] Jeffrey Weeks and others describe the formation of a modern public identity known as the "sexual citizen." The term *sexual citizen* is a modern concept that exists in the intersection of private claims to space, self-determination, and pleasure while also inheriting public rights to justice and recognition.[48] Weeks further illuminates that "the sexual citizen is a hybrid being, who tells us a great deal about the pace and scale of cultural transformation and new possibilities of the self and identity."[49]

According to Weeks, as early as the 1960s, an individual would not likely have defined their personhood, social involvement, and presence through proclamations such as "I am gay/lesbian" or "queer" or "transgender."[50] But modern blurring between what is personal (sexual preferences) and public (revealing one's sexuality through a media outlet) is what makes the idea of sexual citizenship so contemporary. Today it is commonplace for many members of sexual minorities to define themselves (in terms of both personal and collective identities) by their sexual attributes—and to claim recognition, rights, and respect as a consequence.[51] Weeks argues that the emergence of the sexual citizen tells us a great deal about ever-accelerating social change, the transformation of the sexual world, and the new possibilities of self and identity.

One of the most recent examples of a sexual citizen staking a claim to rights is Caitlyn Jenner. Jenner was a former college football player and gold medalist in the men's decathlon event at the 1976 Summer Olympics, where she went on to set a world record. Having revealed that she had struggled with gender dysphoria since her youth, Jenner undertook a process of transition to a female identity. Her claim to her sexual citizenship debuted on the cover of *Vanity Fair*, with the words "Call Me Caitlyn" bolded across the page.[52] After all the years of struggling, Jenner said, being on the cover of a magazine as a woman would be the start of her new life: "As soon as the *Vanity Fair* cover comes out, I'm free."[53] The cover secured a place in Jenner's personhood and public recognition and has allowed her to redefine herself—just as Griner and Collins employed *Sports Illustrated* to claim their sexual citizenship.

The idea of sexual citizenship mirrors many other claims to traditional citizenship: "It is about enfranchisement, about inclusion, about belonging, about equity and justice, about rights balanced by new responsibilities."[54] What is different about sexual citizenship is that it brings to light issues and obstacles that were implicit or silenced in earlier notions of citizenship. The idea of sexual citizenship has moved from the margins to the center of our concerns because of very powerful social changes.[55]

Online Readers' Comments

Controversial online news readers' comments sections have evolved to become a staple that accompanies most online news stories. In the beginning, comment sections sparked a firestorm of debates across newsrooms in the United States but are now resignedly accepted as a common feature. Though commonplace today, not all news organizations have happily incorporated this new space. In fact, some newsrooms have opted to completely eradicate comment sections after a period of hosting readers' comments. Many have argued that the sections are filled with too much vitriol. Examples of people who have done away with this section include *Chicago Sun-Times* managing editor Craig Newman, who claims that the "tone and quality" of reader comments often results in "an embarrassing mishmash of fringe ranting and ill-informed, shrill bombing" and says that he and his staff were drained by the noxious posts.[56] Adam Felder states in the *Atlantic* that readers' comments are "often racist, sexist, threatening or otherwise worthless."[57]

While readers' comments sections are often brimming with appalling content, it bears reminding that these kinds of comments are not out of the ordinary for any space that hosts public conversations. Journalists especially are always optimistic that their pieces will spark thoughtful, intelligent discussions, but in truth, conversations held by the masses often do not measure up to democratic ideals. However, stories that generate an astronomical number of comments, vile or not, do provide insight into society's perceptions regarding the issue being debated.

Readers' comments sections are similar to letters to the editor, as they allow readers to participate in the news process.[58] The letters to the editor section in a newspaper is considered a vital space for public discourse and is perceived as a key institution of the public sphere. Many editors consider the section to be "among the few outlets available to the public for voicing opinion," "the community's heartbeat," and a "debating society that never adjourns."[59] In a study conducted by Lee Sigelman and Barbara Walkosz to gauge the public's opinion on declaring Martin Luther King Day a holiday in Arizona, the researchers found that letters to the editor *did* represent the public's opinion.[60]

In the present study, readers' comments were selected from all news stories from the Huffington Post, CNN, the *New York Times*, FOX News, and NBC News from April 18, 2013, through April 30, 2013, that covered the coming-out announcements of Griner and Collins. None of the readers' comments analyzed here originated from dedicated sports news websites. The intent was to gather comments on general news websites with the heaviest traffic and not limit the comments to only sports websites. By eliminating sports news websites such as ESPN, the selected comments represent those of not only sports fans but also general news readers who have no idea who these two athletes are. Thus, this study was able to analyze comments from a wider range of perspectives.

The comments were analyzed in two groups—comments related to Griner's coverage and comments related to Collins's coverage. The comments revealed two widely divergent receptions of Griner and Collins. The theme that dominated the discourse following Brittney Griner's coming-out announcement coalesced around the notion that it was only a matter of time before her revelation happened. It was to be expected. On the other hand, comments surrounding Collins's coming-out announcement were crammed with support and congratulatory wishes. Jason Collins was described as a hero, a legend, a leader, and an inspiration.

Jason Collins, the Darling

Sports, the perpetual tower of testosterone, have been proven to cast aside the men who do not fit the stereotype of the masculine male. In April 2013, then Celtics coach Doc Rivers received a phone call from Jason Collins. Collins told his former coach that he was going to announce to the world that he was gay. When Collins made his revelation and came out of the closet, it seemed as if the tide had turned—in online comments sections, at least. The users in these sections laud Collins for his courage and his candor:

Jason—today you stand a lot taller than 7'0".—justdoit

Not being gay, I guess I cannot claim "gay pride." But I sure as heck am PROUD of Jason Collins! We ALL should be.—MotMista

Many commenters herald Collins as a hero—not just any hero, but the equivalent of a civil rights champion:

> Jason Collins, Thank you for helping to break down barriers & open the mids [*sic*] of millions of young boys & girls (gay & straight). I'll include adults too. You are a hero! Forward!—Conrad_mason

> This guy has my utmost respect. An ACTUAL sports hero.—MathIsTruth

> Way to go Jason Collins. You're the latest in a long line of civil rights heroes.—N Yorker

Ample commenters compare Collins to sports legend Jackie Robinson (the first African American to play in the Major Leagues and a significant contributor to the civil rights movement) and Martin Luther King Jr.:

> It is likely not trivial to a young gay athlete, the same way that Jackie Robinson's breaking the color barrier in baseball was not trivial to those black athletes who followed him.—Sarah

> Booker T. Washington. Martin Luther King. Thurgood Marshall. Jason Collins.—Oldtime Democrat, HP.

Users who express the most negativity (less than 10 percent of the comments analyzed) tout the belief that same-sex preferences conflict with Christian values. For example,

> Jason Collins should not be getting all this attention for his sinful choice. Everyone from the white house to other nba [*sic*] players support Collins. Homosexuality is a deadly choice a person makes that will have eternal devastating consequences. Sin is not something to gloat about and be praised. Jesus Christ will have the last word. Unrepentant gay people will not go to Heaven. The only praise that counts is God's. what profit a man if he gains the whole world and loses his soul or what will he give in exchange for his soul.—avenger777

> The Bible declares that homosexuality is an abomination in God's eyes, and the sentence is death unless they repent. Leviticus 20:13; Romans

1:18–27. This sin must be confessed and forsaken, and Jesus said, "You must be born again" (born from above of the Spirit of God). John 3:3. If you do not repent of your sins and put your faith in the Lord Jesus Christ while you are still alive, you will perish (die in your sins). John 3:16.—annie walker

The few other negative posts center on the belief that Collins only decided to come out to revive his faltering career. Some commenters mention that Collins only dared to come out of the closet because his career was ending, and so he really had nothing to lose. Some examples of these comments include the following:

> Let us see what happens when a "franchise player" comes out—someone that is popular with the fans, etc.—Househusband from the burbs

> My reaction? YAWN. I am not a basketball fan, but if it were Kobe, Blake Griffin or someone even I had heard of, it may be of passing interest. However, I believe this guy needed to jump-start his career, and Sports Illustrated needed to create buzz, thus the reports in the media of "rumors" of a male major league athlete coming out the last few weeks. Good marketing, Sports Illustrated!—HEF

> Looks like an old, below average (at best) basketball player desperately looking for a contract. He was on his way out of the NBA, as no team would've signed him. So now he comes out, forcing the NBA to give him a pity contract (otherwise he'd be screaming discrimination).—Chris

The overall tone of comments about Collins is highly positive; they are packed with encouraging words. Many of the commenters expressed how they felt like they were sharing in Collins's heroic act by claiming they were proud of him. The users almost implied that they had been in this battle with Collins all along, and now, together, they had achieved victory. It is very similar to language expressed when games are won by the athletes, but fans claim "*We* won" instead of "*They* [the athletes] won."

The coverage of Jason Collins's coming out by the *Boston Globe* mirrors the reactions of the online news commenters. The first *Globe* article covering

Collins's revelation (titled "Ex-Celtic Jason Collins Reveals He Is Gay") features a prominent image of Collins laughing and giving a thumbs-up sign. While the image is not directly related to the announcement of Collins's sexuality, the choice by the *Globe* to feature it matters, as it highlights Jason Collins in a positive, strong, and joyful manner.

The next mention of Collins's revelation in the *Globe* article is in a column by Adrian Walker titled "Jason Collins' Quiet Facilitator."[61] The column reveals how Collins had consulted with his friend, U.S. Representative Joe Kennedy III, to discuss how Collins was going to come out publicly. Walker emphasizes that Collins received the full support of the congressman. The entire column is laudatory, with quotes from Congressman Kennedy such as "He is someone I've literally and figuratively looked up to" and "He's a historical figure now."[62] Walker also mentions then Celtics coach, Doc Rivers, being proud of Collins. Dan Lebowitz, former director of the Center for the Study of Sport in Society at Northeastern University in Boston, calls Collins's revelation a "civil rights watershed moment."[63]

After the immediate coverage of Collins's coming out in the two articles discussed previously, the next article that appeared approximately a week later took the same positive tone. The *Boston Globe* features Jason Collins and Joe Kennedy being honored at the Greater Boston PFLAG (Parents, Families and Friends of Lesbians and Gays) gala and auction.[64] While the piece is short, the image that was chosen to accompany it is another positive image of Collins—one that features him holding a glass of champagne surrounded by a group of men laughing. Subsequent articles from the *Globe* follow the same trajectory. The articles describe Collins as "thrilled" with his new life and as a favorite at Boston's Gay Pride parade. Published several months later in February 2014, another article discusses how Collins's homosexuality is not a matter of concern to other basketball players.

The *Boston Globe*'s overall tone and reception of the former Celtics player's coming out were very positive. Collins had a strong support system in the readers' comments, and connecting him to civil rights leaders demonstrates how supportive commenters were about his coming-out announcement. News coverage, in the *Globe* and elsewhere, was similarly supportive. On the other hand, the comments and media coverage of Brittney Griner's coming out painted a vastly different picture. Griner, unlike Collins, did not receive the same congratulatory wishes as her male counterpart, and her announcement was not lauded as heroism.

Brittney Griner, the Dyke

The themes that emerge from the 567 comments on all the previously mentioned news sites' comment sections following Griner's coming-out story center on the notion that it is no surprise that Griner is gay. There are criticisms of Griner's appearance and claims that lesbian women are predatory. An overwhelming majority of Griner's commenters focus on the expectedness of her lesbian sexuality, as the persistent stereotype maintains that the entire WNBA is gay. The following comments exemplify the long-standing belief that women who excel in a physically demanding sport such as basketball are immediately cast into the lesbian category:

> What's the news here, aren't at least 60% of wnba players Ls [lesbian] anyway? Isn't this common knowledge?—airmjbsanders from SI.com

> A player in the WNBA is a lesbian? Next thing you know a Hockey player will turn out to be Canadian!—SouthStJo from SI.com

> A lesbian player on the WNBA? Thanks for the bulletin from the Department of The Obvious.—Peter L. from SI.com

Women, lesbian or not, are still judged by traditional beauty standards through a patriarchal lens. As a woman, Griner is bound to stereotypical expectations of female beauty. Because she does not conform to those standards, her looks are picked apart and ridiculed in the comments sections. According to Maria Veri, aggressive and physical women's sports such as basketball, softball, ice hockey, and rugby are defiant challenges to "traditional sensibilities of ideal femininity such as passivity, modesty and submissiveness."[65] By challenging objectifications of the female body, Veri suggests, "women who do not acknowledge the male gaze violate the disciplinary codes of femininity and subsequently risk vilification."[66]

We see here how Griner is vilified in the comments as she violates the disciplinary codes of femininity. In John Lisec and Mary McDonald's study of gender inequality in the WNBA, the fear of lesbians is often so palpable that female athletes are consistently portrayed in the presence of a significant male figure (coach, father, husband, boyfriend, older brother, etc.). This is an attempt to encourage images of heterosexuality or reliance on male figures against the backdrop of athletic success.[67]

The effects of these double standards are far-reaching. Girls entering puberty are inundated with consumerist, individualist, and media-driven cultural messages, which result in the body becoming a crucial part of identity.[68] Many girls and women view their bodies as significant obstacles and key sources of distress.[69] A multitude of studies conducted in developed, wealthy nations reveal that by the age of six, girls are already expressing dissatisfaction with their physical appearance.[70] A growing number of adolescents in the West suffer from eating disorders, and on a global scale, millions of women base their self-esteem, social status, and opportunities afforded to them on how they look.[71]

The conversations in comments sections following Griner's coming-out news coverage further solidified that looks are crucial to a woman—heterosexual or lesbian:

dude looks like a lady or is it a lady that looks like a DUDE?????????? No kidding . . .—jdbcfc

gay or guy?!?!??—ComicalSense

. . . if that' a woman I'm a goddamn Chinaman—Chuck_Schick669

The image of the predatory lesbian woman lurking in the shadows, waiting for her next victim, has apparently stood the test of time, as several mentions of it are peppered throughout the comments sections following Griner's story. Below are a few comments that demonstrate this persistent claim:

Nobody is looking at the root cause of homosexuality. Is it nurture? Especially in female sports where at universities so many athletes prey on the younger freshmen/sophomores on road trips . . .—americanLatina.

And women on basketball teams are 95% gay. I played on one and I was the only one of the 4 who were not. The girls did turn the other girls gay. How? I don't know but I was like naw Im a Christian and that's wrong and besides. . . . I love men too much.—bowens2c

Though there are a few positive comments for Griner, they do not comprise a significant portion of the public's overall reception of her announcement. Unlike for her counterpart, Collins, supportive comments for Griner are few and far between. Even the approving comments for Griner demonstrate nowhere near the degree of positivity that those meant for Collins contain:

Silence in the face of injustice is injustice. I'm glad that Britney was able to find the confidence to be herself.—Brittany C.

Good for Brittney and really, for all three of them. I look forward to the day when someone's sexuality is as little a deal to everyone else as it is to Brittney, Elena, and Skylar. Now let's play ball!—Jay W.

Good for her. Hopefully soon this kind of thing will not need to be hyped up by the sports media—it will just be accepted and players' accomplishments on the court will dominate the headlines.—qaan 1

It is very good for her to announce this in such a public way, though, because this will help to start real dialogue for other athletes, as well. I think the Mavericks are confused about what a lesbian is, though—she is still a WOMAN!!—luv1another

In these comment sections, Griner lacks the outpouring of pride and messages of acceptance that Collins enjoys. The positive comments for Griner center mostly on congratulating her and her alone. They do not equate her to a heroine or a civil rights leader, and commenters do not say they are proud of her honesty, as they do with Collins. There is an apparent lack of association between the commenters and Griner. While Collins can bask in the excitement of the commenters who say they are proud of him, Griner's well-wishers do not claim a stake in her announcement or say they are proud of her for coming out. African American female athletes are often relegated to the sidelines. Although not a major theme, several commenters question why Griner's coming out is even news, as the WNBA is irrelevant.

The three themes that dominate Griner's reception in the comments sections (the expectedness of lesbians in the WNBA, the heavy criticism of her appearance, and the stereotype of the predatory lesbian) differ from those centering on Collins. While Collins is lauded as a hero, a civil rights leader, and a pioneer, few congratulatory wishes are present in Griner's pool of comments. It bears emphasis that there is not a single comment on Collins's looks, while Brittney Griner's appearance is the dominant theme in the discourse that accompanies her story.

Analysis

Though a correlation between the contents of readers' comments and society's pulse on LGBTQIA+ issues is beyond the scope of this research, this relatively new public space has clearly indicated that people are gathering to participate in conversations that would not take place in such a blatant form without the anonymity afforded by online news comments sections. The age of the public sphere, where face-to-face talk was the only way dialogue took place, is clearly in the past. Critics of the original Habermas public sphere theory such as Fraser, Negt, and Kluge argue for decentralized and multiplied spaces in the public sphere to include new paths of critiques and new politics, which is apparent now in readers' comments sections.[72] This online public space allows us a peek into the conversations that would not have made it into the mainstream otherwise.

The vastly different reactions shown in readers' comments sections about the two athletes are startling. Surprisingly, there is a lack of comments focused on race. I had initially expected commenters to touch on how the athletes had let the African American community down or even betrayed it, but this is absent from the comments sections. Perhaps the outcome would have been different if the comments had been gathered from online news outlets that had a majority of African American readers.

Gender Disparity

Even though race is not evident in the comments sections, gender disparity is very much apparent. I argue that the disparity between the two receptions lies in the roots of our patriarchal society. As support for LGBTQIA+ rights is seeing an upsurge in the nation, the initial embrace of tolerance is first offered to the hegemonic group—men.

This pattern is reminiscent of the right to vote in the United States. That privilege, initially reserved only for white men, was then extended first to Black men. White women, who were always deemed "free" individuals, won this right decades after that. Again, in our patriarchal society, it is men who first enjoy the early fruits of acceptance, while women are again relegated to the waiting rooms of tolerance.

The present discussion posits the idea that gay men are gaining acceptance more quickly than lesbians—an assertion that goes against the plethora of research arguing that lesbians on the whole are more accepted than gay men. For example, in 2014 Martin Monto and Jessica Supinski studied homophobia based on the twelve-item homonegativity as discomfort scale (HADS), concluding that there is a much greater general discomfort with gay men compared with lesbians.[73] But perhaps lesbian athletes do not share the same experiences as lesbians who are not athletes. In a recent example of hostile environments for lesbian athletes, Rene Portland's policy at Penn State University was deemed the "most public example of unwelcoming coaching tactics for lesbian athletes."[74] Portland had three rules: no drugs, no drinking, and no lesbians. Jennifer Harris would have been the basketball team's leading player if Portland had not dismissed her from the team in 2005 due to Harris's perceived sexuality as a lesbian.

Perhaps past research suggesting that lesbians are more tolerated than gays is not so much grounded in tolerance as in simple oblivion. Hardly a blink would ensue if two women were on the dance floor together. Women can hold hands and not garner raised eyebrows. But for men, it would be unimaginable in many settings to be dancing together or holding hands without triggering some sort of negative reaction. Lesbians (but not lesbian *athletes*) are able to move more invisibly and navigate more fluidly between spaces, simply because it has long been culturally acceptable for women to be physically close to each other, particularly as long as they maintain their femininity.

In 2010, Missouri's then new female head basketball coach, Robin Pingeton, was criticized for this statement: "I'm a Christian that happens to be a coach. . . . This is something very unique, I think, for Division I women's basketball to have a staff that the entire staff is married with kids. Family is important to us and we live it every day."[75] Currently, there is only one openly lesbian coach in Division I women's basketball: Sherri Murrell of Portland State University. She remains the first and the only lesbian coach out of over three hundred teams in the division. Perceptions of female and male athletes have always been embedded in cultural expectations of masculinity and femininity.[76]

While physical strength and competitiveness are celebrated in male athletes, for female athletes, they become jarring qualities, as they disrupt ideals of traditional femininity. Unless the female athlete can balance these stereotypical male qualities with blatant exhibitions of femininity and heterosexuality, female athletes are looked upon as oddities.[77] Perhaps this overwhelming need to exhibit femininity is the reason notable and accomplished athletes such as soccer player Hope Solo, track-and-field Olympian Lolo Jones, professional volleyball player Gabrielle Reese, and tennis star Serena Williams posed nude in various media outlets.

Additionally, patriarchal society is so infused with porn culture that two women are often construed as a sexual fantasy for straight men. Heterosexual pornography is filled with images of multiple women pleasuring a single man. So while on the surface it may seem as if lesbians are extended tolerance, it is perhaps through a distorted lens that is clouded with sexual fantasy rather than tolerance grounded in genuine understanding or acceptance.

Griner, a woman who does not conform to the stereotypical male fantasy, is subjected to heterosexism because she still is a woman. Because she has deviated from the stereotypical beauty standards, as she has demonstrated female muscularity and can no longer serve as a fantasy to heterosexual male desires, the comments regarding her coming-out announcement are not as warm as Collins's.

While Brittney Griner violates almost every expectation of the feminine ideal, Jason Collins fits the vision of the stereotypical masculine man—at least on the outside. Towering at a height of seven feet, Collins is a muscular professional athlete in a physically demanding sport (basketball) who can be deemed a success by all traditional athletic (and most masculine) standards. Nothing externally suggests that he has deviated from the masculine ideal. Collins still fits the vision of a stereotypical man. His stereotypically manly appearance and athletic prowess (a clear indication of masculinity in contemporary American society) contributed to an easier transition from a traditional to alternate form of masculinity.

His stereotypical masculine appearance functions as a system of classification that makes his introduction as a gay man to the public easier to accept. Collins appears to embody all the stereotypical male attributes—but he's gay. This discord is revealed but not actually outwardly visible. Had Jason Collins kissed another man or displayed some other action that amplified his sexual orientation, perhaps the reception would have differed.

The analysis of two conversations that coalesced around Griner's and Collins's coming-out announcements reveals a startling discovery. While commenters on Jason Collins's declaration are filled with warmth and support, the comments sections devoted to Griner's news demonstrate a completely different climate. Collins is congratulated, accepted, and said to make many people feel proud. Griner is the focus of a discourse about how she looks; the few congratulatory wishes lack the warmth that her counterpart garners. Women and men are still held to very different standards. Women are still scrutinized and criticized for not conforming to stereotypical femininity, and women's worth is still very much based on outward appearance.

As the fight for LGBTQIA+ tolerance progresses, different and additional burdens will continue to plague members of the group. The intersectionality of gender and sexuality matters when it comes to homophobia. Just as how a truly meaningful feminist movement needs to constantly be aware of the different struggles that affect white women as opposed to minority women, there too cannot exist only one solution for all LGBTQIA+ members. We must constantly look at LGBTQIA+ progress through a critical lens to ensure tolerance is extended to all, not just a select few.

Notes

1. Edward Kian, Edward Clavio, John Vincent and Stephanie Shaw, "Homophobic and Sexist Yet Uncontested: Examining Football Fan Postings on Internet Message Boards,"

Journal of Homosexuality 58, no. 5 (2011): 681, https://doi.org/10.1080/00918369.2011 .563672.

2. Lori Dann and Tracy Everbach, "Opening the Sports Closet: Media Coverage of the Self-Outings of Jason Collins and Brittney Griner," *Journal of Sports Media* 11, no. 1 (2016): 169–92, https://doi.org/10.1353/jsm.2016.0003.

3. Andrew Billings et al., "The Art of Coming Out: Traditional and Social Media Frames Surrounding the NBA's Jason Collins," *Journalism & Mass Communication Quarterly* 92, no. 1 (2015): 142–60, https://doi.org/10.1177/1077699014560516.

4. Jenna McGregor, "Corporate America's Gay-Rights Evolution," *Washington Post*, February 27, 2014, https://www.washingtonpost.com/news/on-leadership/wp/2014/02/27/corporate-americas-gay-rights-evolution/.

5. Jackie Calmes and Peter Baker, "Obama Says Same-Sex Marriage Should Be Legal," *New York Times*, May 9, 2012, https://www.nytimes.com/2012/05/10/us/politics/obama-says-same-sex-marriage-should-be-legal.html.

6. McGregor, "Corporate America's Gay-Rights."

7. Kristen Purcell et al., "Understanding the Participatory News Consumer," *Pew Research Project*, March 1, 2010, https://www.pewresearch.org/internet/2010/03/01/understanding-the-participatory-news-consumer/; Carla Rice, *Becoming Women: The Embodied Self in Image Culture* (Toronto: University of Toronto Press, 2014).

8. Sarah Atske, "Majority of Americans Favors Same-Sex Marriage, but Divisions Persist," Pew Research Project, May 14, 2019, https://www.pewresearch.org/politics/2019/05/14/majority-of-public-favors-same-sex-marriage-but-divisions-persist/.

9. Nelson Burton, *The Stronger Women Get, the More Men Love Football* (New York: Avon, 1994), 6.

10. Billings et al., "Art of Coming Out," 142–60.

11. David Plummer, *One of the Boys: Masculinity, Homophobia, and Modern Manhood* (Binghamton: Haworth, 1999), 122.

12. "Piazza: 'I'm Not Gay,'" *Hartford Courant*, May 22, 2002, https://www.courant.com/2002/05/22/piazza-im-not-gay/.

13. Cyd Zeigler, "NBC Apologizes for Mitcham 'Gay' Snub," *Outsports*, August 28, 2008, https://www.outsports.com/2008/8/27/3860722/nbc-apologizes-for-mitcham-gay-snub.

14. Greg Rosenthal, "NFL Team Asks Colorado's Nick Kasa: 'Do You Like Girls?,'" nfl.com, February 27, 2013, https://www.nfl.com/news/nfl-team-asks-colorado-s-nick-kasa-do-you-like-girls-0ap1000000145664.

15. Mary Jo Kane and Helen Lenskyj, "Media Treatment of Female Athletes: Issues of Gender and Sexualities," in *MediaSport*, ed. Lawrence Wenner (New York: Routledge, 1998), 186–201.

16. Raewyn Connell and James Messerschmidt, "Hegemonic Masculinity: Rethinking the Concept," *Gender & Society* 19, no. 6 (2005): 833, https://doi.org/10.1177/0891243205278639.

17. Nicole Melton and George Cunningham, "When Identities Collide: Exploring Minority Stress and Resilience among College Athletes with Multiple Marginalized Identities," *Journal for the Study of Sports and Athletes in Education* 6, no. 1 (2013): 45–66, https://www.tandfonline.com/doi/abs/10.1179/ssa.2012.6.1.45.

18. Michael Messner, *Power at Play: Sports and the Problem of Masculinity* (Boston: Beacon, 1992), 566.

19. Gert Hekma, "As Long as They Don't Make an Issue of It . . . ," *Journal of Homosexuality* 35, no. 1 (1998): 2, https://www.tandfonline.com/doi/abs/10.1300/J082v35n01_01.

20. Eric Anderson, and Michael McCormack, "Intersectionality, Critical Race Theory, and American Sporting Oppression: Examining Black and Gay Male Athletes," *Journal of Homosexuality* 57, no. 8 (2010): 949–67, https://doi.org/10.1080/00918369.2010.503502.

21. Keith Boykin, *Beyond the Down Low: Sex, Lies, and Denial in Black America* (New York: Carroll & Graf, 2005).

22. Kimberley Crenshaw, "Mapping the Margins: Intersectionality, Identity Politics, and Violence against Women of Color," *Stanford Law Review* 43, no. 6 (1991): 1241–99, https://doi.org/10.2307/1229039.

23. Leslie McCall, "The Complexity of Intersectionality," *Signs: Journal of Women in Culture and Society* 30, no. 3 (2005): 1771–1800, https://lsa.umich.edu/content/dam/ncid -assets/ncid-documents/Ten%20Diversity%20Scholarship%20Resources/McCall %20(2005)%20The%20Complex%20of%20Intersectionality%20.pdf.

24. Carissa Froyum, "'At Least I'm Not Gay': Heterosexual Identity Making among Poor Black Teens," *Sexualities* 19, no. 5 (2007): 603–22, https://journals.sagepub.com/doi/ 10.1177/1363460707083171.

25. Sara Bridges, Mary Selvidge, and Connie Matthews, "Lesbian Women of Color: Ther- apeutic Issues and Challenges," *Journal of Multicultural Counseling and Development* 31, no. 2 (2003): 113–30, https://go.gale.com/ps/i.do?p=HRCA&u=googlescholar&id= GALE%7CA101860840&v=2.1&it=r&sid=HRCA&asid=19c70ad2.

26. Keith Boykin, *One More River to Cross: Black and Gay in America* (New York: Anchor, 1996).

27. Gill Clarke, "Queering the Pitch and Coming Out to Play: Lesbians and Physical Education in Sport," *Sport, Education and Society* 3, no. 2 (1998), 145–60, https://www .tandfonline.com/doi/abs/10.1080/1357332980030202.

28. Delroy Constantine-Simms, "Is Homosexuality the Greatest Taboo?," in *The Greatest Taboo: Homosexuality in Black Communities*, ed. Delroy Constantine-Simms (Los Angeles: Alyson, 2000), 76–87.

29. bell hooks, *Where We Stand: Class Matters* (New York: Routledge, 2000), 69; Earl Hutchinson, "My Gay Problem, Your Black Problem," in Constantine-Simms, *Greatest Taboo*, 9.

30. Michael Eric Dyson, *Race Rules: Navigating the Color Line* (Reading: Addison-Wesley, 1996).

31. Robert Miller, "African American Churches at the Crossroads of AIDS," *Focus* 16, no. 10 (2001): 1–4, https://europepmc.org/article/MED/11668967.

32. Elijah Ward, "Homophobia, Hypermasculinity, and the U.S. Black Church," *Culture, Health, and Sexuality* 7, no. 5 (2007): 493–504, https://search-library.ucsd.edu/discovery.

33. Michael Eric Dyson, *Open Mike: Reflections on Philosophy, Race, Sex, Culture and Religion* (New York: Basic, 2003).

34. Beverly Greene, "Lesbian Women of Color: Triple Jeopardy," in *Women of Color: Integrating Ethnic and Gender Identities in Psychotherapy*, ed. Lillian Comas-Diaz and Beverly Greene (New York: Guilford, 1994), 398.

35. Cornel West, *Race Matters* (New York: Vintage, 2001), 129.

36. Pat Griffin, "Changing the Game: Homophobia, Sexism and Lesbians in Sport," in *Gender and Sport: A Reader*, ed. Sheila Scranton and Anne Flintoff (London: Routledge, 2002), 193–208.

37. Julie Bindel, "Sportswomen Are Stereotyped as Gay—But That Doesn't Make Coming Out Easy," *Guardian*, February 12, 2014, https://www.theguardian.com/commentisfree/2014/feb/12/sportswomen-stereotyped-gay-coming-out-casey-stoney.

38. Bindel, "Sportswomen Are Stereotyped."

39. Darcy Plymire and Pamela Forman, "Breaking the Silence: Lesbian Fans, the Internet, and the Sexual Politics of Women's Sport," *International Journal of Sexuality and Gender Studies* 5, no. 2 (2000): 141–53, https://link.springer.com/article/10.1023/A:1010124712461#citeas.

40. Victoria Brownworth, "Bigotry on the Home Team: Lesbians Face Harsh Penalties in the Sports World," *Advocate*, June 4, 1991, 34–39.

41. Brownworth, "Bigotry."

42. Brownworth, "Bigotry."

43. Griffin, "Changing the Game," 217–34.

44. Griffin, "Changing the Game."

45. Griffin, "Changing the Game."

46. Jason Collins and Franz Lidz, "Why NBA Center Jason Collins Is Coming Out Now," *Sports Illustrated*, April 29, 2013, 248, https://www.si.com/more-sports/2013/04/29/jason-collins-gay-nba-player.

47. Joah Iannotta and Mary Jo Kane, "Sexual Stories as Resistance Narratives in Women's Sports: Reconceptualizing Identity Performance," *Sociology of Sport Journal* 19, no. 4 (2002): 347–69, https://journals.humankinetics.com/view/journals/ssj/19/4/article-p347.xml.

48. Jeffrey Weeks, "The Sexual Citizen," *Theory, Culture & Society* 15, nos. 3–4 (1998): 35–52, https://journals.sagepub.com/doi/10.1177/0263276498015003003.

49. Weeks, "Sexual Citizen."

50. Weeks, "Sexual Citizen."

51. Weeks, "Sexual Citizen."

52. Buzz Bissinger, "Caitlyn Jenner: The Full Story," *Vanity Fair* (July 2015), 49, http://www.vanityfair.com/hollywood/2015/06/caitlyn-jenner-bruce-cover-annie-leibovitz.

53. Bissinger, "Caitlyn Jenner."

54. Weeks, "Sexual Citizen," 35–52.

55. Weeks, "Sexual Citizen."

56. Cathy Newman, "Sick of Internet Comments? Us, Too—Here's What We're Doing about It," *Chicago Sun-Times*, April 12, 2014.

57. Adam Felder, "How Comments Shape Perceptions of Sites' Quality—and Affect Traffic," *Atlantic*, June 5, 2014, https://www.theatlantic.com/technology/archive/2014/06/internet-comments-and-perceptions-of-quality/371862/.

58. Sanjay Kapoor, "Most Papers Receive More Letters," *Masthead* 47, no. 2 (1995): 9, https://www.thefreelibrary.com/Most+papers+receive+more+letters.-a017312900.

59. Brian Knowlton, "U.S. Job Site Bans Bias Over Gender Identity," *New York Times*, January 5, 2010, https://www.nytimes.com/2010/01/06/us/06gender.html.

60. Leo Sigelman and Barbra Walkosz, "Letters to the Editor as a Public Opinion Thermometer: The Martin Luther King Holiday Vote in Arizona," *Social Science Quarterly* 73, no. 4 (1992): 938–46, https://www.jstor.org/stable/42863131.

61. Adrian Walker, "Jason Collins' Quiet Facilitator," *Boston Globe*, May 1, 2013, https://www.bostonglobe.com/metro/2013/04/30/representative-joe-kennedy-iii-was-quiet-facilitator-jason-collins-first-active-major-sports-athlete-come-out/lDoysBRLQQGWiy7M1tv5jM/story.html.

62. Walker, "Jason Collins' Quiet Facilitator."

63. Walker, "Jason Collins' Quiet Facilitator."

64. Mark Shanahan, "Jason Collins, Joe Kennedy III Honored by Local PFLAG Group," *Boston Globe*, May 12, 2015, https://www.bostonglobe.com/lifestyle/names/2015/05/12/jason-collins-honored-greater-boston-pflag-event/iHiXMXZa4HDvonMKDGEB3M/story.html.

65. Maria Veri, "Homophobic Discourse Surrounding the Female Athlete," *Quest* 51, no. 4 (1999): 355–68, https://www.tandfonline.com/doi/abs/10.1080/00336297.1999.10491691.

66. Veri, "Homophobic Discourse."

67. John Lisec and Mary McDonald, "Gender Inequality in the New Millennium: An Analysis of WNBA Representations in Sports Blogs," *Journal of Sports Media* 7, no. 2 (2012): 153–78, https://www.semanticscholar.org/paper/Gender-Inequality-in-the-New-Millennium%3A-An-of-WNBA-Lisec-Mcdonald/36ff8b0657534c914ceecd175bc89fbb3c55e311.

68. Lori Irving, "Promoting Size Acceptance in Elementary School Children: The EDAP Puppet Program," *Eating Disorders* 8, no. 3 (2000): 221–32, https://psycnet.apa.org/record/2000-05737-003.

69. Rice, *Becoming Women*.

70. Lina Ricciardelli and Marita McCabe, "Children's Body Image Concerns and Eating Disturbance: A Review of the Literature," *Clinical Psychology Review* 21, no. (2001): 325–44, https://pubmed.ncbi.nlm.nih.gov/11288604/.

71. Nancy Etcoff et al., "The Real Truth about Beauty: A Global Report: Findings of the Global Study on Women, Beauty and Well-Being," Club of Amsterdam, September

2004, https://www.clubofamsterdam.com/contentarticles/52%20Beauty/dove_white_paper_final.pdf.

72. Nancy Fraser, "Rethinking the Public Sphere: A Contribution to the Critique of Actually Existing Democracy," in *Habermas and the Public Sphere*, ed. Craig Calhoun (Cambridge: MIT Press, 1992), 124.

73. Martin Monto and Jessica Supinski, "Discomfort with Homosexuality: A New Measure Captures Differences in Attitudes toward Gay Men and Lesbians," *Journal of Homosexuality* 61, no. 6 (2014): 899–916, https://www.tandfonline.com/doi/abs/10.1080/00918369.2014.870816?journalCode=wjhm20.

74. Kethevane Gorjestani, "Opening the Last Closet," Columbia Sports Journalism, July 1, 2010, https://www.scribd.com/document/320805801/Opening-the-Sports-Closet-PDF&ved=2ahUKEwjAoZuCuf2HAxXqQjABHYkjCrUQFnoECBcQAQ&usg=AOvVaw156xZT1Eo2I9IQnJYAuEbX.

75. Gorjestani, "Opening the Last Closet."

76. Gorjestani, "Opening the Last Closet."

77. Griffin, "Changing the Game," 193–208.

14

The Enduring Sounds of Whiteness

Boston Sports Radio and Race

DONNA L. HALPER

It was mid-September 1934, and Sam Lacy was not happy about what he had just heard on the radio. Lacy, a veteran baseball writer for the Black press and a big fan of the Negro Leagues, was listening to Washington DC station WJSV when suddenly, after talking respectfully about the upcoming Major League games, the white announcer, Arch McDonald, made a snide remark about an upcoming Negro League game. Lacy, who had covered the Negro Leagues for the *Washington Tribune* and would soon embark on a long career with the *Baltimore Afro-American*, knew firsthand that many Black players had the talent to play in the majors; it was only because of segregation that they were denied the opportunity. Yet Arch McDonald apparently believed that his presumably white audience would find Negro League baseball amusing.

Lacy was not amused and expressed his outrage in his *Tribune* column.[1] Other sportswriters from the Black press agreed. Many wrote responses to his column, including the *Boston Chronicle*'s Mabray "Doc" Kountze. He provided a long list of Black teams' accomplishments with examples of how some had easily defeated white teams in exhibition games.[2] While Lacy, Kountze, and others provided an eloquent defense of the Negro Leagues, McDonald probably never saw it; there was little evidence that white sportscasters paid much attention to the Black press.

In 1934, there was only one Black sportscaster on radio in the United States—Sherman "Jocko" Maxwell. He hosted a sports-talk show on several radio stations in the greater New York City area, talking about the games and sometimes interviewing players (including a few from the Negro Leagues). Overall, from the 1920s through the early 1950s, Black sports fans nationwide were poorly served by radio. Major League Baseball (MLB) games had been on the air in some cities since 1921. However, since the majority of radio sports announcers ignored Black athletes, the only way for most Negro League fans to follow the sport was to either attend the games in person or rely on the Black press.

In the Washington-Baltimore area, Sam Lacy hosted a show on station WOL for a few months in 1935.[3] He was one of the announcers when WWDC aired the first-ever Negro League radio-broadcasted game in August 1942.[4] Most network sports programs featured events like the World Series, where the play-by-play announcers were white, and since baseball was still segregated, so were the players. The one exception was boxing. Sometimes the networks would broadcast a championship match featuring a star Black boxer like Joe Louis.[5] Otherwise, it was rare to hear Black athletes mentioned on a mainstream station. That was certainly true in Boston. Although the city did not have a Negro League team, there was a thriving Black semipro baseball scene with well-attended games. Yet no available evidence suggests that Boston's sportscasters ever mentioned those teams. The teams' exploits were mainly covered in the Black press, often by Doc Kountze.[6]

In contrast, Boston radio featured Black entertainers almost from the start. In 1922, the famous Black actor Charles S. Gilpin delivered a segment from *The Emperor Jones*, a play in which he had the starring role, on station WGI.[7] Cast members from the Black musical *Shuffle Along* sang several hits from a show on WNAC.[8] But there were no Black announcers, no sports programs that covered Black athletes, and few news programs that ever mentioned the Black community. The concerns of Boston's Black residents were mainly found in the pages of the local Black newspapers, the *Boston Guardian* and *Boston Chronicle*. No evidence exists that influential (and outspoken) Black editors like the *Guardian's* William Monroe Trotter or sportswriters like Doc Kountze were invited on air to offer their perspectives. Discussions of issues like racism were seldom heard on Boston radio (or, to be fair, on stations in most other cities) until the 1960s.

There are several possible explanations for why national radio, and specifically Boston radio, offered so little coverage of the Black experience in America. One factor was station owners' belief that broadcasting "controversial" programs might offend white listeners and sponsors. The networks, too, avoided any programs that might alienate their affiliates, many of which were in the segregated South. Most stations preferred to broadcast hit songs by Black entertainers rather than discussions of potentially contentious issues. In Boston, white station owners may have believed the city's Black population (which the 1950 census said was slightly less than 5 percent) was too small to worry about, or perhaps they saw no way to monetize the Black audience given the stereotypes advertisers held about Black consumers.[9]

Occasionally, a controversial topic managed to get some airtime—usually as part of an external program that a station had agreed to broadcast. In January 1926, W. E. B. Du Bois, editor of the monthly publication of the National Association for the Advancement of Colored People's (NAACP), *The Crisis*, gave a talk entitled "The Hypocrisy of White Folk," a provocative topic WBZ would ordinarily have avoided. Because of the station's agreement with Boston's Ford Hall Forum to broadcast its Sunday night lecture series, this talk got on the air. Unfortunately, the technology to easily record and preserve radio programs did not yet exist, thus we have no idea how it sounded. We do know it was broadcast, thanks to fan mail sent to Dr. Du Bois praising him for "using the radio to bring facts to so many you could not reach otherwise."[10] A newspaper summary of the event noted that one of the themes in Dr. Du Bois's talk was the "alleged hypocrisy of Great Britain and its brutal treatment of the black race in East Africa." The broadcast, however, did not only discuss British colonialism. Du Bois also observed that "all the fine, abstract ideals of white civilization—its truthfulness, honesty, courtesy, chivalry towards women—vanish in reality when it comes to the white man's treatment of the colored race." He proceeded to provide numerous examples of those vanishing ideals to a packed crowd at the forum.[11]

Several decades later, Boston's Black newspaper reporters would still have agreed with Du Bois: while Boston claimed to be a liberal and tolerant city, racism was pervasive. Yet radio, still a dominant medium, seldom mentioned everyday reality. It wasn't just the lack of Black radio announcers or programs—there were many other manifestations of racism in the city. For example, Boston's schools were integrated in theory, but in practice, there were neighborhood schools that remained rigidly white where Black students were unwelcome. The city's all-white school committee remained adamant about maintaining this status quo.[12] In the mid-1970s, a court-ordered plan to desegregate the schools by busing Black students into previously white districts stirred angry protests from white parents, politicians, and activists. This became a major news story, covered thoroughly by both national and local media. Prior to that era, rarely would Boston's white political leaders speak to the press about racism, and there was a lot that should have been said. Not only were the city's schools de facto segregated; Black musicians who performed in Boston's nightclubs were unwelcome at city hotels, which meant they had to stay in local people's homes.[13] Black and white musicians also kept to separate labor unions.[14] With few Black representatives in the state legislature, these (and other) discriminatory practices went unchallenged.

Still, there were positive signs in professional sports, even though the progress did not reflect the sentiments of the whole city. The Boston Celtics was the first team in the National Basketball Association (NBA) to draft a Black player, Chuck Cooper, in 1950. In Major League Baseball, the National League Boston Braves signed their first Black player, Sam Jethroe, the same year. It is worth noting, however, that while Jethroe would later have fond memories of how he was treated by Boston fans, he understood that in the city itself, there were many places where even a well-known Black athlete was not welcome. He coped by living in one of Boston's Black neighborhoods, where he "stayed pretty close to home" when he wasn't playing. If he wanted entertainment, he went to the Hi-Hat, a local jazz club that featured Black performers. "I didn't go around to many white places—bars, movies, etc.," he told the *Boston Globe* in 1979.[15]

Meanwhile, evidence suggests that the Boston Red Sox intentionally delayed integrating their team. The Sox had no Black players until 1959, making them the last Major League Baseball team to integrate. The delay was not due to a lack of opportunities—the Sox had a chance to sign Jackie Robinson and Jethroe in 1945.[16] The team's upper management, however, included men like Eddie Collins and Joe Cronin, both of whom were vehemently opposed to signing Black players. Year after year, the Red Sox offered one excuse after another for keeping the team all white.

White and Black communities likely held vastly different perspectives on the Red Sox' race relations. It is doubtful that any Boston radio sports programs in the 1950s, all of which were hosted by white men, ever discussed why the Red Sox had no Black players until 1959. Meanwhile, the perception that the Red Sox were a racist organization took hold in the Black community. In 1978, a Black columnist for the *Bay State Banner* noted that while huge crowds were attending Red Sox games, most of the fans were white: "Although there are more black fans in Boston than I would hazard to guess, we don't see them at Fenway [Park], enjoying beer and hot dogs, and roaming the streets after the games to celebrate at the nearby bars. Somehow I don't think that you have to be EINSTEIN to figure it out."[17] Regardless of whether white sports commentators discussed Red Sox hiring decisions, the Black press covered the story.[18]

Black athletes were aware that Boston was unfriendly to people of color. In his 1979 memoir, former basketball legend Bill Russell, who played for the Boston Celtics in the 1950s and 1960s, referred to Boston as a "flea market of racism. It had all the varieties, old and new, and in their most virulent form."[19] Long before that, in 1964, he spoke to a magazine reporter, comparing how he was treated as a star basketball player versus how he was treated as a Black man. He recalled being honored at a well-attended testimonial dinner in Reading, Massachusetts, for his accomplishments on the basketball court. When white residents heard that he and his family wanted to buy a home in that town, "the neighbors objected like hell." They further relayed the resident's sentiment: "As an athlete—a celebrity even—sure, you're a great guy to have in this town. 'As long as you don't [live] close to me.'"[20]

I grew up in Boston and I was a loyal Celtics fan; I listened to the games on the radio faithfully. While I easily remember play-by-play announcer Johnny Most effusively praising Russell's skills and crediting him with turning the Celtics into champions,[21] I do not recall a conversation about the treatment of Russell or the team's other Black players or Russell's perspectives about civil rights. Years later, these topics were often discussed, but not in the 1950s or early 1960s. Russell was among the few Black athletes willing to speak publicly about the racism he encountered, earning him the scorn of some white fans. Jethroe said nothing about it until years later. The same was true for many other Black athletes of that era.

In late summer 1961, Boston finally got a full-time Black radio station, WILD. As early as 1952, the station, previously known as WBMS, was playing several hours a day of Black music. White owner Norman Furman was among the first station executives in Boston to hire Black announcers, including Gretchen Jackson, who hosted a women's program, and Sabby Lewis, a local bandleader and jazz pianist.[22] WBMS also aired live broadcasts from the Hi-Hat, hosted by a well-known white deejay named "Symphony Sid" Torin.[23] After WBMS was sold, its new owner, Nelson Noble (who was also white), tried several formats, including pop music, before hiring a staff of Black announcers and transitioning to rhythm and blues along with some jazz.[24] It turned out to be a good move. Some of the new deejays became very popular, especially Jimmy "Early" Byrd and "Wildman Steve" Gallon. Unfortunately, WILD, like WBMS before it, was a "daytimer," a station that only operated from sunrise to sunset, limiting its influence. But there were now more Black voices on the radio dial, and the Black community (along with many white listeners, me among them) liked WILD's music.

In addition to entertainment, the station began offering news and public affairs programs. By 1965, WILD was broadcasting a Saturday afternoon talk show that was unique for its time. "NAACP Topics" was hosted by Thomas "Tom" Atkins, then executive secretary of the NAACP's Boston chapter. Atkins, who went on to become one of the first Black members of Boston's City Council, discussed current issues that affected the Black community and interviewed prominent guests. His frequent cohost was Lovell Dyett, then an executive with Action for Boston Community Development (ABCD). The two hosts did not shy away from controversy, whether in their choice of topics or of guests. Among the people they interviewed were Louis Farrakhan of the Nation of Islam and Stokely Carmichael of the Student Nonviolent Coordinating Committee, both of whom were famously outspoken.[25] They also interviewed Rt. Reverend Francis J. Lally, a representative of the Boston Archdiocese, and accused the Catholic Church of not taking a strong enough stand against racism.[26]

On the other hand, sports topics did not seem to be a priority. WILD had a sports department in the 1960s, but little was written about what it broadcast; the focus was on the civil rights movement and the needs of Boston's Black residents. By the late 1960s, call-in sports programs were gaining in popularity on several Boston stations; but as in past decades, all the hosts were white even though a growing number of the players were Black. WILD eventually developed its own call-in sports program in 1973, with Ken Hudson as the host; he was already well known, having become the NBA's first Black referee in 1968.[27] More than a decade later, in 1984, WILD hired "Coach" Willie Maye, who became one of the station's most popular sports hosts for more than two decades, doing everything from being part of the morning show to making appearances at community events, interviewing local athletes, and even handling some play-by-play of local sports.

Given the turbulence of the 1960s and early '70s, it was not surprising that WILD focused on news and public affairs—two areas where Boston's Black audience had not been well served before. That focus was especially important in April 1968, after Dr. Martin Luther King Jr. was assassinated. Rumors began spreading in several of Boston's Black neighborhoods that a riot was imminent: in other cities, like Chicago and Memphis, violence had already broken out. As Kevin White, Boston's new mayor, along with community leaders like Paul Parks of the NAACP, Thomas Atkins (then newly elected city councillor), and police commissioner Edmund McNamara strategized to maintain calm, WILD took immediate action. The station "dropped its usual broadcast and fed listeners continuous news updates, quelled rumors (including reports that two policemen had been killed in Dudley Square) and urged listeners to keep the peace."[28]

Because WILD was a trusted resource, Black listeners took it seriously. The station invited community leaders like former state representative Michael Haynes, now a Baptist minister, to address the Black audience directly. Another influential speaker that day was singer James Brown. He was about to give a concert at Boston Garden and told WILD listeners that he would donate some of the proceeds to Dr. King's widow.[29] Also helpful was WGBH-TV, Boston's educational public television station, which decided to broadcast the concert live. The fact that Bostonians could watch a live concert by a famous entertainer like Brown (who not only sang his hits but interspersed the performance with positive and encouraging messages) was also credited with helping keep the city calm.[30] In the end, while Boston did have some sporadic looting and a small number of fights, the city remained far more peaceful than many other American cities—thanks in large part to Black leaders like Tom Atkins, members of the Roxbury chapter of the New England Grass Roots Organization (NEGRO), and media outlets like WILD Radio and WGBH-TV.

Another new resource for the community, the *Bay State Banner*, debuted in 1965 as Boston's newest Black newspaper. Its owner, Melvin B. Miller, soon began offering critiques of Boston's political establishment and its white-run media. Unlike Black editors of previous generations, Miller *was* able to get on the air, beginning in August 1966, when he cohosted a series of programs on station WNAC.[31] He continued to advocate in the pages of the *Banner*, on local radio and TV, and at educational events. During the Harvard Law School Forum in November 1967, Miller accused the mainstream press of only covering the Black community when there was a story about crime, thus contributing to the stereotype that Black neighborhoods were inherently dangerous and violent. In 1968, he organized a series of workshops and meetings for Boston's radio and television stations to help their personnel better understand the issues that mattered to Boston's Black residents.[32]

By the late 1960s, Tom Atkins, now a full-time politician, was frequently heard on radio and TV commenting on the conditions in Boston's Black neighborhoods. Meanwhile, his former WILD cohost, Lovell Dyett, continued broadcasting the once-a-week NAACP talk show. In late July 1968, WILD entered a partnership with the educational station on Boston University (BU), WBUR-FM, coproducing "The Drum," a nightly program that provided local news, interviews, music, and commentary. It won critical praise and several awards, but in late August 1971, John Silber, president of the university, stated that the show was costing BU too much money to produce, and he made the controversial decision to cancel it.[33] Later that year, Lovell Dyett debuted a Sunday night talk show on WBZ Radio, one of Boston's most influential stations. Though Dyett's program was a plus for the Black community, it only aired once a week. Boston's major talk hosts, all of whom were white, broadcast their shows five times a week.

Meanwhile, sports talk was growing in popularity, and radio stations were hiring new commentators, many of them retired professional athletes. But as a Black member of the Celtics noted in a 1967 interview, these former players were always white.[34] So were the hosts of the sports-talk shows on Boston's biggest stations, including the two most popular programs, *Calling All Sports*, hosted by Guy Mainella, and the *Sports Huddle*, cohosted by Eddie Andelman, Mark Witkin, and Jim McCarthy. Both programs were on WBZ Radio, and both debuted in 1969 (the *Sports Huddle* began on a smaller station earlier in the year before landing at top-rated WBZ in December). Ten years later, although some of the announcers, commentators, and stations were different, the biggest sports-talk shows were still hosted by white announcers.

One small but important change occurred in 1972, when then host of *Calling All Sports*, Guy Mainella, added a Black host, a recent BU graduate named Jimmy Myers, to do fill-in work, mostly on weekends. In 1972–73, few if any Black sports-talk announcers were on Boston radio, and Myers received more scrutiny than the average white announcer. He also turned out to be more controversial than some of Boston's white sports fans expected. While Myers knew sports inside and out, he quickly got a reputation for being outspoken. Like Bill Russell, he was willing to express his opinion, whether remarking on the prejudice he believed Black athletes had to endure or commenting about why Boston still had no full-time Black sports hosts on radio or TV.[35] Myers became a polarizing figure, which his detractors described as "combative" as well as "cocky, arrogant, and egotistical." While some sportswriters shared that view, others wondered if racism was affecting how listeners perceived him.[36]

Years later, in 1995, when Cedric Maxwell, a former star player for the Boston Celtics, was hired to be the color commentator for the team's radio broadcasts on WEEI, he too was criticized—but for a different reason. Maxwell was the only Black analyst for any Boston sports broadcast, and listeners had trouble understanding his southern accent. Evidently, so did his colleagues, who jokingly began calling him the "Poofessor."[37] Maxwell was new at this role, but he was also aware that he would be subjected to harsher critiques than a white rookie announcer. He hired a speech coach and worked to improve his pronunciation, but sportswriters continued to remark on the way he spoke—even while acknowledging that he seemed to genuinely enjoy being on the radio, and his unique way of expressing himself was effective, even if it differed from how other (white) announcers did it.[38]

In September 1991, when WEEI changed over to all-sports talk along with some play-by-play, the station quickly became a ratings powerhouse, yet also another example of an all-white air staff. In 1996, there were no Black hosts on WEEI other than Cedric Maxwell, who covered the Celtics games. In late September 2003, WEEI found itself in the midst of a huge controversy when its morning team, John Dennis and Gerry Callahan, made an egregiously racist remark on air. It all started after a gorilla named Little Joe escaped from the Franklin Park Zoo. He was ultimately recaptured at a bus stop in one of Boston's Black neighborhoods, but not before he terrorized a young girl who was waiting for a bus. Dennis and Callahan found this amusing. They suggested it was a "METCO gorilla," catching the bus to the suburbs (METCO was a voluntary desegregation organization that bused Black children to white suburbs, where the schools were supposed to be better).[39] The comparison of a Black child to a gorilla outraged many Black listeners, and some white listeners too. If WEEI's staff had been more diverse, it is doubtful that kind of "joke" would ever have been made. But it *was* made, and it caused WEEI enormous problems: sponsors pulled their ads, and the station was criticized by various advocacy groups as well as members of the Massachusetts legislature. WEEI's management suspended the morning team for two weeks. Some people believed they should have been fired. Excepting Maxwell, the station's staff remained completely white until two years after this incident, when *Boston Globe* sportswriter Michael Holley was hired as a cohost.

The Boston radio landscape continued to change. WILD experienced a heyday of sorts in the 1980s under the ownership of Black businessman Kendall Nash. Boston's only Black-owned station, it served as a beacon for the Black community. Nash's wife ultimately sold the station after he died of cancer in 1992. By 2006, WILD ceased to exist as a Black station, much to the consternation of many in the community.[40] In 2009, a new FM sports-talk station, "98.5, the Sports Hub," made its debut and gradually rose to the top of the ratings. But once again, most of its announcers were white. In 2020, a *Boston Globe* study of who was who on Boston sports radio and TV showed, "If you read, listen, or watch anything to do with the Greater

Boston sports scene, there's only a 1 in 10 chance that a Black person is telling you those stories." The study further revealed, "Only twelve of the 126 full-time TV reporters and anchors, sports radio hosts, play-by-play announcers, analysts, and newspaper and website reporters and columnists in Greater Boston are Black."[41]

Of course, hiring the same people with the same perspectives led to the same results. In February 2023, one of 98.5 the Sports Hub's hosts, Tony Massarotti, was suspended for making an attempt at a joke that seemed to associate Black people with car thieves. Massarotti later apologized on air for his "insensitive remarks."[42] As one Boston sportswriter noted sarcastically, perhaps there should be a whiteboard where we keep tabs on "Days since a Boston Sports Radio Host Has Had to Apologize for a Racist or Sexist Comment." But he also added that the problem in Boston's sports-talk universe isn't just the proverbial sounds of whiteness. Rather, Boston's sports radio is a "bro culture," where guys, usually white guys, talk sports as if they are in a bar or a diner. They use a style that is "edgy" but sometimes crude and demeaning, with the hosts thinking their misguided attempts at humor are funny.[43] To the people being subjected to these rude and snide remarks, there is nothing funny about them.

Experiencing so few minorities on the air today harkens to 1934 and Sam Lacy's disgust and alienation when a white announcer mocked the Negro Leagues. A lack of diverse voices creates a white-washed viewpoint lacking in varied perspectives. At least these days, it's not just the Black press that gets outraged when talk show hosts push the envelope. At least these days, many white listeners are just as upset when a host uses racist stereotypes to get a laugh. And yet, the problem persists.

Notes

1. Sam Lacy, "Looking 'Em Over," *Washington Tribune*, September 22, 1934, 12.
2. Sam Lacy, "Looking 'Em Over," *Washington Tribune*, October 6, 1934, 13.
3. "On the Air," *Washington Tribune*, November 19, 1935, 8.
4. Donna L. Halper, "August 7, 1942: First Negro League Baseball Game Is Broadcast on Radio," *Society for American Baseball Research*, accessed August 7, 2024, https://sabr.org/gamesproj/game/august-7-1942-first-negro-league-game-is-broadcast-on-radio/.

5. "Broadcast of Fight May Begin Before 10 O'Clock," *Harrisburg, Pennsylvania Evening News*, June 22, 1937, 12.

6. See, for example, his book, *50 Sports Years along Memory Lane: Afro-American Sports History; Hometown, Local, National* (Medford MA: Mystic Valley, 1979), which includes invaluable information about the Black semipro teams.

7. "Bits from Emperor Jones Broadcasted," *Boston Herald*, April 4, 1922, 11.

8. "Programs for Today," *Boston Globe*, August 25, 1922, 11.

9. "Push Promised by Black Caucus for Minority Ownership," *Broadcasting*, September 26, 1977, 27. Black advocacy groups were still complaining about the impact of these stereotypes even in the late 1970s, as many national advertising agencies continued to ignore the growing spending power of the Black audience.

10. Walter A. Smith, letter to W. E. B. Du Bois, January 10, 1926, MS 312, W. E. B. Du Bois Papers, Special Collections and University Archives, University of Massachusetts Amherst Libraries, https://credo.library.umass.edu/view/full/mums312-b035-i515.

11. "Prof. Du Bois Indicts White Civilization," *Boston Globe*, January 11, 1926, 20.

12. Howard Bryant, *Shut Out: A Story of Race and Baseball in Boston* (Boston: Beacon Press, 2002), 57.

13. Virgil Wright, "South End Woman Recalls Neighborhood's Jazz Heyday," *Bay State Banner*, November 11, 1999, 2.

14. Bridgit Brown, "Jazz Legend Haynes Recalls Hub Childhood," *Bay State Banner*, October 18, 2007, 17, 20.

15. Larry Whiteside, "The First to Play," *Boston Globe*, July 22, 1979, 41.

16. Bill Nowlin, "Sam Jethroe," Society for American Baseball Research, accessed August 7, 2024., https://sabr.org/bioproj/person/sam-jethroe/.

17. Stephen Shepard, "Lay It on the Lion," *Bay State Banner*, April 27, 1978, 14.

18. "NAACP Accuses Bosox of Bias," *Chicago Defender*, April 25, 1959, 24.

19. Bill Russell and Taylor Branch, *Second Wind: The Memoirs of an Opinionated Man* (New York: Random House, 1979), 183.

20. Edward Linn, "I Owe the Public Nothing," *Saturday Evening Post*, January 18, 1964, 62.

21. Jack Craig, "Most's Rasp Was Music to the Ears of Fans," *Boston Globe*, January 5, 1993, 55.

22. William Buchanan, "Norman Furman, 79; Was Manager of Boston, New York Radio Stations," *Boston Globe*, July 7, 1980, 26.

23. Buchanan, "Norman Furman."

24. June Bundy, "Vox Jox," *Billboard*, November 6, 1961, 24.

25. Bryant Rollins, "Opinion from the Editor's Desk," *Bay State Banner* (Boston), August 27, 1966, 5.

26. Ken Botwright, "School Vote Disastrous, Fr. Lally Says," *Boston Globe*, November 21, 1965, 8.

27. "Ken Hudson, N.B.A.'s Smallest Referee: A Tree Stump in a Valley of Redwoods," *New York Times*, January 10, 1971, S4.

28. David Yosifon, "Boston Kept Cool in Wake of Assassination," *Bay State Banner*, January 15, 1998, 7A.
29. "James Brown Helps Out," *Bay State Banner*, April 11, 1968, 1.
30. Percy Shain, "James Brown Hub Show Wins National Acclaim," *Boston Globe*, April 12, 1968, 14.
31. "Banner Sponsors Show on WNAC," *Bay State Banner*, August 6, 1966, 1.
32. "Communications," *Bay State Banner*, October 8, 1970, 2A.
33. "'Drum' Cancellation Deplored by Staff," *Bay State Banner*, September 2, 1971, 1.
34. "Madison Avenue Ignores Black Athletes," *Bay State Banner*, October 5, 1967, 1.
35. Neil Singelais, "WBZ's Myers—Unhappy as Second Fiddle," *Boston Globe*, July 30, 1978, 87.
36. Nathan Cobb, "The Combative Jimmy Myers: A Man of Many Words Has Something to Say about Sports, Race and Respect," *Boston Globe*, January 27, 1993, 21.
37. John Koch, "Interview with Cedric Maxwell," *Boston Globe*, April 18, 1999, M8.
38. Bill Doyle, "Watch Celtics on Radio: WEEI's Crew Adds to Telecast," *Telegram & Gazette* (Worcester MA), February 22, 2001, D1.
39. Frank Hoffmann, Jack M. Dempsey, and Martin J. Manning, *Sports-Talk Radio in America, Its Context and Culture* (New York: Routledge, 2011), 49.
40. René Serghino, "Faithful Listeners Bid Farewell to WILD-FM," *Bay State Banner*, October 12, 2006, 1, 21.
41. Michael Silverman, "Diversity Lags in Local Sports Media," *Boston Globe*, December 11, 2020, C1, C6.
42. Chad Finn, "Massarotti Taken Off Air for the Week," *Boston Globe*, February 22, 2023, C3.
43. Chad Finn, "Sports Talk Radio Earns Its Dubious Reputation," *Boston Globe*, March 25, 2023, C1.

15

Act as If

Allison Feaster, the Politics of Inclusion, and Achieving the
American Dream in the National Basketball Association

EILEEN NARCOTTA-WELP AND ELISABETH ERICKSON

A spectacular walnut tree stands amid a grove of native pine trees in Chester, South Carolina, with a warped and tattered piece of wood bearing a bent wire rim affixed to its trunk about ten feet from the ground. The tree is positioned on a slight hill with a slope that seems unfit for any kind of sport. Yet this beat-up basketball hoop was once the site of daily competition. Until the sun went down each day, Allison Feaster competed against her older brother in one-on-one matchups or attempted to beat her older sister in a game of horse.[1] This was her training ground—the humblest of beginnings—an outdoor, self-made court where she had to compete *uphill* to achieve.

Feaster's later success, both in academics and in professional basketball, was rooted in the lessons she learned on that hill. In seventh grade, standing five feet nine inches tall, Feaster tried out and played as a starter on the Chester High School girls' basketball team.[2] She led her high school team to a state basketball championship in 1993, won two South Carolina Player of the Year awards in 1993 and 1994, and was named an All-American by both Parade in 1994 and Street & Smith in 1993 and 1994.[3] Feaster also graduated first in her class. Although recruited to play basketball by the likes of the University of Connecticut and the University of Tennessee (both women's college basketball powerhouses at the time), she followed her mother's guidance and focused on academically rigorous institutions that did not grant sports scholarships.[4] She considered Duke, Dartmouth, and Yale, but her final choice was Harvard University.

Tucked away in Cambridge, Massachusetts, Harvard University is an idyllic representation of academia. With a strong intellectual history, Harvard is one of the top academic institutions in the United States. In choosing Harvard, Feaster, a young Black woman, entered a predominantly white space. "It was complete culture shock," she has said. "I was coming from a small Southern town. . . . I remember being terrified because I didn't really feel like I belonged."[5] But by pushing through that struggle, she accomplished some unfinished business for her mother: "My mother used to say that she would have attended Harvard if she did not have to forego college. . . . She wanted us to strive for the best in all things . . . I believed Harvard was the best academic institution . . . [and] . . . basketball was not a huge factor in my decision."[6]

While basketball may not have been a major factor in her college decision, Feaster made an immediate impact on the Harvard basketball program. In her first season, she averaged 17 points and an Ivy League–leading 11.8 rebounds per game. She was named First-Team All-Ivy and unanimously voted Ivy League Rookie of the Year. In the following three years, Feaster led the Crimson to three consecutive Ivy League titles and National Collegiate Athletic Association (NCAA) appearances.[7] It was her final NCAA appearance that sealed her legacy at Harvard and college basketball lore. On March 14, 1998, Feaster led the sixteenth-seeded Crimson to victory over the top-seeded Stanford Cardinals. Harvard won 71–67, with Feaster compiling 35 points and 13 rebounds. This win marked the first time in the history of the NCAA basketball tournaments, male or female, that a sixteenth seed defeated a top-seed team.[8] While Harvard eventually lost to the University of Arkansas in the second round of the NCAA Tournament, Arkansas coach Gary Blair summed up Harvard's season and Feaster's remarkable rise to college basketball dominance, remarking, "Harvard is the American Dream. Harvard is the chance for every [one] out there in America to realize, 'We can.'"[9] Feaster seemed to embody that American Dream, capping her career with 2,312 points and 1,157 rebounds.[10]

Feaster's basketball dreams continued when the Los Angeles Sparks selected her as the fifth overall pick in the 1998 Women's National Basketball Association (WNBA) Draft.[11] She played in the WNBA for ten years (1998–2008) with the Los Angeles Sparks, Charlotte Sting, and Indiana Fever, then continued her basketball career in France and Spain. In 2016, settled in Spain, Feaster was about to accept a role in the Madrid office of the National Basketball Association (NBA) when Greg Taylor, senior vice president of player development of the NBA G League, called to offer her a spot in a new one-year program to learn the behind-the-scenes work at the NBA, WNBA, and NBA G League. After finishing the program, she served as lead of the culture relations and player personnel office in the NBA G League—a stepping stone to her glass-ceiling-breaking role as Boston Celtics vice president of player development and organizational growth.[12] Hired in 2019, Feaster is one of a handful of women of color in high-ranking positions in men's professional sports. Part of her imagined this position, and more, for her life; yet another part of her wondered if she might only "get a 'regular job.'"[13] And while her position with the Celtics is a dream come true, it seems her path may lead to her ultimate dream, which she identified in 1997: "To be 'the first female commissioner of the NBA.'"[14]

Feaster is the epitome of the American Dream: a young Black woman from a small town in South Carolina who seemingly has overcome barriers of class, race, and gender to obtain respect, admiration, and power within the professional structure of men's basketball. The hours she practiced, the years she toiled in a foreign country playing the game she loved, and the connections she sought and made in the WNBA and NBA are heralded for their representation of the distinctly American value of meritocracy: the idea that success comes with hard work. She carries a never-give-up attitude along with individual academic and athletic achievement. There is no question that Allison Feaster is an exceptional athlete and professional. Moreover, the narrative that has accompanied her success appears to reflect an optimistic, hopeful, and inspiring racial narrative.[15]

Upon closer analysis, counternarratives are revealed. These are identified through sport studies scholars Susan Birrell and Mary McDonald's methodology of "reading sport," wherein the authors argue that athletes and sporting events serve as texts to be critically analyzed. Using varied theoretical approaches, mediated narratives are interrogated to expose power relationships and "alternative accounts of particular incidents and celebrities that have been decentered, obscured, and dismissed by hegemonic forces."[16] This methodology allows critical scholars to recognize the gendered and racial politics that invisibly organize and circulate around Feaster's mediated persona.

Our analysis will focus on the strategic ways in which Feaster's gender and race are made to matter (and not matter) through the all-encompassing white narrative of the American Dream. We will do so by first contextualizing the postfeminist and postracial nexus of the late 1990s and early 2000s, when Feaster played college basketball and participated in the WNBA—both significant points of identity development. We reveal how ideological narratives that promote individualism and a white, middle-class, heterofeminine subject circulate in this conjuncture of gender and race and are adopted in order to succeed in American sport. Second, Feaster has identified two influential figures in her professional life: her mother, Sandra Booker; and her collegiate basketball coach, Kathy Delaney-Smith. It is through her mother's example of work ethic and commitment and Delaney-Smith's motto of "Act as if" that Feaster models whiteness and the American Dream. But Feaster is a complex individual with multiple social identities. We note, interestingly, that she rejects the notion of individualism on sports teams—an ideology negatively applied to Black female athletes—in favor of the white, middle-class, feminine notions of humility, humbleness, and team over self.[17] Beyond the construct of the American Dream, we use Foucault's theory of the docile body to reveal that Feaster is, in fact, subject to cultural surveillance through motherhood in both her personal and professional life.[18] Implied in the concept of motherhood is heterosexuality and the reproduction of gender norms. Yet in the conclusion, we note that significant changes in the American political, cultural, and social context in the early 2020s have shifted Feaster's narrative, allowing for Blackness and individualism to play a more prominent role in her story.

Growing Up Feaster

Allison Feaster grew up on the basketball court, but that basketball court encompasses a multitude of political, social, cultural, and economic contexts. Lawrence Grossberg, a critical cultural studies scholar, argues that "context is everything and everything is context," meaning that any point of study cannot be fully analyzed and understood without the "lived milieux of power."[19] The meaning of Feaster's success in the sport of basketball and how it has been mediated can only be understood by examining the intersections of her personal identities.

Born in 1976, Feaster grew up during the rise of neoliberal economic and cultural policies that took shape after the racial and feminist social movements of the 1960s and 1970s. Under the leadership of President Ronald Reagan, there was a significant shift in the national consciousness away from the overt political activism of the 1960s to a politics that justified economic policies favoring the wealthy.[20] The idea was that corporate expansion along with individual freedoms would "trickle down" to the masses. Buffered by the moral fabric of the nuclear family—the moral fiber of America—white, middle-class citizens were heralded as the embodiment of the "Great Society."[21] This type of "backlash" politics is too simplistic to contextualize Feaster and her journey to the NBA. In fact, the time when Feaster grew up (1980s to mid-2000s) is an immensely complex and often contradictory period regarding gender and racial politics.

In the postfeminist period, women experienced numerous material gains and social freedoms. Positive gains were also felt in the context of women's sports. Passed just four years prior to Feaster's birth, Title IX legislation allowed for greater access to resources and opportunities for women in publicly funded educational institutions. By 1994, when Feaster made her decision to attend Harvard, legislative oversight was finally paying off in greater numbers of women's teams and increasing female participation in women's sports on college campuses.[22] The 1996 Atlanta Olympics became known as the "Summer of Women," as females "stole" the show—achievements that the media conveniently linked to Title IX. While the American public was well aware that U.S. gymnasts competed every fourth summer, many viewers watched women compete on a national team in women's basketball, soccer, and softball for the first time. Olympians recall seeing girls and boys wearing jerseys with U.S. women's players' names stitched on the back, signaling a shift in the value of female athletes.[23] The NBA capitalized on the U.S. women's basketball team's gold medal and began a women's league in 1997. After the turn of the millennium, however, women's professional sport was a hard sell because most women's leagues did not make a profit and it was difficult to justify their existence.[24] The umbrella of the NBA provided the WNBA with the financial cover it needed to remain viable and gain a cultural foothold in American sports culture.

These feminist gains in sports did not occur in a cultural vacuum. While media attention and access to sporting opportunities increased, suggesting that equality in men's and women's professional sports had been achieved, feminist cultural theorists like Angela McRobbie argue that postfeminist ideology operates through a "double entanglement," a duplicitous process that incorporates and assumes aspects of second-wave feminism while simultaneously commodifying a "new" type of feminism depicting women as empowered consumers.[25] High-profile and/or newsworthy achievements of women and girls validate the notion that the systemic and structural discrimination against females is an issue of the past, and social institutions are recognized as "progressive" for their commitment to social change. This move toward a depoliticized feminism carries "subtle messages that situate a clash between generations, where feminist ideology is figured as belonging in the past, something necessary for an older generation of white women."[26] This approach slowly but surely unravels the structural and ideological work of feminism, introducing a new type of feminism that is based on lifestyle politics and the "hyper aestheticization" of everyday life—what McRobbie calls the "girling of femininity."[27] Black feminist scholar Kimberly Springer underscores McRobbie's analysis, noting that postfeminism identifies the ideal female as a Global North, white, middle-class, heterosexual consumer.[28]

When considering Allison Feaster, we cannot leave race out of the analysis. As a Black woman navigating her early life, Feaster had to negotiate the dominant narrative of white, middle-class heterofemininity in sport.[29] Springer explains, "As part of a racialized discourse, one must grapple with post-feminism's place in the post-civil rights era."[30] The term *post–civil rights*, like postfeminism, embodies multiple meanings: (1) a demarcation of time, (2) backlash against civil rights initiatives and politics, and more increasingly, (3) an ideology asserting that society is color-blind, or "postracial."[31] Like postfeminism, a post–civil rights era embodies liberal notions of multicultural equality. Postracial politics appropriates the language of civil rights social movements, such as an emphasis on "equal opportunity," to suggest that "equal rights" have been achieved.

In this context, it is not racism but rather anti-racist politics that are responsible for racial inequalities that are not supposed to exist. Black athletic celebrities of the 1980s and 1990s like Michael Jordan and O. J. Simpson were touted as examples of commodifiable Black men who negotiated the white, middle-class sports environment by opting out of racial politics.[32] However, Black male athletes are not Feaster's cultural counterparts. To understand how a Black female athlete negotiated this postfeminist and postracial moment, a Black feminist analysis must be applied. As political scientist Alexander-Floyd argues, "A Black feminist analysis exposes the ways in which what we view as post-Civil Rights and post-feminist timeframes and ideologies are not only deeply enmeshed but, indeed, co-constitutive . . . it is formulated through the politics of not only race, but gender and class, where Black families would come to be situated for political participation and social uplift by attaining middle-class respectability . . . patterned after an idealized white middle-class family."[33] Feminist sport studies scholar Eileen Narcotta-Welp conducted a Black feminist analysis when examining the 1999 Women's World Cup and the U.S. women's national soccer team's only Black starter, goalkeeper Briana Scurry. For Scurry to be successfully marketed to a white, middle-class, suburban audience, her Blackness and femininity were made to matter in some respects and not matter in others. Both the media and Scurry herself adopted an attitude of racialized postfeminism that underscored her adherence to middle-class heterofeminine standards and rendered her Blackness apolitical.[34]

We suggest that, like Scurry, Allison Feaster's successful rise in the NBA cannot be fully understood outside of the confluence of postfeminism and postracism. As with us all, Feaster is a product of the time in which she lives. In the next section, this coconstitutive process is evident in Feaster's reproduction of the white narrative of the American Dream.

Feaster and the White American Dream

The notion that the United States presents its citizens with a uniquely American opportunity to improve their social standing from that of their parents through hard work and capitalist endeavors is ingrained in our nation's cultural story. Sports historian Steven Reiss notes, for example, that in the early 1900s, high salaries led to improved social prestige for American League baseball players, drawing the attention of young men to the career of "professional athlete." In short, the notion of the American Dream expands to include the conception that a life in sports conclusively offers upward financial mobility.[35] As a result, the American Dream's cultural storyline is integral to our understanding of sports: sports provide an ostensibly level playing field for those who participate, whether it is in the arena or the front office. The American Dream narrative adheres to the idea that society and sports are meritocracies based on skill and hard work. Those who succeed must have worked harder and been more talented than those who do not. The reverse of this, of course, means that those who fail did not work hard enough to win. Clearly, the truth lies somewhere in the middle and somewhere else altogether.

The mythos of the American Dream is central to nearly all media coverage of Feaster. Sports are viewed as an avenue of economic opportunity, a catalyst to improve social capital, and a way to alleviate the racial and social injustices in our society. Feaster's story is told like stories about other Black athletes are told across the decades, though her status as an Ivy League–educated Black woman complicates the simplistic, dominant narrative of a young Black female athlete overcoming her working-class roots. Feaster's stories of her childhood as the daughter of working-class, divorced parents in South Carolina stand in stark contrast to the image of an institution like Harvard University.

Both of Feaster's parents played basketball in high school, but her mother, Sandra, was the most influential resource in her life. After her parents divorced when Feaster was ten, her mother drove two hours each day to work as a secretary at a financial analyst firm and then worked weekends as a switchboard operator for Greyhound to earn extra money for the family. Sandra stressed the importance of academics to all her children. Unable to attend college as a young woman because of an unplanned pregnancy, Sandra earned a bachelor's degree from Winthrop University in 1992. Feaster witnessed the value of a college degree firsthand as her mother was quickly promoted from secretary to financial analyst and no longer had to work weekends.[36] Feaster later noted that Sandra's example of a blue-collar work ethic helped her balance life as a student and an athlete.[37]

The specter of that lost college opportunity for her mother loomed in Feaster's head during her senior year in high school. An excellent student and athlete, Feaster had her pick of big-name academic institutions, and ultimately, Harvard beat out Duke, Rice, Dartmouth, and Yale as her college choice. To pay for her degree from one of the most expensive schools in the nation—though they are NCAA Division I, the Ivy League schools do not offer athletic scholarship dollars—Feaster worked in the Harvard mailroom and took out loans. She hoped that the education and social capital she earned at the university would move her far beyond her working-class background.[38] In 2021, Feaster discussed her rise to the Celtics' front office with Marc Spears, a journalist for ESPN's online magazine, *The Undefeated*, now renamed *Andscape*, stating, "I didn't get here by myself. My mom had to work so hard. She worked hard and by herself. And there's so many people along the way who invested in me . . . and so, it's not me. It's not me and I don't ever think that it's me doing this. I am a product of those who are important to me, and I am a champion for those who are coming after me."[39] As an astute seventeen-year-old, Feaster recognized that to achieve her dreams of moving her family from its blue-collar roots to a higher social status, she would need to capitalize upon the academic opportunity and accept an offer to join the Harvard Crimson women's basketball team. "I saw going to Harvard as a springboard to the workforce, to get a job and help my family out," she said. Naturally, she seized the opportunity.[40] She is one of the lucky few for whom sports has served as a vehicle for upward social mobility, and it happened largely because she selected Harvard over the University of Connecticut or the University of Tennessee.

Her Harvard years were also formative in helping her navigate the world as a Black female athlete. Feaster credits Harvard's head basketball coach, Kathy Delaney-Smith, a white woman, with instilling a personal mantra that Feaster still cites: "Act as if."[41] This mantra is a mental commitment to concentrating on manifesting a goal as if it has already become reality and blocking out any conflicting thoughts. Feaster absorbed Delaney-Smith's words, which became the words by which she has since lived, noting, "That is what really stuck with me above and beyond the NCAA Tournament appearances, the Ivy titles, the individual accolades."[42] The notion that Feaster could "act as if" she belonged in Cambridge, Massachusetts, though arriving from a small town in South Carolina, was powerful. Feaster notes the culture shock of the transition from her small southern town to Massachusetts: "My mom had to drive me up with my stuff and drop me off in Harvard Square and I remember being terrified because I didn't really feel like I belonged. And so, it took a while for me to become adjusted and thank God I had my basketball community and team to wrap their arms around me and my coach, because it would have been that much more difficult."[43]

Delaney-Smith's *act as if* mantra underscores an important addendum to the American Dream mythos: those who believe they can, will. It does not consider either the explicit or implicit barriers of race, class, and gender that individuals face as they attempt to improve their social situation; if one *acts as if* often enough, one will be able to achieve one's goal. Feaster's success in achieving a better socioeconomic status for her family results from her ability to parlay her athletic talent into a world-class education. The *act as if* mantra works when its adherent succeeds. It does not have an answer for how its adherent should reconcile *acting as if* with an unsuccessful endeavor.

As a Black woman at Harvard, in the WNBA, in Europe, and now as an executive in the C-suite of an NBA franchise in a city with a problematic racial history, *act as if* set forth a pattern for her life achievements that reinforces the meritocratic and individualistic notions of the American Dream. As recently as 2017, Feaster spoke about *acting as if* regarding her role on the NBA's Basketball Operations Associate Program that led to her position in the G League:

> It's a challenge, but I also see it as an opportunity. I'm not the most outgoing person unless I have to be, and this role really forces me to swallow that trepidation that I have. [Boston] is the center of the basketball universe, and we have some of the greatest basketball minds in our company. I had to understand that I'm one of them. I've spent many years in this game, not just in the States, but abroad as well. Coming to terms with being confident enough to navigate the space was something

I kind of had to overcome. In order to successfully navigate it, you have to believe in yourself. I did it when I was a player because I practiced day in and day out. But I've also done it off the court in preparing myself to step into this role. So, it's been a challenge to be a little bit more confident than you have to be.[44]

When discussing her role at the Celtics, Feaster said, "I pinch myself every day I walk in the gym. I'm living a dream, and at times it doesn't seem real. Of course, I don't lead with 'I'm the first or the only.' It's 'I'm so thankful to be in this space and really appreciative of this opportunity,' and understand the responsibility I have to touch others and to pull others up along the way with me."[45] Feaster clearly understands the special place she holds as one of the only Black women at the executive level of an American professional sport franchise, while at the same time, she acknowledges that she is still having to *act as if* to negotiate her professional life as a Black woman in her midforties.

It is one thing to *act as if*. It is another thing entirely to have the social capital to break into the personnel side of the front office of one of the NBA's most storied franchises. It seems an even more improbable leap—even for the mythos of the American Dream—that this would be the career trajectory of a Black woman from working-class South Carolina. When discussing her postplaying career, however, Feaster credits her success in obtaining a high-level front-office role in the NBA to hard work: "There's really no one path, no recipe for success, but I can just share what worked for me and that is never stop hustling. Never stop grinding. Always be open to learn new things, to step outside your comfort zone, to grow. I was not the most social person. I had to make phone calls. I followed up with emails. I thanked people for opportunities. You really have to be on your grind and be top of mind and be prepared when an opportunity rolls around."[46] At the same time, though, Feaster has chalked up her postplaying career path to "serendipity," achieving her position mostly through luck—much, like she says, her boss Danny Ainge, Celtics' former general manager and a white man, achieved his: "I sat with Danny at the facility for a couple hours, just getting to know each other. I remember a very valuable lesson he mentioned—that all of the positions he's had post-playing really came about serendipitously. He never really planned to be in a certain place, but things just kind of worked out. A lot of my experiences were the same. Being here, it's kind of come full circle."[47]

Of course, neither Ainge nor Feaster landed in their postplaying career positions serendipitously. Each was an elite college player—Ainge was a Wooden Award winner (the best collegiate male basketball player in the nation), and Feaster was a Kodak First-Team All-America selection; each earned a degree from a prestigious academic institution; each was a first-round selection to the NBA or WNBA, respectively; and each had a lengthy professional playing career filled with accolades. Their on-court talents and success landed them squarely amid conversations about basketball leadership in the NBA. This is not to discount their education, their hard work, or their professional development efforts, but we must recognize that while the American Dream asserts that *anyone could* have achieved what Ainge and Feaster have, the reality is that *not many do*.

Recognizing the gap between those who could and those who do is especially important when focusing on Feaster's accomplishments. Black women from working-class backgrounds are often "othered" by media coverage; to participate in professional environments, they are often presented with even more challenges than their white counterparts face.[48] As a Black woman working in the predominantly white, male environment of the NBA, it becomes even more important for Feaster to adhere to notions of white femininity. She must navigate her race and gender in ways that Ainge has never had to consider. She walks a thin line of being ambitious, confident, and professionally assertive, complicated by cultural notions of the "angry Black woman."[49]

Black Female Motherhood in Professional Sport

In his book *Discipline and Punish,* French poststructural theorist Michel Foucault traces the complex and ever-shifting relations between power, knowledge, and the body. He argues that modern societal structures were created to discipline the body into docility. Discipline is not a physical punishment or enslavement but rather a coercive power reproduced through the supervision of time, space, and movement as well as surveillance. The architectural structure of modern surveillance places the burden of discipline upon the individual, or what Foucault notes as governmentality.[50] He states that governmentality "should be a machine for creating and sustaining a power relation independent of the person who exercises it; in short, that [individuals] should be caught up in a power situation of which they are themselves the bearers."[51] Social norms, then, become a measure of difference that produces reality, objects, rituals of truth, and knowable subjectivities.[52] As such, individuals become more invested in the categories of a "normalized" discourse leading to fewer moments of resistance against the status quo.

Bodies are inevitably self-directed as they move through space and time. But not all bodies are considered equal in society. White female bodies are idealized as the norm, while white society sees "*the* Black woman's body as multiply displaced."[53] The Black female body is enmeshed in a matrix of raced, classed, gendered, and sexualized politics. This intersectional matrix attempts to silence Black aesthetics, even as global athletic celebrities like Serena Williams and Simone Biles present alternatives that deconstruct the normalizing gaze of whiteness.[54] However, the deconstruction of the white gaze is not universal. The postfeminist and postracial milieu of the 1990s and 2000s provide a cultural context in which docile bodies, especially those of Black women, must mirror the status quo. Feaster is a representation of a "raced" docile body.[55]

Media accounts of Feaster's achievements, on and off the court, resist the "Africanized Horatio Alger trope of athletes" that sport studies scholar Mary McDonald observed in her studies of Michael Jordan and Ervin "Magic" Johnson.[56] These athletes embody the intertwined ideologies of individualism and the American Dream, perpetuating the mythos that anyone can work hard enough to improve their social standing. Individualism, of course, is venerated as the basis for personal freedom, autonomy, and achievement of the American Dream. In sports it is derided for being the root of the "selfish" athlete who hurts a team by not "sharing," while it is also held up as an ideal responsible for one's athletic prowess. The notion of the "selfish athlete" has long served as a metaphor for "Black athlete."[57] McDonald's textual analysis of media coverage of Jordan notes that he was long held up as a symbol of the American Dream, and his success in both sports and advertising helped cultivate an image that allowed white Americans to "forget" he was Black.[58] At the same time, however, global affairs scholar Joshua Wright notes that Jordan was seen as the "godfather of Generation 'Me,'" setting the stage for Black male athletes who were roundly criticized for being selfish, including Allen Iverson, Cam Newton, and Floyd Merriweather.[59]

As a Black woman playing sport in America, Feaster did not have the luxury that Jordan had to establish a persona that captured the nation's interest. As Birrell and Hall note, we see women's experiences—in this case, in basketball—as variations or deviations from men's experiences, which are held up as the norm.[60] For Feaster, fewer viewers for women's sports translated to fewer opportunities to rewrite the cultural narrative of what it means to be a female athlete. Long-standing cultural stereotypes of Black female athletes still shape our cultural imagery, with strength as the historically pervasive narrative.[61] Further, the social roles that Black female athletes are allowed to embody are more limited than the social roles available to male athletes. Kinesiologist M. Ann Hall argues that culturally, we police the femininity of our female athletes in a way we do not practice with the masculinity of our male athletes.[62] This is particularly true of the 1990s and early 2000s, when Feaster was a collegian and in the first part of her professional playing career.

While an active player, Feaster, in interviews, both soft-pedals and highlights the long hours and hard work that went into her playing career and education, a narrative that complicates the typical American Dream story. She resists the notion of individualism—regularly giving credit to her family, her coaches, her teammates, her husband, and her luck—while also asserting ownership over her efforts since childhood. After all, Feaster likely would not find herself in the role of the Celtics' director of player development without having played basketball at a high level. College teammates interviewed about Feaster also noted that her public persona was consistently different from the demeanor she showed around her team. Former teammates described her as "quiet if you don't know her, but to her best friends, she's kind of crazy" and as "vocal and opinionated" around the team but "shy" around others.[63] Delaney-Smith, her collegiate coach, said, "[She] is very, very special in that she uniquely combines a tremendous amount of skill and talent with sincere humility. I believe she would rather not be the focus, but she understands why . . . I think she believes that she is just part of the puzzle."[64] These descriptions of Feaster as a player reinforce Hall's conceptions of female athletes as embodying femininity—care for others, not self.[65] Although sport is conceived of as a masculine and competitive enterprise, as a player, Feaster often downplayed her own role and successes within the sport and elevated those of her teammates.

From her first time in the national media spotlight following the sixteenth-seed Crimson's upset of the top-seed Cardinals in 1998, Feaster understated her role in the win, despite her team-leading contribution of thirty-five points and thirteen rebounds. "I can't tell you the amount of adversity we faced, just coming in here," she said. "But somehow, we did it."[66] Even when talking about her personal achievements during her first three years playing for Harvard, during which she was named Ivy League Rookie of the Year and twice named Ivy League Player of the Year, she put the team first. In 1997, nine months before sixteenth-seed Harvard knocked off top-seed Stanford, she told a reporter from the Harvard *Crimson* newspaper, "Every year we have team goals, and every year we always seem to fall just a little short of those goals. More than ever, this year we've been able to accomplish everything we wanted to do. Personally, I feel that based on the team's success, each of us has enjoyed our own degree of success, and the same is true of myself."[67] In foregrounding the team's accomplishments and understating her individual accolades, Feaster perpetuates our expectations of female athletes as competitors who always put the team first. In doing so, we see a restatement of the ideals of the white female athlete, as Feaster focuses on the "we, not me" of her team.

Another significant area for modeling feminine docile bodies is motherhood. Motherhood is a unique rite of passage for women who choose to experience it. According to feminist scholar Sharon Hays, motherhood in the Global North is lived through behaviors and attitudes that signify an "intensive mother."[68] Intensive mothering is time-consuming, highly emotional, and child-centered. This ideal practice privileges white, middle-class, heterosexual, married women.[69] Within this context, Black women's bodies are constantly surveilled and most often seen as "other." Negative stereotypes of Black motherhood have been shaped by cultural images of Black women as "mammy," "the matriarch," and the "welfare queen."[70] Feaster's mediated persona resists these cultural tropes. Instead, she exemplifies the postfeminist, athletic superwoman who can and does "have it all."

During the early years of the WNBA in the late 1990s, narratives of motherhood and family circulated in the media as a marketing initiative to deflect attention from the masculine, athletic, and formidable bodies on the court and reimagine women's sports as heterosexual.[71] Chris Wright, chief marketing officer of the WNBA's Minnesota Lynx, denotes the difference between NBA and WNBA audiences: "The target on the WNBA side is first women, then families, then business."[72] While Feaster did not figure prominently in this discourse, stories about her relationship with her husband, Danny Strong, who is also a former professional basketball player, and Feaster's eventual pregnancy with her daughter did attract media attention.[73] Feaster notes that she and her husband, who played basketball overseas, found it difficult to navigate being in the same country, let alone the same continent, throughout the year. Regardless of this difficulty, the health and stability of Feaster and Strong's heterosexual relationship is signified through its longevity. Strong is "her high school sweetheart."[74] The use of *her* in this quote is significant, for it places a singular meaning on a relationship between two people. Strong must be *her* sweetheart to reproduce a docile body—one that is heterosexual in the queer space of women's basketball.

In 2005, just days after winning the French women's basketball league title and a few days before starting the WNBA season with the Charlotte Sting, Feaster found out that she was pregnant.[75] She continued to play in the WNBA until she was placed on the injured reserve list four months into her pregnancy.[76] She remained with the Sting for the remainder of the season, and in February 2006, her daughter, Sarah, was born.

In the construction of docile feminine bodies, governmentality as seen through historical gender norms confines women to caregiving and nurturing the family. Feaster recognized motherhood as an area of potential gendered surveillance and concludes that her daughter should stay with her when she plays abroad. Feaster notes, "My husband is pretty practical, and he understands the role that a mother plays in a young child's life . . . it was just an unspoken: she'll stay with me when we have to be apart."[77] Feaster verbalizes the unspoken norm of a mother's responsibility for caregiving. In Foucault's words, she is the "bearer" of this norm, surveilling herself to cultivate a docile body that does not resist the status quo.

Interestingly, this notion of motherhood has followed Feaster into her work with the Boston Celtics organization. Many in the upper echelons of the Celtics franchise adhere to a binary assumption about gender.[78] At the organizational level, the Celtics are beginning to value and embrace the differences between men and women. Sports management scholars George Cunningham and Michael Sagas note that "traditionally feminine characteristics, such as listening, collaborating, and peacemaking, add value to the workplace."[79] The notion of being embraced for one's difference reduces any gendered and/or racial tensions in the organizational ranks. Feaster notes that the Celtics have not treated her or former fellow employee Kara Lawson, who previously served as the organization's first female assistant coach and is also Black, as tokens: "The beauty of this position and this organization and the way that Kara and I have been welcomed, it's just like any other employee, I imagine . . . I don't feel like 'the other' as maybe I felt as being the only African-American on my Harvard team."[80] While the gendered and racial aspects are not overt, the Celtics reinforce normative assumptions that reduce power for women—and most certainly, women of color—in the workplace. Specifically, Ainge, former general manager and president of basketball operations, and Brad Stevens, former head coach and current president of basketball operations, demonstrate this notion. Ainge states, "I believe that women bring a different perspective. . . . Brad feels the same way. . . . And we have a lot of players also that are raised by single mothers. But I think that the biggest thing, I believe men and women are different. And they bring a different perspective. . . . And I think [Feaster and Kara Lawson] are going to bring great perspective to our coaching staff and the entire organization."[81] Ainge alludes twice to the notion that men and women have different perspectives, clearly dividing men and women into two separate and distinct categories. What is of most interest, linguistically, is his off-the-cuff mention of "single mothers." In this statement, Ainge, a white man, manages to reduce two Black women not only to the biological function of motherhood but also to the negative tropes of Black matriarchy and single mothers who have had problematic life histories.[82]

In her role as vice president of player development and organizational growth in the Boston Celtics organization, Feaster is responsible for creating and maintaining relationships with the players and acting as a liaison between the players and the administration. This position embodies the characteristics of motherhood, as she is to maintain contacts with players that revolve around their personal growth as athletes and as functioning adults in society. Rich Gotham, president of the Boston Celtics, states that Feaster is, "[that] liaison between player and the team leadership to make sure that those resources that are necessary, players have access to [them]."[83] Feaster was hired for her stellar reputation and abilities, but those abilities do not exist outside or away from particular stereotypes and embedded values, assumptions, and beliefs about gender and race held by organizational members.[84] Professionally, she is to be a mother-like figure who can be reached at any moment for emotional support and access to much-needed resources. Moreover, Feaster is to be a player's greatest advocate, a responsibility that goes far beyond the court and dives into the intimate space of relationship building. Feaster notes, "I genuinely have come to love these guys and I am the No. 1 champion for them. They know my door is always open. They know I care and am here to help them be the best they can be."[85] For a Black woman, these beliefs are accentuated, adopted, and circulated through the narratives of the lack of parental control over young Black men in the 1990s. The narrative of the absent father in Black, single-family households cemented blame on Black culture for the increase in divorce rates and the overall decline of the nuclear family in America.[86] Feaster, whether she is a mother or not, carries the burden of this stereotype, and the Celtics continue to reproduce it.

Feaster's ability to remain apolitical provided her social capital throughout her playing career and education. In Feaster's interviews prior to June 2020, she remains an enigma, toeing the oft-repeated line of working hard for team success and occasionally acknowledging her own abilities and achievements. We question whether her role as "postfeminist athletic superwoman" truly subverts these long-held cultural notions regarding Black women. She may unwittingly be feeding into a different trope for Black women, one that is just as harmful as the previous stereotypes because it is unattainable.

Feaster joined many Americans in a personal racial reckoning when she learned of the murder of George Floyd by Minneapolis police officer Derek Chauvin on May 25, 2020. She notes the horrific killing and resulting media coverage marked a turning point in her consciousness about the role that she played in the world as a Black woman. At the time, she said she spent three months in South Carolina with her mother and stepfather and realized that she had not paid attention to the adversity that other people of color experienced throughout their lives: "It has just been a matter of doing what we gotta do. . . . We have to grind; we have to get up. We don't have time to show pain or weakness. [Floyd's death] was really the first time, being there with my mom, seeing a nation crying out, that I was conscious of some inner pain."[87]

Starting in June 2020, as the Celtics doubled down on diversity, equity, and inclusion programs for their players and front-office staff, Feaster's own cultivated social media identity begins to hint at a political rejection of the white cultural narrative that has shaped the public's view of her. She is, again, a product of her time. Feaster's continued comments indicate she is unwilling to return to her previous apolitical stance. She seems more comfortable in her Blackness than at any other point in her public life, and she has achieved a professional status within an NBA organization that no other Black American woman has to date. Through this resistance, we can only hope that her mediated representation develops a new trope about women in sport, one where intersectionality is centered.

Notes

1. Justin Camenker, "Feaster Reminisces about Phone Call That Led to Her Joining the C's," nbcsportsboston.com, March 19, 2021, https://www.nbcsportsboston.com/nba/boston -celtics/feaster-reminisces-about-phone-call-that-led-to-her-joining-the-cs/175467/. We use the moniker "Allison Feaster": Feaster is married and hyphenates her last name as Feaster-Strong, but Strong is rarely used in the mediated coverage of her.
2. Lydialyle Gibson, "The Irresistible Allison Feaster: A Life in Basketball, So Far," harvardmagazine.com, November–December 2022, https://www.harvardmagazine .com/2022/11/feature-allison-feaster.

3. South Carolina State Senate General Assembly, "110th Session, 1993–1994," scstatehouse.gov, May 19, 1994, https://www.scstatehouse.gov/sess110_1993-1994/bills/1426.htm.
4. Gibson, "Irresistible Allison Feaster."
5. Marc Spears, "Celtics' Allison Feaster: 'I Didn't Get Here by Myself,'" andscape.com, March 24, 2021, para. 26, https://andscape.com/features/celtics-allison-feaster-i-didnt-get-here-by-myself/.
6. Meredith Rainey-Valmon, "Allison Feaster-Strong," ivy50.com, May 16, 2007, para. 5, http://ivy50.com/blackhistory/story.aspx?sid=5/16/2007.
7. Ivy League Sports, "The Ivy Influence: Allison Feaster-Strong," webarchive.org, February 2, 2012, https://web.archive.org/web/20160918034119/http://www.ivyleaguesports.com/history/blackhistory/2011-12/allison_feaster-strong.
8. Eduardo Perez-Giz, "Remembering a Historic Season," thecrimson.com, March 20, 1998, accessed March 12, 2022, https://www.thecrimson.com/article/1998/3/20/remembering-a-historic-season-pfollowing-the/.
9. Perez-Giz, "Remembering a Historic Season," para. 2.
10. Craig Lambert, "Charlie the Great," harvardmagazine.com, January 1997, accessed March 12, 2022, https://www.harvardmagazine.com/sites/default/files/html/1997/01/jhj.sports.html.
11. WNBA, "1998 WNBA Draft," wnba.com, 1998, accessed March 12, 2022, https://www.wnba.com/draft/1998.
12. Justin Lester, "Former WNBA Players Allison Feaster and Stacey Lovelace on the NBA's Basketball Operations Associate Program," global.nba.com, November 7, 2017, https://global.nba.com/news/former-wnba-players-allison-feaster-and-stacey-lovelace-on-the-nbas-basketball-operations-associate-program/#; Nyala Pendergrass, "Allison Feaster Brought Her Own Seat to the Boston Celtics Table," si.com, August 10, 2022, https://www.si.com/nba/2022/08/10/allison-feaster-celtics-100-influential-black-women.
13. Pendergrass, "Allison Feaster," para. 2.
14. Lambert, "Charlie the Great," para. 10.
15. Kyle Kusz, "Much Adu About Nothing? Freddy Adu and Neoliberal Racism in New Millennium America," in *Commodified and Criminalized: New Racism and African Americans in Contemporary Sports*, ed. David J. Leonard and C. Richard King (New York: Rowman and Littlefield, 2011), 147–64.
16. Mary McDonald and Susan Birrell, "Reading Sport Critically: A Methodology for Interrogating Power," *Sociology of Sport Journal* 16, no. 4 (1999): 295.
17. David J. Leonard, "Dilemmas and Contradictions: Black Female Athletes," in *Out of Bounds: Racism and the Black Athlete*, ed. Lori Latrice Martin (Santa Barbara CA: Praeger, 2014), 209–30; Patricia Vertinsky and Gwendolyn Captain, "More Myth Than History: American Culture and Representations of the Black Female's Athletic Ability," *Journal of Sport History* 25, no. 3 (1998): 532–61.
18. Michel Foucault, *Discipline and Punish: The Birth of the Prison* (New York: Vintage, 1977).

19. Lawrence Grossberg, *Bringing It All Back Home: Essays on Cultural Studies* (Durham NC: Duke University Press, 1997), 255.

20. Henry Giroux, *The Terror of Neoliberalism: Authoritarianism and the Eclipse of Democracy* (Boulder CO: Paradigm, 2004); Mary McDonald, "Michael Jordan's Family Values: Marketing, Meaning, and Post-Reagan America," *Sociology of Sport Journal* 13 (1996): 344–65.

21. Mary D. Edsall and Thomas B. Edsall, *Chain Reaction: The Impact of Race, Rights, and Taxes on American Politics* (New York: W. W. Norton, 1992).

22. R. Vivian Acosta and Linda J. Carpenter, "Women in Intercollegiate Sport: A Longitudinal, National Study Thirty-Seven Year Update, 1977–2014," acostacarpenter.org, 2014, http://www.acostacarpenter.org/2014%20Status%20of%20Women%20in%20Intercollegiate%20Sport%20-37%20Year%20Update%20-%201977-2014%20.pdf, last accessed March 12, 2022.

23. Paul Newberry, "Summer of Women: Females Stole the Show at the 1996 Olympics," washingtonpost.com, August 13, 2020, https://www.washingtonpost.com/sports/olympics/summer-of-women-females-stole-the-show-at-1996-olympics/2020/08/13/83cbcc80-dd9e-11ea-b4f1-25b762cdbbf4_story.html.

24. Rachel Allison, *Kicking Center: Gender and the Selling of Women's Professional Soccer* (New Brunswick NJ: Rutgers University Press, 2018).

25. Angela McRobbie, "Postfeminism and Popular Culture: Bridget Jones and the New Gender Regime," in *Interrogating Postfeminism: Gender and the Politics of Popular Culture*, ed. Yvonne Tasker and Diane Negra (Durham NC: Duke University Press, 2007), 27.

26. Nikol G. Alexander-Floyd, *Re-imagining Black Women: A Critique of Post-feminist and Post-racial Melodrama in Culture and Politics* (New York: New York University Press, 2021), 5–6.

27. David Andrews, "Contextualizing Suburban Soccer: Consumer Culture, Lifestyle Differentiation and Suburban America," *Culture, Sport, Society* 2 (1999): 31–53; C. L. Cole and Amy Hribar, "Celebrity Feminism: Nike Style Post-Fordism, Transcendence, and Consumer Power," *Sociology of Sport Journal* 12, no. 4 (1995): 347–69; McRobbie, "Postfeminism and Popular Culture."

28. Kimberly Springer, "Divas, Evil Black Bitches, and Bitter Black Women: African American Women in Postfemininst and Post-Civil-Rights Popular Culture," in Tasker and Negra, *Interrogating Postfeminism*, 249–76.

29. Cole and Hribar, "Celebrity Feminism"; Mary McDonald, "Marketing of the Women's National Basketball Association and the Making of Postfeminism," *International Review for the Sociology of Sport* 35, no. 1 (2000): 35–47; Eileen Narcotta-Welp, "A Black Fly in White Milk: The 1999 Women's World Cup, Briana Scurry, and the Politics of Inclusion," *Journal of Sport History* 42, no. 3 (2015): 382–93; Eileen Narcotta-Welp, "Going Solo: The Spectre of the 1999ers and Hope Solo as the Conscious Pariah," *Sport in Society: Cultures, Commerce, Media, Politics* 21, no. 7 (2018): 996–1012.

30. Springer, "Divas, Evil Black Bitches," 253.
31. Giroux, *Terror of Neoliberalism*.
32. Leola Johnson and David Roediger, "Hertz, Don't It? Becoming Colorless and Staying Black in the Crossover of O.J. Simpson," in *Reading Sport: Critical Essays on Power and Representation*, ed. Susan Birrell and Mary McDonald (Boston: Northeastern University Press, 2000), 40–73; McDonald, "Michael Jordan's Family Values."
33. Alexander-Floyd, *Re-imagining Black Women*, 9.
34. Narcotta-Welp, "Black Fly."
35. Steven Reiss, "Sport and the American Dream: A Review Essay," *Journal of Social History* 14, no. 2 (1980): 295–303.
36. Gibson, "Irresistible Allison Feaster."
37. "Allison Feaster Appears on 'Exceptional Women' Show on Boston's WMJX-FM Magic 106.7," BeyondtheW.com, accessed May 14, 2023, https://beyondthew.com/allison-feaster-appears-on-exceptional-women-show-on-bostons-wmjx-fm-magic-106-7/.
38. Rainey-Valmon, "Allison Feaster-Strong."
39. Spears, "Celtics' Allison Feaster," para. 2.
40. "Allison Feaster Appears," para. 5.
41. Spears, "Celtics' Allison Feaster," para. 9.
42. Spears, "Celtics' Allison Feaster," para. 9.
43. Spears, "Celtics' Allison Feaster," para. 26.
44. Lester, "Former WNBA Players," para. 15.
45. Spears, "Celtics' Allison Feaster," para. 2.
46. Spears, "Celtics' Allison Feaster," para. 40.
47. Jared Weiss, "'How Can We Find a Way to Hire This Person?' Why the Celtics Were So Driven to Add Allison Feaster," *New York Times*, October 17, 2019, para. 2, https://www.nytimes.com/athletic/1293596/2019/10/17/how-can-we-find-a-way-to-hire-this-person-why-the-celtics-were-so-driven-to-naballison-feaster/.
48. Akilah R. Carter-Francique and F. Michelle Richardson, "Controlling Media, Controlling Access: The Role of Sport Media on Black Women's Sport Participation," *Race, Gender & Class* 23, nos. 1–2 (2016): 7–33.
49. Vertinsky and Captain, "More Myth Than History."
50. Foucault, *Discipline and Punish*, 195–228.
51. Foucault, *Discipline and Punish*, 201.
52. Shirley Anne Tate, *Black Women's Bodies and the Nation: Race, Gender and Culture* (New York: Palgrave Macmillan, 2015), 4.
53. Tate, *Black Women's Bodies*, 3 (emphasis in the original).
54. Andrea Elizabeth Shaw, *The Embodiment of Disobedience: Fat Black Women's Unruly Political Bodies* (Boulder CO: Lexington, 2006).
55. Tate, *Black Women's Bodies*, 7.
56. Mary McDonald, "Horatio Alger with a Jump Shot: Michael Jordan and the American Dream," *Iowa Journal of Cultural Studies* 15, no. 1 (1996): 33–47.

57. Joshua Wright, "Be Like Mike? The Black Athlete's Dilemma," *Spectrum: A Journal on Black Men* 4, no. 2 (2016): 1–19.

58. McDonald, "Horatio Alger"; McDonald, "Michael Jordan's Family Values."

59. Wright, "Be Like Mike?," 10.

60. Susan Birrell, "Studying Gender in Sport: A Feminist Perspective," *Sport and the Sociological Imagination* (1984): 125–35; M. Ann Hall, "The Discourse of Gender and Sport: From Femininity to Feminism," *Sociology of Sport Journal* 5, no. 4 (1988): 330–40.

61. Vertinsky and Captain, "More Myth Than History."

62. M. Ann Hall, *Feminism and Sporting Bodies: Essays on Theory and Practice* (Cambridge: Cambridge University Press, 1996).

63. Jamal K. Greene, "Women's Cager's Charlie Horse," thecrimson.com, June 5, 1997, para. 2, https://www.thecrimson.com/article/1997/6/5/womens-cagers-charlie-horse -pshes-quiet.

64. Greene, "Women's Cager's," para. 11.

65. Hall, "Discourse of Gender."

66. Michelle Smith, "The Crimson Leave," *Washington Post*, March 16, 1998, D08.

67. Greene, "Women's Cager's," para. 30.

68. Sharon Hays, *The Cultural Contradictions of Motherhood* (New Haven CT: Yale University Press, 1996), 19–51.

69. Miriam Peskowitz, *The Truth behind the Mommy Wars: Who Decides What Makes a Good Mother?* (New York: Seal, 2005), 1–19.

70. Patricia Hill Collins, "The Meaning of Motherhood in Black Culture and Black Mother/ Daughter Relationships," *Sage* 4, no. 2 (1987): 3–11.

71. Mary McDonald, "Queering Whiteness: The Particular Case of the Women's National Basketball Association," *Sociological Perspectives* 45, no. 4 (2002): 379–96; Kelly Whiteside, *WNBA: A Celebration; Commemorating the Birth of a League* (New York: Harper, 1998).

72. Terry Wood, "Smart Marketing Key to Success in WNBA," *Seattle Times*, June 13, 1998, E5.

73. Associated Press, "In This League, the Mothers Know Best," nytimes.com, June 4, 2006, https://www.nytimes.com/2006/06/04/sports/basketball/04wnba.html; Springer, "Allison Feaster."

74. Pendergrass, "Allison Feaster"; Springer, "Allison Feaster: Life as a Pro Basketball Player," wbur.org, May 12, 2017, para. 15, https://www.wbur.org/onlyagame/2017/05/ 12/allison-feaster-sting-harvard-mom.

75. Springer, "Allison Feaster."

76. Associated Press, "In This League."

77. Springer, "Allison Feaster: Life," para. 34.

78. George B. Cunningham and Michael Sagas, "Gender and Sex Diversity in Sport Organizations: Introduction to a Special Issue," *Sex Roles* 58 (2008): 3–9; Debra E. Meyerson and Deborah M. Kolb, "Moving Out of the 'Arm Chair': Developing a Framework to

Bridge the Gap between Feminist Theory and Practice," *Organization* 7, no. 4 (2000): 553–71; Sally Shaw and Wendy Frisby, "Can Gender Equity Be More Equitable? Promoting an Alternative Frame for Sport Management Research, Education, and Practice," *Journal of Sport Management* 20, no. 4 (2006): 483–509.

79. Cunningham and Sagas, "Gender and Sex Diversity," 5.
80. Justin Quinn, "Allison Feaster Exceling as Celtics' Director of Player Development," celticswire.usatoday.com, February 20, 2020, para. 23, https://celticswire.usatoday.com/2020/02/20/nba-boston-celtics-allison-feaster-director-player-development/.
81. Mike Tony, "Celtics Name Former Harvard Standout Allison Feaster Director of Player Development," ivyhoops.com, September 2019, https://ivyhoopsonline.com/2019/09/07/celtics-name-former-harvard-standout-allison-feaster-director-of-player-development/#more-12727, last accessed March 12, 2022, para 4, para. 8.
82. McDonald, "Michael Jordan's Family Values"; Vertinsky and Captain, "More Myth Than History."
83. Weiss, "How Can We Find," para. 33.
84. Cunningham and Sagas, "Gender and Sex Diversity."
85. Camenker, "Feaster Reminisces," para. 10.
86. McDonald, "Michael Jordan's Family Values."
87. Allison Feaster, "Allison Feaster, Celtics VP of Player Development," ESPN Radio, July 23, 2020, https://www.espn.com/radio/play/_/id/29526023.

Afterword

Balancing Sports Commemoration and Race

KATHRYN LEANN HARRIS

The chapters included in this book reflect an unearthing of narratives that have mostly been cast out of the limelight. In a world where so many contemporary Black athletes are celebrated for their athletic greatness, this raises the question: Why? Why are the pioneer athletes of the modern Black sports era relegated to a forgotten past, when so many of their modern trailblazing counterparts of today are heralded? What we honor publicly reflects the combination of societal values and cultural power dynamics. To understand what is remembered and why, we must start by noticing which stories are publicly visible and when they appear, then consider what is to be gained and lost by shifting the focus onto what has previously been hidden.

In Boston, commemoration efforts that honor early Black sports figures began appearing widely in the last couple of decades, alongside recent Black political and social gains and amid current events calling attention to under-representation. Though this commemoration is welcome and long overdue, the price of looking reflectively at these players and their sports era has been high. Black sports pioneers can get lost against the backdrop of white nostalgia at the center of the city and nation's struggle with its own victory narratives defined by sociologist Lindsey Freeman as "the notion that the United States is a land of freedom and uses force only in response to an attack. Victory culture goes hand in hand with the American culture of innocence, the myth of the benevolent nation stripped of any lust for power."[1] This idea, of America as a culture of perpetual goodness and victory, was conceived with the nation's founding. Black athletes' experiences challenge that narrative, exposing a long-standing political undercurrent in sports that still exists today. Recent Black sports commemoration in Boston illuminates this significant impact of the early athletic pioneers, a movement that, as it expands, will contribute to a more balanced understanding of our shared past.

Black sports commemoration in and around Boston is experiencing an emergence where there was previously a void. Nearly all of the region's public representations of Black athletes appeared over the last fifteen years. The city of Cambridge installed a granite marker in Daheny Park honoring Olympic medalists Dr. Charles L Jenkins and John Thomas in 2003.[2] Worcester erected a statue of Major Taylor in 2008 and opened the Major Taylor Museum in 2021.[3] Bill Russell's statue was unveiled at Boston's City Hall Plaza in 2013.[4] That same year, Lorenz Finison completed his successful campaign to install a Katherine "Kittie" Knox monument in Mount Auburn Cemetery at the site of her previously unmarked grave, and in 2023 the Cambridge location of Recreational Equipment Inc. (REI) opened the Kittie Knox Cycle Center.[5] The Willie O'Ree Community Hockey Rink was dedicated in Allston in November 2018, the same month O'Ree was inducted into the Hockey Hall of Fame.[6] In 2018, the Red Sox changed the name of the famed street outside the park's entrance from Yawkey Way back to Jersey Street, consciously separating themselves from the anti-Black legacy and segregationist policies of the team under owner and president Tom Yawkey, who led the organization from 1933 to 1977.[7] In July 2020, the Red Sox sponsored a Black Lives Matter mural on a very visible billboard along the Massachusetts Turnpike adjacent to Fenway Park. They unveiled the sign in conjunction with the "sixty-first anniversary of Elijah 'Pumpsie' Green's debut as the Red Sox's first black player in 1959—making Boston the last MLB [Major League Baseball] team to integrate."[8] The city of Malden dedicated its River Loop park to Louise Stokes in September 2020.[9] Basketball courts at Walker Playground in Roxbury named after Medina Dixon opened in August 2022.[10] Andrea's Pizza in Stoneham commissioned a graffiti art–styled mural of Bill Russel in 2022.[11] The following year the city of Boston named Harambee Park football field in honor of Harry G. Wilson III and Dennis G. Wilson, brothers who started the Roxbury Raiders and Silver Stars community football and cheerleading programs and Roxbury Basketball Association summer league.[12] Later that year the Lowell YMCA recognized Harry "Bucky" Lew with a plaque, honoring his legacy as the first Black professional basketball player.[13] In 2024, the city of Brockton dedicated a statue to boxer Marvin Hagler. Two earlier acts of commemoration stand as exceptions to the lateness of these delayed recognitions: Malden High School installed a statue of Louise Stokes in the 1980s, and Medford named their film festival after Mabray "Doc" Kountze in 1997.[14]

Much of what a society chooses to hide can be seen by examining what they make visible and when. At the dedication of the basketball courts named in her honor, Dixon's family wondered why she had not been remembered sooner. Her impact was significant. "Medina didn't just affect Boston, or Massachusetts, or NCAA [National Collegiate Athletic Association] Women's basketball, she really transformed women's basketball across the country," her brother Rob noted.[15] Given her accomplishments, recognizing her much sooner than 2022 would have been fitting. O'Ree's story reveals more about how and when we choose to remember the past than it does about O'Ree himself. Though he was the first Black player in the National Hockey League (NHL) and a pathbreaker for others, there was little immediate "splash" when he broke the color barrier. After a few small Associated Press (AP) stories in 1958, his contribution went largely unrecognized, perhaps because, unlike Jackie Robinson's, his achievement didn't open a floodgate of Black hockey players but also, perhaps, because he was not what one could call a superstar. Had he been more successful as a player, he may not have been so ignored by mainstream society. Often, though, widespread white celebrations of athletes who broke sports color barriers did not happen immediately, in real time. Only decades later did O'Ree's star rise in popular estimation, when journalists and others started looking for historic, nostalgic, Black "firsts."

In the gulf between accomplishments and recognition lies an American tendency toward escapism that threads directly through sports. Like all other parts of society, sports have been filtered through the nation's power structure. As sports began to rise in popularity in the late 1800s, they became intertwined with politics. Then as minorities of all kinds gained agency through sports and society, harnessing affection under a victorious limelight, white and male dominant culture began a campaign to shift the power structures of sports to keep themselves on the top—of sports *and* society. Central to their strategy was propagating the message that sports are not political; they are a place to have fun, escape, and enjoy fair competition. This distractive campaign was an act of cultural gaslighting that heralded sports as an equal playing field and thus needed to remain pure and separate from other cultural dynamics so that the "best man" might win. In reality, politics were the driving factor that kept each member of society in their place within a societal caste system and allowed the dominant society's victory narrative to thrive.[16]

In the mid-twentieth century, the foundations of America's victory narrative started to erode. The use of the atomic bomb, followed closely by the truth telling and violent clashes of the civil rights movement, exposed America as a perpetrator, and not always a victorious one, of the violence centrally embedded in its cultural fabric.[17] Believing the notion that America was perpetually victorious and always on the side of right was no longer possible for all Americans. Efforts to deconstruct and dissolve the victory narrative by proponents of the civil rights, women's, and LGBT movements emerged gradually throughout the end of the twentieth century, even as the dominant society continually strove to reestablish the nation's founding identity.[18]

Commemoration is a central American remembrance practice dating to the nation's birth, when it became synonymous with the victor identity. Colonists imported these practices from their ancestors in England and Europe. Nearly as soon as the Revolutionary War ended, the founders relayed their national identity on monuments as a demarcation of America's newly birthed values, vision, and triumph. The act of honoring a person, idea, event, or community codifies that entity in the collective consciousness and reflects the commemorator's heralded values. For America, as historian John Gillis explains, "commemorations have served to solidify America's national victory identity, casting a nation's ideals in bronze and stone, and, later, in interpretive text at museums and at historic sites."[19] In short, to the victor go the spoils, and with them, a chance to write the narrative.

The primary areas in which American commemorations take place are politics, sports, and war. Overcommemoration, the practice of celebration without balanced perspective, is most rampant within sports. Practices such as focusing on win-loss records and glory stories or erecting monuments without much context feed a singular victorious ideal. Early twentieth-century white power players exploited overcommemoration to propagate the victory narrative in such forms as war monuments and Confederate memorials, a trend that reversed as the mythos of their message dissolved. As noted in my previous work, a majority of the nation's overtly anti-Black monuments were erected by white Americans during the same period that Native sports mascots emerged, between the 1890s and 1920s, which period historians have depicted as the nadir of race relations in the United States.[20] During this time, white supremacy proponents erected monuments to remind African Americans that they were subjugated and concurrently reduced Native Americans to mascots, depicted as historically inaccurate caricatures.[21] Native mascots continued to proliferate until "American Indians later gained power in both political and economic life."[22] Social pressure then increased, associated sports brands dropped in value, and the mascots started falling away. The same trend can be traced within the Black liberation movement and the "athlete activism" Joseph Cooper outlines in his contribution to this book. As Black activists began "securing and transferring power via economic and technological means," monuments honoring figures of white supremacy began to fall, and Black commemoration efforts rose across all sectors, including sports.[23]

Black pioneers of sport had a lived experience that ran counter to the grand narrative and flew in the face of the dominant culture's efforts to uphold their ideals. The undercurrent of early Black sports movements was not a story of victory for white America; instead, these stories revealed the embodiment of Black agency and visibility against seemingly insurmountable odds imposed by centuries of cultural violence and against an enduring culture of segregation, economic disenfranchisement, and white supremacy ideology. Sport is and always has been such a powerful change agent that the dominant powers have deemed it necessary to control. Black Boston players used their athletic prowess and agency to navigate this terrain, gaining increased social space by advancing into the playing fields.

Sports should not be relegated to depoliticized entertainment, tales of escape, or topics of mere reflection; rather, they are central to understanding how America's societal and cultural movements have been expressed across all domains of human activity. The actions of Boston's Black sports pioneers suggest that they were aware of this. Over and over again, they utilized their athletic success to position themselves as powerful societal actors and to advocate for equity and fair treatment.

Bids for the separation of politics and sports still permeate the dominant culture. Central to the politics of sports is a call to act as though sports are inherently not political. Ironically, the depoliticization propagated in the late 1800s never really happened. Sports and politics remain undeniably intertwined. Focusing on any part of American sports history without recognizing these attempts at deception serves only to direct attention away from an inequitable system, one that uses sports as a central mouthpiece.[24]

Examining these stories requires giving agency and voice to the Black liberation movement long before the white victory narrative allows for it. Voice matters. Those who are heard write the narrative and change public perception. This means listening to groundbreaking Black athletes and acknowledging both the expanse of their accomplishments as well as their treatment at the hands of mainstream society at the time. The call here is not only to recognize but also to contextualize with balanced perspective. While these accomplishments are significant and noteworthy, if viewed only through a competition model, some of these pioneers may seem small next to the accolades and firsts won by some of their white counterparts. In reality, they were all major players who ushered in cultural sea changes, more awe inspiring given the giant currents they battled in order to even play.

Moreover, these stories ask us to reconsider all that we think we know about the arc of sports in America. They ask us to see the politics at play that do not reconcile with the "equal playing field" sports were supposed to offer, politics that perpetuate the inequalities that thwart this promise. Exposing the racial and social politics that previously dominated the sports arena is also to expose the politics that remain at the center of sports today. A true assessment of sports and politics in America means considering just how far the dominant culture was, and is, willing to go to remain dominant. The stories in this book expose Boston, the cradle of the nation's liberty message, as a player in this game.

Repairing the harms of these legacies requires more than a statue, plaque, or named park. Although these commemorative elements are significant, meaningful, and important, they carry a greater impact when combined with contextualized interpretation and socially relevant activism. Russell's monument at Boston's city hall, for example, addresses more than the accomplishments of his career. He was hesitant to support the movement to publicly honor him, given his complicated relationship with the city and preference to stay out of the limelight. He asked that it reflect his more recent investment with the community rather than his past relationship with it and "only agreed to it on the condition that the project generated a grant program to go towards mentorship initiatives for children," Ann Hirsch, the public artist who designed the monument in collaboration with Pressley Associates Landscape Architects, reflected.[25] She continued, "We had a commitment to honor not just Bill Russell the athlete, not just Bill Russell the player-coach, but also Bill Russell the national mentorship leader and the human rights and civil rights activist. The sculpture speaks to all of those different dimensions to who Bill Russell was."[26] This is also reflected at his monument, which features a multitude of plaques that address these various components of his life.

Rather than merely citing their "historic first" contribution, commemorations must examine the whole person, community, and organizations surrounding them. Doing this highlights their humanity and reflects the involved culture that bolstered their success and contributed to a more equitable and inclusive sporting environment. Providing this additional context goes beyond commemorating a moment, a demarcation, or a statistic and takes us into the lives of the people and the culture in which they lived.

There remains an enormous gap in Boston's Black sports commemoration, which can now be addressed through pursuing creative and inventive options to both recognize the athlete and engage the community. "After nearly 250 years," as described in *Interpreting Sports at Museums and Historic Sites*, "the American 'victory culture' narrative is yielding to a more subjective, inclusive, and nuanced understanding of the nation's identity, and commemoration practices are changing with it."[27] Toward the end of the twentieth century, an antimonuments movement emerged; Gillis attests, "As the unity of American idealism dissolved, so did the relevancy of monuments that reflected a singular point of view, cultural subset, or overarching narrative."[28] In its place is a more open and inclusive space that runs counter to the absolutism of commemoration. Commemoration can take, and is taking, different forms, opening the door for creative expression that does not have to filter through traditional power structures in order to occupy real estate and gain attention.

For those who choose to expand the landscape of Black sports commemoration, ensure that your efforts are both visually compelling and impactful to the surrounding community. Install interpretive panels with enough space to explore the complexities inherent to each athlete's story. Create a forum series that offers insights, asks hard questions, and welcomes open discussion. Make reparative statements like that of the Red Sox' Black Lives Matter billboard. Generate a public program that raises funds to support the community in ways that align with the honored athlete's efforts. Create spaces that support today's athletes, such as the Kittie Knox Cycle Center, where cyclists can get a tune-up, take a shower, and convene.[29] Hold sporting events like the annual George Street Bike Challenges sponsored by the Major Taylor Museum in Worcester.[30] These actions do more than honor the person's past; they invite the present community to embody the type of equitable playing field these athletes' legacies fostered. In all cases, pay homage to the courage of Black sports pioneers who played against the grain of their time and forged a more humane world for ours.

Notes

1. Lindsey A. Freeman, *Longing for the Bomb: Oak Ridge and Atomic Nostalgia* (Chapel Hill: University of North Carolina Press, 2015), 127.
2. Beth Folsom, "For Two Rindge Athletes, Olympic Medals Meant More Than Just Athletic Victory," *Cambridge Day*, August 5, 2024, https://www.cambridgeday.com/2024/08/05/for-two-rindge-athletes-olympic-medals-meant-more-than-just-athletic-victory/.
3. "Major Taylor Museum," Discover Central Massachusetts, accessed November 30, 2023, https://www.discovercentralma.org/listing/major-taylor-statue/311/; Nicole Shih, "City Honors 'Worcester Whirlwind' Again with New Major Taylor Museum," *Telegram & Gazette*, October 29, 2021, https://www.telegram.com/story/news/2021/10/29/major-taylor-rides-again-new-museum-honors-worcester-world-cycling-champ/6192060001/.
4. Jeremy Siegel and Gal Tziperman Lotan, "The Story behind Bill Russell's Statue, a Monument to Mentorship," WGBH, August 2, 2022, https://www.wgbh.org/news/local/2022-08-02/the-story-behind-bill-russells-boston-statue-a-monument-to-mentorship.

5. Friends of Mount Auburn, "Kittie Knox 1874–1900," Mount Auburn Cemetery, accessed February 1, 2013, https://www.mountauburn.org/kittie-knox-1874-1900/; Ashley Giordano, "The Legacy of Cyclist Kittie Knox," Expedition Portal, February 17, 2022, https://expeditionportal.com/the-legacy-of-cyclist-kittie-knox/; "Kittie Knox Cycle Center Grand Opening Group Ride with REI Co-Op & MassBike," MassBike, May 17, 2023, https://www.massbike.org/reiride_230517.

6. Eric Russo, "Willie O'Ree Community Rink Dedicated in Allston: Bruins Help Unveil Street Hockey Rink in Soon-to-Be Hall of Famer's Honor," *Bruins Centennial*, November 1, 2018, https://www.nhl.com/bruins/news/willie-o-ree-community-rink-dedicated-in-allston-301517586; Fluto Shinzawa, "In Boston, Willie O'Ree Street Hockey Rink Is One Part of Giant Project to Diversity Hockey," *The Athletic*, February 18, 2019, https://theathletic.com/813331/2019/02/18/in-boston-willie-oree-street-hockey-rink-is-one-part-of-giant-project-to-diversify-hockey/.

7. Tovia Smith, "Boston Changes 'Yawkey Way' to 'Jersey Street' after Concerns over Racist Legacy," NPR *Morning Edition*, April 26, 2018, https://www.npr.org/2018/04/26/605851052/boston-red-sox-want-to-strike-former-owners-name-off-street-sign.

8. Nicole Darrah, "'Silence Is Unacceptable': Boston Red Sox Unveil Huge Black Lives Matter Mural Next to Fenway Park ahead of MLB Opening Day," *U.S. Sun*, July 23, 2020, https://www.the-sun.com/news/1186459/black-lives-matter-boston-red-sox-fenway-park/.

9. Amanda Hurley, "Malden River Loop Dedication: The Story of Louisa Stokes," Neighborhood View: Malden from Your Viewpoint, September 2, 2020, https://neighborhoodview.org/2020/09/02/malden-river-loop-dedication-the-story-of-louise-stokes/.

10. "At Long Last, Medina Dixon's Legacy Is Put on Hold," *Dorchester Reporter*, August 24, 2022, https://www.dotnews.com/2022/long-last-medina-dixon-s-legacy-put-record.

11. WBZ-News Staff, "Mural Outside Pizza Shop in Stoneham Honors Celtics Legend Bill Russell," CBS *Boston News*, November 15, 2022, https://www.cbsnews.com/boston/news/mural-andreas-pizza-shop-stoneham-honors-celtics-bill-russell/.

12. "Harambee Park Football Field Named in Honor of Wilson Brothers," *City of Boston*, August 10, 2022, https://www.boston.gov/news/harambee-park-football-field-named-honor-wilson-brothers.

13. Chris Boucher, "Lowell YMCA to Honor 1st Black Pro Basketball Player," *Inside Lowell*, November 3, 2023, https://insidelowell.com/12007-2/.

14. "Louisa Stokes: The Malden Meteor," Sports Museum, accessed November 18, 2023, https://www.sportsmuseum.org/curators-corner/louise-stokes-the-malden-meteor/; "Doc Kountze Art/Film Festival March 27," InsideMedford.com, March 22, 2010, https://www.insidemedford.com/2010/03/22/doc-kountze-artfilm-festival-march-27-2/.

15. "At Long Last."

16. Kenneth Cohen, "Afterword," in *Interpreting Sports at Museums and Historic Sites*, ed. Douglas Stark and Kathryn Leann Harris (New York: Rowman & Littlefield, 2023), 215–20.

17. Tom Engelhardt, *The End of Victory Culture: Cold War America and the Disillusioning of a Generation* (Amherst: University of Massachusetts Press, 2007), 3–15.
18. Engelhardt, *End of Victory Culture*, 3–15.
19. John Gillis, *Commemorations: The Politics of National Identity* (Princeton NJ: Princeton University Press, 1994).
20. Kathryn Leann Harris, "Challenging Branded Appropriation by Uncovering Native Mascot Origins," in Stark and Harris, *Interpreting Sports*, 137–47.
21. Allison Keyes, "Two Museum Directors Say It's Time to Tell the Unvarnished History of the U.S.," *Smithsonian Magazine*, March 5, 2018, https://www.smithsonianmag.com/smithsonian-institution/two-museum-directors-say-its-time-tell-unvarnished-history-us-180968341/; Rayford Logan, as referenced in Mark V. Tushnet, "Progressive Era Race Relations Cases in Their 'Traditional' Context," *Vanderbilt Law Review* 51, no. 4 (1998), https://scholarship.law.vanderbilt.edu/vlr/vol51/iss4/6/.
22. Kevin Gover, undersecretary for museums and culture at the Smithsonian Institute and previous director of the National Museum of the American Indian, interview with the author, July 28, 2021.
23. Harry Edwards, "The Fourth Wave: Black Athlete Protests in the Second Decade of the 21st Century," keynote address, North American Society for the Sociology of Sport (NASSS), Tampa Bay, Florida, 2016, quoted in Joseph Cooper, *A Legacy of African American Resistance and Activism through Sport* (New York: Peter Lang, 2021), 48–54.
24. Cohen, "Afterword."
25. "Story Behind."
26. "Story Behind."
27. Kathryn Leann Harris and Douglas Stark, "Preface," in Stark and Harris, *Interpreting Sports*, xix, quoting John Gillis, ed., *Commemorations: The Politics of National Identity* (Princeton NJ: Princeton University Press, 1994).
28. Gillis, *Commemorations*, 3–20.
29. "Alberta Scott Station Plaza & Kittie Knox Cycle Center Open at CX," BLDUP, May 23, 2023, https://www.bldup.com/posts/alberta-scott-station-plaza-the-kittie-knox-cycle-center-open-at-cx.
30. "19th Edition: George Street Bike Challenge for Major Taylor," Major Taylor Association, July 23, 2023, https://www.majortaylorassociation.org/events/georgestreet23.shtml.

Born in Boston, **Bijan C. Bayne** is an award-winning Washington-based freelance columnist and critic and a leading literary historian on U.S. race relations. He is the author of several books, including *Sky Kings: Black Pioneers of Professional Basketball* (1997), *Elgin Baylor: The Man Who Changed Basketball* (2015), and *Martha's Vineyard Basketball: How a Resort League Defied Notions of Race and Class* (2015). He is a contributor to ESPN and Andscape.com.

Jomills H. Braddock II is a professor of sociology in the Department of Sociology and Criminology at the University of Miami in Coral Gables, Florida. His research focuses on social equity issues across a range of areas, including race, gender, class, education, and sport. He has published widely, including the books *Sex Segregation in Sports: Why Separate Is Not Equal* (coauthored with Adrienne Milner, 2016), and *Women in Sports: Breaking Barriers, Facing Obstacles*, vols. 1 and 2 (coedited with Adrienne Milner, 2017). Among the awards received by Braddock in recognition of his scholarly achievements is Fellow of the American Educational Research Association in Washington DC.

Brian D. Bunk is a senior lecturer in the History Department at the University of Massachusetts Amherst. His research focuses on the history of soccer in the United States. He is the author of *From Football to Soccer: The Early History of the Beautiful Game in the United States* (2021). Other relevant publications include "Sardinero and Not a Can of Sardines: Soccer and Spanish Identities in New York City during the 1920s," which appeared in the *Journal of Urban History* (2015), and "The Rise and Fall of Professional Soccer in Holyoke Massachusetts, USA," in the journal *Sport in History* (2011).

Joseph N. Cooper is the inaugural Dr. J. Keith Motley Endowed Chair of Sport Leadership and Administration, a special assistant to the chancellor for Black Life, and an associate professor at the University of Massachusetts Boston. His research focuses on the intersection between race, gender, sport, education, and culture, with an emphasis on sport involvement as a catalyst for holistic development. He has presented research at international, national, and regional conferences and published numerous peer-reviewed journal articles, book chapters, edited books, and op-eds. He has also been cited in various media outlets, including the *New York Times, Boston Globe*, ESPN, *Le Monde*, ABC News, NBC, Yahoo, *Diverse Issues in Higher Education, Insider*, and USA *Today*. He is the author of *From Exploitation Back to Empowerment: Black Male Holistic (Under)development through Sport and (Mis)education* (2019) and *A Legacy of African American Resistance and Activism through Sport* (2021). He is the editor of *Anti-racism in Sport Organizations* (2022).

Robert Cvornyek is professor emeritus of history at Rhode Island College. He currently serves as an assistant teaching professor at Florida State University Panama City, where he specializes in sport history. He received his PhD in history from Columbia University. Cvornyek has written extensively on the intersection of race, sports, and cultural expression and, recently, edited the autobiography of baseball Hall of Famer Effa Manley. He is currently working on a documentary film that explores the money game in New England African American baseball. Cvornyek also codirects the program It Don't Mean a Thing If It Ain't Got That Swing: Baseball, Jazz, and Black Cultural Expression.

Marvin P. Dawkins is a professor of sociology in the Department of Sociology and Criminology at the University of Miami in Coral Gables, Florida. His research focuses on issues of race and social equity in education, career attainment, sports, and other areas. He has published widely, including the book *African American Golfers during the Jim Crow Era* (coauthored with Graham C. Kinloch, 2000). Dawkins currently serves as the University of Miami's faculty athletics representative to the Atlantic Coast Conference and the NCAA.

Sundiata Djata researches and teaches African, African American, Caribbean, and Latin American histories and is the author of *Blacks at the Net: Black*

Achievement in the History of Tennis, 2 vols. (2006–8), and *The Bamana Empire by the Niger: Kingdom, Jihad and Colonization, 1712–1920* (1997).

Kelly Dwyer is a graduate student in the DeVos Sports Business Management Program at the University of Central Florida. While pursuing a master's degree in business administration and a master's degree in sports business management, she is also a graduate teaching assistant within the UCF sports minor undergraduate program. A former student athlete, Dwyer earned many academic and athletic achievements while playing collegiate softball. She also currently serves as the general manager of a baseball team in the Florida Collegiate Summer League.

Elisabeth Erickson is an associate professor of sport management at the Plaster College of Business and Entrepreneurship at Lindenwood University. She earned her PhD in health and sport studies from the University of Iowa in 2014. A feminist cultural studies scholar, Erickson examines the impact of race, class, gender, and sexuality on collegiate and recreational sport.

Ed Farnsworth studied political science and American studies at Temple University before earning a master's degree in library science at Drexel University. A contributor to *Soccer Frontiers: The Global Game in the United States, 1863–1913* (2021) and *The Encyclopedia of Greater Philadelphia* (2018), Farnsworth was formerly the managing editor of the *Philly Soccer Page*. His work has also appeared on the Society for American Soccer History's website, RSSSF.com, Inquirer.com, TheCup.us, Centro de Investigaciones de Historia y Estadística del Fútbol Español, EPYSA.org, and in the 2011 MLS All-Star Game program.

Marcis Fennell is an assistant professor of sport administration at the University of Louisville. Fennell's personal background in sport as an athlete includes a brief professional football career, four years as an NCAA Division I student athlete, and a member of the prestigious Long Beach (CA) Polytechnic High School football program. Fennell has authored or coauthored articles in several academic disciplines. He has studied topics such as trash talk in sport, leadership in sport, diversity in leadership, student athletes and self-esteem, and faculty climate in higher education. Beyond the confines of the classroom, Fennell assists coaches at the high school and college levels, implementing integrated character education and seeking to influence the moral development and moral reasoning of athletes within the environment of competitive sport.

George Fosty is a Canada-born historian, documentary filmmaker, and publisher. He earned a master's degree in history from MSU-Texas, a bachelor's degree in history from the University of Hawai'i at Hilo, and an AA in history from Western Wyoming College. In addition, he holds a diploma in international law from London City Polytechnic and a legal generalist certificate from Adelphi University. He is the author or coauthor of eleven books, including *Black Ice: The Lost History of the Colored Hockey League of the Maritimes, 1895–1925* (2004), *Where Brave Men Fall: The Battle of Dieppe and the Espionage War against Hitler, 1939–1942* (2013), and *Nais-Myth: Basketball's Stolen Legacy* (2022).

Aram Goudsouzian is the Bizot Family Professor of History at the University of Memphis. He grew up in Winchester, Massachusetts, and earned a bachelor's degree from Colby College and a PhD from Purdue University. He is the author of *The Men and the Moment: The Election of 1968 and the Rise of Partisan Politics in America* (2019), *Down to the Crossroads: Civil Rights, Black Power, and the Meredith March against Fear* (2014), *King of the Court: Bill Russell and the Basketball Revolution* (2010), *The Hurricane of 1938* (2004), and *Sidney Poitier: Man, Actor, Icon* (2004). He is the editor of Karnig Panian's *Goodbye Antoura: A Memoir of the Armenian Genocide* (2015) and the coeditor, with Charles McKinney, of the collection *An Unseen Light: Black Struggles for Freedom in Memphis, Tennessee* (2018).

Donna L. Halper has spent four decades as a professor of communication and media studies, working at several Boston-area universities. A widely quoted media historian with expertise in the history of broadcasting, she is the author of six books, including *Invisible Stars: A Social History of Women in American Broadcasting*, 2nd ed. (2014), and *Boston Radio, 1920–2010* (2011). She has written numerous book chapters and articles for magazines and journals. When not researching radio and TV history, Halper writes about baseball, focusing on Negro League history, baseball "firsts," and biographical sketches of early sportswriters. A former radio deejay and music director, she is credited with having discovered the rock band Rush. Halper reinvented herself and got her PhD at age sixty-four.

Kathryn Leann Harris is the Founder & CEO of Interpreting Sports, a museum consulting firm that helps organizations create socially responsible and culturally responsive sports history content. She works with a simple, but not small, aim—to re-center the international sports conversation around empathy, balanced humanity, and authentic connection, one interpretive project at a time. Harris's work as lead author/editor for *Interpreting Sports at Museums and Historic Sites* (Rowman & Littlefield, 2023) serves as a calling card for her commitment to diversity and inclusivity. The book's essays and her consulting work guide practitioners to craft sport-related projects while considering their social responsibility to sports figures' diverse backgrounds and whole humanity as well as their wider cultural impact. Her work experience includes projects or positions with the Housatonic Museum of Art, Rediscover Mapledale, International Tennis Hall of Fame, James Madison's Montpelier, adidas History Management Department, and Alabama Sports Hall of Fame.

C. Keith Harrison is a professor of business, hip-hop, and sport at UCF Orlando and a former NCAA ScholarBaller in football at Cerritos College and West Texas A&M, where he made the honor roll lettering as a center on the football team. Harrison has published numerous peer-reviewed articles and books on the topics of education and sport, the business of hip-hop innovation, and sport data analytics. Harrison teaches a graduate-level seminar on sport data analytics and undergraduate courses on the business of hip-hop and innovation and entrepreneurship in sports and entertainment. Harrison is the principal investigator and coauthor of the NFL's annual career mobility study and report on hiring practices (2012–present) and has consulted with several brands and organizations throughout his career. Harrison is a Nasir Jones Hiphop Fellowship alumnus at Harvard University's Hutchins Center for African and African American Research.

Jaime Loke is an associate professor of journalism at the Bob Schieffer College of Communication at Texas Christian University. Much of her research is based on the intersection of journalism and gender while also investigating the role of mass media in establishing and reinforcing hierarchies of power within a given society. Loke completed her PhD from the University of Texas in 2011 and joined the faculty at the University of Oklahoma prior to teaching at TCU beginning in 2018.

Eileen Narcotta-Welp is an associate professor in the Department of Exercise and Sport Science at the University of Wisconsin–La Crosse. She earned her PhD in health and sport studies from the University of Iowa in 2016. As a feminist cultural studies scholar, Narcotta-Welp's research interests include the intersections of race, class, gender, and sexuality in relation to high-performance women's sport in both the United States and transnational contexts. Her work has appeared in the *Journal of Sport History, Sport in Society*, and *Soccer and Society* as well as in multiple edited book collections.

Violet Showers Johnson is a professor of history at Texas A&M University. She earned a bachelor's degree from the University of Sierra Leone; a master's degree from the University of New Brunswick, Canada; and a PhD from Boston College. After many years at Agnes Scott College, she joined Texas A&M University as a professor of history and the director of Africana studies. At Texas A&M she has also served as the associate dean for faculty in the College of Liberal Arts, and the senior associate dean for faculty excellence and development on the Texas A&M campus in Qatar. A naturalized U.S. citizen, Showers Johnson's international personal and academic backgrounds have shaped much of her work as a teacher and scholar. She focuses on race, ethnicity, and immigration; African American history; African history; and the history of the African diaspora. She has authored or coauthored books and articles on the Black immigrant experience in America. Her publications include *The Other Black Bostonians: West Indians in Boston, 1900–1950* (2006), and *African & American: West Africans in Post-Civil Rights America* (coauthored with Marilyn Halter, 2014). She is currently completing a monograph with the working title "Black While Foreign: The Complicated History of the Killing of Two African Immigrants in Late Twentieth-Century America."

Andrew Smith is the dean of the College of Professional Studies at Millikin University. He earned a PhD in history from Purdue University, where he began writing about the history of boxing and race in the United States. His work has appeared in the *Journal of Sport History* and *International Journal of the History of Sport* and in edited collections, including *A Companion to American Sport History* (2014), *American National Pastimes—a History* (2015), and *Philly Sports: Teams, Games, and Athletes from Rocky's Town* (2016). Smith is the author of *No Way but to Fight: George Foreman and the Business of Boxing* (2020) and has appeared on media outlets like ESPN Radio, *Fox Sports*, National Public Radio, and Sirius XM.

Douglas Stark focuses on making history more engaging, relevant, and accessible to a diverse audience. His experience includes strategic planning, fiscal management, project management, facility development, historic preservation, collections care, content and exhibition development, branding and messaging, product development, programming and outreach, and audience engagement. He served as museum director at the International Tennis Hall of Fame in Newport, Rhode Island, for thirteen years. He also worked at the Naismith Memorial Basketball Hall of Fame and the U.S. Golf Association. He is the 2016 recipient of the International Sports Heritage Association's W. R. "Bill" Schroeder Distinguished Service Award. He is the past president of the New England Museum Association and received the association's Excellence Award in 2021. Stark is a graduate of Brandeis University, where he earned a bachelor's degree in American history with a minor in the history of art. He pursued graduate studies at New York University, where he earned a master's degree in American history, with dual certification in museum studies and archival management, historical society administration, and historical editing. Stark holds an MBA with a concentration in nonprofit management from the University of Massachusetts at Amherst. He is the author of five books on basketball.